SUBSIDIES, DIPLOMACY, AND STATE FORMATION IN EUROPE, 1494–1789: ECONOMIES OF ALLEGIANCE

Subsidies, diplomacy, and state formation in Europe, 1494–1789: Economies of allegiance

EDITED BY
SVANTE NORRHEM AND ERIK THOMSON

Lund University Press

Copyright © Lund University Press 2020

While copyright in the volume as a whole is vested in Lund University Press, copyright in individual chapters belongs to their respective authors, and no chapter may be reproduced wholly or in part without the express permission in writing of both author and publisher.

Lund University Press

The Joint Faculties of Humanities and Theology

LUND
UNIVERSITY
PRESS

P.O. Box 117
SE-221 00 LUND
Sweden
http://lunduniversitypress.lu.se

Lund University Press books are published in collaboration with Manchester University Press.

British Library Cataloguing-in-Publication Data
A catalogue record for this book is available from the British Library

ISBN   978-91-984698-3-7   hardback
ISBN   978-91-984698-4-4   open access

First published 2020

An electronic version of this book is also available under a Creative Commons (CC-BY-NC-ND) licence, thanks to the support of Lund University, which permits non-commercial use, distribution and reproduction provided the author(s) and Lund University Press are fully cited and no modifications or adaptations are made. Details of the licence can be viewed at https://creativecommons.org/licenses/by-nc-nd/4.0/

The publisher has no responsibility for the persistence or accuracy of URLs for any external or third-party internet websites referred to in this book, and does not guarantee that any content on such websites is, or will remain, accurate or appropriate.

Typeset
by Toppan Best-set Premedia Limited

Contents

Acknowledgements	*page* vii
Notes on contributors	viii
Introduction – Svante Norrhem and Erik Thomson	1

1	The role of subsidies in seventeenth-century French foreign relations and their European context – Anuschka Tischer	25
2	'Unter den Schutz Frankreichs': German reception of French subsidies in the Thirty Years' War – Tryntje Helfferich	43
3	'Mercenary' contracts as Fiscal-Military Instruments – Peter H. Wilson	68
4	The uses of French subsidies in Sweden, 1632–1729 – Svante Norrhem	93
5	The problems with receiving subsidies: Sweden and the lesser powers in the long eighteenth century – Erik Bodensten	118
6	Pensions in Switzerland: practices, conflicts, and impact in the sixteenth century – Philippe Rogger	146
7	Subsidy treaties in early modern times: the example of the German principality of Waldeck – Andreas Flurschütz da Cruz	172

8   Small powers and great designs: diplomacy, cross-border patronage, and the negotiation of subsidy alliances in the north-western part of the Holy Roman Empire (late seventeenth century) – Tilman Haug   188

9   The 'fiscal-military hub' of Amsterdam: intermediating the French subsidies to Sweden during the Thirty Years' War – Marianne Klerk   213

10 Jean Hoeufft, French subsidies, and the Thirty Years' War – Erik Thomson   234

Select bibliography   259
Index   271

Acknowledgements

The editors wish to thank the Swedish Foundation for the Humanities and Social Sciences (Riksbankens Jubileumsfond) which through generous funding enabled us to gather all the authors for a meeting in Lund during the process of working on this volume. We are also deeply grateful to Professor Lucien Bély who very kindly came to that meeting and provided important advice, feedback, and criticism.

Notes on contributors

Erik Bodensten has a PhD in history and is a Researcher at Lund University. He has specialized on Swedish eighteenth-century history and is currently studying how France, Russia, Great Britain, and Denmark tried to influence Swedish foreign policy 1719–1772. His publications include 'Political Knowledge in Public Circulation: The Case of Subsidies in Eighteenth-Century Sweden', in *Circulation of Knowledge: Explorations into the History of Knowledge*, ed. by Johan Östling, Erling Sandmo, David Larsson Heidenblad, Anna Nilsson Hammar, and Kari Nordberg (Lund: Nordic Academic Press, 2018).

Andreas Flurschütz da Cruz has a PhD in history and is a Researcher at Otto-Friedrich-Universität Bamberg. He studies witchcraft, networks, and military history. His dissertation examined the ways and means that were available to the early imperial nobility when promoting their interests. His publications include *Zwischen Füchsen und Wölfen: Konfession, Klientel und Konflikte in der fränkischen Reichsritterschaft nach dem Westfälischen Frieden* (Constance and Munich: UVK Verlag, 2014).

Tilman Haug has a PhD in history and is a postdoctoral scholar at Universität Duisburg-Essen. He is an expert on early modern diplomacy, corruption, and patronage, as well as on state formation. He currently studies early modern lotteries, speculation, and state finance. His publications include *Ungleiche Außenbeziehungen und grenzüberschreitende Patronage: Die französische Krone und die geistlichen Kurfürsten (1648–1679)*, Externa 6 (Cologne: Böhlau, 2015), and *Protegierte und Protektoren: Asymmetrische politische Beziehungen zwischen Partnerschaft und Dominanz (16. bis frühes*

20. *Jahrhundert)*, ed. by Tilman Haug, Nadir Weber, and Christian Windler, Externa 9: Geschichte der Außenbeziehungen in neuen Perspektiven, 9 (Cologne: Böhlau, 2016).

Tryntje Helfferich is an Associate Professor of History at the Ohio State University. She is an expert on central Europe and France during the early modern period, with a particular focus on the Reformation era (1500–1650) and the period of the Thirty Years' War (1618–1648). Her publications include *The Thirty Years War: A Documentary History* (Indianapolis: Hackett, 2009); *On the Freedom of a Christian* (Indianapolis: Hackett, 2013); *The Iron Princess: Amalia Elisabeth and the Thirty Years War* (Cambridge, MA: Harvard University Press, 2013); and *The Essential Thirty Years War* (Indianapolis: Hackett, 2015).

Marianne Klerk has a PhD in history and is an Associate Member of St Antony's College, University of Oxford. Her expertise includes economic, international, and military history. Currently she studies the reliance of (nascent) early modern states on external partnerships for resource mobilization with a focus on seventeenth-century Amsterdam. Her publications include '"The unheard Changes in Europe, and the strange Revolutions which happened in our United Provinces in our times": Reason of State and Rule of Law in Petrus Valkenier's 't Verwerd Europa (1675)', in *Recht, Konfession und Verfassung im 17. Jahrhundert: West- und mitteleuropäische Entwicklungen*, ed. by Robert von Friedeburg and Matthias Schmoeckel (Berlin: Duncker & Humblot, 2015).

Svante Norrhem is an Associate Professor of History at Lund University. He has a long-standing interest in early modern women's and gender history, as well as in diplomatic history focusing on Franco-Swedish relations. His publications include (co-written with Peter Lindström) *Flattering Allliances: Scandinavia, Diplomacy and the Austrian–French Balance of Power* (Lund: Nordic Academic Press, 2013) and *Mercenary Swedes: French Subsidies to Sweden 1631–1796* (Lund: Nordic Academic Press, 2019).

Philippe Rogger has a PhD in history and is a Researcher at Universität Bern. He is an expert on pensions and transnational patronage in the sixteenth-century Swiss confederacy. Currently he studies Swiss confederate military entrepreneurship in the early modern period. His publications include *Geld, Krieg und Macht: Pensionsherren, Söldner und eidgenössische Politik in den Mailänderkriegen 1494–1516* (Baden: Hier und Jetzt, 2015).

Erik Thomson is an Associate Professor of History at the University of Manitoba. He is an expert on early modern Europe, with special interests in French and Swedish history. His publications include 'Le Travail du diplomate et la diffusion des idées politiques à l'époque moderne: la Fronde vue par le résident suédois Schering Rosenhane (1648–1649)', *Histoire, Economie & Sociétés* (April 2010); and 'For a Comparative History of Early Modern Diplomacy: Commerce and French and Swedish Emissarial Cultures during the Early Seventeenth Century', *Scandinavian Journal of History* 31.2 (June 2006).

Anuschka Tischer is a Professor of History at Universität Würzburg. She has a long-standing interest and expertise in early modern French and German history. Her publications include *Französische Diplomatie und Diplomaten auf dem Westfälischen Friedenskongreß: Außenpolitik unter Richelieu und Mazarin*, Schriftenreihe der Vereinigung zur Erforschung der Neueren Geschichte e.V. 29 (Münster: Aschendorff Verlag, 1999), *Offizielle Kriegsbegründungen in der Frühen Neuzeit: Herrscherkommunikation in Europa zwischen Souveränität und korporativem Selbstverständnis* (Münster: Aschendorff Verlag, 2012), and *Ludwig XIV* (Stuttgart: Kohlhammer Kenntnis und Können, Band 774, 2016).

Peter H. Wilson is a Professor of History at the University of Oxford. He is an expert on war and military history from the seventeenth century to around 1900, and early modern German history, particularly the political, military, social, and cultural history of the Holy Roman Empire between 1495 and 1806, as well as on war and military history. His publications include *Lützen: Great Battles* (Oxford University Press, 2018), *The Holy Roman Empire: A Thousand Years of Europe's History* (London: Penguin, 2017), and *The Thirty Years War: Europe's Tragedy* (London: Penguin, 2009).

Introduction

Svante Norrhem and Erik Thomson

Historians have long recognized that the early modern period formed a pivotal moment in the development of European warfare, states, and diplomacy, with profound effects upon global history. As might be expected when rulers and occasionally subjects sought to gain glory by taking up arms to vindicate the justice of their claims – whether dynastic, customary, or historical – in a political system widely conceived as hierarchical, warfare was nearly endemic.[1] The intractable theological disputes that followed the Reformation added grounds for debating the nature of justice. The ubiquity of warfare created an intense and persistent pressure to gain a significant advantage, driving an evolutionary process of statebuilding characterized by punctuated equilibria; these moments of rapid change were occasionally revealed by battlefield victories or civil wars. Cannon founders, gunsmiths, architects, and shipwrights experimented with new techniques. Princes and other military leaders refined tactics and sought to increase the effectiveness of their forces with advantages in numbers, discipline, and supply. Ambassadors and theorists invented more elaborate methods of demonstrating the justice of their sovereigns' claims. They also devised new forms for sovereigns to co-operate. Tax-collectors, projectors, bankers, and entrepreneurs proposed new ways to provide the money and resources to sustain these wars, usually by increasing the taxes and other impositions demanded of subjects who often had meagre margins of survival.

---

1 Johannes Burkhardt, 'Die Friedlosigkeit der Frühen Neuzeit: Grundlegung einer Theorie der Bellizität Europas', *Zeitschrift für Historische Forschung* 24 (1997), 509–574.

Money was so central to these changes that the English historian Mark Greengrass has claimed that 'money was the dissolvent of Christendom', providing Europe's states with resources and motives to engage in destructive conflict with one another.[2] Historians have created an extensive and rich literature on European fiscality. They have examined constitutional battles about the control and amount of taxation, theories of finance, the development of public debt, and the organization and corruption of tax and revenue administrations.[3] Much less attention has been paid to the manner in which resources were shared among sovereignties, and the manner in which diplomacy rested upon allies promising to share money and grant access to resources as a prominent part of diplomacy, military provisioning, and the construction of early modern states. Subsidies were ubiquitous features of diplomatic and military history throughout the early modern period, although such payments could assume a wide variety of names and forms. The early modern era also saw numerous variations of subsidy alliances. The most frequent as well as important subsidizers – in terms of sums – were France, Spain, the United Provinces, and England. On the receiving end Sweden, Denmark, the Swiss confederation, the United Provinces, and a number of German and northern Italian states stand out.[4] The

---

2 Mark Greengrass, *Christendom Destroyed: Europe 1517–1648* (London: Allen Lane, 2014), p. 101.

3 Richard Bonney and W.M. Ormrod, 'Crises, Revolutions and Self-sustained Growth: Towards a Conceptual Model of Change in Fiscal History', in *Crises, Revolutions and Self-sustained Growth: Essays in European Fiscal History, 1130–1830*, ed. by Mark Ormrod, Margaret Bonney, and Richard Bonney (Stamford: Shaun Tyas, 1999), pp. 1–21; *Economic Systems and State Finance*, ed. by Richard Bonney (Oxford: Oxford University Press, 1995); *The Rise of the Fiscal State in Europe, c. 1200–1800*, ed. by Richard Bonney (Oxford: Oxford University Press, 1999); and *The Rise of Fiscal States: A Global History, 1500–1914*, ed. by Bartolomé Yun-Casalilla, Patrick K. O'Brien, and Francisco Comin (Cambridge: Cambridge University Press, 2012).

4 Derek McKay and H.M. Scott, *The Rise of the Great Powers, 1648–1815* (London and New York: Longman, 1983), p. 26; Peter H. Wilson, *German Armies: War and German Politics 1648–1806* (London: UCL Press, 1998), pp. 63, 87, 107, 179, 206–207, 228, 267–269; Dwyryd Wyn Jones, *War and Economy in the Age of William III and Marlborough* (Oxford: Basil Blackwell, 1988), pp. 8–11; Jeremy Black, 'Parliament and Foreign Policy in the Age of Walpole: The Case of the Hessians', in *Knights Errant and True Englishmen: British Foreign Policy, 1660–1800*, ed. by Jeremy Black (Edinburgh: John Donald Publishers Ltd, 1989), pp. 46–47; C.W. Eldon,

Introduction 3

subsidies could make up large proportions of the state revenue of not just the receiving countries but also the subsidizers. Subsidies served early modern diplomacy as a major structure, that is to say a series of rules and resources, which conditioned discourse, practice, and agency in a consistent manner over a long period of

---

England's Subsidy Policy towards the Continent during the Seven Years War (Philadelphia: University of Pennsylvania, 1938); Christopher Storrs, '"Große Erwartungen". Britische Subsidienzahlungen an Savoyen im 18. Jahrhundert', in *Das 'Blut des Staatskörpers': Forschungen zur Finanzgeschichte der Frühen Neuzeit*, ed. by Peter Rauscher, Andrea Serles, and Thomas Winkelbauer (Munich, 2012: *Historische Zeitschrift*, Beiheft, vol. 56, 2012), 87–126; Stanley J. Stein and Barbara H. Stein, *Silver, Trade, and War: Spain and America in the Making of Early Modern Europe* (Baltimore and London: The Johns Hopkins University Press, 2000), pp. 52–53; Hildegard Ernst, 'Spanische Subsidien für den Kaiser 1632 bis 1642', in *Krieg und Politik 1618–1648: Europäische Probleme und Perspektiven*, ed. by Konrad Repgen (Munich: R. Oldenbourg Verlag, 1988), pp. 299–302; Gottfried Lorenz, 'Schweden und die französischen Hilfsgelder von 1638 bis 1649', in *Forschungen und Quellen zur Geschichte des Dreißigjährigen Krieges*, ed. by Konrad Repgen (Münster, 1981), pp. 98–148 (p. 99); Stuart P. Oakley, *War and Peace in the Baltic, 1560–1790* (London and New York: Routledge, 2005), p. 41; Patrik Winton, 'Denmark and Sweden in the European Great Power System, 1720–1765', in *Revue d'histoire nordique (2012)*, ed. by Erik Schnakenbourg, pp. 39–61; Patrik Winton, 'Parliamentary Control, Public Discussions and Royal Autonomy: Sweden, 1750–1780', in *Histoire & Mesure*, XXX.2 (2015), 51–78 (p. 57); Knud J.V. Jespersen, 'Danmark og Europa 1648–1720', in *Dansk udenrigspolitiks historie, ii: Revanche og Neutralitet, 1648–1814*, ed. by Carsten Due-Nielsen (Copenhagen: Gyldendal Leksikon, 2002), pp. 99, 102, 106, 114, 125; Ole Feldbaek, 'Helstaten 1720–1814', in *Dansk udenrigspolitiks historie, ii: Revanche og Neutralitet, 1648–1814*, ed. by Carsten Due-Nielsen (Copenhagen: Gyldendal Leksikon, 2002), pp. 275–278; Christian Windler, '"Ohne Geld keine Schweizer": Pensionen und Söldnerrekrutierung auf den eidgenössischen Patronagemärkten', in *Nähe in der Ferne: Personale Verflechtung in den Außenbeziehungen der Frühen Neuzeit (Zeitschrift für Historische Forschung*, Beiheft 36), ed. by Hillard von Thiessen and Christian Windler (Berlin, 2005), 105–133 (p. 112); Martin Körner, 'The Swiss Confederation', in *The rise of the fiscal state in Europe, c. 1200–1815*, ed. by Richard Bonney (Oxford: Oxford University Press, 1999), pp. 327–357; Martin Körner, 'Der Einfluss der europäischen Kriege auf die Struktur der schweizerischen Finanzen im 16. Jahrhundert', in *Proceedings of the Seventh International Economic History Congress*, vol. 2, ed. by Michael Flinn (Edinburgh, 1978), pp. 274–281; Martin Körner, *Luzerner Staatsfinanzen 1415–1798: Strukturen, Wachstum, Konjunkturen* (Lucerne and Stuttgart: Luzerner Historische Veröffentlichungen, 1981); Philippe Gern, *Aspects des relations franco-suisses au temps de Louis XVI*

4   Subsidies, diplomacy, and state formation

time.[5] Subsidies also played complex roles in the internal politics of states irrespective of whether they were receiving or paying subsidies; for such transfers of resources could both prompt and still political debates, favour particular social and political groups within states, and either accelerate or slow the construction of durable state institutions.

By 'subsidy' we mean primarily the payment of money by one sovereign to another in return for military and political aid, typically agreed upon by means of a formal agreement and even treaty. We do not think it is useful to circumscribe the definition of the word too narrowly, for early modern statesmen could use many different words including pensions, gratifications, gifts, favours, and other terms relatively loosely to refer to obligations to furnish money or other resources in return for political considerations or military co-operation. Nor did all transfers of resources from one sovereign to another in exchange for money entail subsidies. Monarchs could purchase a naval vessel or weapons, for example, without the same sort of political associations that subsidy arrangements entailed. The authors of the chapters in this book aim to illuminate different aspects of the role of subsidies in early modern political history. Most of the chapters focus on France, and on the consequences of the subsidies that formed a crucial part of its alliances from the Thirty Years' War until the end of the reign of Louis XIV. While France was far from the only power to pay subsidies in the early modern period, French diplomats created what amounted to a distinctive system of alliances in which 'subsidies' played a large role.

(Neuchâtel: Editions de la Baconnière, 1970), p. 151; Andreas Suter, 'Korruption oder Patronage? Außenbeziehungen zwischen Frankreich und der Alten Eidgenossenschaft als Beispiel (16.–18. Jahrhundert)', in *Korruption: Historische Annäherungen an eine Grundfigur politischer Kommunikation*, ed. by Niels Grüne and Simona Slanička (Göttingen: Vandenhoeck & Ruprecht, 2010), pp. 167–203; Philippe Rogger, *Geld, Krieg und Macht: Pensionsherren, Söldner und eidgenössische Politik in den Mailänderkriegen 1494–1516* (Baden: Hier und Jetzt, 2015); Stephan Karl Sander-Faes, 'Die Soldaten der Serenissima: Militär und Mobilität im frühneuzeitlichen Stato da mar', in *Militärische Migration vom Altertum bis zur Gegenwart* (Studien zur Historischen Migrationsforschung, vol. 30), ed. by Christoph Rass (Paderborn: Ferdinand Schöningh, 2016), pp. 111–126; Egidio Ivetic, 'The Peace of Passarowitz in Venice's Balkan Policy', in *The Peace of Passarowitz, 1718*, ed. by Charles Ingrao, Nikola Samardžić and Jovan Pešalj (West Lafayette, IN: Purdue University Press, 2008), pp. 63–72.

5 William H. Sewell, Jr, 'A Theory of Structure', in his *Logics of History: Social Theory and Social Transformation* (Chicago: University of Chicago Press, 2005), pp. 124–151.

Consequently, not only was money Christendom's dissolvent but it might serve as a political adhesive that diplomats could use to bind sovereigns together, despite their different identities, interests, and even faiths.

French subsidies played a central role in European politics from Charles VIII's invasion of Italy in 1494 until the French Revolution. The Valois kings had emerged from the Hundred Years' War with what were probably the largest revenues and army of any European monarchy and with an extensive set of dynastic claims that the members of the Valois family sought to pursue, despite the resistance they provoked amongst other monarchs, and particularly the Habsburgs. Maximilian of Habsburg thought Charles VIII's continued claims to Burgundy unjust; Maximilian would be further provoked by Charles's claim to Naples and Milan, and he was moved to organize a coalition against France which included not only the pope but the father of his son Felipe's new wife Joanna – Ferdinand of Aragon, who also claimed Naples. Although Charles VIII possessed excellent cavalry and artillery, he lacked infantry; and in 1495, his agents at Turin entered into an agreement with the Swiss, who had turned to his father against the Burgundians nearly two decades earlier, to provide twelve thousand soldiers for his service in return for subsidies. France's attempts to control the Swiss cantons, both for geopolitical reasons and because the cantons were seen as a recruiting ground for soldiers, established a pattern for making financial considerations an important part of a treaty of alliance. The practice spread across the continent and beyond in the sixteenth, seventeenth, and eighteenth centuries. Machiavelli, famously, referred to the Swiss as mercenaries in *The Prince* and thought the French unwise to rely on the troops of allies paid for their service rather than on native troops.[6]

Yet money's role in European politics would increase, rather than decrease, as Maximilian's grandson Charles created a composite monarchy that combined the Burgundian inheritance, the Low Countries, the office of the Holy Roman Emperor and the Habsburg Austrian homelands, and the Spanish kingdoms with not only Aragon's contentious Italian claims and possessions but also Castile's territories in the New World. Where his grandfather Maximilian had financed his struggle against Charles VIII and Louis XII with

---

6 See *The Prince*, chapter 13. On this subject, see Jérémie Barthas, *L'argent n'est pas le nerf de la guerre: Essai sur une prétendue erreur de Machiavel* (Rome: École Française de Rome, 2012).

loans from financiers such as Jacob Fugger secured on silver from the Tyrol from the Habsburg homelands, Charles could rely not only upon the expanded tax base of all the different states he ruled but also on an additional supply of precious metals from the New World as well as on the *Quinto real*, the 20 per cent tax levied upon them. The combination of the geographic dispersion of Charles's states and the new creditworthiness of his crown created a new financial moment as financiers drew up loans and moved money between the different states of Charles's empire to suit financial need, joining together financial markets in a new way. Bills of exchange from Seville, Madrid, and Medina del Campo were drawn in Genoa, Antwerp, the fairs of Besançon, and correspondents of the Fuggers in Ausburg, Vienna, and Prague. The dynastic ambitions of Charles and his successors depended upon international bankers capable of using his realm's revenues to raise credit from private capital holders in a variety of financial centres both inside and outside his jurisdiction and finally using specialized bankers to move these funds to realms where he could pay his armies.[7] These mechanisms could be used to pay subsidies – including to the Guise early in the French wars of religion and the French Catholic league in the 1590s.

French kings from François I to Louis XIV attempted to frustrate what they viewed as a Habsburg bid to pursue universal monarchy without mines of silver to rival Potosi. Commentators sympathetic to France in the sixteenth and seventeenth century were fond of referring to the fields of France as the French king's mines, and trusted that grain and wine were necessities for all of France's neighbours. While modern estimates of premodern GDP figures, and perhaps particularly for France, ought to be treated with caution, these numbers suggest that France predominantly relied upon its large population to raise money, as French per capita GDP seems to have been somewhat lower than those of many of its monarchs' rivals, and, indeed, many of the states to which it paid subsidies.[8]

---

7 Giovanni Muto, 'The Spanish System', in *The Origins of the Modern State in Europe: 13th–18th Centuries: Economic Systems and State Finance*, ed. by Richard Bonney (Oxford: Clarendon Press, 2002), pp. 231–259.

8 We follow 'The Maddison-Project', www.ggdc.net/maddison/maddison-project/home.htm, 2013 version, accessed 20 October 2017. Extrapolating from the French data using a constant growth rate, French per capita GDP looks to have been less than half that of the Netherlands in 1650, and less than that of Sweden. The 'Maddison-Project' draws upon Lennart Schön and Olle

Introduction

Ultimately, French subsidies, as all of the expenditures of the crown, came from revenues raised overwhelmingly from comparatively poor peasants and farmers. In France, these taxes were both direct taxes such as the *taille*, a name for a variety of taxes on land collected in various forms in different parts of France, or indirect taxes, such as the *gabelle*, a tax raised on salt, usually from its sale by a government monopoly. Monarchs began to borrow money from merchants, either as individual bankers or in consortia. They continued to draw significant sums from this form of borrowing, particularly from *financiers* who advanced money in return for collecting taxes. During the reign of François I, the king also began to raise consolidated debts in the form of *rentes sur l'hôtel de ville de Paris*, based on municipal revenues which were viewed as more credible than direct obligations based on royal promises. These were initially modest, but ballooned along with other debts – including debts to allies such as the Swiss and the English crown – during the religious wars of the second half of the sixteenth century.[9] The financial turmoil associated with the Wars of Religion largely persuaded the Italian and other foreign bankers, who had been major creditors of the crown until that point, that the French crown was not worth the risk. The French crown largely turned to domestic sources of capital, and to fiscal expedients such as increasing sales of offices.

Despite the crown's dire fiscal state and outstanding debts to allies, Henri IV would pay subsidies to opponents of the Habsburgs, notably the United Provinces. During the seventeenth century, the

---

Krantz, 'The Swedish Economy in the Early Modern Period: Constructing Historical National Accounts', *European Review of Economic History* 16 (2012), 529–549. The French estimates seem to be unmodified from those provided in Angus Maddison, *The World Economy: A Millennial Perspective* (Paris: OECD, 2001), Table B-21, p. 264. France is not included in Stephen Broadberry et al., *British Economic Growth: 1270–1870* (Cambridge: Cambridge University Press, 2015); Leonardo Ridolfi, *L'histoire immobile? Six Centuries of Real Wages in France from Louis IX to Napoleon III: 1250–1860*, Laboratory of Economics and Management Working Papers Series, Scuola Superiore Sant'Anna, Pisa, 2017/14 (June 2017), suggests how much remains to be learned of French premodern macroeconomic data – without reversing Maddison's gloomy estimation of low French growth rates. While aimed at global historians, the cautions about such figures expressed by Morton Jerven, 'An Unlevel Playing Field: National Income Estimates and Reciprocal Comparison in Global Economic History', *Journal of Global History* 7 (2012), 107–128, are relevant in this context.

9 Richard Bonney, *The King's Debts: Finance and Politics in France, 1589–1661* (Oxford: Clarendon Press, 1981).

French monarchy would embrace the payment of subsidies on a different scale than previously, using alliances in which subsidies played a prominent role to pursue crucial aspects of royal policy. Louis XIII made alliances promising subsidies to support the United Provinces' resumed war against the king of Spain, and for the Danish, Swedish, and various German princes to fight against the Holy Roman Emperor.[10] Louis XIV continued some of these subsidies and used subsidies as a tool in order to implement his own politics. When Louis XIV appeared to Dutch and some English statesmen as aspiring to universal monarchy, the Dutch and particularly the English used the tool of subsidies to frustrate the French monarch.[11] During the eighteenth century, principally the French and the British, but also the Austrians, used subsidies to procure allies and attempt to maintain the balance of power. Some powers, such as Prussia, became important recipients of subsidies. Even after the purchase of internationally liquid public debts became a way of supporting allies, statesmen continued to find treaties articulating promises of subsidy payments in return for political and military service a useful part of the repertoire of diplomacy.

When Immanuel Kant advocated a clean break with previous and present theories and practices of diplomacy in his 'Zum ewigen Frieden' ('Of Perpetual Peace') of 1795, he criticized subsidies as one of many practices that encouraged war.[12] Kant argued that there was a necessary connection between the constitution of a state and whether it is bellicose or pacific. A despot who spoke on behalf of unrepresented subjects could easily make war, because 'a war will not force him to make the slightest sacrifice as far as his banquets, hunts, pleasure palaces and court festivals are concerned ... He can decide on war ... as a kind of amusement, and unconcernedly leave

---

10 Lucien Bély, *L'art de la paix en Europe: Naissance de la diplomatie moderne XVIe–XVIIIe siècle* (Paris: Presses Universitaires de France, 2007), pp. 157–179, and Peter H. Wilson, *The Thirty Years War: Europe's Tragedy* (London: Penguin, 2009), pp. 379–381 and 464–465.
11 Janine Fayard, 'Attempts to Build a "Third Party" in Northern Germany', in *Louis XIV and Europe*, ed. by Ragnhild Hatton, trans. by Geoffrey Symcox and Derek McKay (London: Macmillan, 1976), pp. 213–240, and Jonathan Israel, *The Anglo Dutch Moment: Essays on the Glorious Revolution and Its World Impact* (Cambridge: Cambridge University Press, 1991).
12 'Perpetual Peace: A Philosophical Sketch', in *Kant: Political Writings*, ed. by Hans Reiss, trans. by H.B. Nisbet (Cambridge: Cambridge University Press, 2nd ed. 1991), p. 103.

Introduction

it to the diplomatic corps ... to justify [it] for the sake of propriety.' Therefore, Kant reasoned, all states must have republican constitutions where 'the consent of the citizens is required to decide whether or not war is to be declared', for this would mean that those who declare war would feel all its miseries.[13] He began the essay with prohibitions against specific diplomatic practices in order to nullify what he called the 'three powers of the state', the *'power of the army*, the *power of alliance*, and *the power of money'*. Kant thought subsidies particularly odious. Like acquiring states by marriage or purchase, subsidy payments mistook a state – which Kant thought was a 'society of men which no-other than itself can command' – and 'made it into a commodity'. Thus he thought subsidies were a kind of perversion, arguing that 'when the troops of one state are hired to another to fight an enemy who is not common to both ... the subjects are thereby used and misused as objects to be manipulated at will'.[14]

Historians have showed only limited interest in subsidies and the transfer of resources between allies as distinct and central problems of early modern diplomacy. There is not an extant list, for example, of all the payments promised from one sovereign to another in early modern Europe, and still less a record of whether the payments were made. The words 'subsidies' and 'pensions' are not in the indexes of recent surveys of diplomatic history in German, French, or English, and the subject does not receive systematic treatment in any of them.[15] Recent works by Anglophone historians, often grouped together under the heading 'New Diplomatic History', have tended to focus on the close reading of diplomatic correspondence, art, and other documents to enrich detailed portrayals of a single diplomat's career, the course of a single peace-treaty negotiation,

---

13 *Ibid.*, p. 100.
14 *Ibid.*, p. 94.
15 Heinz Schilling, *Konfessionalisierung und Staatsinteressen: Internationale Beziehungen 1559–1660* (Paderborn: Ferdinand Schöningh, 2007); Claire Gantet, *Guerre Paix et construction des états, 1618–1714: Nouvelle histoire des relations internationales*, vol. 2 (Paris: Seuil, 2003); Jean-Pierre Bois, *De la paix des rois à l'ordre des empereurs, 1714–1815: Nouvelle histoire des relations internationales*, vol. 3 (Paris: Seuil, 2003); Matthew Smith Anderson, *The Origins of the Modern European State System, 1494–1618* (London: Longman, 1998); Jeremy Black, *A History of Diplomacy* (London: Reaktion Books, 2010). See, however, Lucien Bély, 'Subsides', in *Dictionnaire de l'ancien régime*, ed. by Lucien Bély (Paris: Presses Universitaires de France, 1996), pp. 1178–1179.

or even a single ceremony or painting.[16] The new diplomatic history's close cultural reading and sense of nuance came at the cost of a more diffuse focus on what had been the centre of the older scholarship on diplomatic history, explaining how powers made fundamental choices about how to relate with others over time, whether through peaceful alliances, treaties, and institutions, or through war.[17]

Historians interested in subsidies' role in diplomacy must resort to older scholarship, or to more recent, often German-language, studies of particular alliances and subsidy contracts, and studies of military or fiscal history. Some classic studies echoed Kant's moral condemnation of subsidies as a form of corruption, in which sovereigns entered into agreements against the interests of their state. For example, Max Braubach's 1923 study of the role of subsidies in the Spanish War of Succession criticizes French and British interference in German politics as something that rendered Germans 'mercenaries'.[18] Sometimes broad claims regarding the alleged corruption of subsidy systems focused on individual people who profited from bribery or peculation, as in Ragnhild Hatton's chapter on gratifications to Swedish politicians in Anglo-French diplomatic rivalry during the Age of Liberty.[19] Still others examine how subsidies entered into the formulation of grand policy in a classic sense. Lossky,[20] Fayard,[21] and Frey[22] all write that France paid subsidies

---

16 See Tracey Sowerby's review of the field, 'Early Modern Diplomatic History', *History Compass* 14.9 (2016), 441–456, and John Watkins's programmatic 'Toward a New Diplomatic History of Medieval and Early Modern Europe', *Journal of Medieval and Early Modern Studies* 38.1 (2008), 1–14.
17 Karl W. Schweizer and Matt J. Schumann, 'The Revitalization of Diplomatic History: Renewed Reflections', *Diplomacy and Statecraft* 19 (2008), 149–186.
18 Max Braubach, *Die Bedeutung der Subsidien für die Politik im spanischen Erbfolgekriege* (Bonn and Leipzig: Kurt Schroeder Verlag, 1923), pp. 41, 71, 186–190.
19 Ragnhild Hatton, 'Gratifications and Foreign Policy: Anglo-French Rivalry in Sweden during the Nine Years War', in *William III and Louis XIV: Essays 1680–1720 by and for Mark A. Thomson* (Liverpool: Liverpool University Press, 1968), pp. 68–94.
20 Andrew Lossky, 'La Picquetière's Projected Mission to Moscow in 1682 and the Swedish Policy of Louis XIV', *Essays in Russian History: A Collection Dedicated to George Vernadsky*, ed. by Alan D. Ferguson and Alfred Levin (Hamden, CT: Archon Books, 1964).
21 Janine Fayard, 'Les tentatives de constitution d'un tiers party en Allemagne du Nord 1690–1694', *Revue d'Histoire Diplomatique* 79 (1965), 338–372.
22 Linda Frey, 'Franco-Prussian Relations, 1701–1706', *Proceedings of the Annual Meeting of the Western Society for French History* 3 (1976), 94–105.

in order to buy the allegiance of northern Europe and steer the Nordic countries and North German states away from anti-French alliances, with the hope of strengthening France's borders with the Holy Roman Empire.[23] The most important international studies of recent vintage are of the subsidies France paid to the Swiss cantons in the sixteenth century: at times, French subsidies accounted for between 15 per cent and 65 per cent of an individual canton's revenues, which left its mark economically, socially, and politically by benefiting a Francophile elite.[24] Similar figures can be shown for Hesse-Cassel, where no fewer than thirty subsidy treaties were signed between 1702 and 1763 and the subsidies amounted to between 40 and 50 per cent of the economy.[25] Subsidies can also be seen as part of a number of strategies used by France to create alliances. Tilman Haug has studied how France acted in order to gain control over the two electorates Mainz and Cologne in the mid-seventeenth century, by patronage towards civil servants within the political centre of the two electorates.[26] The intention was to create a division within the Holy Roman Empire by allying parts of the Empire with France. In an earlier study, Richard Place has shown how France tried to buy out German allies of the Emperor from the anti-French coalition in 1687–1688. Even though this attempt failed, it forced Emperor Leopold to make offers to Bavaria that he probably would not have had to do otherwise.[27] A similar attempt, as shown by Linda Frey, was made towards Prussia during the War of the Spanish

---

23 Georges Livet, 'International Relations and the Role of France, 1648–60'; see also Livet's 'The Decline of Spain and the Thirty Years' War, 1609–1648/59', in vol. 4 of *The New Cambridge Modern History*, ed. by J.P. Cooper (Cambridge: Cambridge University Press, 1970), pp. 411–434. Geoffrey R.R. Treasure argues along the same lines that France primarily wished to strengthen its north-eastern and eastern borders; see Treasure, *Mazarin: The Crisis of Absolutism in France* (Abingdon: Routledge, 1995).
24 Windler, '"Ohne Geld keine Schweizer"' [see p. 17, n. 40], pp. 105–133. For further references, see note 3.
25 Jörg Ulbert, 'Französische Subsidienzahlungen an Hessen-Kassel während des Dreißigjährigen Krieges', in *Frankreich und Hessen-Kassel zur Zeit des Dreißigjährigen Krieges und des Westfälischen Friedens*, ed. by Klaus Malettke (Marburg: N.G. Elwert Verlag, 1999), pp. 159–174.
26 Tilman Haug, *Ungleiche Außenbeziehungen und grenzüberschreitende Patronage: Die französische Krone und die geistlichen Kurfürsten (1648–1679)* (Cologne: Böhlau Verlag, 2015).
27 Richard Place, 'Bavaria and the Collapse of Louis XIV's German Policy, 1687–88', *The Journal of Modern History* 49 (September 1977), 363–393 (pp. 378–393).

Succession. Louis XIV then, among other things, promised subsidies in order to tie Prussia to France.[28] The works by Peter Wilson and Charles Ingrao served as pioneering efforts to demonstrate how subsidies strengthened princes' dynastic ambitions and influenced politics within their own realms.[29] They show how subsidies considerably strengthened the position of German states such as Hesse and Württemberg in the seventeenth and eighteenth centuries: their armies became major employers and offered opportunities for advancement (especially to the lower nobility), taxes could be kept low, and a focus on commercial activity was made possible. This gave the Württembergian and Hessian princes a distinct propaganda advantage, along with the chance to pursue their own dynastic ambitions in competition with other groups. The surplus from the subsidies could also be used for luxury consumption – palaces, art, expensive ceremonial – which in turn became part of a status competition with other princely dynasties throughout the Holy Roman Empire and beyond. The arguments against subsidies made by opposition groups included the very high mortality rates among young fighting men and a worrying overdependence on the subsidizer. Towards the end of the eighteenth century, new Enlightenment ideas encouraged this resistance, especially when the British began to use German armies in North America.[30] In a study of Saxony-Gotha, Andrea Thiele notes that the gains in providing soldiers to the United Provinces were a stronger grip on politics in Saxony-Gotha's own territory as well as higher prestige within the international community, together with a financial profit. The

---

28 Frey, 'Franco-Prussian Relations'.
29 Peter H. Wilson, *War, State and Society in Württemberg, 1677–1793* (Cambridge: Cambridge University Press, 1995); Charles W. Ingrao, *The Hessian Mercenary State: Ideas, Institutions, and Reform under Frederick II 1760–1785* (Cambridge: Cambridge University Press, 1987).
30 Frederic Groß, 'Einzigartig? – Der Subsidienvertrag von 1786 über die Aufstellung des "Kapregiments" zwischen Herzog Karl Eugen von Württemberg und der Niederländischen Ostindienkompanie', in *Militärische Migration vom Altertum bis zur Gegenwart* (Studien zur Historischen Migrationsforschung, vol. 30), ed. by Christoph Rass (Paderborn: Ferdinand Schöningh, 2016), pp. 143–164; Lothar Höbelt, 'Vom militärischen saisonnier zum miles perpetuus: Staatsbildung und Kriegsführung im ancien régime', in *Krieg und Gesellschaft*, vol. 2, ed. by Thomas Kolnberger and Ilja Steffelbauer (Vienna: Mandelbaum, 2010), pp. 59–79; Hans-Martin Maurer, 'Das württembergische Kapregiment: Söldner im Dienste früher Kolonialpolitik (1787–1808)', *Zeitschrift für Württembergische Landesgeschichte* 47 (1988), 291–307.

Introduction   13

risks were considerable, though: the dukes of Saxony-Gotha became entrepreneurs and had to pay for recruiting soldiers without knowing when the money was going to be repaid.[31]

Illuminating as this work has been, subsidies also offer an opportunity to engage with recent work in adjoining fields. For example, alliances and the transfer of resources have been the subject of work in the theory of international relations, as well as in the burgeoning field of war and economics, drawing upon game theory. Beginning with the work of the American economists Mancur Olson and Richard Zeckhauser, economists have tried to devise formal models to explain how changing economic and strategic conditions shape decision-makers' choices, and under what circumstances alliances are formed.[32] These studies suggest that alliance expenditures can prompt larger and wealthier participants in alliances to bear a disproportionate part of the common burden of the alliance, both in respect to the expected benefits of the alliance and the two countries' different resource bases and fiscal capacities.[33] Olson's and Zeckhauser's model was devised to analyse the postwar alliances of the United States, relying on assumptions that may not easily transfer to early modern conditions; it regards states as units making rational choices. Yet the model suggests that alliances can endure with stronger and richer countries contributing a disproportionately large share of the total resources, and thus that subsidy payments and other transfers often favour smaller states over long periods of time.

Both the ubiquity of subsidies in early modern diplomacy and the economic theory of alliances suggest that some revisions should be made to the sophisticated accounts of state building that sociologists and historians have developed over the last three decades. Scholars such as Charles Tilly have placed war at the centre of their models

---

31 Andrea Thiele, 'The Prince as Military Entrepreneur? Why Smaller Saxon Territories Sent "Holländische Regimenter" (Dutch Regiments) to the Dutch Republic', in *War, Entrepreneurs, and the State in Europe and the Mediterranean, 1300–1800*, ed. by Jeff Fynn-Paul (Leiden & Boston: Brill 2014), pp. 191–194.

32 Mancur Olson, Jr and Richard Zeckhauser, 'An Economic Theory of Alliances', *The Review of Economics and Statistics* 48.3 (August 1966), 266–279, and for a more recent review of the literature, Todd Sandler, 'The Economic Theory of Alliances', *The Journal of Conflict Resolution* 37.3 (September 1993), 446–483. For an international-relations point of view, see Glenn H. Snyder, *Alliance Politics* (Ithaca: Cornell University Press, 1993).

33 Olson and Zeckhauser, 'An Economic Theory of Alliances', esp. p. 269.

of state-formation, and Tilly articulated this orientation pithily by asking 'How War Made States, and States Made War'. In passing, he suggested that, during the transition period of intensifying military cost and the effort to develop the financial systems to pay for it, some princes, who were poor but skilled in mustering the forces of coercion, 'rented' their armies to other states who were rich in capital. Even so, the transfer of resources from one sovereign to another plays little part in his accounts of sovereigns bargaining with their subjects or in his account of the development of state systems.[34] Rather than looking at the state of politics at a given moment, scholars interested in state building often privilege the development of the military, fiscal, and bureaucratic institutions that allow a state to survive in the long term. Their analysis tends to privilege the negotiation between a sovereign and their subjects, and the development of state capacity that allowed sovereigns to extract resources from their own territories and populations. Tilly and other theorists of state formation scrutinize such features of state as constitutional forms, ideological quality, bureaucratic sophistication, capital richness, forms of military organization, and homogeneity of leadership as significant factors that condition the ability of states to support the increasing burden of wars.[35] While scholars have devoted significant attention to certain forms of transnational transfers of resources, such as military expertise, arms, and loans whether mediated directly from bankers to sovereigns or in the international purchase of state debt, subsidy payments have attracted less attention from the writers of state-building literature. This probably reflects doubts that subsidies strengthened the states that received them, doubts which seem logical enough on the surface. One could

---

34 Charles Tilly, *Coercion, Capital and European States, AD 990–1990* (Oxford: Basil Blackwell, 1990), p. 81.
35 One could go back to Otto Hintze, 'Military Organization and the Organization of the State' (originally 1906), in *Historical Essays of Otto Hintze*, ed. by Felix Gilbert (Oxford: Oxford University Press, 1975), pp. 178–215; Michael Mann, *The Sources of Social Power, I: A History of Power from the Beginning to A.D. 1760* (Cambridge: Cambridge University Press, 1986); Charles Tilly, *Coercion, Capital and European States*; Jan Glete, *War and the State in Early Modern Europe: Spain, the Dutch Republic and Sweden as States, 1500–1660* (London: Routledge, 2002); Wolfgang Reinhard, *Geschichte der Staatsgewalt: Eine vergleichende Verfassungsgeschichte Europas von den Anfängen bis zur Gegenwart* (Munich: C.H. Beck, 1999), pp. 305–387; Harald Gustafsson, *Makt och människor: Europeisk statsbilding från medeltiden till franska revolutionen* (Gothenburg: Makadam, 2010).

argue that states which were provided with external resources had less incentive to develop effective institutions of their own, and might even allow monarchs to avoid the political quarrels that often accompanied the creation of new systems of taxation, for instance.

Even if one accepts the odd premise of the state-building literature that early modern sovereigns should be considered as rational institution builders who attempted to maximize the power they were able to project, the argument that subsidies are irrelevant or even detrimental to the development of states seems overly hasty. If in some cases subsidies only allowed states with too few resources to survive the increase in military scale and expense to defer their eventual absorption into larger polities, in others subsidies afforded an opportunity to react to immediate political crises while still considering reforms on a longer time-scale. Institutionally unsophisticated and revenue-poor states could use subsidies to establish relations with international financial circles who otherwise might well have had little cause to engage themselves, providing an opportunity for the transfer of knowledge of financial practices. By paying subsidies, the French monarchy avoided controversies that might otherwise have provoked earlier and more profound resistance. Participation in the French system of subsidies neither necessarily accelerated nor necessarily retarded state development; but such participation could undoubtedly change political dynamics, the creation of institutions, and the form of states that would emerge.

In order to explore the Reformation's implications for international relations, Daniel Nexon has recently suggested that it is useful to view early modern international structures as 'networks of networks', and that even the composite monarchies of early modern Europe can usefully be modelled as interlocking patron–client networks centred on the monarch, bounded by nested networks settled in different bounded polities, and disrupted by religious networks that resisted patronage and unsettled relations between provinces.[36] Nexon's stimulating suggestion that dynastic agglomerations could be seen as networks of social elites – including local intermediaries, a transnational class of substitutable elites, and the local 'ordinary people' – provides one way of analysing the role of transnational networks based on the transfer of resources such as subsidies. Rather

---

36 Daniel H. Nexon, *The Struggle for Power in Early Modern Europe: Religious Conflict, Dynastic Empires, and International Change* (Princeton: Princeton University Press, 2009), for 'network of networks', p. 48.

than seeing early modern states as mustering the resources of neatly bounded polities, Nexon's model calls attention to the importance of bargaining for resources over the boundaries of polities, with ample room for ideological opposition as well as the accommodation of both elites and more common people.

Nexon's emphasis on bargaining and networks provides a manner of analysing more profound changes in early modern politics than had been captured in previous processes of state formation, but it is supported by a great deal of empirical research into the organization of early modern warfare, politics, and states. Many scholars have shown how relations among early modern – and indeed all – polities rested upon a wide range of interpersonal contacts on a variety of levels. Many scholars have shown how 'private contractors' or 'entrepreneurs' organized large domains of early modern statecraft, from armies, through the financial system.[37] Given that many of these contractors could be transnational, or, to articulate their status in terms more germane to the early modern context, could be actors who sought the favour and business of many confessional and dynastic rulers, this suggests important ways in which administrative expertise and resources could flow across the boundaries of states. Among the important factors that conditioned dynastic monarchs' behaviour was access to capital and expertise that could easily cross the boundaries of individual polities. Subsidies were only one form of access to transnational resources which could inflect the forms of early modern politics, giving access to expertise, resources, and capital beyond the neat boundaries of the 'state' and allowing monarchs to compete for resources on the basis of confessional location, dynastic reputation, and, perhaps, even bureaucratic and military efficiency.

Given the importance of these transnational influences, one could argue that the efficiency of the links to pan-European markets for goods, military power, and capital and credit was as important as, and doubtless in some way correlated to, the efficiency with which

---

37 David Parrott, *The Business of War: Military Enterprise and Military Revolution in Early Modern Europe* (Cambridge: Cambridge University Press, 2012); *The Contractor State and Its Implications, 1659–1815*, ed. by Richard Harding and Sergio Solbes Ferri (Las Palmas de Gran Canaria: Universidad de Las Palmas de Gran Canaria, 2012); *War, Entrepreneurs and the State*, ed. by Jeff Fynn-Paul; and Rafael Torres-Sánchez, Pepijn Brandon, and Marjolein 't Hart, 'War and Economy: Rediscovering the Eighteenth Century Military Entrepreneur', *Business History* 60.1 (2018), 4–22.

a state exploited its own resources.[38] That argument should encourage efforts to explore and document how early modern polities drew upon pan-European and even global networks for resources, money, and credit. Richard Ehrenberg's *Das Zeitalter der Fugger: Geldkapital und Kreditverkehr im 16 Jahrhundert* thus remains a foundational book.[39] Not only does it show the deep embeddedness of European diplomacy in the financial networks of the sixteenth century; it also brings out the vital importance of the transfer of resources to the functioning of early modern states and diplomatic relations more generally. The money provided by subsidies was often of peculiar importance because of its provision in ready, fungible cash in major financial centres, the 'hubs' of early modern finance and commerce. This allowed the recipients of subsidies to make payments for armies, diplomats, and other goods in particularly liquid forms, where bargaining within their own boundaries was often constrained by the liquidity of the assets they could offer – which often required significant investments of capital and expertise.

The payment and receipt of subsidies could have consequences that went far beyond the military and fiscal effects commonly referred to, affecting public opinion, political and economic relations, and social mobility.[40] Yet in older histories of diplomatic relations or war finance, the subsidies' part in state formation is usually discussed as a peripheral phenomenon in the context of a wider examination of particular diplomatic missions, or as one element of the factors that helped create alliances. Focusing on subsidies allows us to perceive the importance of access to international expertise, organization, and capital to early modern statecraft, and to see how access to foreign resources could create the possibility of altering domestic constitutions, politics, and patronage relationships.

Subsidies were a source of political conflict between competing power groupings. Perhaps the most explicit example of these dynamics was the secret Treaty of Dover between Louis XIV of France and Charles II of England, Scotland and Ireland. Louis XIV's offer of subsidies was intended not merely to draw Charles II's territories

---

38 One thinks of the work of Edward Barbier, *Scarcity and Frontiers: How Economies Have Developed through Natural Resource Exploitation* (Cambridge: Cambridge University Press, 2011).
39 Richard Ehrenberg, *Das Zeitalter der Fugger: Geldkapital und Creditverkehr im 16. Jahrhundert*, 2 vols (Jena: Gustav Fischer, 1896).
40 Ingrao, *The Hessian Mercenary State*, pp. 164–174; Windler, '"Ohne Geld keine Schweizer"', pp. 105–134; Wilson, *War, State and Society*, pp. 28–42.

into a coalition against the United Provinces but also to undermine Parliament's efforts to limit its monarch's prerogative, and the identity of the Anglican Church and Presbyterian Churches and the monarch and putative head. James II sought subsidies from France in order to be able to ignore the British Parliament, which held the nation's purse strings. When Louis XIV refused, James II had to fall in line with Parliament's foreign policy, which in turn undermined French interests. The upshot was that Louis XIV reconsidered, and subsidies were paid on condition that British troops were withdrawn from the United Provinces.[41] In the 1690s the English Parliament in conflict with William III decided to dissolve most of the army – of which the majority were paid foreign soldiers – something that prevented William from taking active part in Scandinavian politics.[42] Thus, debates about taking subsidies – which, as Olson and Keckhauser's model would suggest, often involves smaller partners taking richer allies' money – frequently raise not only issues of autonomy and dependence but also questions concerning the very shape and content of the constitution itself. As a result, subsidies could hardly escape becoming a major subject of debate, particularly in those polities whose foreign policies and even survival were acutely dependent upon aid from another sovereign.

The English examples illustrate how subsidies were not always paid by a substantially stronger state to a substantially weaker state. Subsidies were sometimes a result of a need for countries like Spain or the United Provinces to hire troops in order to be participants in a war.[43] The subsidy system also stemmed from a need to find allies who could not only provide troops but also act more or less on behalf of the subsidizer in war – as Denmark and Sweden did from time to time on behalf of France. Subsidies could be a fleeting response to a particular need for troops and political support at a particular moment, or become a longer-lasting 'structural' element of European diplomacy. For example, French and Swedish statesmen came to view the payment of subsidies as almost a traditional element of their crowns' relationship, doubtless because of the frequency with which France paid subsidies to Sweden; not only did Sweden receive subsidies from France for eighty-nine of the years from 1631

---

41 Robert H. George, 'The Financial Relations of Louis XIV and James II', *The Journal of Modern History* 3 (1931).
42 See Stewart P. Oakley, *William III and the Northern Crowns during the Nine Years' War, 1689–1697* (New York and London: Garland, 1987).
43 Thiele, 'The Prince as Military Entrepreneur?', p. 170.

to 1796 but occasionally these subsidy payments occurred for periods of more than twenty consecutive years.[44] Subsidies prompted significant debates about the legal, political, and moral implications of the payment of subsidies. In a time when religion supposedly played an important role in all politics, and indeed war was sparked off by confessional differences, it is striking how many subsidy treaties were in fact signed between parties of different faiths. The French subsidies paid to the two Lutheran countries Denmark and Sweden to defend Lutheranism during the Thirty Years' War is only one such example; the ones paid to Anglican England to go to war against the Puritan United Provinces is another. Hesse-Cassel provided troops to both England and France, and Sweden accepted subsidies not only from France but also from Spain, the United Provinces, and England – all countries of another confession.

The Belgian legal historian Randall Lesaffer has noted how Roman ideals of *amicitia* or 'peaceful friendship' came to be central conditions in true alliances.[45] These ideals conferred obligations as if both parties to the treaty were equal and autonomous moral agents who could freely enter into a contract, even though they occupied different places in the hierarchy of dynastic precedence that constituted the Society of Princes.[46] Early modern treaties conferred different rights and privileges upon different parties to them, while those parties

---

44 For example: in 1738 members of the Swedish Council of the Realm spoke about how the relation between France and Sweden had become hereditary and, in 1774, an instruction for a new French ambassador to Stockholm says that the relation between the two countries had been formed by nature: 'la nature elle-même semble l'avoir formée'. See Carl Trolle Bonde, *Anteckningar om Bondesläkten, Riksrådet Grefwe Gustaf Bonde III* (Lund, 1898), p. 285, and La Courneuve, Archives diplomatiques (AD), Memoire et documents, Suède, 25 (Instructions for comte d'Usson before travelling to Stockholm as ambassador 1774).
45 Randall Lesaffer, '*Amicitia* in Renaissance Peace and Alliance Treaties (1450–1530)', *Journal of the History of International Law* 4 (2002), 77–99.
46 Lucien Bély's *La société des princes, XVIe–XVIIIe siècle* (Paris: Fayard, 1999); Wolfgang Weber, 'Interne und externe Dynamiken der Frühneuzeitlichen Herrscherdynastie: ein Aufriss', in *Bourbon und Wittelsbach: Neuere Forschungen zur Dynastiengeschichte*, ed. by Rainer Babel, Guido Braun, and Thomas Nicklas (Münster: Aschendorff, 2010), pp. 61–77; Wolfgang Weber, 'Dynastiesicherung und Staatsbildung: Die Entfaltung des frühmodernen Fürstenstaats', in *Der Fürst: Ideen und Wirklichkeiten in der europäischen Geschichte*, ed. by Wolfgang Weber (Cologne: Böhlau Verlag, 1998), pp. 91–136.

continued to be viewed as freely choosing autonomous moral agents who sought peace for reasons of friendship and mutual interest. Hugo Grotius was adamant that the only legitimate reason for war was a just cause, whether or not that war was on behalf of a sovereign, an ally, or even the cause of humanity, and consequently that a sovereign who declared war for economic benefit would be worse than a common mercenary, for '[d]id they sell only their own lives it were no great Matter: but they sell also the Lives of many an harmless inoffensive Creature: So much more odious than Hangmen, by how much it is worse to kill without a Reason, than with one.'[47] But if it would be criminal to go to war only for money, Grotius concludes, it would be completely acceptable and even praiseworthy to accept monetary support from a friendly prince for a just war. Theorists and practices differed, however, as to whether paying a subsidy entailed an act of war. Some manifestos included the payment of subsidies among the grounds for a just war, and certain treaties explicitly forbade the continuation of subsidy payments as a condition of peace, although powers evaded such conditions by continuing to pay subsidies. Other theorists, however, argued that princes were free to bestow gifts on whomever they chose, and that these gifts could not be interpreted as constituting grounds for war. Some subsidies were in fact so widely known as to be considered public knowledge, without this entailing war between the power who paid the subsidy and its ally's enemy.[48]

Study of the early modern state requires documenting not just how states raised resources to make war but also how access to transnational resource-transfers reshaped the practices, discourse, and constitutional form of early modern states. As such, subsidies are not just a subject for the 'new diplomatic history', particularly

---

47 Hugo Grotius, *The Rights of War and Peace*, ed. by Richard Tuck (Indianapolis: Liberty Fund, 2005), book II, chapter XXV, p. 1165.

48 For example, Louis XIII's subsidies to the Swedes and the Dutch were mentioned in pamphlets by Richelieu's *dévots* opponents, and were mentioned in anti-French pamphlets after the outbreak of open war; see Caroline Maillet-Rao, *La pensée politique des dévots Mathieu de Morgues et Michel de Marillac: Une opposition au ministériat du cardinal de Richelieu* (Paris: Honoré Champion, 2015), pp. 326–343; Randal Lesaffer, 'Defensive Warfare, Prevention and Hegemony: The Justifications for the Franco-Spanish War of 1635 (Part II)', *Journal of the History of International Law* 8.2 (2006), 155–157, and [Cornelius Jansen], *Le Mars Francois ou la Guerre de France: En laquelle sont examinées les raisons et la justice pretendue des armes & des alliances du roi de France* (n.p., n.pub., 1637), pp. 436–437.

Introduction

if that field only interests itself in the formation of a diplomatic culture without aspiring to analyse what caused war and peace, or participate in the analysis of deeper structural changes in the relations between polities. Scholars should consider subsidies as a major feature in the formation of the early modern state.

Content of the volume

Though the volume contains a wide variety of chapters covering different perspectives of the early modern subsidy system, its aim is not to be all-encompassing but to provide in-depth case studies. However, the authors have been careful to place each case study in a wider European context so as to make it clear to the reader how the individual example relates to a larger whole. We make no claims to have covered all aspects of the French use of subsidies, not to mention other important powers who engaged with subsidies in the early modern era. Rather, the chapters in this volume aim to suggest, rather than exhaust, different aspects of early modern history that can be engaged by examining subsidies as a central problem.

France, being one of the major providers of subsidies in the early modern period, and its capacity of giver are at the focus of Anuschka Tischer's chapter, which examines France's use of subsidies in politics and diplomacy in the seventeenth century. Subsidies were an important factor in the French struggle against the House of Habsburg, a resource that was made possible by the fact that the realm was quite advanced in the state-building process, and that the king thus had a solid income from taxes. Placed in a larger context, France, by using subsidies, influenced the state-building process in other territories and contributed to the formation of a balance between Protestants and Catholics in Germany and in Europe.

Tryntje Helfferich discusses how French subsidies to German states during the Thirty Years' War were understood by the recipients and what this can teach us about the war. Helfferich shows how subsidies, although they were primarily seen and described as necessary to maintain armies, were perceived as posing a threat to a prince's honour, independence, and power, as well as to German culture. Such fears, Helfferich argues, reinforced a process towards calls for the creation of a unified German nation centred on a shared linguistic-cultural inheritance.

Peter H. Wilson places subsidies in the broader context of what he terms 'Fiscal-Military Instruments', or a wide variety of ways in which resources needed for war were transferred among states, both by statesmen and by various kinds of entrepreneurs. Wilson argues that subsidies must be viewed not only as part of a diplomatic and political history of states interacting with states but as part of what he calls a European Fiscal-Military System, distinguished by the flow of money, weapons, and men needed for wars through a diverse set of channels, determined by basic forces of geography, demography, economy, and politics.

Sweden is in focus in two chapters by Svante Norrhem and Erik Bodensten. Norrhem argues that France as the main supplier of subsidies over a lengthy period promoted Swedish state formation in various ways: subsidies were a prerequisite for war; they helped maintain an army, and they funded military building projects and thus increased the demand for military, administrative, and other expertise. Looking at the long eighteenth century, Erik Bodensten shows that the receipt of subsidies caused a variety of strategic problems, dilemmas, and challenges for the receiving party. With Sweden as his point of departure, he argues that a decrease in demand for subsidy troops posed a major challenge for minor powers as the states system of Europe changed.

Another example of the impact of payments from a stronger party on a weaker one is given by Philippe Rogger, who has investigated the Franco-Swiss relation during the sixteenth century. Individuals, Rogger argues, benefited from foreign-policy relations, and resources amassed as a result of French patronage were fundamental to the ruling elites' accumulation of political power.

In his chapter about the principality of Waldeck in the seventeenth and eighteenth centuries, Andreas Flurschütz da Cruz shows how even very small European states could gain considerably from subsidy deals with states such as Venice, the Netherlands, and Great Britain. Waldeck thus serves as an example of how subsidies could help secure smaller states' place within the Holy Roman Empire and build their positions within the noble hierarchy of Europe. Tilman Haug, while discussing the often difficult position in which a ruling prince in a small German state was placed when he received subsidies from France or England, looks partly beyond the state. Alliances between smaller and larger states were often brokered by what he terms cross-border networks or clients of foreign powers within the Empire. Through three case studies, he investigates the role that such cross-border networks or clients played in negotiating subsidy treaties, especially within the Holy Roman Empire.

Erik Thomson and Marianne Klerk in their respective chapters both supply examples of the workings of and the central role played by non-state actors for the procurement and transfer of resources for war-making. Following Wilson's model of a Fiscal-Military System, Marianne Klerk has studied how the handling of subsidies along with other war-making resources was organized in specific urban European centres, which she terms 'fiscal-military hubs'. Amsterdam, Hamburg, and Genoa became the most important such hubs for the flourishing war-organization industry because they attracted wealthy merchant-financiers. She particularly focuses on how Dutch and Swedish merchants attempted to use copper and other goods from Sweden to support the Swedish crown's credit, in various kinds of mercantile relations which bridged the gap between support and taking profits. The role of hubs is important for our understanding of the wider context of individual fiscal-military agents, Klerk argues, and she offers further insights into the relation between the business of war and European state formation. Erik Thomson focuses on the Hoeufft family, who remitted French subsidy payments to many of France's allies during the Thirty Years' War, including Sweden and the Dutch Republic. Thomson reveals how the skills and connections of Jean and Mattheus Hoeufft, acquired during years of large-scale arms dealing, were necessary to the remittance of the subsidies, but also how subsidies came to play a central role securing their business, as diplomatic pressure was enlisted to make the French crown pay them quickly. At this diplomatic moment the Hoeuffts made political power and mercantile credit act in parallel, serving their own Calvinist political goals as well as the aims of the most Christian monarch.

Money may have been one of the forces that served to dissolve Christendom; but money also proved a powerful reagent which shaped the reactions that caused the new states and system of states to arise. The prevalence of subsidy payments might be seen merely as a sign of the transitory brokerage phase of early modern state building. It might simply be regarded as a moment when sovereigns who were rich in capital 'rented' armies from those who had the ability to make war. Subsidy payments might be seen as a corrupt system which reduced those princes and states to the roles of dependents of those who paid them. They can be condemned as a method of finance that slowed or even prevented the emergence of modern states, delaying but not preventing the destruction of states that lacked the fiscal capacity and institutional strengths to survive until the modern age.

The chapters in this book, however, suggest that the role of subsidies was more complex. Subsidies were paid only after careful consideration that the receiver would actually provide whatever the giver needed – military strength or neutrality, or access to land, fortresses, harbours, or people. In addition, the volume highlights the ways in which states and dynasties were strengthened by resources that offered prestige and military, and sometimes financial and cultural, power. Subsidies allowed both those who paid and those who received money a degree of flexibility and choice in making institutional reforms; and, if not every sovereign took advantage of time and opportunity, that is not necessarily the fault of the mechanism of subsidies. Through attracting subsidies and using them wisely, lesser German princes could rise in the intricate web of princely hierarchy within Europe. Moreover, the book goes beyond the state level to seek out the mechanisms that made the subsidy system function, and to show how the practices of early modern diplomacy influenced a wide range of commercial and financial relations. This book has brought together experts, each of whom has contributed to a volume that aims at introducing studies of subsidies as an important field of research which contributes greatly to a new understanding of early modern diplomacy and of European war-making, dynastic ambition, and state formation.

1
The role of subsidies in seventeenth-century French foreign relations and their European context

Anuschka Tischer

The focus of this chapter is on the notion and practice of subsidies in French politics and diplomacy in the seventeenth century. It begins, however, with some general observations on the subject concerning the notion and practice of subsidies to demonstrate what I see as the desiderata, relevant issues, and methodological problems. I then continue with a short overview of the French practice of subsidies in the sixteenth and seventeenth centuries and finally present some examples of how the notion and practice were used and described in relation to French diplomacy at the Congress of Westphalia.

General observations

As was pointed out in the Introduction, subsidies are one of those political notions and practices common in the early modern period that are yet to be systematically researched. The methodological problem can be compared to the notion and practice of protection, which has also only recently been put on the scholarly agenda.[1] The comparison is useful as protection and subsidies have several common features and are, in fact, entangled in their use in the early modern international system. Research on protection could thus

---

1 *Protegierte und Protektoren: Asymmetrische politische Beziehungen zwischen Partnerschaft und Dominanz (16. bis frühes 20. Jahrhundert)*, ed. by Tilman Haug, Nadir Weber, and Christian Windler, Externa: Geschichte der Außenbeziehungen in neuen Perspektiven, 9 (Cologne: Böhlau Verlag, 2016); Rainer Babel, *Garde et protection: Der Königsschutz in der französischen Außenpolitik vom 15. bis zum 17. Jahrhundert*, Beihefte der Francia, 72 (Ostfildern: Thorbecke Verlag, 2014).

serve as a kind of model for research on subsidies in diplomatic and political terms. There are a number of particular connections between the two: there is no clear concept, but the notion is used in multiple ways; the notion is used for personal or state relations, for a practice inside political communities, and for external relations; the notion and practice do change during the early modern period, and this change is significant for the state-building process and for an understanding of the sovereign modern state; the practice is significant for asymmetric relations, as these were customary as long as societies and state relations were regarded as hierarchical; the practice was theoretically delegitimized on the basis of the notion of sovereignty and equality of states. However, the political practice of protection and subsidies did not end with the modern state, and one might even discuss whether there are still relics of this practice to this day.

In general, a subsidy was offered as assistance or support for war. In the first place, a 'subsidy' was an extraordinary form of support that subjects gave to their prince in times of war. That is how the notion is used in Jean Bodin's *Les six livres de la République*, where the right to raise subsidies from subjects is listed as one of the signs of sovereignty.[2] As no regular tax was established in the Holy Roman Empire, the financing of war continued to be based on a subsidy system.

As a result of further developments, a 'subsidy' came to mean a form of support in terms of money or troops that one power gave to another for a war or at least in a conflict. Such cases were usually regulated by a treaty and thus took the form of an alliance. The French subsidies in focus in this analysis were part of alliances.

---

2 'Sous cette même puissance de donner et casser la loi, sont compris tous les autres droits et marques de souveraineté: de sorte qu'à parler proprement on peut dire qu'il n'y a que cette seule marque de souveraineté, attendu que tous les autres droits sont compris en celui-là, comme décerner la guerre, ou faire la paix, connaître en dernier ressort des jugements de tous magistrats, instituer et destituer les plus grands officiers, imposer ou exempter les sujets de charges et subsides, octroyer grâces et dispenses contre la rigueur des lois, hausser ou baisser le titre, valeur et pied des monnaies, faire jurer les sujets et hommes liges de garder fidélité sans exception à celui auquel est dû le serment, qui sont les vraies marques de souveraineté, comprises sous la puissance de donner la loi à tous en général, et à chacun en particulier, et ne la recevoir que de Dieu.' Jean Bodin, *Les six livres de la République: Un abrégé du texte de l'édition de Paris de 1583*, ed. by Gérard Mairet (Paris: Librairie générale française, 1993), p. 101.

The role of subsidies 27

There was, however, a difference if France paid money to an ally to fight the war (i.e. a proxy war for France) or if France and its ally or allies fought a war together, where every partner contributed what they could best provide, be it money or military forces. Finally, there is yet another use of the notion of subsidies: troops hired from one power to another were also called subsidies or subsidy troops. Obviously, this was a different form of bilateral relation from an alliance. Thus, subsidies can mean different things in the early modern period.[3] The difference between the various practices of subsidies is not always clear, in particular when we compare political entities with completely different structures and constitutions. The estates of the Holy Roman Empire could support the emperor in two ways: by troops or money approved by an Imperial Diet (*Reichshilfe*) or by an official alliance with the emperor. In both cases, they could impose conditions for their support. On the other hand, the estates were in both cases not really free to refuse any support to the emperor. The estates were vassals, and the emperor could claim to represent and defend a common cause.[4] The Holy Roman Empire thus represents a remarkable case in terms of how the notion and practice of subsidies could move in multiple directions.

France represents another, and completely different, case. It was one of the largest payers of financial subsidies in the early modern period. The king of France had an established right to claim regular taxes inside the country. The kings of France had an elaborate concept regarding their own authority and sovereignty, and in the French view it was somehow disreputable or at least humble to

---

3 Michael Busch, 'Subsidien', in *Enzyklopädie der Neuzeit*, ed. by Friedrich Jäger, vol. 12 (Stuttgart: Metzler Verlag, 2010), cols 1210–1212.
4 When the League of Rhine, concluded in 1658, deliberated about military support for the emperor against the Ottoman Empire in 1663, members of the League spoke explicitly of subsidies, and they discussed a long list of conditions they wanted Leopold I to fulfil. See the *Protocollum In Consilio Fœderatorum circa subsidium contra Turcam* in the Haus-, Hof- und Staatsarchiv in Vienna, *Mainzer Erzkanzlerarchiv, Friedensakten*, vol. 64, file 1. Neither in their separate negotiations nor in the Imperial Diet, however, could they finally refuse subsidies for this traditionally well-established cause, although the estates knew that Leopold pursued his very own interests in Hungary. See Anton Schindling, *Die Anfänge des Immerwährenden Reichstags zu Regensburg: Ständevertretung und Staatskunst nach dem Westfälischen Frieden*, Veröffentlichungen des Instituts für Europäische Geschichte Mainz, 143 (Mainz: Verlag Philipp von Zabern, 1991).

accept money, as we see further below in this chapter with regard to the time of the Peace Congress of Westphalia. The French policy, however, operated for about two centuries, for a long time because other powers did not share this view and accepted French money. Thus, it would be overly simple to brand the French policy as modern in contrast to those of other powers. In fact, France, or at least the French policy as we know it, depended on the subsidy system: the early modern struggle of the French kings and politicians against the House of Habsburg could hardly have been undertaken in a direct military confrontation or by France alone. After Cardinal Richelieu had exposed France to this struggle, the greatest fear for the French was to be without allies during an attack by Spain and a subsequent war.[5] Thus, the struggle against the House of Habsburg and its alleged universal monarchy formed alliances of convenience in which France had the money, whereas its partners had the military means.[6]

The French military system could hardly stand alone prior to the reforms at the time of Louis XIV.[7] Despite its long coastline, the country had no considerable naval fleet, and the war against Spain between 1635 and 1659 would have been impossible without Dutch and later English military support at sea. Moreover, for its army, the populous realm of France needed foreigners and thus subsidies in the sense of subsidy troops. Cardinal Richelieu had his doubts that the French mentality in general was fit for serious fighting

---

5 Anuschka Tischer, *Französische Diplomatie und Diplomaten auf dem Westfälischen Friedenskongreß: Außenpolitik unter Richelieu und Mazarin*, Schriftenreihe der Vereinigung zur Erforschung der Neueren Geschichte e.V., 29 (Münster: Aschendorff Verlag, 1999), p. 186.
6 For the political stereotype of a *Monarchia Universalis*, see Franz Bosbach, *Monarchia Universalis: Ein politischer Leitbegriff der Frühen Neuzeit*, Schriftenreihe der Historischen Kommission bei der Bayerischen Akademie der Wissenschaften, 32 (Göttingen: Vandenhoeck & Ruprecht, 1988); Peer Schmidt, *Spanische Universalmonarchie oder 'teutsche Libertet': das spanische Imperium in der Propaganda des Dreißigjährigen Krieges*, Studien zur modernen Geschichte, 54 (Stuttgart: Franz Steiner Verlag, 2001).
7 For the unsatisfactory state of the French military during the time of Richelieu, see David Parrott, 'French Military Organisation in the 1630s: The Failure of Richelieu's Ministry', *Seventeenth-Century French Studies* 9 (1987), 151–167; David Parrott, *Richelieu's Army: War, Government and Society in France 1624–1642* (Cambridge: Cambridge University Press, 2001). For a more general overview, see John A. Lynn, *Giant of the Grand Siècle: The French Army 1610–1715* (Cambridge: Cambridge University Press, 1997).

and saw it as essential that the French army included foreign forces.[8] When, however, Louis XIV later emphasised the close tie between sovereignty and the performance of war, this simultaneously implied a pursuit of autonomy in warfare.[9] While Richelieu was successful, because France rather paid than fought, Louis XIV promoted the idea of a vigorous warrior king who consequently went to open war – although the king's diplomacy and its use of money remained an important additive to his wars.

Notwithstanding the complex political and military system of which subsidies usually constituted a part, they first of all fulfilled an economic purpose: one power funded the expenses of another. Thus, funders had a political interest in what they paid for; and vice versa, the one accepting the money of another power might not have been able to act the way they did without this money. The financial value – or more precisely, the value of what the money could buy – evidently served as the leading factor of subsidies. This is in clear contrast to diplomatic gifts, which had a strong symbolic dimension and were means of communication, no matter how expensive they were.[10] It was impossible to simply sell such a gift and buy something 'useful' or to use the money to pay off debts.

However, this does not mean that subsidies were purely economic. Early modern society was essentially based on honour, reputation, and symbolic acts. Thus, there was a symbolic dimension already when subsidies were given or accepted. Like any symbolic act, the giving and taking of subsidies could be perceived in different ways, and the perception could have political consequences. As we shall see, French diplomats and politicians were uncertain regarding the impression caused by the French subsidies. Was it the impression that the French allies needed money or, vice versa, that France had to buy its allies? Nevertheless, French money in combination with

---

8 *Testament Politique de Richelieu*, ed. by Françoise Hildesheimer (Paris: Société de l'Histoire de France, 1995), pp. 305–306.

9 Joël Cornette, *Le roi de guerre: Essai sur la souveraineté dans la France du Grand Siècle* (Paris: Éditions Payot & Rivages, 1993).

10 For the wide range of diplomatic gifts and material exchange in foreign relations, see *Materielle Grundlagen der Diplomatie: Schenken, Sammeln und Verhandeln in Spätmittelalter und Früher Neuzeit*, ed. by Mark Häberlein and Christof Jeggle, Irseer Schriften: Studien zur Wirtschafts-, Kultur- und Mentalitätsgeschichte new series, 9 (Constance and Munich: UVK Verlagsgesellschaft, 2013). Cf. also several chapters in *Medien der Außenbeziehungen von der Antike bis zur Gegenwart*, ed. by Peter Hoeres and Anuschka Tischer (Cologne: Böhlau Verlag, 2017).

French protection in general had quite a positive impact on French reputation during the Thirty Years' War.[11] The reasons why political powers supplied one another ranged from economic interests to proxy wars and joint wars, and thereby to common political interests. There were, however, few purely economic subsidy relations. The Swiss Confederation was the first and only long-term political power to organize subsidy troops for money and not pursue a foreign-power policy. However, even the Swiss had some foreign interests, and those who hired Swiss mercenaries also had to combine their financial efforts with diplomatic ones, because the Confederation would only leave its troops in a war for one conflicting party, and as a political community it would not act against its own political interests. The position of the French ambassador in Solothurn was crucial. He solemnly represented a traditional good understanding of both powers and would try to convince the Swiss that they shared common interests with the French.[12]

Studies on subsidies usually focus on one aspect concerning the notion and practice related to this phenomenon. Some thorough studies exist on subsidies in a military context, which present statistical material and military aspects.[13] If we take a look at subsidies

---

11 Cf. Tryntje Helfferich, Chapter 2 below.
12 Thomas Lau, 'Fremdwahrnehmung und Kulturtransfer – der Ambassadorenhof in Solothurn', in *Wahrnehmungen des Fremden: Differenzerfahrungen von Diplomaten im 16. und 17. Jahrhundert*, ed. by Michael Rohrschneider and Arno Strohmeyer, Schriftenreihe der Vereinigung zur Erforschung der Neueren Geschichte e.V., 31 (Münster: Aschendorff Verlag, 2007), pp. 313–341; Andreas Affolter, *Verhandeln mit Republiken: Die französisch-eidgenössischen Beziehungen im frühen 18. Jahrhundert*, Externa: Geschichte der Außenbeziehungen in neuen Perspektiven, 11 (Cologne: Böhlau Verlag, 2017). For the Swiss case, also see Philippe Rogger, Chapter 6 below.
13 See, for instance, Hildegard Ernst, *Madrid und Wien 1632–1637: Politik und Finanzen in den Beziehungen zwischen Philipp IV. und Ferdinand II.*, Schriftenreihe der Vereinigung zur Erforschung der Neueren Geschichte e.V., 18 (Münster: Aschendorff Verlag, 1991); Gottfried Lorenz, 'Schweden und die französischen Hilfsgelder von 1638 bis 1649: Ein Beitrag zur Finanzierung des Krieges im 17. Jahrhundert', in *Forschungen und Quellen zur Geschichte des Dreißigjährigen Krieges*, Schriftenreihe der Vereinigung zur Erforschung der Neueren Geschichte e.V., 12 (Münster: Aschendorff Verlag, 1981), pp. 98–148; Jörg Ulbert, 'Französische Subsidienzahlungen an Hessen-Kassel während des Dreißigjährigen Krieges', in *Frankreich und Hessen-Kassel zur Zeit des Dreißigjährigen Krieges und des Westfälischen Friedens*, ed. by Klaus Malettke, Veröffentlichungen der Historischen Kommission für Hessen, 46 (Marburg: Elwert, 1999), pp. 159–174; Max Braubach,

The role of subsidies

in a wider political and diplomatic context, there are still further problems of definition, delimitation, and coherence with other notions and practices. Thus, subsidies are not clearly separated from pensions, although subsidies are usually regarded as part of an alliance of equals, whereas pensions indicate some kind of patron–client relationship. When Jörg Ulbert analysed the French subsidies for Hesse-Cassel during the Thirty Years' War, he referred to pensions as 'subsidies in disguise' (*verkappte Subsidien*).[14] It is remarkable that Sweden used at least 14 per cent of its French subsidies not for military but for diplomatic expenses, in particular for financing its delegation during the peace talks in Osnabrück.[15] On the other hand, in an earlier study on the role of subsidies in the War of the Spanish Succession, Max Braubach referred to them as a 'substitute' (*Ersatz*) for pensions, a judgement made on the basis of a short overview of the historical development and function of the two.[16] Both views have their pros and cons and should be discussed further.

Moreover, subsidies represent a form of support with money or soldiers, but they should also be regarded in relation to symbolic capital, not only because they themselves were seen as symbolic but because they were entangled and competed with other values that were less material or practical in nature. This is very well illustrated by the case of Braunschweig: during the Nine Years' War, Duke Ernst August received subsidies from France, which hoped to neutralise the duke from the conflict. Actually, however, the French support strengthened the duke's position vis-à-vis Emperor Leopold I, who promoted the territory of Braunschweig-Lüneburg to a new electorate in 1692. By this act, the new elector finally became a part of the imperial alliance against France. Lucien Bély mentioned this specific case in an overview over subsidies in the *Ancien Régime* as an example of just how unpredictable the outcomes of subsidies were with regard to political calculations.[17] Moreover, in this case it was the emperor's decision that brought the Wolfenbüttel branch of Braunschweig to accept French subsidies and thereby join a French alliance, as Wolfenbüttel did not accept that the internal balance

---

Die Bedeutung der Subsidien für die Politik im spanischen Erbfolgekriege (Bonn and Leipzig: Schroeder, 1923).
14 Ulbert, 'Französische Subsidienzahlungen', p. 166.
15 Lorenz, 'Schweden und die französischen Hilfsgelder', p. 99.
16 Braubach, *Die Bedeutung der Subsidien*, p. 7.
17 Lucien Bély, 'Subsides', in *Dictionnaire de l'Ancien Régime*, ed. by Lucien Bély (Paris: Presses Universitaires de France, 1996), pp. 1178–1179.

of the House of Braunschweig was destroyed by the creation of the new electorate.[18]

The case of Braunschweig gives us an idea of the complexity of the means of giving and taking in early modern society and state system, in particular when we keep in mind that the political conditions of the great powers were completely different: France had a comparatively well-functioning tax system, which allowed the king to hire troops and pay subsidies. At the same time, however, an elaborate concept of the king as a sovereign prince existed. It would have been impossible for a French king to accept subsidies other than hired troops on a purely economic basis. This may be compared to the fact that it would also have been impossible for a French king to accept a protector and protection, even during his minority reign. Thus, a French king could not have been 'supported' in a war in the same way as he himself supported, for instance, Sweden or Hesse-Cassel during the Thirty Years' War: What might have blemished the honour and reputation of a king of France was for others just a useful means of foreign policy.[19]

Unlike the situation in France, the emperor had no income or military basis ex officio. When he asked for subsidies, he did so based on the original meaning of the notion: he had to ask the members of the Holy Roman Empire for extraordinary support. As the Imperial Estates were international actors at the same time, the emperor was in competition with international actors even when he asked for 'internal' support, as demonstrated in the case of Braunschweig. On the other hand, the emperor was part of the House of Habsburg, which often provided him with a solid basis of troops and money, either from his own hereditary lands or from his Spanish cousins.[20] In addition, the emperor also had ex-officio access to an enormous symbolic capital and could offer status improvements and enhancements. The creation of a new electorate for Braunschweig is a spectacular example, but Leopold I in particular used this means in many ways. Thus, the money and troops of Louis XIV also competed against the symbolic capital amassed by the emperor.

When we finally ask why subsidies were spent, it is evident that the one giving money to someone else wanted to attain a political

---

18 Braubach, *Die Bedeutung der Subsidien*, pp. 59–60.
19 For the functional view of the receivers on subsidies, see Tryntje Helfferich, Chapter 2 below.
20 Cf. Ernst, *Madrid und Wien*.

The role of subsidies

or military objective or at least had the impression that there was an objective to which he should contribute.[21] This indicates a further difference between subsidies and gifts, as gifts were usually not given to reach a specific objective. Subsidies, however, were not just a price paid by a power to then get what it wanted. There remained a lot of uncertainties, in particular since a political actor who took money did not become a service provider as a result, but still remained an independent power. He could disappoint the hopes of the payer. In the worst case, the subsidies helped a power to acquire a form of authority that could frighten the one who was paying for it. The relationship between France and Sweden in the Thirty Years' War serves as a good example of this: from the very beginning, France was not able to calculate or control the Protestant power it supported with money, and the growing Swedish success aggravated the situation. French politicians were confronted with the fact that they paid for Sweden's unwanted war against Denmark in 1643 and, even worse, for Sweden's strong pro-Protestant politics at the Congress of Westphalia, all of which were not the reasons for paying out the subsidies.[22]

The more subsidies became an established system, the more there were political actors who more or less expected pensions or subsidies, even if the money did not influence their policies in any significant way. The elector of Mayence, Johann Philipp von Schönborn, is an example of a minor political actor who received money from both France and the emperor, but who nevertheless balanced quite well between the two. Emperor Leopold I judged in

---

21 See, for instance, the statement by the French ambassador Abel Servien who negotiated on the Franco-Dutch alliance in The Hague for some time during the Congress of Westphalia and wrote to Cardinal Mazarin on 9 April 1647: 'Je croy tellement que sans miracle on ne fera rien cette année avec les armes du costé de cet Estat, qu'une des plus nécessaires applications que nous devions avoir, selon mon advis, est de profficter des troupes qui sont entretenues du subside de France, qu'on est sur le poinct de licencier.' *Acta Pacis Westphalicae*, ed. by Max Braubach, Konrad Repgen, and Maximilian Lanzinner, series II B (French Correspondence), vol. 5, prep. by Guido Braun (Münster: Aschendorff Verlag, 2002), part 2, p. 1019.
22 For the French government's insistence on the view that their subsidies were meant to pay for the war against the emperor, not against Denmark, see *Acta Pacis Westphalicae*, II B, vol. 1, prep. by Ursula Irsigler (Münster: Aschendorff Verlag, 1979), pp. 266, 301. For the further difficulties between France and Sweden during the time of the Westphalian Peace Congress, see Tischer, *Französische Diplomatie*, pp. 295–310.

1671 that it was necessary to pay money to the elector, although he was already separated from France owing to the political situation.[23]

Subsidies in French politics

In 1552, Henri II of France initiated a significant policy of subsidies with the Treaty of Chambord.[24] He concluded an alliance with several Protestant German princes against Emperor Charles V, which was the climax of a French policy of trying to win over imperial estates against a suspected universal monarchy of the Habsburg ruler. According to the Treaty of Chambord, the German princes raised troops, whereas the French king promised them 70,000 *écus* per month plus an initial sum of money. The Treaty of Chambord, which allowed the king to occupy the imperial cities of Metz, Toul, and Verdun, was also the beginning of the modern French policy of protection.[25] This highlights the entanglement between the practices, an entanglement which was, however, soon interrupted: after the 1559 Peace of Cateau-Cambrésis, by which France accepted the Habsburg predominance, the French kings focused on the realm's

---

23 'Kurmainz zeigt sich guet und ganz abgesondert von Frankreich, also ist wohl vonnöthen, ihn nit stecken zue lassen ... Idem faciat Pötting und sehe, dass man aufs wenigste etwas thue. Dann revera, ohne Geld erhalten wir diese Leut nit, und nehmen sie nochmals Frankreichs Geld an, so heißt es, oleum et operam perdidimus.' In: *Privatbriefe Kaiser Leopold I. an den Grafen F.E. Pötting. 1662–1673*, ed. by Dr Alfred Francis Pribram and Dr Moriz Landwehr von Pragenau, part 2, Fontes Rerum Austriacarum, Diplomataria et Acta LVII (Vienna: In Kommission bei Carl Gerold's Sohn, 1904), p. 197. For the elector's relations to France, see Tilman Haug, *Ungleiche Außenbeziehungen und grenzüberschreitende Patronage: Die französische Krone und die geistlichen Kurfürsten (1648–1679)*, Externa: Geschichte der Außenbeziehungen in neuen Perspektiven, 6 (Cologne: Böhlau Verlag, 2015).

24 For the treaty text, see *Politische Korrespondenz des Herzogs und Kurfürsten Moritz von Sachsen*, ed. by Historische Kommission bei der Sächsischen Akademie der Wissenschaften zu Leipzig, vol. 5, prep. by Johannes Herrmann, Günther Wartenberg, and Christian Winter (Berlin: Akademie Verlag, 1998), pp. 574–585.

25 For the occupation and its further consequences, see Christine Petry, *'Faire des sujets du roi': Rechtspolitik in Metz, Toul und Verdun unter französischer Herrschaft (1552–1648)*, Pariser Historische Studien, 73 (Munich: R. Oldenbourg Verlag, 2006). For the development of the French protection politics of this period, see Babel, *Garde et protection*.

internal problems and pursued no noteworthy foreign policy for several decades.[26]

When France returned to the international stage with Henri IV, it faced the problem of a lack of money. Money was the key to the success of French foreign policy before Cateau-Cambrésis, and later for the foreign policy of Richelieu; but the debts of the French crown to Swiss mercenaries from the time of the Wars of Religion became a serious obstacle to the financial credibility it needed for its future foreign policy. The first payments at the end of the sixteenth and beginning of the seventeenth centuries were solemn events purporting to restore confidence. Yet, although France would have debts to the Swiss of up to 70 million *livres* for a long time, the realm was quite successful in recruiting further mercenaries and also in building up a network of political powers receiving French money.[27] This was important to French foreign policy during the Thirty Years' War. Obviously, subsidies did not necessarily represent an immediate cash flow; they could also be a promise in relation to a distant future. In this case, credibility was crucial, not liquidity, which required a partner who accepted subsidies although he did not have any immediate need for the money.

France once again started to finance the enemies of the House of Habsburg – and in particular, once again, the Protestant enemies – at the beginning of Cardinal Richelieu's government in 1624. In the same year, Louis XIII concluded the Treaty of Compiègne with the States-General of the United Provinces, in which the latter received a loan that was to be repaid after a peace with Spain.[28] Starting in 1630, Louis gave them one million *livres* annually for their war 'as a gift' (*en don*).[29] With the Treaty of Bärwalde in 1631, France was

---

26 For the treaty of Cateau-Cambrésis, see Bertrand Haan, *Une paix pour l'éternité: La négociation du traité du Cateau-Cambrésis*, Bibliothèque de la Casa de Velázquez, 49 (Madrid: Casa de Velázquez, 2010).
27 For the debts and payment, see Lau, 'Fremdwahrnehmung und Kulturtransfer', pp. 315–316.
28 A reproduction of this treaty with further information can be found in the database *Europäische Friedensverträge der Vormoderne online* of the Leibniz-Institut für Europäische Geschichte in Mayence: www.ieg-friedensvertraege.de/treaty/1624%20VI%2010%20Allianz-%20und%20Subsidienvertrag%20von%20Compi%C3%A8gne/t-958-1-de.html?h=1, accessed 5 November 2017.
29 Renewal of the alliance from 17 June 1630: www.ieg-friedensvertraege.de/treaty/1630%20VI%2017%20Erneuerung%20der%20bestehenden%20Allianz/t-964-1-de.html?h=1, accessed 5 November 2017. The subsequent

obliged to pay one million *livres* per year to Sweden, whereas Sweden had to raise an army.[30] The French policy thus more or less adhered to the model of 1552. However, it went further in a different way: it took decades until the war and the subsidies came to an end. From 1630 onwards, France paid subsidies for eighteen subsequent years. Moreover, there was not just one but several subsidy arrangements – those with the Dutch Republic and with Sweden followed an agreement with Hesse-Cassel, which cost France an additional 500,000 *livre*s per year.[31] Finally, this war soon became more than a proxy war for France; so from 1635 onwards, the realm had to pay its own war expenses in addition to the subsidies.

France could use subsidies in its foreign policy because it had the money to do so. As a member of the French government, probably Cardinal Mazarin himself, would say in the summer of 1648, when the parties of the Thirty Years' War were increasingly exhausted: 'It is not that we have much more money, but we still have more than our enemies.'[32] The reason why France usually had more money for foreign policy than its enemies was found in the fact that it was particularly advanced in its state-building process and the establishment of taxes. At the same time, France had more inhabitants, and thus tax-payers, than any other European country. The good material conditions of the French foreign policy were proved by the fact that France, unlike its costly allies Sweden and Hesse-Cassel, did not ask for any financial satisfaction during the Congress of Westphalia. Hence, the French claim to have fought the war for German liberty was probably more credible for the German estates that had to pay the money Sweden needed for the compensation of its military. The French government's generosity outside its own country came with risks: in 1648, the very year of the Peace of Westphalia, the revolt of the Fronde broke out, starting with protests against new fiscal laws whereupon state bankruptcy followed.

---

alliance treaty was concluded on 15 April 1634: www.ieg-friedensvertraege.de/treaty/1634%20IV%2015%20Allianz-%20und%20Freundschaftsvertrag%20von%20Den%20Haag/t-1079-1-de.html?h=1, accessed 5 November 2017.

30 Treaty of Bärwalde: www.ieg-friedensvertraege.de/treaty/1631%20I%2013%20Allianzvertrag%20von%20B%C3%A4rwalde/t-1293-1-de.html?h=1, accessed 5 November 2017.

31 Ulbert, 'Französische Subsidienzahlungen', p. 167.

32 'Ce n'est pas qu'on veuille dire que nous ayons beaucoup plus d'argent, mais tousjours en avons nous plus que nos ennemis.' Quoted from Tischer, *Französische Diplomatie*, p. 199.

The role of subsidies   37

The transfer of money to foreign powers remained an important element of French foreign policy after Westphalia.[33] Nevertheless, the main instrument of the power politics of Louis XIV was the military means under the direct control of the state (i.e. a strong standing army and fortresses). During the War of the Spanish Succession, France paid subsidies to the grandson of Louis XIV, Philippe, who claimed the Spanish throne, as well as to French allies, the most important being the electors of Bavaria and Cologne. At 4–6 million *livres* annually, the French subsidies for Philippe were high; however, compared to the 70–90 million *livres* annual overall cost of the war, the subsidies represented a relatively small expense.[34]

In an overview, I would say that the peaks of the French subsidy policy were in the 1550s and again in the 1630s and 1640s with a long interruption due to internal conflicts. The French subsidy policy started in 1552 with a relatively high engagement of 70,000 *écus* (i.e. about 210,000 *livres* per month), which meant more than two and a half million *livres* per year. Even if we take currency changes into consideration, this seems impressive compared to the same sum paid to the Dutch Republic, Sweden, and Hesse-Cassel combined during the Thirty Years' War, in particular as the income of the French crown had increased since the sixteenth century. On the other hand, in 1552 France won Metz, Toul, and Verdun immediately, whereas in the Thirty Years' War it faced long-term financial obligations and finally its own involvement in the war. This makes it difficult to compare the two most relevant cases of French subsidy policy. I would argue, however, that these mark a period of an international entanglement of France with parallels in the French politics of protection, a period which ended with the Peace of Westphalia. In the future, France would pursue a modern state policy, that is, a policy relying substantially on institutionalized means which the government could control, such as a standing army or fortified borders. Nevertheless, unpredictable means like protection and subsidies depending on co-operation with foreign powers – and not necessarily geared to any material advantage for France – were also still in use, but they no longer formed a central element in France's foreign policy. It is worth discussing whether

---

33 For the relations to the electors of Mayence and Cologne, see, for instance, Haug, *Ungleiche Außenbeziehungen*.
34 Guy Rowlands, *The Financial Decline of a Great Power: War, Influence, and Money in Louis XIV's France* (Oxford: Oxford University Press, 2012), pp. 23, 158.

this was a result of a long-term state-building process or of the concrete experiences of French politicians and diplomats in relation to those means during the Thirty Years' War and the Congress of Westphalia.

An outlook on subsidies in French diplomacy at the Congress of Westphalia

Subsidies were a subject of political correspondence and internal diplomatic discussion and, as they were part of diplomacy, the diplomats also took part in the subsidy policy. During the Thirty Years' War, one of the Swedish negotiators in Osnabrück, Johan Adler Salvius, was simultaneously responsible for the administration of the French subsidies, a responsibility that constituted a heavy burden for him in addition to the peace negotiations.[35] This task must have influenced his relations with his French colleagues, who served as his contacts for any questions or problems concerning the subsidies. Complaints regarding the frequent delay of payment were made by the Swedish resident in Münster where the French delegation resided.[36] Vice versa, the French found themselves in an awkward position when they would have welcomed subsidies, and recognised their political benefit, but had to wait for decisions and money from Paris: in 1644, when the Swedes urged in favour of subsidies for Transylvania, the French diplomats made it clear that they had no power to make a decision on this point and that they furthermore did not have the money for this kind of extraordinary payments. This was something they had to point out, since it was quite common for them to pay for political and diplomatic expenses in advance.[37] Nevertheless, they agreed that the matter was of high importance in order to encourage the prince of Transylvania to fight against the emperor.

It is evident that subsidies were a means of diplomacy, but using this means was tricky. At least in its last phase, the Swedish war in Germany was completely dependent on French subsidies, and the

---

35 Cf. Lorenz, 'Schweden und die französischen Hilfsgelder'.
36 *Acta Pacis Westphalicae*, II B, vol. 1, p. 430.
37 'Nous n'avons pas apporté icy la bource si bien garnie que nous puissions pourvoir de nous mesmes à des despenses impréveues de cette nature.' *Acta Pacis Westphalicae*, II B, vol. 1, p. 173.

The role of subsidies

French diplomats knew it.[38] They used the frequent delays of payment as a kind of policy of pinpricks, and the Swedes understood this correctly.[39] When the French became more and more dissatisfied with the Swedish demands, the French ambassador Claude d'Avaux openly announced a delay to his Swedish counterpart Johan Oxenstierna in 1647.[40] However, there was no serious consideration of stopping the subsidies, as the French and the Swedes were finally tied together in the war. Besides those threats, Cardinal Mazarin also tried to make it clear to the Swedish government that the subsidies were a heavy burden for the French people and that France nevertheless tried its best to fulfil its obligations.[41]

The subsidies for the Dutch Republic were used in the opposite way: when it became more and more evident that the ally was prepared to conclude a peace treaty without France, and when the French were particularly upset with the behaviour of the Dutch delegation, they were anxious that the subsidies should be paid without any delay.[42] However, it was the Dutch Republic itself that sent a clear signal of its political independence: before it made an official arrangement with Spain, it refused to accept further subsidies and even forbade its still-ally to recruit its troops.[43]

On the basis of this, it is not surprising that the French were somehow frustrated regarding the subsidy policy. Ambassador Abel

---

38 'en effect e[l'alliance] fust autant désirée des Suédois que de nous et qu'elle leur fust beaucoup plus nécessaire à cause du subside qu'on leur donne.' *Acta Pacis Westphalicae*, II B, vol. 3, prep. by Elke Jarnut and Rita Bohlen with an introduction and an appendix by Franz Bosbach (Münster: Aschendorff Verlag, 1999), p. 711. The overview of Lorenz shows that this perception reflected reality.
39 *Acta Pacis Westphalicae*, II B, vol. 1, pp. 430, 435; series II C (Swedish Correspondence), vol. 3, prep. by Gottfried Lorenz (Münster: Aschendorff Verlag, 1975), p. XLVII.
40 *Acta Pacis Westphalicae*, II B, vol. 5, 1, p. CXLIV.
41 *Acta Pacis Westphalicae*, II B, vol. 4, p. 516.
42 'Cependant, il est bon que vous soyés informés, pour le faire valloir de delà, que depuis trois jours on a faict payer quatre cens mil francz du dernier quartier du subside pour Messieurs les Estatz sans qu'on y ayt voulu apporter un seul moment de retardement pour la conduicte de quelques-uns de leurs députez, dans l'asseurance que les dictz Sieurs Estatz remédieront aux inconvéniens ausquelz ilz ont voulu nous exposer par leur mauvaise volonté.' *Acta Pacis Westphalicae*, II B, vol. 5, 1, p. 427.
43 *Acta Pacis Westphalicae*, II B, vol. 5, 1, p. XCII.

Servien wrote clear words to his nephew Hugues de Lionne, the future secretary for foreign affairs, and angrily stated that, with regard to subsidies, everyone would behave 'as if we were the treasurers of other nations and as if we were obliged to buy the friendship of those who should be more than happy to have ours'.[44] Servien's outburst also shows that the French did not really regard those accepting subsidies as equals. There was even some disdain for them, since they took money for their 'friendship' and alliance, and they were openly interested in money. With this type of disdain towards such an economic attitude, Servien was definitely not alone in the French government.[45] In particular when it comes to the Dutch Republic, this view fitted into the general disdain of a noble society towards a state of republicans and 'merchants'.[46] When later, in the 1670s, the political constellation had changed, and Louis XIV went to war against the Dutch Republic, French politicians and diplomats were more than eager to show that a war was not a merchant's business – notwithstanding the fact that France had needed the Dutch fleet and military force against Spain some decades before.[47]

---

44 'comme si nous estions les trésoriers des autres nations et comme si nous estions obligez d'achepter l'amitié de ceux qui se doivent tenir trop heureux d'avoir la nostre.' *Acta Pacis Westphalicae*, II B, vol. 4, p. 764.

45 See, for instance, the description provided in a royal memorandum regarding the ambassador of the Dutch Republic in Paris: 'Messieurs les Plénipotentiaires ne doivent pas craindre que l'ambassadeur d'Hollande qui est en cette cour puisse avoir rien cogneu de nos sentimens sur le contenu dans cet article. C'est un homme qui ne se met guières en peyne de les descouvrir et que l'on ne veoid jamais que quand il vient demander l'argent des subsides ou parler en faveur de quelques marchands sur des "prises" de vaisseaux.' *Acta Pacis Westphalicae*, II B, vol. 4, p. 810.

46 See, in general, Helmut Gabel and Volker Jarren, *Kaufleute und Fürsten: Außenpolitik und politisch-kulturelle Perzeption im Spiegel niederländisch-deutscher Beziehungen 1648–1748*, with an introduction by Heinz Duchhardt and Horst Lademacher, Niederlande-Studien, 18 (Munich and Berlin: Waxmann, 1998). For the French perception of their enemies and allies, including the Dutch Republic, during the time of the Congress of Westphalia, see Anuschka Tischer, 'Fremdwahrnehmung und Stereotypenbildung in der französischen Gesandtschaft auf dem Westfälischen Friedenskongress', in *Wahrnehmungen des Fremden: Differenzerfahrungen von Diplomaten im 16. und 17. Jahrhundert*, ed. by Michael Rohrschneider and Arno Strohmeyer, Schriftenreihe der Vereinigung zur Erforschung der Neueren Geschichte e.V., 31 (Münster: Aschendorff Verlag, 2007), pp. 265–288.

47 See, for instance, the judgement of French diplomat Honoré Courtin as early as 1665: 'Ce n'est pas le mestier des marchans de faire la guerre, il faut de bons chefs, de bons officiers, de braves soldats et de hardis matelots.

Conclusion

Subsidies were an important means in the French struggle against the House of Habsburg, a means that was made possible by the fact that the realm was quite advanced in its state-building process and that the king, consequently, had a solid income from taxes. On the other hand, the French subsidy treaties still reveal a deficit, because the French foreign policy was based on the military forces of its allies. Of course, this was not necessarily a structural deficit: the alliances just enabled France to pursue an ambitious policy that would have been impossible otherwise. Nevertheless, subsidies were an incalculable means with its own dynamics. During the Thirty Years' War, the costs grew continuously whereas the effect was sometimes disappointing, or even the opposite of what was intended. It is thus not surprising that French politicians during the time of the Congress of Westphalia expressed serious doubts regarding the use of subsidies – just as they did regarding the use of protection.[48] There were several good reasons to look for other means.

However, if we do not merely focus on the development of France itself, we still have to pose the question what the French subsidies meant for European history and the states system. Financial needs, and in particular the necessity to finance war, are seen as key for understanding the modern state-building process.[49] Usually, this factor is analysed from two perspectives: first, how a ruler was able

---

Les Hollandois manquent de tout cela', in *Bescheiden uit vreemde archieven omtrent de groote nederlandsche zeeoorlogen 1652–1676*, ed. by H.T. Colenbrander, vol. 1 (1652–1667) (The Hague: Martinus Nijhoff, 1919), pp. 218–219. Cf. also James Rees Jones, *The Anglo-Dutch Wars of the Seventeenth Century* (London and New York: Longman, 1996), p. 66. The war declared by Louis XIV on the Dutch Republic in 1672 is notorious for the fact that the French king saw his 'glory' being questioned by the fact that the republic's diplomacy had forced him into a peace with Spain four years before.

48 Cf. Anuschka Tischer, 'Protektion als Schlüsselbegriff politischer Sprache und Praxis in Frankreich im 17. und 18. Jahrhundert', in *Protegierte und Protektoren: Asymmetrische politische Beziehungen zwischen Partnerschaft und Dominanz (16. bis frühes 20. Jahrhundert)*, ed. by Tilman Haug, Nadir Weber, and Christian Windler, Externa: Geschichte der Außenbeziehungen in neuen Perspektiven, 9 (Cologne: Böhlau Verlag, 2016), pp. 49–64.

49 See Michael Stolleis, *Pecunia nervus rerum: Zur Staatsfinanzierung in der frühen Neuzeit* (Frankfurt am Main: Klostermann, 1983); Johannes Burkhardt, 'Die Friedlosigkeit der Frühen Neuzeit: Grundlegung einer Theorie der Bellizität Europas', *Zeitschrift für historische Forschung* 24 (1997), 509–574.

to obtain money from inside their territory, in particular by the establishment of taxes, or, second, how the international rivalry over external resources became the motor of the wars of the early modern period. Subsidies render this view more complex: one may ask if the French subsidies, which were the subject of the present discussion, caused a kind of revenue equalization in some parts of Europe. They did not replace the struggle for financial resources; they were part of this struggle and balanced or counterbalanced other developments. By means of its subsidies, France influenced the state-building process in other territories and also contributed to the fact that a balance between Protestants and Catholics was reached in Germany and Europe. The French subsidies thus have to be regarded in a much wider context than just French foreign policy in itself.

2

'Unter den Schutz Frankreichs': German reception of French subsidies in the Thirty Years' War

Tryntje Helfferich

Introduction

Historians have embraced the term 'Thirty Years' War' for the multifaceted conflict that devastated Central Europe between 1618 and 1648. At its heart, this was a civil war fought within the confines of the Holy Roman Empire, driven in large part by religious conflict and by fundamental disagreements over the very nature of the empire and the balance between princely liberties and imperial power. This internal German war was also of enormous interest to its neighbours, who intervened on one side or another, thus complicating the war further and intertwining it with larger European conflicts – especially the ones between the French Bourbons and the Spanish and Austrian Habsburgs, between the Swedes and the Danes, and between the Spanish and their rebellious Dutch subjects. In general, there were two clear sides in this war, sides which, despite some major shifts over the years, remained evenly balanced in strength until the final Peace of Westphalia in 1648. On one side stood the Catholic Austrian Habsburg emperor, supported by his Spanish Habsburg cousins and by most of the Catholic German princes and estates. On the other side stood the Protestant German princes and estates, assisted briefly by the Lutheran Danes and more extensively by the Calvinist Dutch, Lutheran Swedes, and Catholic French.

Despite the war's broad reach, many German princes and rulers tried to avoid direct engagement unless absolutely forced to muster troops for self-defence. Moreover, even those who actively joined the conflict had difficulty fielding an army for more than a brief period. Not only were personal princely incomes usually insufficient to allow extensive warfare, but the representative bodies (estates) of territories wielded traditional rights to approve taxation, and they frequently placed limits on the ability of princes to shift the financial burden to their subjects. And indeed, the cost of maintaining an army was enormous. The ten-to-fifteen-thousand-man imperial army of the Lower Rhinish-Westphalian Circle, for example, required approximately 1–1.5 million *reichstaler* annually, while the 78,000-man army of the Heilbronn League – an alliance made in 1633 among a number of German Protestant princes, France, and Sweden – cost 9.8 million *reichstaler* annually. Thus on average, an army incurred a cost of approximately 100–125 *reichstaler* per soldier per year, roughly equivalent to the cost of one and a half pounds of bread a day for each man.[1]

To meet such expenses, armies subsisted largely off the land, drawing their maintenance from loot or from more regularized war taxation, known as contributions, imposed on occupied territories. Yet while contributions provided a principal method of war financing in this era, they could be insufficient to allow effective offensive military action, or could fail entirely through over-extraction or popular resistance. This was true even for the emperor or imperial leagues that could pool the resources of multiple territories and princes – for individual princes the problem was far greater. Those intent on taking part in the conflict, therefore, were forced to depend on the financial resources of their officers or to seek external sources of funding from other European powers. For the emperor and his allied German states, such external military subsidies came primarily from the Spanish Habsburgs and to a lesser extent from the papacy. For the German opponents of the emperor, some subsidies came

---

1 Hubert Salm, *Armeefinanzierung im Dreißigjährigen Krieg: Der Niederrheinisch-Westfälische Reichskreis 1635–1650* (Münster: Aschendorff, 1990), pp. 165–176; Johannes Kretschmar, *Heilbronner Bund, 1632–1635*, I (Lübeck: H.G. Rahtgens, 1922), pp. 230–231; Kersten Krüger, 'Schwedische und dänische Kriegsfinanzierung im Dreißigjährigen Krieg bis 1635', in *Krieg und Politik 1618–1648*, ed. by Konrad Repgen (Munich: R. Oldenbourg Verlag, 1988), pp. 275–298. For the cost of bread, see Tryntje Helfferich, *The Thirty Years War: A Documentary History* (Indianapolis: Hackett, 2009), pp. 296, 300. Theoretical wages for ordinary infantry soldiers ranged between 6 and 10 florins (4–5 *reichstaler*) a month, but food, lodging, and other expenses were deducted, and any remaining wages were often in arrears. David Parrott, *The Business of War: Military Enterprise and Military Revolution in Early Modern Europe* (Cambridge: Cambridge University Press, 2012), pp. 161–163.

'Unter den Schutz Frankreichs' 45

from the Dutch and English; but by far the greatest subsidy amounts were distributed by the French.[2]

In this chapter I discuss the German understanding of these French moneys and what this can teach us about the war. I argue that subsidies were primarily seen and described as functional, as a means by which the German princes could levy troops, manage their supply and maintenance, and employ them in the fight to preserve princely liberties from what they saw as Habsburg tyranny. Yet French subsidies were also freighted with additional, and often contradictory, meanings. First, the payments were seen by the Germans as proxies for the value the French monarch placed on his allies, and thus were in themselves honours and indications of the recipient's worth and status. But the payments were also described as worrisome attempts by the French to buy influence and wield control over the princes – thereby denigrating the latter's sovereign status and demoting them to the role of mercenary captains. French moneys were also portrayed as a means for this crown to meddle in imperial affairs, and perhaps even as a step towards the complete subjugation of the German empire and the subsequent loss of all its traditional liberties. Finally, we see that these subsidy treaties strengthened an existing fear of French cultural dominance among some members of the German elite, inspiring calls for the creation of a unified and an explicitly anti-French German national identity.

Subsidies as necessary tools of war

The functional and mutual nature of French moneys is most clearly demonstrated in the actual subsidy agreements signed between France and its Protestant German allies. In the October 1636 Treaty of Wesel made between Landgrave Wilhelm V of Hesse-Cassel and the French king Louis XIII, for example, the landgrave was granted

---

[2] For more on military financing and the importance of military enterprisers see Parrott, *Business of War*. See also Cordula Kapser, *Die bayerische Kriegsorganisation in der zweiten Hälfte des Dreißigjährigen Krieges 1635–1648/49* (Münster: Aschendorff, 1997); Dieter Albrecht, 'Zur Finanzierung des Dreißigjährigen Krieges: Die Subsidien der Kurie für den Kaiser und Liga 1618–1635', *Zeitschrift für bayerische Landesgeschichte* 19, Vierteljahresschrift für Sozial- und Wirtschaftsgeschichte, Beihefte 47/48, 2 vols (1956), 534–567; Fritz Redlich, *The German Military Enterpriser and His Work Force: A Study in European Economic and Social History* (Wiesbaden: F. Steiner, 1964).

subsidies of 200,000 *reichstaler* a year (500,000 *livres*) in return for fielding an army of seven thousand infantry and three thousand cavalry for their common cause against the Habsburg emperor. This subsidy treaty was later renewed under Wilhelm's widow, Landgravine Amalia Elisabeth, and fixed to continue until the end of all hostilities, with both parties vowing not to make peace without the other.[3]

Surveying the correspondence of the Hessian court during this period, we see that, when these French subsidies were discussed, it was almost always in terms of their functional and necessary role as a tool of the Hessian anti-Habsburg war effort. The landgrave and, after him, the landgravine, along with their military officers and councillors, all stressed how the money allowed them to pay and supply existing troops, levy new recruits, buy munitions, maintain an occupying presence in strategically significant areas in the empire, and undertake offensive pushes either independently or in conjunction with their foreign and German princely allies. For example, in an internal document in which Hessian councillors debated the continuation of the French alliance, one pointed out that it 'would not be possible to acquire the means by which one could subsist and support the troops without the agreement, subsidies, and assistance of the allies'.[4] This was no exaggeration, for, although the Hessians drew enormous contributions from occupied territories in East Frisia and Westphalia, they still depended on French subsidy payments for as much as a third of their military funding.[5]

Subsidy treaties with the French were thus practical tools that allowed German princes to engage in military adventurism despite monetary shortfalls. At times, however, the issue was not merely

---

3 Archives du Ministère des Affaires Etrangères, Correspondance Politique, Paris [AAECP] Hesse 1, fols 113–119, Treaty of Wesel, 21 October 1636. The earlier version of the treaty, with a smaller subsidy, is in AAECP Hesse 1, fols 76–77, Treaty of Minden, 12 June 1636. See also AAECP Hesse 1, fols 233–245, Treaty of Dorsten, 22 [29] August 1639.
4 Hessisches Staatsarchiv Marburg [HStAM] 4d Nr. 46, fols 1–10, Dorsten, 26 July/5 August 1639. See also HStAM 4h Nr. 1406, fols 19–21. This and all subsequent translations into English are by the author.
5 The landgravine extracted 180,000 *reichstaler* annually from East Frisia plus c. 100,000 from Westphalia, while French subsidies yielded 200,000-plus *reichstaler* annually. See HStAM 4d Nr. 51, fols 1–3, Instructions for Vultejus, Groningen, 12/22 January 1638; RK FrA Fasz. 50a Konv. A, fols 160–161, Trauttmansdorff to Ferdinand III, Münster, 7 August 1646, published in *Acta Pacis Westphalicae* [*APW*], II A, vol. 4 (Münster: Aschendorff, 2001), pp. 493–495.

freedom of action but survival; for, as the war dragged on, France's Protestant German allies were forced to contemplate the complete loss of their lands and liberties. Given these enormous stakes, subsidy alliances with France became all the more important. In February 1638, for example, some of the landgravine's councillors suggested that only through a French alliance could she 'be assured of land and people, along with religion'.[6] The following year, her councillor Johannes Vultejus went even farther, arguing that given the grim military situation, and the inability of the Protestant German estates to unify their military actions, a mere subsidy alliance was insufficient. Instead, they must throw themselves 'under the protection of the Crown of France'. Reasonable terms for such a submission needed to be worked out, he admitted, to ensure that their Reformed 'religion and liberty would remain unharmed' and 'foreign troops' would not occupy their fortresses; but all this, and even 'in extrema' helping the French king gain the imperial title, were necessary because 'the [Habsburg] house of Austria fully intends to subjugate Germany completely and to extirpate liberty and the Evangelical religion'.[7]

Despite their great fear of imperial tyranny, however, the German princes were not unaware of the irony of depending on Catholic France for the salvation of German Protestantism. Such cross-confessional alliances were equally awkward for the French, who reassured themselves that pragmatism and religious flexibility were necessitated by the Habsburg menace.[8] To assuage consciences and court preachers on both sides, therefore, subsidy treaties included various religious assurances for the treatment of conquered areas, such as a promise to allow the free exercise of the other's religion without any change or innovation, and to leave the local clergy unmolested and in full possession of their properties. Even this was insufficient, however, for the landgravine of Hesse, who in 1639 told the French that 'she had wanted nothing more than the liberty

---

6 HStAM 4d Nr. 90, Vice Chancellor and Secret Council to Amalia Elisabeth, Cassel, 18/28 February 1638.
7 This plan was not pursued. HStAM 4d Nr. 56, *Gutachten des Geheimen Rats Vultejus betr. Unterstellung unter den Schutz Frankreichs*, 24 November/4 December 1639. For more on French protection of small states, see *Protegierte und Protektoren: Asymmetrische politische Beziehungen zwischen Partnerschaft und Dominanz (16. bis frühes 20. Jahrhundert)*, ed. by Tilman Haug, Nadir Weber, and Christian Windler, Externa 9 (Cologne: Böhlau, 2016), pp. 89–162.
8 Paul Sonnino, *Mazarin's Quest: The Congress of Westphalia and the Coming of the Fronde* (Cambridge, MA: Harvard University Press, 2009), p. 90.

of her religion in her states', and so, unless she had a written guarantee of actual French support for this at a general peace, there was no point in sending her any money. Indeed, such subsidies 'would be useless', because she would instead 'make another agreement in order to have the free exercise of religion ... [as] this is the primary reason that has obliged her to negotiate with the king [of France].'[9] After some hesitation, the French agreed.[10]

While the religious articles of subsidy treaties were generally, though not consistently, followed by both sides, other treaty terms were regularly violated. Subsidy recipients frequently provided smaller armies than promised, for example, or failed to take the field at all. Such behaviour could easily be justified, however, by the fact that throughout the war the French crown maintained a consistently abysmal record of paying on time or as promised.[11] This infuriated its allies, who repeatedly attempted to explain that the entire war effort depended on the French infusions of money, which contemporaries termed 'the sinews of war'. For example, in a letter of the Hessian agent Joachim de Wicquefort to the French superintendent of finances in 1644, he stressed that the landgravine's financial distress was causing a dangerous situation both for her and for her allies. 'Only France remains that can contribute to her support', Wicquefort wrote, for the military situation was such that the landgravine was fully 'exposed to [the enemies'] discretion, and to her total ruin'. Unless the French offered 'something quickly and powerfully for her conservation', he went on, 'one will shortly see the ruin of her armies and the loss of her state'.[12] This warning to the French was then reinforced by the Hessian councillor Adolf Wilhelm von Krosigk, who cautioned the French court that without overdue and additional funds, the landgravine 'will be obliged to act simply in the defensive, to make a reduction of her troops, and to lower the number of the officers (through whom, however, the

---

9 AAECP Hollande 21, fols 307–308, d'Amontot (extract), 10 December 1639.
10 A declaration was added to the Treaty of Wesel. See AAECP Hesse 1, fols 223–224, 254–256, 257, 307–310, 311–312, 313–314.
11 The French paid Hesse-Cassel 6,442,566 *livres* by the end of the war (82 per cent of the sum promised). Jörg Ulbert, 'Französische Subsidienzahlungen an Hessen-Kassel während des Dreißigjährigen Krieges', in *Frankreich und Hessen-Kassel zur Zeit des Dreißigjährigen Krieges und des Westfälischen Friedens*, ed. by Klaus Malettke (Marburg: N.G. Elwert, 1999), pp. 166–168.
12 AAECP Hollande 30, fols 106–107, Wicquefort to Bailleul, The Hague, 25 January 1644.

levies and recruits are necessarily raised) – even though by this means the small number [of men] that her highness will keep will not be secure'.[13]

Such letters also suggest the willingness of France's German allies to use threats to obtain payment. 'Pay us or we will collapse' was a general refrain from the Hessians that appears in the documents year after year; 'pay us or we will be forced to make peace and you will face the emperor alone'. The very frequency of such threats, as well as the insistent focus on allied funding we see in the Hessian correspondence, indicates how significant they understood the French subsidies to be for the continued functioning of the Hessian war effort in the empire, and how great a part they played in the French–Hessian relationship. Such dependence, however, left France's German allies vulnerable to manipulation, and the French openly used their subsidy payments to encourage behaviour that favoured them or discourage behaviour that did not. For example, when in 1640 the landgravine of Hesse-Cassel sent delegates to the Regensburg Reichstag, one of her counsellors reported that the French had been displeased by this delegation, which they feared indicated an effort to abandon her French allies and make a separate peace with the emperor. 'Because of this,' her counsellor reported, 'the promised extraordinary subsidy moneys of 50,000 *reichstaler* are being withheld'.[14] Similarly, the French regularly withheld pledged subsidies to their ally Duke Bernhard of Saxe-Weimar, both in an attempt to limit his independence and in response to his failures to field the promised number of troops.

The use and reception of pensions and honours

In addition to subsidies, the French also used other monetary and symbolic inducements such as pensions, honorary titles, and gifts in order to guide behaviour, mould and strengthen their ties with their German allies, and build trust. Yet whilst subsidies, like their related mercenary contracts, were usually given with strict terms spelled out in writing (such as the dates on which certain funds would be made available, the number of infantry and cavalry the

---

13 AAECP Hollande 30, fols 108–109, Krosigk to Mazarin, The Hague, 25 January 1644. Note also Krosigk's careful refutation of rumours that the landgravine was skimming funds.
14 HStAM 4e Nr. 1411, fragment from letter to Amalia Elisabeth, c. December 1640 / January 1641.

recipient was expected to field, and so forth), pensions and other financial handouts enabled the French to exert a softer form of influence. Moreover, unlike subsidies, where the crown demanded (though of course did not always receive) overt and specified return on investment, pensions and similar inducements usually came with no stated expectations of direct reciprocal action. This gave the recipients some freedom to manoeuvre. In 1633, for example, the French agent Feuquières visited Landgrave Wilhelm V with an honorary military title and gift of an annual pension of 12,000 *écus* (36,000 *livres*). The clear intention of the visit and the gifts was to persuade Wilhelm to join the Heilbronn League. However, while he gratefully and 'very humbly' accepted the money and honours, he did not in fact join the League.[15]

Once bestowed, honours were generally lasting, even when the recipient ignored French desires; but pensions, like subsidies, could be and were withheld. Wilhelm V's promised ordinary pension of 1633, for example, was not in the end paid either in that year or the next, nor was an extraordinary payment of 100,000 *reichstaler*, which was promised to the landgrave in December 1634 to aid him in maintaining his troops.[16] Nevertheless, the fiction remained that at least the pension moneys were entirely honorary. At times, moreover, the French court made a special effort to deny even the suggestion that these were anything but freely given gifts and expressions of regard. In the negotiations over the military alliance between Wilhelm V and the French in 1636, for example, in addition to thorough discussions of subsidy payments and other military details, the French instructions to their agent, St Chamond, ordered him to stress to the landgrave that the pension they offered him was 'a demonstration of the good will of His Majesty, which will not carry any obligation'. Again, St Chamond was told that 'this is not in the form of an obligation or as a condition of the treaty, but as a true demonstration of the good will that His Majesty has toward the said landgrave'.[17]

Thus pensions and gifts were portrayed by the French as signs of respect and honour. They also seem to have been accepted as such by the Germans. During treaty negotiations in 1636, the landgrave began by thanking the French king for the 'evident zeal

---

15 Ulbert, 'Französische Subsidienzahlungen', pp. 161, 169.
16 *Ibid.*, p. 161.
17 AAECP Hesse 1, fols 73–75, Annotations on the treaty, [May?] 1636, fols 73–75.

that His Majesty had for the interests of the German Estates for re-establishing a secure and general peace and for preserving by all means the ancient liberties of the princes of the empire', proclaiming that he was 'infinitely obliged to His Majesty for all of the very special affection that he was pleased to harbour for his highness [the landgrave] and all of his house, and grateful for all of the lovely and honourable offices'.[18] For such German princes, moreover, the value of a pension or the exalted nature of a title directly reflected upon the recipient's worth, dignity, and personal prestige. Accordingly, German princes competed among themselves for the status that these conferred. In his 1636 negotiations, for example, the Hessian landgrave had complained that the duke of Wittenberg was being preferred to him for the title of General of the Army.[19] Similarly, in 1637, the prince of Anhalt complained that the French had offered him only 'a pension of 4,000 *écus* along with the position of field marshal', unlike the 12,000 that had been given to Wilhelm of Hesse-Cassel and to Bernhard of Saxe-Weimar. Anhalt was only a colonel commanding a regiment of infantry within the landgrave's army, so the lower title and pension made sense from the French perspective; but he clearly still took offence.[20]

Status inducements became such an important and expected part of Franco-German relations that, in the negotiations with Hesse-Cassel mentioned above, the French court expressed the concern that, if the gifts were to be deemed insufficient, the landgrave might scuttle the entire treaty over them as a matter of personal honour. Similarly, in negotiations with Wilhelm's widow, Amalia Elisabeth, the French not only agreed to make subsidy payments in return for military action, they also offered the landgravine a large pension and an expensive cross of diamonds, as well as a pension for her young son and the same honorary French military title (*Général des Troupes Allemandes*) that his father had enjoyed at the time of his death.[21]

---

18 AAECP Hesse 1, fols 57–58, William V mémoire, Cassel, 17/27 March 1636.
19 AAECP Hesse 1, fols 53–54, Mémoire, 16 February 1636.
20 AAECP Hollande 21, fols 400–409, d'*Estampes mémoire pour Monsieur de Bouthellier*, April 1639.
21 AAECP Hesse 1, fols 179–182bis, Louis XIII (minute) to de la Boderie, 19/29 October 1637; AAECP Allemagne 14, fols 396–411, Memoire to D'Avaux, 19/29 October 1637, letter sent in Bibliothèque Nationale [BN] Ms. Baluze 167, fols 127ff. See also Ulbert, 'Französische Subsidienzahlungen', pp. 161, 169 n. 15.

In addition, it is noteworthy that titles and pensions bestowed by the French in order to curry German princely favour often came together, as a package of honours.[22] Pensions, gifts, and honours were also directed to the councillors and military officers of princes, whose influence at German courts could be considerable. For example, as part of subsidy-treaty negotiations with the landgrave of Hesse-Cassel in 1636, the French agent de la Boderie was asked to approach and satisfy those councillors at the landgrave's court who were 'affectionate towards France and to whom one has promised a pension'.[23] At the death of the landgrave in 1637, the French court sent de la Boderie to the court of his widow with instructions to ensure the continuation of the Franco-Hessian relationship. To this end, he was instructed to 'gratify' the landgravine's counsellors, Hans Heinrich von Günderode and Reinhardt Scheffer, through the gift of 3,000 *livres* 'divided between them'.[24] Later, de la Boderie approvingly noted that Günderode 'has not lost any occasion to serve with a lot of fervour, he is perfectly instructed on affairs and well disposed to serve the king'.[25]

In the following year, when the alliance with the Hessians seemed in danger, not only did the French court instruct de la Boderie to offer the landgravine larger subsidies and pensions if only she would ratify the treaty, it also instructed him to focus his attention on her lieutenant general, Peter Melander, and 'to win him and to make him affectionate towards France'. For 'considering that Mr Melander has a lot of power to bring her to the continuation of the alliance with His Majesty', the instructions stated, 'Mr de la Boderie has orders to sound him out and discover what he would like from His Majesty … [and] to promise him, if it is necessary, not only the said 18,000 *livres* already at hand, but double or triple the said

---

22 French–princely relationships in a later period are analysed in Tilman Haug, *Ungleiche Außenbeziehungen und grenzüberschreitende Patronage: Die französische Krone und die geistlichen Kurfürsten (1648–1679)* (Cologne: Böhlau, 2015). For a similar situation, see Christopher Storrs, *War, Diplomacy and the Rise of Savoy, 1690–1720* (Cambridge: Cambridge University Press, 2007), pp. 74–121.
23 AAECP Hambourg 1, fols 97–104, Instruction pour Mr Rorté, 15 April 1636.
24 AAECP Hesse 1, fols 179–182bis, Louis XIII (minute) to de la Boderie, 29 October 1637.
25 AAECP Hesse 1, fols 193–194, Summary of de la Boderie letter, 27 March 1638.

sum'.²⁶ Such determined wooing led Melander to boast that 'he was only to serve great kings who had the means to recompense their faithful servants'.²⁷ French presumption and use of money to gain influence among their officers and officials did not always go down well with the German princes, however. In a letter to her closest adviser, for example, the Hessian landgravine complained of a visit by a French ambassador, who had brought such 'excessively great' sums of money to pay pensions to her military officers that it had caused a giant uproar among the men.²⁸

Subsidies as a threat to princely independence

Whilst the German princes needed, expected, and gloried in their French subsidies and pensions, and used them to bolster their power at home vis-à-vis each other and their own estates, the relationship between a German prince and the French king was inevitably unequal and prone to misunderstanding and misuse. In 1638, for example, the Hessian privy council advised the landgravine of its general scepticism of foreign alliances and of French motives in particular, arguing that one could never depend on the French to fulfil their promises to reject peace with the emperor until the landgravine was assured of her lands, people, and religion. How, they continued, could allies of such unequal power ever work in conjunction? Such a relationship was inherently 'an uncertain thing on which one cannot depend nor put any reliance, particularly because of the disparity of the confederates who would pull on a single yoke'.²⁹

Fully aware of the dangers of their unequal status, the Germans (as we shall see below) quickly pushed back when the French attempted to use subsidies to impose explicit or implicit obligations and control beyond what the princes and their councillors thought appropriate. If pensions and honours were free gifts, and if subsidy

---

26 AAECP Hollande 20, fols 387–390, Mémoir to Mr. d'Estampes, 18 August 1638. Melander would be named by the French a field marshal and a 'sub-lieutenant of the German troops', along with his 18,000 *livres* in pension.
27 AAECP Allemagne 14, fols 368–371.
28 Her annoyance at d'Estampes is in HStAM 4d Nr. 50, fols 30–31, Amalia Elisabeth to Vultejus, Dorsten, 21/31 December 1638.
29 HStAM 4d Nr. 90, Vice Chancellor and Secret Council to Amalia Elisabeth, Cassel, 18/28 February 1638. The same document then went on to cast doubt on the French willingness to stand with the Hessians on matters of religion if it came to a general peace.

treaties were military alliances between sovereigns (even unequal ones), then the relationship was clear and princely honour maintained. But if pensions were bribes and subsidy treaties were mercenary contracts between a king and his employee, then the German princes' treasured dignity and sovereignty were thrown into question. This was doubly a concern since, during the war, France's German allies based their opposition to the emperor explicitly on the necessity to preserve the so-called German liberties – that is to say, the sovereign independence of the German princes and imperial estates. By allying with the French, the Germans wondered, were they merely trading one kind of subservience for another?

The Germans' determination to preserve all indications of princely sovereignty may be observed within the framework of negotiations over one of the Hessian subsidy treaties. While a preliminary version of that treaty specified that Landgrave Wilhelm, 'as Lieutenant General of the King's Armies in Germany', would command their joint forces under the name of the king, the landgrave utterly refused to accept this and so place himself in the role of military contractor or employee. Instead, the landgrave insisted that both his own troops and any new levies paid for by French subsidies should fight under his own command and name, not that of the king. The French eventually relented, and this point was removed in the final agreement.[30] At the same time, moreover, the landgrave complained that the king seemed to prefer another German subsidy recipient, Duke Bernhard of Saxe-Weimar, to him. The king's agent, St Chamond, was thus instructed to assure Wilhelm that the honorary title and moneys given to him were hereditary to his house and so 'entirely different from the employment of the said Duke Bernhard'. Moreover, St Chamond was to take pains to mollify Wilhelm by stressing that the king knew well that the landgrave was a sovereign prince, while Bernhard merely served as the Heilbronn League's general.[31]

This disagreement indicates the degree to which the German princes believed that their status was affected by their acceptance of French subsidies, as well as the degree to which the French were at

---

30 AAECP Hambourg 1, fols 97–104, Instruction for Mr Rorté, 15 April 1636. See also AAECP Hesse 1, fols 76–77, Treaty of Minden, 12 June 1636; AAECP Hesse 1, fols 113–119, Treaty of Wesel, 21 October 1636. See also BN Ms. Fr. 10212, fols 55–71, Instruction to Cologne, between 11 November and 22 December 1636; HStAM 4h Nr. 2116, fols 65–74, *Das herrn Vice Cantzlars bedencken*, n.d.
31 AAECP Hambourg 1, fols 97–104, Instruction for Mr Rorté, 15 April 1636.

pains to address the princes' scruples and umbrage over perceived slights to their honour and independence. Yet French frustration at this is evident. Not only was St Chamond told that 'His Majesty considers it necessary to begin the negotiations by mentioning that His Majesty continues His concern for the conservation of the princes and estates of the empire – His friends and allies'; but St Chamond was also instructed to encourage the landgrave to be ready to give assistance to Duke Bernhard along the Rhine, with Bernhard acting 'in the capacity of General of the League' and Wilhelm acting 'under his own name or under whatever other title it will please him to hold'.[32]

The German princes' concern over the precise nature of their titles and honours was not merely a matter of personal ego and pride but an indication of a European society in which reputation and recognized social status were of the utmost importance. Thus even the most minor discourtesy shown towards a prince by the French crown could influence his individual status and honour within the empire's intricate and closely observed web of hierarchical relationships. Navigating such subtle points was made all the more difficult for the princes, however, by the fact that the distinction between sovereign princely ally and noble military contractor might be fluid or unclear, and that subsidies from the French flowed into the pockets of both.[33] At one end of the spectrum were princes such as Wilhelm of Hesse-Cassel, who studiously maintained and insisted on his princely status throughout all of his treaties with the French. At the other end were princes such as Count Ernst von Mansfeld, who often wielded an army as large as that of Hesse-Cassel but who was not a major territorial lord and was not treated as such in any of his subsidy agreements, which clearly understood him as a mercenary contractor.[34]

The nature of the Franco-German relationship was far more uncertain for Bernhard of Saxe-Weimar, who was without doubt one of the most significant of France's German subsidy recipients.

---

32 *Ibid.*, fol. 101r.
33 For more on this topic, see Andrea Thiele, 'The Prince as Military Entrepreneur? Why Smaller Saxon Territories Sent "Holländische Regimenter" (Dutch Regiments) to the Dutch Republic', in *War, Entrepreneurs, and the State in Europe and the Mediterranean, 1300–1800*, ed. by Jeff Fynn-Paul (Leiden and Boston: Brill, 2014), pp. 170–192.
34 Walter Krüssmann, *Ernst von Mansfeld (1580–1626): Grafensohn, Söldnerführer, Kriegsunternehmer gegen Habsburg im Dreißigjährigen Krieg* (Berlin: Duncker & Humblot, 2010).

Bernhard was only a lesser German prince and not initially the ruler of a territorial state. After a long military career, mostly in the service of the Swedes, he had gained an impressive reputation and, as reward for his service, the duchy of Franconia. In 1633 he was also made general-in-chief for the army of the Heilbronn League. Then, in October 1635, after the League had withered (when most of its members joined the Peace of Prague, which brought them back under the emperor), Bernhard made an individual treaty with the French at Saint-Germain-en-Laye. According to the terms of this agreement, in return for an annual subsidy of 4 million *livres* (1.6 million *reichstaler*) and part of the territory of Alsace, Bernhard would field an army of eighteen thousand men to their mutual benefit. Interestingly, however, while most scholars consider Bernhard a military enterpriser or contractor, Bernhard, as with Wilhelm of Hesse-Cassel above, maintained in this treaty a claim to sovereign status and independence by refusing to swear an individual oath of loyalty to the French king.[35]

Yet despite this, the French, as we saw above in their negotiations with Wilhelm of Hesse-Cassel, still referred to Bernhard in condescending terms as non-sovereign and fundamentally different to the landgrave. The immediate result of the confusion between Bernhard-the-contractor and Bernhard-the-sovereign-ally was tension and discontent on both sides. While the French attempted to direct the duke and control his military actions, he chafed openly at any oversight and tried to use his influence to advance both his own princely power and the interests of the Protestant German princes. Matters between the French and the duke only deteriorated with time, as Bernhard began openly defying the requests of the French, pursing military goals they opposed, and generally indicating scorn for his supposed partners. Such intransigence, despite the 'large amounts distributed' to the duke, 'greatly displeased' the French king, who called on the duke to consider the common cause. Nevertheless, after taking the fortress of Breisach in 1638, Bernhard concluded the surrender in his own name, not that of the French,

---

35 Bernhard Röse, *Herzog Bernhard der Große von Sachsen-Weimar*, vol. II (Weimar: Verlag des Großh. Sächs. priv. Landes-Industrie-Comptoirs, 1829), pp. 457–461, 554–556. See also Heinrich Bücheler, 'Bernhard von Sachsen-Weimar: der Cottodiere des Protestantismus', *Damals* 22 (1990), 63–79; Amblard-Marie-Raymond-Amédée Noailles, vicomte de, *Bernard de Saxe-Weimar (1604 à 1639) et la réunion de l'Alsace à la France* (Paris: Perrin, 1908); Parrott, *Business of War*, pp. 107–110.

'Unter den Schutz Frankreichs'

and installed a governor loyal and answerable to himself. The French were relieved when he died in 1639.[36] Although such a spectacularly poor relationship was not the norm, the unequal status between subsidy giver and subsidy recipient often led to at least some uncertainty and disagreement over the extent of independence these agreements allowed.

Subsidies as a means to French domination of the empire

The subsidy-related anxieties of France's German allies also fit into a far larger storm then brewing over French influence in the empire. To date, most scholarship on anti-French sentiment has focused on the rise of the aggressive France of Louis XIV later in the seventeenth century, and it was certainly at that time that concerns about the French exploded, with numerous calls for Germans to beware such things as 'the secret intrigues of the French King's ministers at the courts of several princes for the enslaving of Europe'.[37] Similarly, Samuel von Pufendorf, in his *Present State of Germany* (1696), warned of the dangers of French subsidies and pensions, arguing that 'the man must be very stupid, who doth not see, that the End of all this Courtship is the opening a Way to the Ruin of the *German* Liberty, especially if the Male Line of the House of *Austria* should happen to fail. And the *French* King should there upon obtain the Empire.'[38] Thus, he added later in the work:

> Germans must be careful not to contribute to their own servitude by assisting France, as happens when they do not conjoin their counsels and strength to repulse the enemy that threatens them all, but either incline together to ruin their fatherland because they have been bought by French gold, or sit by quietly, corrupted by noxious bribes, without

---

36 AAECP Allemagne 15, fols 285–288, Louis XIII to d'Avaux, 16 July 1639.
37 Jean Baptiste Colbert, *Monsieur Colbert's ghost* ... (London: Printed for Edward Golden, 1684). The classic work on the so-called soldier trade of the eighteenth century is Friedrich Kapp, *Der Soldatenhandel deutscher Fürsten nach Amerika* (Berlin: Julius Springer, 1874). For more modern treatments see Charles W. Ingrao, *The Hessian Mercenary State: Ideas, Institutions, and Reform under Frederick II, 1760–1785* (Cambridge: Cambridge University Press, 1987); James Allen Vann, *The Making of a State: Württemberg, 1593–1793* (Ithaca: Cornell University Press, 1984); Peter H. Wilson, *War, State and Society in Württemberg, 1677–1793* (Cambridge, Cambridge University Press, 1995).
38 Samuel von Pufendorf, *The Present State of Germany*, trans. by Edmund Bohun, ed. by Michael J. Seidler (Indianapolis: Liberty Fund, 2007), p. 380.

a care for the public good – even though others are struggling and they, too, will be devoured by Polyphemus after the rest have been consumed.[39]

Decades later, in an empire reeling from numerous French-initiated conflicts, such sentiments would be common, finding their way, for example, into the writings of Friedrich Wilhelm I who, in a letter of instruction for his son, Friedrich II ('the Great'), famously stressed the importance of freeing the Prussian military from dependency on French and other foreign subsidies.[40]

Yet such anti-French propaganda and fears of French attempts to use money to achieve universal dominion, or at least domination of the empire, clearly had deeper roots; and especially during the middle years of the Thirty Years' War, when French cash poured into German coffers and French armies crossed over into the empire, this sentiment gained ground. The most prominent of such critiques came from pro-Habsburg Catholics, who used the popular press to discredit France and its German Protestant supporters and to divide the allies. The 1626 polemical pamphlet 'Altera secretissima instructio', for example, was ostensibly an anonymous supporter's letter of advice to Calvinist Elector Palatine Friedrich V, but was in fact an attempt by a member of the imperial privy council in Vienna to cause internal allied distrust. The author warned the elector that past French financial support for the Dutch Calvinists provided clear evidence that 'it is never safe to trust to French papists', for they had only used the conflict for their own purposes. During the Dutch Revolt against the Spanish, he argued,

> the [French] king's letters [of credit] were thrust upon every man, nay money was brought, but all to that end that the French might have time to make their own Peace, that they might settle their own affairs in a safe point, and derive the extremity of danger upon the Hollanders, and boast that the French were craftier then the craftiest. With the same fraud they will deal with you, suddenly leave you or ruin you ... Count Maurice [prince of Orange] advised often, that French aid was to be used, but their faith not to be trusted to. The Great League rested upon the lilies, but they have pulled

---

39 Ibid., n. 814. See also Peter Claus Hartmann, *Geld als Instrument europäischer Machtpolitik im Zeitalter des Merkantilismus* (Munich: Kommission für Bayerische Landesgeschichte, 1978).
40 Philip G. Dwyer, *The Rise of Prussia 1700–1830* (London and New York: Routledge, 2014), pp. 56–57.

away their heads; and when one hath most need of them they turn enemies.[41]

Such critics thus warned Germans that the mendacious French wielded their subsidies in the empire only to benefit themselves, and would surely abandon their deluded allies when it suited them. The result would be a stronger France but an empire left damaged, its people dead and displaced, its ancient liberties and Catholic Church crippled. Similar critiques also appear in private correspondence. In July 1647, for example, the Catholic Bishop von Wartenberg noted in his diary after a meeting with two of the French delegates to the Peace of Westphalia, the duc de Longueville and Claude d'Avaux, that although one might hope for better from fellow Catholics, 'through French interposition [in the empire], nothing has been improved. On the contrary, through its subsidies and confederates, it has inflicted irreparable damage on Catholicism in Germany – if not by intention, then at least in effect.'[42]

Catholics were the most outspoken critics of the French and their subsidies; but after the 1635 Peace of Prague, when most German Protestants abandoned their foreign allies and joined the imperial side, anti-French critiques became more multi-confessional. French intervention then became more explicit, for, in response to the loss of its allies, France sent its own troops across the Rhine into the empire, rather feebly defending this action by claiming that it was still attempting to protect the German liberties – even if the princes themselves had abandoned the effort. The leader of the Protestant princes' volte-face at this time was Elector Johann Georg of Saxony, who transformed himself from an imperial rebel into an imperial general and a prominent voice of anti-foreign sentiment. In a 1638 letter to the Hessian estates, for example, he castigated them for their refusal to come to peace or reject their French allies. Rather than look to German solutions, as almost all other princes had done, the elector argued, the Hessians trusted that their goals would be more likely 'to be pushed through under the domination of foreigners. And thus at the same time the beloved fatherland and the whole

---

41 Noel Malcolm, *Reason of State, Propaganda, and the Thirty Years' War: An Unknown Translation by Thomas Hobbes* (Oxford: Clarendon Press, 2007), pp. 140–142, 144 (English modernized for ease of reading).
42 *APW* III C 3, 2, Diarium Wartenberg, vol. 2, 2, ed. by Joachim Foerster (Münster: Aschendorff, 1987), pp. 936–937.

German nation would go to rack and ruin. And you would want to rend asunder all volumes of the holy imperial constitution under the name of German freedom.'[43]

Yet even among those Germans who rejected the Peace of Prague and maintained French alliances, we see an awkward disconnect between, on the one hand, an acceptance and even eagerness to accept subsidies and honours, and, on the other, a striking distrust of French pretentions and unease at the spectre of French dominance over the German lands and people. For example, one pamphlet, published ostensibly by a leading officer of Bernhard's army shortly after his death in 1639, offered a strong defence of imperial territorial integrity and fear that Bernhard's conquests along the Rhine would now fall to France. What would all 'righteous German hearts' think of them, he asked, if, through their actions, they

> burdened the fatherland with such a powerful neighbour and so brought the ancient acquired liberty into the most extreme danger … [with] the result that foreign potentates, peoples, and nations, after they suck the marrow from the bones of us Germans, shall also rule over and dominate us, divide the Roman Empire among themselves, eliminate German liberty, and impose on us … the unprecedented mockery of the yoke of slavery, while we, with our own sweat and blood and acting in a blind, mindless way, help them like poor slaves.[44]

Despite such public demands for German liberty, however, the directors of Bernhard's army eventually signed a treaty with the French. By requiring oaths of loyalty from the generals, that treaty placed them more firmly under French control and authority while still leaving them full operational independence. This was a move that the historian C.V. Wedgwood called, with typical flair, 'the final abdication of the German patriots, such as they were, from any even partial control of their allies' war'.[45]

---

43 HStAM 4d Nr. 90, Johann Georg of Saxony (copy) to the Estates of Hesse-Cassel, Dresden, 12/22 January 1638.

44 *AbtruckSchreibens Von einem fürnehmen Officier vnter der von Hertzog Bernhardt Sachsen Weinmar hinterlassenen Armee* … (1639), fols Bi r, Bii r. Of course, it is quite possible that this too was a bit of Habsburg propaganda, not the work of a Protestant French ally.

45 C.V. Wedgwood, *The Thirty Years War* (New York: New York Review of Books, 1938), pp. 412–413. Note that the oath was a matter of great controversy, and not actually sworn until August 1640. On this matter, see David Parrott, *Richelieu's Army: War, Government and Society in France, 1624–1642* (Cambridge: Cambridge University Press, 2001), pp. 295–296.

As a sign of their lingering internal concern about French arrogance, untrustworthiness, and empty promises, the Hessians also briefly (beginning in 1639) entertained a scheme, in conjunction with the Catholic duke of Pfalz-Neuburg, to form a new third party in the empire. This league of princes would create a purely German, and bi-confessional, power bloc within the empire, a bloc that would counter the Franco-Swedish party on the one hand and the Imperial-Spanish party on the other. Draft manifestos (for the league never came to fruition) argued that 'foreign kings and potentates' had used the war as an excuse to seize 'one place after another in the empire'. Yet 'in spite of all this, so many noble German cavaliers find themselves in the service of such foreign potentates whereby, under the false delusion of the conservation of their freedom, they themselves co-operate in the oppression and subjection of their fatherland'. If German princes did not soon extract themselves from service to foreign crowns, the manifesto warned, 'they and other German princes will be plunged and precipitated into a far greater servitude and slavery than had ever before occurred'. To save themselves and their fatherland from 'further oppression and dismemberment' by these foreign powers, all imperial electors, princes, and estates 'without distinction of religion' must co-operate and unite into a 'faithful coalition'.[46]

Subsidies as one part of a greater threat to the fatherland

In common usage, the term fatherland (*Vaterland* in German or *patria* in Latin) indicated the town or land of one's birth; but, by the sixteenth century, the term was also being used to indicate a larger, more abstract political body, territory, or kingdom to which its adherents owed loyalty and service, and which they were obliged to defend. The term also became highly politicized, and was especially wielded by those attempting to justify military and political opposition to a central authority. In this sense a person who demonstrated love for the fatherland (*amor patriae*), that is, who was a 'patriot', would not simply show civic piety by defending his fatherland's religion and laws – the classic definition of patriot found in the works of Cicero; he would safeguard the constitutional privileges of the

---

46 Landesarchiv Nordrhein-Westfalen, Abteilung Westfalen [LANRW] Julich Berg II 3370, fols 10r–13v, 14 July 1639; LANRW Julich Berg II 3370, fols 47–54v, 13 February 1640.

fatherland against the unjust acts of a despotic ruler or power.[47] During the Thirty Years' War, it was this broader idea of *amor patriae* that was seized upon by internal opponents of imperial power, but the league manifesto demonstrates how this idea was also directed against subsidy alliances with the French and other foreigners. Germans who joined these foreigners or accepted their money, titles, and honours, the manifesto warned, might mean well, but had in truth been tricked into co-operating in their own, and the empire's, subjugation and enslavement.

We thus see a recurring theme in critiques of French subsidies – that the French intended to gain and dominate the empire not so much through force of arms but through the softer, more insidious strategy of trickery, delusion, and money. Even worse, the Germans themselves seemed willing to assist in this plan, gladly fighting for the French and stupidly trusting their inducements and false assurances that the king desired nothing more than the preservation of the German liberties. If Germans did not awaken to the danger, the critics argued, the French would not merely enslave them but dismember them, devour them, and suck the marrow from their bones. The French, in other words, would take from them both their freedom and their very essence. Interestingly, this new anti-subsidy rhetoric clearly drew on, and then merged into, an existing anti-French polemic that was concerned not primarily with the dangers of French military-financial might but with the threat of France's dominant cultural power. For by the end of the sixteenth century, French art, music, clothing, and language had become all the rage at European princely courts and within wealthy urban social circles. This Francophilism among the European elite meant that young German nobles had French tutors, learned, spoke, and wrote in the French language from their early years, wore the latest in French fashion, often went to France as

---

47 For more on ideas of *patria*, see Robert von Friedenburg (ed.), *'Patria' und 'Patrioten' vor dem Patriotismus: Pflichten, Rechte, Glauben und die Rekonfigurierung europäischer Gemeinwesen im 17. Jahrhundert* (Wiesbaden: Harrassowitz Verlag, 2005); Alexander Schmidt, *Vaterlandsliebe und Religionskonflikt: Politische Diskurse im Alten Reich (1555–1648)* (Leiden: Brill, 2014); Gundula Caspary, *Späthumanismus und Reichspatriotismus: Melchior Goldast und seine Editionen zur Reichsverfassungsgeschichte* (Göttingen: Vandenhoeck & Ruprecht, 2006); Orest Ranum (ed.), *National Consciousness, History and Political Culture in Early Modern Europe* (Baltimore and London: Johns Hopkins University Press, 1975); Alastair Duke and Andrew Spicer, *Dissident Identities in the Early Modern Low Countries*, ed. by Judith Pollmann and Andrew Spicer (Farnham: Ashgate, 2009), pp. 1–76.

part of their Grand Tour, and then brought home and aped French etiquette, courtly styles, and political patterns. By the beginning of the seventeenth century, such wholescale elite adoption of foreign trends brought about a conservative reaction and led to calls among some intellectuals for Germans to show a greater love of their fatherland by reviving and celebrating native German culture, language, traditions, and values. One clear example of this trend is the 1617 establishment in Weimar of the Fruchtbringende Gesellschaft ('Fruitbearing Society'). This elite literary society, founded on an Italian model, had as its goals the establishment of linguistic norms, the purification of the German language and purging of foreign words and phrases, and the advancement of German in literary and scholarly works – where it sadly lagged behind other European vernaculars. From the beginning, however, the Society had at its heart both a literary or linguistic goal and what we might call a political, patriotic purpose. This was both negative, in terms of driving out foreign influences, and positive, in attempting to forge a unified German literary tradition, to advance the honour and reputation of the German language (and thus also of German speakers), and to spark an empire-wide regeneration through the improvement of morals and the restoration of unique German cultural norms.[48]

German language theorists within the Society and elsewhere criticized France, in particular, as exerting an enervating influence on German behaviour, character, and unity. Moreover, Society writings warned, true Germans needed to be careful, for foreign linguistic domination was only the first step in the complete political enslavement of the German nation and loss of its shared identity.[49] Especially as the war dragged on, the Society presented itself as a

---

[48] Calls for German purity stretch back to the medieval era, but the seventeenth century saw the rise of numerous specifically literary societies, including the Aufrichtige Tannengesellschaft (est. 1633), the Deutchgesinnete Genossenschaft (est. 1643), and the Pegnesische Blumenorden (est. 1644). For more on what he terms the 'linguistic patriotism' of these baroque language societies, see Thorsten Roelcke, 'Der Patriotismus der barocken Sprachgesellschaften', in *Nation und Sprache: Die Diskussion ihres Verhältnisses in Geschichte und Gegenwart*, ed. by Andreas Gardt (Berlin and New York, 2000), pp. 139–168.

[49] The Pietist mystic Jakob Böhme, for example, argued for the special sanctity of German as the pure 'sensual' mother language that gave Germans their national identity. See Leon Stein, 'Religion and Patriotism in German Peace Dramas during the Thirty Years War', *Central European History* IV.2 (June 1971), 131–148 (p. 133).

defender of common German interests and of the freedoms threatened by foreign influence, and offered the German language as the best way for Germans – divided in so many other ways – to unite.[50] As the Society member Karl Gustav von Hille argued, '[a]lthough our German empire sheds blood and tears, and is almost to the point of death because war afflicts it without end, yet the Palm Tree [the symbol of the Society] blossoms in the weapons of the virtuous, gives a welcome shaded space, and is greened by the dew from heaven'.[51]

Many of the arguments used by the Society and others who were concerned about foreign cultural domination thus employ the same imagery as that used against foreign subsidies, and advance much the same goal as those attempting to form a purely German imperial third party. Like the anti-subsidy authors, moreover, these linguistic patriots' warnings against German slavery and folly suggest a widespread sense of insecurity and defensiveness, as well as an effort to heal imperial divisions and weakness by forging a new unified German national identity. A poem by Sigmund von Birken (known to the society as 'Der Erwachsene' or 'the Adult') provides an excellent example of this. 'Learn from the Latins and let the Gauls teach you how one should honour the fatherland and its language', he wrote:

> Where is the Walloon who uses German? And where is the Frenchman who loves our tongue? Why then do you hold only to foreign mouths and ears? Is your language then born ignobly? ... Pift! German! Shame on you! And if you will not be shamed, then God will take from you your honour and your freedom. If you make your language a maid, you will become a servant of the foreigners, because your fatherland is not good enough for you. No, patriot, oh no, treat yourself better! If you will be a nation, then you will be greater in honour and in reputation. Help old German loyalty, my German, help make new the adornment of the German language![52]

According to Birken, therefore, Germans did not currently form a true 'nation' – a unified ethnic community or people. They could become one, however, by rejecting foreign language and service and by coming together under their shared, worthy German cultural and linguistic traditions. Thus in many ways, this movement, which

---

50 This was the argument of the great German poet Opitz. See Joachim Whaley, *Germany and the Holy Roman Empire*, vol. I (Oxford: Oxford University Press, 2012), p. 466.
51 Karl Gustav von Hille, *Der Teutsche Palmbaum* (Munich: Kösel Verlag, 1970), pp. 28–29.
52 Georg Neumark, *Der Neu-Sprossende Teutsche Palmbaum* (Weinmar [Nürnberg]: Joachim Heinrich Schmid, 1668), VIII.

tied identity and political freedom to cultural preservation, demonstrates an interesting prefiguring of nineteenth- and twentieth-century cultural nationalism.[53]

Nevertheless, such arguments did little to stem the use of the French styles and French language, both at the princely courts and in literary and diplomatic circles. French also remained the language of the European and German officer class, partly because of the ongoing influence of French military schools and manuals. The dominance of French military terminology caused some critics, such as the Stettin military engineer Wendelin Schildknecht, to complain that 'although we were born of our mother in Germany', we behave as if 'we were suckled in France by an ape and raised by a baboon'.[54] The Hessian general Peter Melander, similarly, had the reputation of shunning the use of foreign languages, and he did not tolerate the use by his soldiers of such common French terms as *corps de garde*, *parade*, and *parole*, requiring instead the solid German terms *Hauptwache*, *Stellung*, and *Wort*.[55] Melander, despite having accepted hundreds of thousands of French *livres* during his early career, would also turn against their subsidies in the end, leaving Hessian service in an angry protest against the continued French alliance, which he claimed would lead to German subjugation.[56]

---

53 This complicates Robert von Friedeburg's argument that cultural meanings of *patria* were extremely unusual in the early modern era. Robert von Friedeburg, 'In Defense of Patria: Resisting Magistrates and the Duties of Patriots in the Empire from the 1530s to the 1640s', *Sixteenth Century Journal* 32 (2001), 357–382. Note that the attempt to form a common identity around language purposely excluded the large number of peoples living within the empire who were not native German speakers. For more on how early modern peoples attempted to shape themselves into nations, see Duke and Spicer, *Dissident Identities*; Robert Stein and Judith Pollmann (eds), *Networks, Regions and Nations: Shaping Identities in the Low Countries, 1300–1650* (Leiden: Brill, 2010); Adrian Hastings, *The Construction of Nationhood. Ethnicity, Religion, and Nationalism* (Cambridge: Cambridge University Press, 1997); Georg Schmidt, 'Die frühneuzeitliche Idee "deutsche Nation": Mehrkonfessionalität und säkulare Werte', in *Nation und Religion in der Deutschen Geschichte*, ed. by Heinz-Gerhard Haupt und Dieter Langewiesche (Frankfurt and New York: Campus, 2001), pp. 33–67.

54 William Jervis Jones, *Images of Language: Six Essays on German Attitudes to European languages from 1500 to 1800* (Amsterdam: John Benjamins Publishing, 1999), pp. 96, 103–104.

55 Ibid., pp. 104–105.

56 HSAM 4f Frankreich, Nr. 1311, de la Boderie to Amalia Elisabeth, 9/19 December 1640.

Disquiet about foreign cultural and political domination, and the countervailing push for the creation of a shared German national identity, also spilled over into the German popular press from the late 1620s onwards, a development which coincided with the beginning of French financial involvement in the war. Thus we find numerous pamphlets and broadsheets ridiculing Germans who wore French fashions, sported French beards, or used the French language in preference to the good old German tongue. A German who put on such foreign fashions and modes – a 'Monsieur Alamodo' – was shown to be both a fop and a fool.[57] 'As for the French, I know well that God will punish Germany through them', one pamphlet writer opined, 'for we have, like gesticulating apes in nightgowns, every day thoughtlessly and artlessly copied that nation in customs, ceremonies, gestures, banquets, language, clothes, and music. How could we fall into their hands better than this? But the Frenchman shall not become emperor in this way. The lilies belong to him; the eagle belongs to the Germans.'[58]

Conclusions

This study of the German understanding of French subsidies sheds new light on the Thirty Years' War by highlighting the internal tension among princes over how best to preserve both their liberties and their national identity. On the one hand, the German subsidy recipients described French moneys as beneficial, functional, and indeed necessary tools for the pursuit of their political and religious goals, which helped them to defend both their territorial rights and the proper balance of power within the larger empire. The princes also celebrated and fought over such subsidies, and the titles and gifts that often accompanied them, as indicators and promoters of their personal honour and social status. On the other hand, those opposed to French involvement in the war complained that such subsidy agreements were not helpful but foolish, and damaging to the German liberties, in that they not only allowed a hostile foreign crown to meddle in imperial affairs but probably concealed sinister efforts by the French to weaken, conquer, or even dismember the empire. France's German allies shared some of these suspicions and

---

57 John Roger Paas, *The German Political Broadsheet 1600–1700*, vol. 4 (Wiesbaden: Harrassowitz, 1994), pp. 34, 291–322, 352–375; vol. 7 (2002), pp. 27–28, 232–236, 240–244.

58 *Der Deutsche Brutus, Das ist: Ein Abgeworffenes Schreiben …* (1636).

expressed unease that subsidy treaties, by leaving them dependent on French aid and placing them under French protection, made them seem mercenaries or supplicants, constantly having to beg or threaten to be paid while simultaneously needing to resist French efforts to use money as a means of control and domination. Such fears about a possible loss of German princely or imperial sovereignty and territorial integrity then drew on and merged with pre-existing anxieties and insecurities about the weakness or disunity of the German people and culture as a whole. As a result, both types of fear were reinforced – a process that helped contribute, well before the French Revolution, to calls for the creation of a unified German nation centred on a shared linguistic-cultural inheritance.

3
'Mercenary' contracts as Fiscal-Military Instruments

Peter H. Wilson

Introduction

Subsidies are widely acknowledged as an important manifestation of European interstate relations between the fifteenth and early nineteenth centuries, and they are beginning to attract serious attention from scholars. To date, research has largely focused on individual agreements or sets of agreements as part of wider diplomatic relations between two states. It is recognized that such relations were invariably asymmetrical, with the stronger party paying the weaker one in return for some kind of support or cooperation, usually in military or political terms. Subsidies are seen as an extension of a states system, like a financial lubricant smoothing and strengthening alliances between sovereign governments. Most research draws heavily on official records and concentrates on quantifying how much was paid and what kind of support was purchased.[1] Ancillary to this are studies examining the public discussion of such arrangements, especially in the eighteenth century when they drew criticism as akin to 'mercenary' service and unworthy of civilized governments.[2] Finally, there are works on the soldiers who served under 'subsidy treaties'. Like the other two approaches, this

---

1 For example, P.C. Hartmann, *Geld als Instrument europäischer Machtpolitik im Zeitalter des Merkantilismus 1715–1740* (Munich: Kommission für Bayerische Landesgeschichte, 1978).

2 C.W. Eldon, *England's Subsidy Policy towards the Continent during the Seven Years War* (Philadelphia: University of Pennsylvania, 1938); H.D. Schmidt, 'The Hessian Mercenaries: The Career of a Political Cliché', *History* 43 (1958), 207–212.

third category usually focuses narrowly on individual cases and views these from a variety of hostile perspectives, such as subaltern studies, often echoing early modern critiques of the 'soldier trade'.[3]

This chapter argues that we need to set subsidies in their wider context as just one of many ways of transferring war-making resources across political jurisdictions. Subsidies belong to the contractual forms which emerged during early modernity and which this chapter will term Fiscal-Military Instruments. These were contractual forms and specific recognized practices which evolved to facilitate the procurement and exchange of a wide variety of war-making resources supplied not only by states but also by a host of non-state actors. This exchange of resources was sufficiently complex and extensive to warrant the term European Fiscal-Military System which is deliberately used here to extend, rather than replace, the existing term Fiscal-Military State by supplementing the study of war's impact on domestic development with an examination of how it affected interaction with other states and non-state actors. Taking this broader perspective removes subsidies from the narrow, and partly anachronistic, confines of diplomatic and conventional political history anchored on the study of sovereign states, which tends to reduce research to a cost-benefit analysis of objectives and outcomes in military, economic, and political terms.

The primary goal of this chapter is to disentangle subsidies from other Fiscal-Military Instruments, notably the various forms of contract to supply troops with which subsidy treaties were often combined. The first part will sketch the wider context by briefly outlining the emergence, scope, and eventual demise of the European Fiscal-Military System, before defining Fiscal-Military Instruments and identifying the most common forms. The third, more substantial, section will examine the different kinds of troop contracts and indicate the extent to which they were combined with subsidies.

---

3 This is particularly true of works on the so-called 'Hessians' fighting for Britain during the American Revolutionary War, much of which is stuck in 'for and against' arguments already articulated in the eighteenth and nineteenth centuries: Peter Keir Taylor, *Indentured to Liberty: Peasant Life and the Hessian Military State, 1688–1815* (Ithaca: Cornell University Press, 1994); Charles W. Ingrao, *The Hessian Mercenary State: Ideas, Institutions, and Reform under Frederick II 1760–1785* (Cambridge: Cambridge University Press, 1987); *Die 'Hessen' im Amerikanischen Unabhängigkeitskrieg (1776–1783)*, ed. by Holger Th. Gräf, Andreas Hedwig, and Annegret Wenz-Haubfleisch (Marburg: Historische Kommission für Hessen, 2014).

The European Fiscal-Military System

European political geography is the product of violent competition which has left the continent divided into distinct states. This process is often described as a Darwinian struggle for survival, with only the 'fittest' states achieving full sovereignty. Leopold von Ranke, one of the founders of modern historical method, argued that 'primacy of foreign policy' dictated how each state developed internally. Each state strove for autarky, modifying its own institutions, economy, and society so as to compete more aggressively and efficiently with its neighbours.[4]

More recently, John Brewer coined the term 'Fiscal-Military State' to describe the institutionalization of permanent taxation and armed forces during the seventeenth and eighteenth centuries. His study is part of a wider debate on whether authoritarian or constitutional states are more efficient at mobilizing resources for warfare.[5] This

---

4 Leopold von Ranke, *Das Politische Gespräch und andere Schriftchen zur Wissenschaftslehre* (Halle: M. Niemeyer, 1925; first published in 1836), pp. 10–35, available in English as 'A Dialogue on Politics', in Theodore H. von Laue (ed.), *Leopold von Ranke: The Formative Years* (Princeton: Princeton University Press, 1950), pp. 152–180, esp. pp. 167–168. The concept was developed further by Ranke's colleague Wilhelm Dilthey, 'Friedrich der Große und die deutsche Aufklärung', in Dilthey, *Studien zur Geschichte des deutschen Geistes* (Göttingen: Vandenhoeck und Ruprecht, 1959; first published in 1927), pp. 176–205, and propagated further by Otto Hintze, 'Military Organisation and the Organisation of the State', in *The Historical Essays of Otto Hintze*, ed. by Felix Gilbert (Oxford: Oxford University Press, 1975), pp. 180–215, esp. p. 180.

5 John Brewer, *The Sinews of Power: War, Money, and the English State 1688–1783* (New York: Alfred A. Knopf, 1989). The subsequent debate has spawned an extensive literature, of which the following offer good introductions: *The British Fiscal Military States 1660–c.1783*, ed. by Aaron Graham and Patrick Walsh (Farnham: Ashgate, 2016); *War, State and Development: Fiscal-Military States in the Eighteenth Century*, ed. by Rafael Torres Sánchez (Pamplona: Ediciones Universidad de Navarra, 2007); *The Fiscal-Military State in Eighteenth-century Europe*, ed. by Christopher Storrs (Farnham: Ashgate, 2009). There are important, though often unacknowledged, connections with the earlier discussions of Joseph Schumpeter's historical sociology of the emergence of the 'tax state', especially in his classic 'The Crisis of the Tax State', *International Economic Papers* 4 (1954), 5–38, which was written in 1918. See also Richard Abel Musgrave, 'Schumpeter's Crisis of the Tax State', *Journal of Evolutionary Economics* 2 (1992), 89–113; E. Ladewig Petersen, 'From Domain State to Tax State: Synthesis and Interpretation', *Scandinavian Economic History Review* 23 (1975), 116–134.

research has greatly extended our understanding of the relationships among political institutions, economies, and societies; but it has largely overlooked the fact that virtually no European state has waged war without external assistance.

This is the paradox of European history. Competition was possible only through co-operation with allies, neutrals, and even enemies, since states have rarely obtained all they needed for warfare from their own populations, while governments have generally been unable to prevent their own subjects from aiding other powers. The 'success' of each state has depended not only on its ability to assert itself militarily but also on its being recognized as a 'state' by its neighbours. The emergence of diplomatic conventions and international law is only one aspect of this process. Europe contained a host of semi-sovereign entities, like the German and Italian principalities and city-states, which not only struggled to preserve or enhance their autonomy but also provided war-making resources to other, larger states.

These exchanges have primarily been studied from the perspective of diplomacy, which only identifies formal alliances and arrangements between states. In fact, the connections were far more complex and profound, as they encompassed numerous non-state actors like merchants, entrepreneurs, bankers, experts, and agents of all kinds.[6] The resources that were transferred ranged from armaments to fully equipped and manned warships, from individual recruits to entire armies, from barrels of cash to sophisticated financial transfers and credit. Additionally, numerous services were provided, such as transportation for men and materials, the right to cross neutral territory or use specialist facilities like ports, as well as the exchange of intelligence and specialist know-how.

These transfers were handled by intermediaries often based in cities which were not necessarily political capitals, but which functioned as 'hubs' or nodal points in the complex Fiscal-Military System that emerged during the 1560s and matured around 1700, when all the essential features were in place.[7] These included

---

6 Useful examples of the different kinds of agent in *War, Entrepreneurs, and the State in Europe and the Mediterranean, 1300–1800*, ed. by Jeff Fynn-Paul (Leiden: Brill, 2014).

7 These ideas are elaborated at greater length in Peter H. Wilson, 'The European Fiscal-Military System and the Habsburg Monarchy', in *The Habsburg Monarchy as a Fiscal-Military State c.1648–1815: Contours and Perspectives*, ed. by William Godsey, Petr Mat'a, and Thomas Winkelbauer

recognized ways of interacting, such as specific forms of military conventions, recruitment contracts, and financial exchanges, all of which were as much part of Europe's political development as diplomatic protocol or court rituals. This system allowed governments to access vital additional resources and greatly contributed to the growing scale and intensity of warfare across this period.

The French Revolutionary and Napoleonic Wars saw both the peak of the system and the onset of its demise. The revolutionary ideology of the citizen-in-arms, as well as the Revolution's assault on social and geographical privileges, greatly expanded the state's war-making potential by removing many of the legal barriers to the mobilization of human and material resources. Simultaneously, the state's greater reach was legitimated by heightened nationalist ideology (sovereignty of the nation), which expanded the state's power to command 'national' resources whilst discouraging reliance on 'foreigners'.[8] The nationalization of war-making resources encouraged efforts to prevent their 'export' to potential enemies by curbing extra-territorial violence through bans on privateering or enlisting in foreign armies.[9] Co-operation continued amidst the competition as states agreed collectively to remove or nationalize the non-state actors, for instance through a more coherent articulation of neutrality after 1815.[10]

Meanwhile, the wars between 1792 and 1866 eliminated most of Europe's smaller states, as well as the remaining areas of fuzzy

---

(Oxford: Proceedings of the British Academy, forthcoming); 'Competition through Cooperation: The European Fiscal Military System 1560–1850', inaugural lecture, University of Oxford, 30 January 2017, podcast at www.history.ox.ac.uk/article/peter-h-wilson-inaugural-lecture. The concept of 'hubs' is discussed further by Marianne Klerk, Chapter 9 below.

8 The introduction of more truly universal conscription is one example of this: *Conscription in the Napoleonic Era: A Revolution in Military Affairs?*, ed. by Donald J. Stoker, Frederick C. Schneid, and Harold D. Blanton (London: Routledge, 2014).

9 For this process, see Janice E. Thomson, *Mercenaries, Pirates and Sovereigns: State-building and Extraterritorial Violence in Early Modern Europe* (Princeton: Princeton University Press, 1994); Jan Martin Lemnitzer, *Power, Law and the End of Privateering* (Basingstoke: Palgrave, 2014); Nir Arielli, Gabriela A. Frei, and Inge van Hulle, 'The Foreign Enlistment Act, International Law, and British Politics 1819–2014', *International History Review* 38 (2016), 636–656.

10 Maartje Abbenhuis, *An Age of Neutrals: Great Power Politics 1815–1914* (Cambridge: Cambridge University Press, 2015).

'Mercenary' contracts 73

sovereignty such as the German Confederation. These areas had been the major suppliers of foreign troops together with Switzerland, which progressively curbed its inhabitants from enlisting in foreign armies between 1848 and 1870 as such enlistment was considered increasingly at odds with the country's official neutrality adopted in 1815. The surviving larger states emerged better equipped to wage war independently of outsiders. Industrialization assisted this, partly by boosting domestic arms manufacture (though few states achieved self-sufficiency) but mainly by easing recruiting problems by replacing manual labour by machine production. European imperialism simultaneously opened access to additional military human resources. The recruitment of indigenous soldiers reduced (relatively speaking) the numbers of Europeans required to expand and defend empires, whilst also increasing overall numbers that could be deployed globally.[11]

The risks of conflict were increased, however, because the presence of nationalism combined with the removal of minor states made it harder to make peace through the traditional means of minor territorial adjustments. Meanwhile, the nationalization of warfare meant that, when conflicts broke out, their impact on each belligerent was even greater than before, leading to what has become known as the age of 'total war' 1914–1945.[12]

Fiscal-Military Instruments

Fiscal-Military Instruments evolved as ways to facilitate the procurement and exchange of war-making resources between state and non-state actors across political jurisdictions. The emergence of these standardized practices contributed greatly to the coherence

---

11 Examples in *Guardians of Empire: The Armed Forces of the Colonial Powers, c. 1700–1964*, ed. by David Killingray and David Omissi (Manchester: Manchester University Press, 1999); Myron Echenberg, *Colonial Conscripts: The Tirailleurs Sénégalais in French West Africa, 1857–1960* (London: Heinemann, 1990).

12 *On the Road to Total War: The American Civil War and the German Wars of Unification, 1861–1871*, ed. by Stig Förster and Jörg Nagler (Cambridge: Cambridge University Press, 1997); *Anticipating Total War: The German and American Experiences, 1871–1914*, ed. by Manfred F. Boemeke, Roger Chickering, and Stig Förster (Cambridge: Cambridge University Press, 1999); *Great War, Total War: Combat and Mobilization on the Western Front, 1914–1918*, ed. by Roger Chickering and Stig Förster (Cambridge: Cambridge University Press, 2000).

of Europe as a Fiscal-Military System and frequently enabled hostile, or at least mutually suspicious, parties to co-operate in what were high-risk arrangements. Fiscal-Military Instruments such as troop levies were contracts between two or more parties which could be governments with their own jurisdictions, but were not necessarily so and could include semi-sovereign powers like the German principalities, or non-state actors like agents and contractors. They took a variety of forms, but all gave rise to a fiscal-military asset (i.e. some form of warmaking resource) of one entity, and a financial and/or political liability of another entity. One party agreed to provide some kind of assistance in return for material and/or political recompense from another who might be based in a different political jurisdiction. Agreements were framed as contracts, setting out the terms and obligations of each party. These were signed and sealed, and thus formally binding, despite the obvious absence of any supranational framework capable of enforcing them. Their key role was to foster trust between the parties through their appearance in commonly accepted, mutually understood forms.

The most obvious forms of Fiscal-Military Instruments were the various ways in which governments extracted human, financial, and material resources from their own subject populations. These frequently lacked explicit contracts, though all political authority rested on some kind of contractual theory of government in which the state provided protection against internal and external threats in return for subordination and support from the inhabitants. In practice, all states in the parts of Europe that were touched by Roman Catholicism developed some form of representative institution to mediate their demands for taxes, human resources, and materials. These forms of extraction can be labelled 'fiscal' and encompassed a wide variety of direct and indirect taxes paid in cash and kind, as well as forms of compulsory service extending from varieties of feudal levy through types of militia to different forms of conscription. Debt and forced loans were additional forms and played a substantial part in all war finance. These aspects have been widely studied as a dimension of the emergence of sovereign states, but this literature has generally interpreted states as autarkic actors and only examined their efforts to raise resources within their own territories.[13] Fiscal

---

13 *The Rise of Fiscal States: A Global History, 1500–1914*, ed. by Bartolomé Yun-Casalilla, Patrick K. O'Brien, and Francisco Comin (Cambridge: Cambridge University Press, 2012); *The Rise of the Fiscal State in Europe, c. 1200–1815*, ed. by Richard Bonney (Oxford: Oxford University Press,

instruments were employed in neutral or hostile territory, notably through the levying of 'contributions' under the threat of violence. These extorted payments in cash and kind and emerged during the later sixteenth century, before being refined during the mid-1620s in the Thirty Years' War. Contrary to their depiction in most secondary literature, contributions were not a form of licensed plundering but generally relied on formal agreements with the authorities of neutral or occupied communities and territories. These authorities employed their own fiscal structures to raise what was demanded, sometimes by introducing new taxes specifically for that purpose.[14]

Material Fiscal-Military Instruments were contracts which covered the provision of war-making materials ranging from warships, weaponry, munitions and other equipment to food and fodder, as well as the supply of horses and transport animals. These resources were often purchased, but they could also be hired – notably in the case of warships such as the fleet, complete with weaponry and crews, that was provided by the Dutch arms merchant Louis de Geer (1587–1652) for the Danes in their war against Sweden in 1643–1645.[15] Similar subcategories can be identified for contracts over the use of port facilities, transit for troops or war materials across another party's territory, or for the supply of intelligence or expertise. The recent literature on the 'contractor state' has noted the significance of entrepreneurs, who were often more important in supplying the material needs of armies and navies than procurement from state-owned factories or yards.[16] To date, this literature has

---

1999). For a detailed example of the role of non-state actors as brokers for international loans, see Aaron Graham, 'The War of the Spanish Succession, the Financial Revolution, and the Imperial Loans of 1706 and 1710', in *The War of the Spanish Succession: New Perspectives*, ed. by Matthias Pohlig and Michael Schaich (Oxford: Oxford University Press, 2018), pp. 299–321.

14 Peter H. Wilson, 'War Finance, Policy and Strategy in the Thirty Years War', in *Dynamik durch Gewalt? Der Dreißigjährige Krieg (1618–1648) als Faktor der Wandlungsprozesse des 17. Jahrhunderts*, ed. by Michael Rohrschneider and Anuschka Tischer (Münster: Aschendorff, 2018), pp. 229–250.

15 R.C. Anderson, *Naval Wars in the Baltic during the Sailing-ship Epoch 1522–1850* (London: C. Gilbert-Wood, 1910), pp. 47–69.

16 *The Contractor State and Its Implications 1659–1815*, ed. by Richard Harding and Sergio Solbes Ferri (Las Palmas de Gran Canaria: Universidad de Las Palmas de Gran Canaria, 2012); Roger Knight and Martin Wilcox, *Sustaining the Fleet, 1793–1815: War, the British Navy and the Contractor State* (Woodbridge: Boydell and Brewer, 2010); Rafael Torres Sánchez, *Military Entrepreneurs and the Spanish Contractor State in the Eighteenth Century* (Oxford: Oxford University Press, 2016).

largely focused on indigenous contractors supplying their own government; but it is clear that many were engaged in supplying other powers, often through networks of intermediaries.[17]

Like fiscal instruments, financial ones could be employed within a state's own jurisdiction or across it to obtain money from other countries. Examples include bills of exchange, bonds, and all manner of loans and debts. Subsidies were another important, specific form, involving the promise of one party to provide financial support to another in return for military and/or political support or co-operation. A major problem in the literature has been confusion between the *purpose* of such agreements and the *form* they took. Subsidies could be paid for a wide variety of reasons, including securing the active support of an ally, enabling such support from a weaker partner which might otherwise be unable to assist, and paying another power to refrain from assisting a hostile third party. Likewise, the party receiving subsidies might have multiple motives of which simple financial gain was rarely the most prominent, despite the frequent characterization by earlier historians of such arrangements as 'mercenary'.[18] The purposes of subsidies varied greatly, but the form was essentially the same. They were agreed in a treaty which specified the amount, timing, duration, and form of payment, as well as the obligations of the recipient. There were often additional, secret articles detailing political co-operation, including political favours that the paying party promised the recipient in addition to the financial transaction.[19]

---

17 One example was de Geer. For others, see Julia Zunckel, *Rüstungsgeschäfte im Dreißigjährigen Krieg: Unternehmerkräfte, Militärgüter und Marktstrategien im Handel zwischen Genua, Amsterdam und Hamburg* (Berlin: Duncker und Humblot, 1997); Pepijn Brandon, *War, Capital and the Dutch State (1588–1795)* (Leiden: Brill, 2015).

18 For example, Max Braubach, *Die Bedeutung der Subsidien für die Politik im spanischen Erbfolgekrieg* (Bonn: Schroeder, 1923). Further discussion of the recipients' motivation is found in Peter H. Wilson, 'The German "Soldier Trade" of the Seventeenth and Eighteenth Centuries: A Reassessment', *The International History Review* 18 (1996), 757–792. For the debate on the term 'mercenary', see Sarah V. Percy, *Mercenaries: The History of a Norm in International Relations* (Oxford: Oxford University Press, 2007).

19 Much of the following is based on an analysis of the treaties signed by the English/British monarchy and numerous continental partners from the 1680s to 1790s (in The National Archive, London, State Papers 103 and 108 series), those signed by the Dutch Republic (in the National Archief, The Hague, 1.01.02 Staten Generaal, VII.A. De ratificaties van tractaten,

Subsidy treaties were arrangements between recognized, established political authorities, even if one or both parties lacked fully modern sovereignty, as in the case of the German princes who were bound within the wider framework of the Holy Roman Empire and who made up the majority of the recipients of such funds. It is important to note that subsidies often required other financial instruments to be delivered, such as bills of exchange or loans. Thus, like Fiscal-Military Instruments generally, though they were agreements between political authorities, they frequently relied on non-state actors for their actual operation.

Historians have sometimes used the term 'subsidy treaty' for what should, for the sake of analytical clarity, be classed as one of the other three types of troop convention discussed below.[20] Another common confusion arises from the fact that subsidy agreements shared a common origin in the 'pensions' paid by powerful states like France to individuals, such as members of the various Swiss cantonal governments. 'Public' and 'private' were not distinguished in the modern sense; indeed such distinctions emerged as part of the wider delineation of political power in sovereign states which included an internal as well as international dimension and was not completed until the early nineteenth century, and in some respects even later.[21] Some princes, such as Wilhelm V of Hesse-Cassel,

---

1700–1797), and those of numerous German principalities including Hesse-Darmstadt (Staatsarchiv Darmstadt, A6 series, as well as negotiations in the E8 B259–B266 series, and papers on foreign enlistment E8 B10/10–16), Münster (Landesarchiv Münster, A58 Nr. 218, 253); Paderborn (Landesarchiv Münster, A267 I Kriegsrechnungen 1694–1798); Württemberg (Hauptstaatsarchiv Stuttgart [HStAS], treaties and papers relating to recruitment for other powers, chiefly A5 Bü.62, 63, 65, 66; A6 Bü.33, 56–60; A7 Bü.10; A8 Bü.5, 8, 59; A74 Bü.189, 190, 197; A19a Bd.1382; A202 Bü.737, 1157, 1159, 1206, 1358, 1361, 1362,2109–2114, 2118, 2219, 2236, 2241, 2254–2256, 2263, 2265, 2282, 2290, 2294, 2462–2471; Landesbibliothek Stuttgart, Cod.Hist.647). I am very grateful to Tom Nora for supplying digital copies of the material from the Dutch National Archives.

20 A common example is the agreement made between France and Bernhard von Sachsen-Weimar in 1635 in which France subsidised what had been till then, and what was still in Sweden's eyes, the army of the Heilbronn League.

21 Giorgio Chittolini, 'The "Private", the "Public", the State', *Journal of Modern History* 67, supplement (1995), 34–61. For pensions and military recruitment, see Christian Windler, '"Ohne Geld keine Schweizer": Pensionen und Söldnerrekrutierung auf den eidgenössischen Patronagemärkten', in *Nähe in der Ferne: Personale Verflechtungen in den Außenbeziehungen*

received both pensions and subsidies from the same power.[22] Moreover, pensions and subsidies could both take the form of a retainer, paid by a government to secure the services of an individual or a prince, should they be required, similar to the 'retainers' (*Wartgelder*) paid to experienced officers and soldiers by many German princes from the end of the fourteenth to the mid-seventeenth century.[23] The development of permanent 'standing' armies around the middle of the seventeenth century transformed retainers into 'half-pay', whereby surplus officers were placed on waiting lists with reduced pay at the termination of each conflict, ready to be recalled should the need arise. France paid several German princes to hold troops in readiness during the early 1750s in anticipation of renewed war in Europe following the unsatisfactory outcome of the War of the Austrian Succession.[24] However, for the sake of analytical clarity it is helpful to distinguish 'subsidies' as transactions between sovereign or at least semi-sovereign authorities and in some way binding on their jurisdictions, and to use 'pensions' to denote payments made to individuals, even if these also had a direct political or military purpose.

Arrangements to pay subsidies were often included in formal alliances, but that did not mean that every subsidy treaty entailed an alliance, or that every alliance involved the transfer of financial or other assistance between the signatories. Neither the provider nor the recipient necessarily agreed to become involved in wars in which the other was engaged. For example, France paid subsidies to the Dutch Republic, Denmark, and Spain during the 1620s without being regarded as a belligerent in the Eighty Years' War (1568–1648) or the Thirty Years' War (1618–1648) by either these three recipients or by their Spanish and Austrian Habsburg opponents.

---

der Frühen Neuzeit, ed. by Hillard von Thiessen and Christian Windler (Berlin: Duncker und Humblot, 2005), pp. 105–133; Friedrich Edelmayer, *Söldner und Pensionäre: Das Netzwerk Philipps II. im Heiligen Römischen Reich*, Studien zur Geschichte und Kultur der iberischen und iberoamerikanischen Länder, 7 (Munich: Oldenbourg, 2002).

22 For an example, see Jörg Ulbert, 'Französische Subsidienzahlungen an Hessen-Kassel während des Dreißigjährigen Krieges', in *Frankreich und Hessen-Kassel zur Zeit des Dreißigjährigen Krieges und des Westfälischen Friedens*, ed. by Klaus Malettke (Marburg: N.G. Elwert, 1999), pp. 159–174.

23 Reinhard Baumann, *Landsknechte* (Munich: C.H. Beck, 1994), pp. 19, 87, 214.

24 Peter H. Wilson, *War, State and Society in Württemberg, 1677–1793* (Cambridge: Cambridge University Press, 1995), pp. 203–209.

Likewise, the German principalities supplied troops to numerous European monarchies and republics between the 1560s and the early nineteenth century, without necessarily formally becoming official belligerents. Indeed, most princes ensured that their agreements allowed them to remain neutral and to honour their commitments to the Holy Roman Empire, even if the latter was actually at war with their subsidy partner. Treaties could include safeguards for troop providers who were attacked as a consequence of fulfilling their agreements.[25] The latter certainly approached the character of an alliance, as did the terms which were often also included to cover political co-operation for specific purposes. However, the alliance elements were not indispensable to the arrangements to transfer war-making resources.

Troop conventions and 'mercenary' contracts as Fiscal-Military Instruments

These preliminary remarks lead us directly to the questions of troop conventions as Fiscal-Military Instruments, and their relationship to subsidies. A major reason for the confusion in much of the literature is that it focuses on subsidy treaties, generally regarding them as asymmetrical *alliances* between major and minor powers, and failing to treat troop conventions as distinct instruments since they were often made entirely independently of any agreements over subsidies. Further problems stem from an often uncritical use of the term 'mercenary' to cover all forms of military recruitment and service before the age of the citizen-in-arms which is widely believed to have begun around 1789.[26] The only serious attempt to date to classify troop conventions is limited to those made by France, with the result that it creates categories which are not fully applicable elsewhere.[27]

It is difficult to design watertight categories for the different forms of foreign troop contracts, as actual practice was so varied

---

25 For instance, all these provisions are included in Württemberg's treaty with France of 4 February 1752, HStAS, A202 Bü. 2219.
26 Alan Forrest, *The Legacy of the French Revolutionary Wars: The Nation-in-Arms in French Republican Memory* (Cambridge: Cambridge University Press, 2009); *The People in Arms: Military Myth and National Mobilization since the French Revolution*, edited by Daniel Moran and Arthur Waldron (Cambridge: Cambridge University Press, 2003).
27 Guy Rowlands, 'Foreign Service in the Age of Absolute Monarchy: Louis XIV and His *Forces Étrangères*', *War in History* 17 (2010), 141–165.

and could slip from one form to another, or even combine several different aspects in one arrangement. Contemporaries were also not consistent in their use of terms like 'auxiliary', 'foreign', 'hired', or 'subsidy'. Variations in motivation and purpose further cloud the distinctions, notably as providers of troops did not necessarily have to be full belligerents or allies of those they were assisting militarily. Broadly, contemporaries used the term 'treaty' (e.g. *Tractat*) for all kinds of agreement, but generally restricted 'capitulation' to contracts covering 'foreign' regiments and 'convention' to the hire of auxiliaries.

Some clarity is obtained when we tease out the different aspects of these arrangements which included how soldiers were recruited and by whom, how they were paid and maintained, and how they related to military command and political authority. It is possible to delineate four main forms, within each of which a number of important variations existed. The four forms co-evolved with the wider Fiscal-Military System, emerging by the mid- to late sixteenth century, and persisting in most cases into the mid-nineteenth century. None of these forms was static, but space precludes exploration of how each changed, and the priority here is to identify their distinguishing characteristics to assist further research in the field.

Direct recruitment

The first form to consider is that of the direct recruitment of individual soldiers who were subjects of one political jurisdiction into the service of another. Many men enlisted individually, often travelling considerable distances to do so, or because they were overtaken by some personal misfortune or economic necessity while away from their own homeland. However, it is almost certain that many more men were recruited by an agent of the hirer sent for that purpose, or by an autonomous intermediary (an enterpreneur or contractor) acting on their own account for financial gain, for career advancement, or to curry favour with the government for which they were recruiting.[28] A key distinguishing feature of this form was that such

---

28 Fritz Redlich's classic study of these intermediaries still provides useful detail: *The German Military Enterpriser and His Workforce*, Vierteljahrschrift für Sozial- und Wirtschaftsgeschichte, Beihefte 47/48, 2 vols (Wiesbaden: Steiner, 1964–1965). The best and most recent reappraisal of these activities is David Parrott, *The Business of War: Military Enterprise and Military Revolution in Early Modern Europe* (Cambridge: Cambridge University Press, 2012).

agents and intermediaries lacked jurisdiction over the area where they were recruited and thus did not have any legal authority to compel men to enlist. They also had no direct call on the support of the authorities in the area where they were recruiting, frequently because those authorities did not want their neutrality compromised. Often, agents and intermediaries secured formal permission to recruit. If granted, permission was usually restricted according to the time and place where recruiters could operate and whether they were allowed to act publicly, accompanied by military musicians in order to attract potential recruits. However, such permission was also frequently refused, or not even sought in the almost certain knowledge that a request would be declined. In such circumstances, recruiters operated clandestinely and could be subject to fines or imprisonment if caught.[29]

The chances of formal permission varied depending on the political circumstances and often also religion of the area where recruitment was to take place, as well as its relationship to the power in whose name the request was being made. For example, the Swiss cantonal authorities declined 133 of the 494 requests from the Prussian army to recruit and postponed at least 30 more between 1717 and 1740, but Catholic authorities were significantly less likely to co-operate than Protestant ones.[30] Many German principalities were reluctant to allow Prussia to recruit, because they rightly feared that Prussian officers and agents would try to induce their own soldiers to desert rather than pick untrained men. Yet, they often agreed for fear of antagonizing such a powerful monarchy.

Sometimes, authorities granted permission even to hostile powers, if the men being recruited were considered politically or economically undesirable. For example, the English monarchy allowed Spain to send officers to recruit Irishmen during years of peace in the seventeenth century, as well as allowing Irishmen to seek appointment as captains in the Spanish service in return for recruiting a company of soldiers.[31] In other cases, the authorities permitted recruitment

---

29 There is a further discussion with examples in Peter H. Wilson, 'The Politics of Military Recruitment in Eighteenth-century Germany', *English Historical Review* 117 (2002), 536–568.
30 Rudolf Gugger, *Preußische Werbungen im der Eidgenossenschaft im 18. Jahrhundert* (Berlin: Duncker und Humblot, 1997), pp. 254–262.
31 Eduardo de Mesa, *The Irish in the Spanish Armies in the Seventeenth Century* (Woodbridge: Boydell, 2014), esp. pp. 39–66; R.A. Stradling, *The Spanish Monarchy and Irish Mercenaries: The Wild Geese in Spain, 1618–68* (Dublin: Irish Academic Press, 1994).

as a form of indirect support for the power that was recruiting, notably in the case of the English monarchy's permission to the Palatinate, Denmark, and Sweden to recruit Scottish, Welsh, and English soldiers between 1618 and 1638. In some cases, recruits were even conscripted to supply armies organized by autonomous contractors, notably Count Ernst von Mansfeld (1580–1626).[32] In the latter case, the authorities' formal co-operation pushed this form of recruitment close to the second category, as we shall see.

The primary contractual elements in this form encompassed a written agreement between the power commissioning the recruitment and the officer or agent conducting it, as well as between that agent and the men enlisting. Agents' contracts specified the number of men they should recruit by a specific date, as well as how they would be recompensed for this service. Frequently, there were stipulations as to what kind of recruit was considered acceptable, with the commissioning power reserving the right to reject men considered unfit for its service. Such stipulations were broadly similar to those employed by that power in its own territory to recruit directly into its army. Recruits were generally signed up on 'capitulations', or time-limited service contracts that were often shorter and on better terms than those offered to native recruits. Additionally, agents and sometimes the commissioning power might sign agreements with the authorities within whose jurisdiction recruitment was to take place. These agreements bound the agents to observe local laws, not to take men by force, and to pay for all goods and services they received. Sometimes they had to provide a 'caution' or deposit as a safeguard for their good behaviour.

Men recruited under this form of troop convention were collected in small groups and then travelled to join specific regiments. Austria and Prussia recruited Germans from across the Holy Roman Empire into their infantry and cavalry regiments to supplement native

---

32 Walter Krüssmann, *Ernst von Mansfeld (1580–1626): Grafensohn, Söldnerführer, Kriegsunternehmer gegen Habsburg im Dreißigjährigen Krieg* (Berlin: Duncker und Humblot, 2010), pp. 544–555; Adam Marks, 'England, the English and the Thirty Years War (1618–1648)' (unpublished doctoral thesis, University of St Andrews, 2012); Steve Murdoch, *Britain, Denmark-Norway and the House of Stuart, 1603–1660* (East Linton: Tuckwell Press, 2000), pp. 187–252; *Scotland and the Thirty Years War, 1618–1648*, ed. by Steve Murdoch (Leiden: Brill, 2001); J.V. Polisensky, 'Gallants to Bohemia', *The Slavonic and East European Review* 25 (1947), 391–404; Steven J. Stearns, 'Conscription and English Society in the 1620s', *Journal of British Studies* 11 (1971), 1–24.

conscripts and volunteers. Other states generally segregated foreign recruits by nationality into separate regiments. France maintained regiments of Germans, Swiss, Irish, Scots, Poles, and Italians, while Germans, Swiss, Irish, and Italians also served Spain. The Dutch had German, Swiss, English, and Scottish units. Sweden recruited widely during the 1620s and 1640s, and then maintained permanent German regiments stationed in its possessions in the Holy Roman Empire. Savoy-Piedmont recruited German and Swiss units after 1690 and the kingdom of Naples did the same after its independence from Austria in 1735.

'Foreign' regiments

Other examples can be found, but, in most of these cases, the direct recruitment of individual soldiers by agents was to sustain units which were already in existence, thus further distinguishing the first form of troop convention from the second which involved an external authority contracting to provide fully formed units for another army. This form of convention involved direct relations between the power commissioning the recruitment and the authority within whose territory it was conducted, in contrast to the first form where relations were either indirect through an agent, or absent altogether in clandestine recruitment. The power requesting recruitment could send an agent to negotiate permission, or it might be approached by another authority who wished to recruit for it, as in the case of several minor German princes who raised regiments for the Dutch and Venetian republics in the 1680s. Unlike direct recruitment, this second form of convention involved the raising of entire regiments or groups of regiments which were recruited with the express permission and often direct assistance of the local authorities.

Intermediaries could still play an important part, as in the case of the Dutch Republic's agreement with the Grisons (Grey Leagues) to recruit an infantry regiment in March 1693 which was secured thanks to the good offices of Colonel Hercules Capol (1642–1706). Capol, who came from an established Grisons family, was promptly named commander of the new unit and it is clear that he relied on his wider kinship and professional networks to recruit it: the company-grade officers included Capol's nephew, cousin, and son-in-law.[33]

---

33 Martin Bundi, *Bünder Kriegsdienste in Holland um 1700: Eine Studie zu den Beziehungen zwischen Holland und Graubünden von 1693 bis 1730* (Chur: Calven Verlag, 1972), pp. 30–40.

Regardless of how the agreement was reached, it generally followed a standard form which emerged as early as around 1500 and specified how the regiment was to be raised, the kind of men who were acceptable as recruits, their terms and length of service, and how this was to be paid for, including what financial or political benefits the recruiting authority would receive from the commissioning power. Agreements often granted the recruiting authority residual rights over the unit once it had been mustered into the commissioning power's forces. Such rights could include the powers to name or at least suggest candidates to fill the initial officer appointments, as well as to replace any subsequent vacancies. Such rights were an important source of patronage, and they linked the regiment and the two contracting authorities through complex personal relationships. However, it was often difficult to exercise actual control once a unit had left the territory where it had been raised, because it passed under the authority of the commissioning power and became an integral part of its army. This point is important, as it constitutes a significant feature which distinguishes this form of convention from auxiliary and subsidy troops who were intended to be returned once they were no longer needed.

The case of the Grisons regiment in Dutch service exemplifies these difficulties. The Dutch unilaterally disbanded five of the regiment's ten companies as an economy measure in 1717, ignoring protests from the Grisons authorities. The importance of such units as a source of income and patronage often obliged providers to comply with hirers' requests for additional human resources to maintain the unit once it had entered their service. The Grisons readily agreed to find more recruits when the Dutch decided to augment each company from 50 to 150 men in 1726, and the unit remained an integral part of the Dutch army until 1797.[34]

Often, the men needed to keep such units up to strength were recruited directly, thus blurring the distinction between the first and second forms of convention. However, once the unit had passed into the commissioning power's army, it remained distinctly 'foreign', additional recruits being sought in the area which had originally provided it. This status was more pronounced in some armies than others, and the overall characteristics changed between the mid-sixteenth and mid-nineteenth centuries. The Spanish, French, Dutch, and later also Savoyard and Neapolitan armies recruited

---

34 *Ibid.*, pp. 123–124.

units characterised as German, Swiss, Italian, and in some cases Scottish, Irish, or English, that were explicitly considered separate from 'national' regiments recruited directly from these states' own subjects. Their distinctiveness was marked by particular uniforms, flags, and generally also legal privileges, pay, and conditions. Other armies recruited such regiments from men who were less obviously linguistically or culturally distinct from their own subjects. For example, both Austria and Prussia incorporated regiments provided by German princes within the Holy Roman Empire which retained connections with their original provider, but were not classed as distinctly 'foreign' units.

The actual composition of these units could vary considerably, particularly over time, as other foreigners, deserters, prisoners, and 'native' recruits were often used to keep them up to strength. For example, only a fifth of the 'Swiss' soldiers in Savoyard service in 1721 actually came from Switzerland, with Germans forming the majority along with a few French and some Savoyards.[35] Official records are often misleading, because definitions of 'foreign' could vary. The Prussian system of conscription introduced around 1733 classed any recruit from outside a regiment's recruiting 'canton' as 'foreign'.[36]

Even allowing for these issues, the numbers of men raised by both the first and second types of convention were considerable. Between the early sixteenth and mid-nineteenth centuries an estimated one million Swiss served in other armies, mainly in distinct regiments. Around half of these were in French service, including around 120,000 who served during the reign of Louis XIV.[37] To put this further into perspective: the French army expanded dramatically from about 55,000 men in the early 1660s to about 150,000 at the start of the Nine Years' War in 1688. At least 655,000 men were recruited during the War of the Spanish Succession (1701–1714), while overall around two million served between 1700 and 1763, of whom about

---

35 Sabina Loriga, 'Soldaten in Piemont im 18. Jahrhundert', L'Homme: Zeitschrift für feministische Geschichtswissenschaft 3 (1992), 64–87 (p. 65).
36 Martin Winter, Untertanengeist durch Militärpflicht? Das Preußische Kantonsystem in brandenburgischen Städten im 18. Jahrhundert (Bielefeld: Verlag für Regionalgeschichte, 2005), pp. 262–265.
37 John McCormack, One Million Mercenaries: Swiss Soldiers in the Armies of the World (London: Leo Cooper, 1993); Albert Hochheimer, Verraten und verkauft: Die Geschichte der europäischen Söldner (Stuttgart: Goverts, 1967), p. 183.

300,000 were recruited from outside France.[38] Though distributed throughout the army, foreigners also formed a significant part of the Prussian army, with their proportion rising from about 20 per cent in the 1720s to around 40 per cent by 1740, and thereafter around half the total until the end of the eighteenth century.[39] Given that the army not only grew from about 40,000 in 1713 to 195,000 by 1786, but also fought four costly wars between 1740 and 1778, this represented a significant increase in foreign recruitment.

The French and Spanish armies continued to maintain foreign regiments throughout the Revolutionary and Napoleonic Wars, while the Neapolitan and Papal armies also raised Swiss and German units when they reconstituted their armies in 1814.[40] Britain also recruited such units, notably from Germans, Swiss, and Dutch, during the wars against Revolutionary and Napoleonic France. After 1815 it became a troop provider, when six thousand Britons, mainly discharged soldiers, joined the armies fighting for independence from Spain in South America.[41] Spanish protests prompted Britain to pass the Foreign Enlistment Act (1819) prohibiting its subjects from joining the forces of foreign powers, but suspended this temporarily in 1835 to permit the recruitment of a ten-thousand-man British Auxiliary Legion to assist the liberal Cristino monarchy against its Carlist rivals in the Spanish civil war of 1833–1840.[42] The progressive nationalisation of war-making, with its ideal of citizens-in-arms, discouraged most states from recruiting foreigners by the 1850s.

That decade was a watershed between premodern Fiscal-Military Instruments and modern forms of military assistance which were more clearly determined by political ideology and by the ideals of the sovereign nation state. Conservative regimes provided foreign units in support of allies facing revolution. Austria and Bavaria

---

38 André Corvisier, *Les Français et l'armée sous Louis XIV* (Vincennes: Ministère de la défense, Etat Major de l'Armée de terre, Service historique, 1975), p. 133, and the same author's *L'armée française de la fin du 17e siècle au ministère de Choiseul*, 2 vols (Paris: PUF, 1964), vol. II, p. 962.
39 Willerd R. Fann, 'Foreigners in the Prussian army 1713–1756', *Central European History* 23 (1990), 76–85.
40 David Alvarez, *The Pope's Soldiers: A Military History of the Modern Vatican* (Lawrence: University of Kansas Press, 2011), esp. pp. 32–40.
41 Ben Hughes, *Conquer or Die! Wellington's Veterans and the Liberation of the New World* (Oxford: Osprey, 2010).
42 Edward M. Brett, *The British Auxiliary Legion in the First Carlist War 1835–1838* (Dublin: Four Courts Press, 2005).

recruited four 'foreign' carabineer regiments for the Bourbon regime in Naples, which had disbanded its Swiss units after a mutiny in 1858 and now faced Garibaldi's insurgency. Austria and Belgium likewise sent foreign legions to back Archduke Maximilian's ill-fated rule as emperor of Mexico 1864–1867, primarily because both monarchies were linked dynastically to him.[43] Meanwhile, a variety of volunteers flocked to fight for various liberal causes across Europe, especially during the 1848 Revolutions and subsequently in Italy, Poland, France, and Greece during the later nineteenth century.[44]

Exile regiments formed a special subcategory of the premodern foreign troops, since they followed their prince into the service of an allied monarch. These examples primarily belong to the era of the Nine Years' War (1688–1697) and the War of the Spanish Succession (1701–1714). Around 25,000 Irish and British troops followed James II into exile after 1691 and became a permanent part of the French army.[45] Smaller numbers of Bavarian and Cologne troops joined the French army when the emperor punished their rulers for backing Louis XIV during the War of the Spanish Succession; but, unlike James II, their princes were restored in 1714 and they were able to return home. The Hanoverian army broadly fits this subcategory during the Napoleonic Wars, when around thirty thousand former personnel and other Germans escaped their occupied homeland to serve in the King's German Legion which formed part of the British army 1803–1815.[46]

Stateless troops recruited as embodied regiments by colonel-entrepreneurs or groups of officers represented a second subcategory of foreign soldiers. One early example was the former army of the Heilbronn League. It was originally formed to assist Sweden during the Thirty Years' War, but after the League's collapse it acted on its own account under its primary commander, Duke Bernhard of Weimar (1604–1639), in arrangement with Sweden's main ally, France, which subsidised its operations. After Bernhard's death, the

---

43 Ernst Pitner, *Maximilian's Lieutenant: A Personal History of the Mexican Campaign, 1864–67*, translated and ed. by Gordon Etherington-Smith (London: I.B. Tauris, 1993).
44 For example, see Andrea Viotti, *Garibaldi: The Revolutionary and His Men* (Poole: Blandford, 1979).
45 John A. Lynn, *Giant of the Grand Siècle: The French Army 1610–1715* (Cambridge: Cambridge University Press, 1997), p. 367.
46 Mark Wishon, *German Forces and the British Army: Interactions and Perceptions, 1742–1815* (Basingstoke: Palgrave, 2013), pp. 165–192.

force was absorbed incrementally into the French army.[47] Other examples include the various units raised after 1685 from and often by Huguenot refugees who served in the armies of Britain, Savoy, the Dutch Republic, Brandenburg-Prussia, Celle and other Protestant German principalities until the early eighteenth century.[48]

Both these subcategories were distinguished by the political circumstances of their formation, but otherwise shared the same features as other foreign troops. Their establishment, organisation, conditions of service, and other matters were all regulated in conventions signed by their leaders with the power whose service they entered. They remained distinct units within their paymaster's army, but were not fully independent and could be discarded when considered no longer needed, as was the case with the four Huguenot regiments in the British army which were disbanded in 1697. Likewise, they sustained themselves through direct recruitment with a similar impact on their actual composition. While almost all of the initial eight thousand men enrolled in the King's German Legion by 1805 were Hanoverians, the force had become cosmopolitan and polyglot by the time it was disbanded in 1815.

Hired auxiliaries

The third major form of troop convention consisted in the hiring of auxiliaries. Like foreign regiments, these were organised by a provider exercising formal jurisdiction over its own territory, notably the German and Italian princes, but also other monarchs such as the rulers of Denmark and Sweden. Units were also provided fully formed, armed, and equipped, and served under their own officers appointed by the provider, who likewise retained some jurisdiction over the units' internal management, such as discipline and promotions. The provider did not have to be an active ally of the power it was assisting, as was the case with the various German principalities supplying troops to Venice in its war against the Ottomans in the 1680s, as well as the better-known example of the Hessians and other Germans serving Britain in America roughly a century later.[49]

---

47 David Parrott, *Richelieu's Army: War, Government and Society in France, 1624–1642* (Cambridge: Cambridge University Press, 2001), pp. 293–298.
48 *War, Religion and Service: Huguenot Soldiering, 1685–1713*, ed. by Matthew Glozier and David Onnekink (Aldershot: Ashgate, 2007).
49 For Venetian service, see for example Alexander Schwencke, *Geschichte der Hannoverschen Truppen in Griechenland 1685–1689* (Hanover: Hahn, 1854).

Finally, as in the case of foreign regiments, the conventions stipulated the initial period of service and sometimes imposed restrictions on where the troops could be deployed, such as prohibiting their dispatch overseas. What distinguished hired auxiliaries from foreign troops was that this was always intended to be a two-way exchange, the units being returned once their contract expired or (as was sometimes allowed in the conventions) their provider recalled them.

The timing of the exchange was carefully choreographed to proceed through clearly defined stages. The overall length of the agreement was specified in a signed treaty or convention. Once this had been ratified, the provider had a fixed period within which the troops had to be assembled at the specified strength and at a designated point. Some agreements allowed for the transfer of mobilisation money to cover at least part of the costs of making the units combat-ready, including bringing them up to the required strength and providing them with field equipment such as wagons and tents. In some cases units had to be raised from scratch, notably where providers concealed their actual lack of preparedness from the hirer. Generally, the provider remained responsible for paying, feeding, and housing the troops throughout this first stage, and was also responsible for their command and for all disciplinary matters. The second stage began once the hirer formally mustered the troops who now entered the hirer's service. This ceremony was much like those held to mark the embodiment of newly raised units in any army, except that auxiliaries remained bound by an oath to their provider and did not become a fully integrated part of the hirer's army. In most cases, auxiliaries were already soldiers and had sworn to abide by the articles of war. They had thus already crossed from civilian to martial law. Instead, what changed was that they now went in under the operational command of the hirer who simultaneously assumed at least partial responsibility for their pay and maintenance. The second stage lasted until the auxiliaries were discharged in another muster from the hirer's service back into the command and maintenance of their provider. This stage was also marked by a formal ceremony, as well as an audit of personnel, equipment, and accounts, so that any outstanding moneys could be calculated. In practice, providers then frequently complained that they were still owed substantial sums, leading in some cases to a fourth stage where these claims were settled, usually in some kind of compromise agreement. Some conventions included demobilisation payments to cover the cost of returning the troops and reducing them to their peacetime strength. Where provided, such payments were usually calculated at between one and three months' pay; but again disagreements could arise when the provider claimed them at the unit's full strength, whereas the hirer paid only according to actual strength.

There were two important subcategories of hired auxiliaries, distinguished by the form and extent of the monetary and material compensation provided. Fully hired auxiliaries became financially independent of the provider and were instead paid, fed, and housed at the hirer's expense. Usually, troop conventions specified that hired auxiliaries were to receive the same rates as the hirer's own forces, to ensure that they were not discriminated against. Subsidised auxiliaries remained partially dependent on their provider for their maintenance. Generally, they received food and fodder in kind, but remained paid by their provider. Additional subsidies might be paid in both cases, but these were not the principal means of maintaining the forces. The lines could blur between hired auxiliaries and foreign regiments if the contracts were extended across many years, including peacetime. Examples include the Anglo-Scottish brigade in Dutch service 1572–1782 and the 3,500 ex-Cromwellian soldiers sent by Charles II to serve Portugal 1662–1668.[50]

Auxiliaries constituted a substantial part of most European armies in wartime between the 1660s and 1790s. The seven thousand Danes hired by William III in 1689 formed 15 per cent of his army at the decisive Battle of the Boyne the following year, and they continued to serve him in campaigns in Flanders until 1697.[51] Between 33,000 and 115,000 German auxiliaries supported the Allied war effort in any given year during the War of the Spanish Succession, dwarfing the British contingent sent to the continent as well as providing a considerable augmentation to the Dutch army, which already contained a large number of German and Swiss foreign regiments.[52]

---

50 *Papers Illustrating the History of the Scots Brigade in the Service of the United Netherlands*, ed. by James Ferguson, 2 vols (Edinburgh: Edinburgh University Press, 1899–1901); Jonathon Riley, *The Last Ironsides: The English Expedition to Portugal 1662–1668* (Solihull: Helion, 2014).

51 Kjeld Hald Galster, *Danish Troops in the Williamite Army in Ireland, 1689–91* (Dublin: Four Courts Press, 2012).

52 Peter H. Wilson, 'Financing the War of the Spanish Succession in the Holy Roman Empire', in *The War of the Spanish Succession: New Perspectives*, ed. by Matthias Pohlig and Michael Schaich (Oxford: Oxford University Press, 2018), pp. 267–297, and *German Armies: War and German Politics 1648–1806* (London: UCL Press, 1998), pp. 104–112.

Subsidy troops

Subsidy troops can be distinguished from auxiliaries by the much looser relationship between the soldiers provided and the monetary compensation received. Such troops were significant, especially during the Revolutionary and Napoleonic Wars, but their numbers were generally fewer than those in the other three forms of troop convention. The inflated importance attached to subsidy troops is largely due to their being confused with auxiliaries and because subsidy payments are generally easier to track than the diverse, but often more substantial, sums paid directly to auxiliaries and foreign troops.[53] Unlike auxiliaries, subsidy troops were not paid in full and did not serve so closely under the payer's command. The treaty generally specified a certain number of men to be provided, but did not entitle the payer to stipulate exactly which units or where they served. The subsidy simply 'subsidised' the provider's costs, but the proportion covered could vary.

Subsidies were more clearly 'political' than the other three forms of convention. A more powerful ally subsidised the cost of a weaker partner in a common war effort, and the arrangements often bore more resemblance to an alliance than was usual in the other forms. Subsidy and auxiliary agreements were often combined, one treaty arranging political co-operation and the payment of a subsidy and another specifying the supply of auxiliaries to the stronger partner, who thus had to meet their direct costs as well as provide the subsidy. However, like the provision of foreign regiments and auxiliaries, such arrangements did not automatically make both partners full belligerents in the same way, thus helping to distinguish these Fiscal-Military Instruments from alliances.

Conclusions

Subsidies were closely associated with the transfer of soldiers from the service of one power to another, but the exact relationship between financial payments and troop conventions has been clouded by lack of precision in identifying and defining the different ways in which war-making resources were exchanged. This chapter has suggested that subsidies should be interpreted as one of several

---

53 An example of this is John M. Sherwig, *Guineas and Gunpowder: British Foreign Aid in the Wars with France, 1793–1815* (Cambridge, MA: Harvard University Press, 1969).

Fiscal-Military Instruments which evolved across early modernity as ways of transferring men, money, materials, services, information, and expertise between partners. Such instruments facilitated what were high-risk arrangements between partners who were often justified in mistrusting each other. Whilst scholarly attention has concentrated on subsidies as aspects of interstate diplomacy, this chapter has argued that we also need to consider the ways in which soldiers were recruited, hired, or lent which were themselves often separate from subsidy treaties and which involved non-state as well as state actors.

4
The uses of French subsidies in Sweden, 1632–1729

Svante Norrhem

Introduction[1]

In his book *Tankar om krig i gemen och Sweriges krig i synnerhet* ('Thoughts about war in general and Sweden's war in particular'), written in 1758 and published in 1767, a civil servant and politician by the name of Anders Nordencrantz (1697–1772) heavily criticized the Swedish acceptance of foreign subsidies. Subsidies become opiates, poisons that delight, corrupt, and drug recipients. Subsidies are like golden hooks pulling the receivers like fish out of their natural environment, Nordencrantz says, and lead them to go wherever the foreigner wishes – especially if there are individuals within the receiving nation who gain from these operations.[2]

By 1758, Sweden had received subsidies from France for twenty successive years, whereas the Franco-Swedish subsidy relationship went back much longer. From 1631 to 1758, Sweden had received subsidies for more than sixty years, most often from France and usually in the form of subsidy troops, as described by Peter H. Wilson in Chapter 3 above. According to Nordencrantz, it had been a grave mistake for Sweden to accept subsidies in the 1630s in order to enter the war in Germany. By its greedy conquest of land, Sweden

---

1 Some of the findings contained in this chapter derive from research more fully presented in Svante Norrhem, *Mercenary Swedes: French Subsidies to Sweden 1631–1796* (Lund: Nordic Academic Press, 2019).
2 Anders Nordencrantz, *Tankar om krig i gemen och Sweriges krig i synnerhet, samt hwaruti Sweriges rätta och sanskyldiga interesse består: skrifwit år 1758, och hörer til et större wärk, som på hög wederbörlig befallning blifwit författadt, men icke förr kunnat komma i dagsljuset* (Stockholm: Lorens Ludvig Greving, 1767), pp. 65, 67.

had ended up in a situation where subsidies were constantly needed for protecting the new territories. Sweden would have been quite a different country, Nordencrantz argues, had that money been invested in agriculture rather than war. The wars and the cost of protecting overseas territories, such as Pomerania in northern Germany, had never been covered by foreign subsidies.³ People in general rejected war, Nordencrantz wrote, claiming that the wars Sweden fought between 1740 and 1756 were decided by just ten individuals within the political elite.⁴

Criticism against accepting subsidies had been voiced before and repeatedly during the lengthy period when Sweden had received them; however, the critique was rarely public before the eighteenth century. Some of the most prominent critical voices belonged to the head of the treasury, Gustaf Bonde (1620–1667), and his grandson, the politician Gustaf Bonde (1682–1764). Bonde the Elder introduced in 1661 a political programme in which he advocated thrift as a method for ceasing to be on the receiving end of foreign money.⁵ Expenses could be reduced by putting an end to the ennoblement of officers, civil servants, or merchants.⁶ His grandson, seventy years later, echoed many of these suggestions but directed his criticism much more pointedly against French subsidies as such. France, according to Gustaf Bonde the Younger, had proved that it sometimes made use of its superior position towards Sweden. An independent nation like Sweden should not accept giving up its freedom for the sake of money.⁷

---

3 *Ibid.*, p. 47.
4 *Ibid.*, p. 62.
5 Gustaf Bonde, 'Riksskattmästaren Gustaf Bondes politiska program 1661', *Historisk Tidskrift* 33 (1913), 42–54 (p. 46).
6 *Ibid.*, 49–50.
7 Carl Trolle-Bonde, *Anteckningar om Bondesläkten af Carl Trolle-Bonde* (Lund: Berlingska Boktryckeri- och Stilgjuteri Aktiebolaget, 1898), pp. 138–139. Similar voices against subsidies were also raised in other European countries from time to time. By the end of the eighteenth century, the recruitment of soldiers in German territories for foreign military service drew increasing criticism. The arguments against subsidies included the high mortality rates among young fighting men and a troubling overdependence on the subsidizer. Enlightenment ideas encouraged this resistance, especially when the British started using German armies in North America. See Tryntje Helfferich, Chapter 2 above, as well as Philip G. Dwyer, *The Rise of Prussia 1700–1830* (London and New York: Routledge, 2014), pp. 56–57; Frederic Groß, 'Einzigartig? – Der Subsidienvertrag von 1786 über die Aufstellung

The uses of French subsidies in Sweden

Despite this criticism of how taking subsidies affected the recipient's political independence and social and economic well-being, research on the early modern period shows that subsidies also brought benefits both to states and to specific people living there. Looking at subsidies at a state level, one may argue that subsidies granted the giver access to much-needed armies and allies at the same time as they enabled relatively small countries, such as Denmark and Sweden, to play a role in European politics.[8] Much of the continental warfare in which the two countries were involved during the early modern period was enabled by foreign subsidies. The same may be said of other countries in Europe at the same time.[9] Rulers and elites benefited from being able to participate in European great-power politics, as they could accrue greater prestige and greater territorial and other material benefits. The so-called 'Soldatenhandel', meaning resource-rich states hiring armies from smaller German states in exchange for subsidies, became a way for lesser German princes to play a role in European politics. Providing soldiers for money could strengthen the political position of princes and give them higher

---

des "Kapregiments" zwischen Herzog Karl Eugen von Württemberg und der Niederländischen Ostindienkompanie', in *Militärische Migration vom Altertum bis zur Gegenwart*, ed. by Christoph Rass (Paderborn: Studien zur Historischen Migrationsforschung, vol. 30, 2016), pp. 143–164; Lothar Höbelt, 'Vom militärischen saisonnier zum miles perpetuus: Staatsbildung und Kriegsführung im ancien régime', in *Krieg und Gesellschaft*, vol. 2, ed. by Thomas Kolnberger and Ilja Steffelbauer (Vienna: Mandelbaum, 2010), pp. 59–79; Charles W. Ingrao, *The Hessian Mercenary State: Ideas, Institutions, and Reform under Frederick II, 1760–1785* (Cambridge: Cambridge University Press, 1987), pp. 138–140; Hans-Martin Maurer, 'Das württembergische Kapregiment. Söldner im Dienste früher Kolonialpolitik (1787–1808)', *Zeitschrift für Württembergische Landesgeschichte* 47 (1988), 291–307.

8 Dwyryd Wyn Jones, *War and Economy in the Age of William III and Marlborough* (Oxford: Basil Blackwell, 1988), pp. 7–11; Christopher Storrs: '"Große Erwartungen": Britische Subsidienzahlungen an Savoyen im 18. Jahrhundert' in *Das 'Blut des Staatskörpers': Forschungen zur Finanzgeschichte der Frühen Neuzeit*, ed. by Peter Rauscher, Andrea Serles, and Thomas Winkelbauer (Munich: Historische Zeitschrift, Beiheft, vol. 56, 2012), 87–126 (p. 124); Peter H. Wilson, *War, State and Society in Württemberg, 1677–1793* (Cambridge: Cambridge University Press, 1995), pp. 85–86.

9 Peter Lindström and Svante Norrhem, *Flattering Alliances: Scandinavia, Diplomacy and the Austrian-French Balance of Power, 1648–1740* (Lund: Nordic Academic Press, 2013), pp. 68–74; Peter H. Wilson, *German Armies: War and German Politics 1648–1806* (London: UCL Press, 1998), pp. 47–49, 176.

prestige within the international community, as shown by the examples of Hesse, Württemberg, and Saxony-Gotha.[10] For Hesse, this resulted in its armies becoming major employers offering opportunities for advancement (especially to the lower nobility). In addition, it meant that taxes could be kept at a low level, while also enabling a focus on commercial activity.[11] However, such obvious benefits were not necessarily found elsewhere among smaller German states.[12]

Prestige – also used as one of several justifications for Sweden to ally with France in the 1630s – was only one possible benefit from gaining subsidies.[13] Armies needed weapons, gunpowder, cannon balls, clothes, shoes, and food, and they needed somebody who could provide them. Subsidies were sometimes used to build or repair fortresses and ships, which implies that there was a demand for building contractors, suppliers of building material, craftsmen, and workers. Of this we know relatively little, since most research on subsidies has focused on the state level and the hiring of soldiers and officers. An exception concerns the merchant entrepreneurs who handled the frequently difficult issue of moving money from one country to another, discussed by Marianne Klerk and Erik Thomson in Chapters 9 and 10 below.[14]

---

10 Ingrao, *The Hessian Mercenary State*, pp. 22–44; Wilson, *War, State and Society*, pp. 22, 41, 74; Andrea Thiele, 'The Prince as Military Entrepreneur? Why Smaller Saxon Territories Sent "Holländische Regimenter" (Dutch Regiments) to the Dutch Republic', in *War, Entrepreneurs, and the State in Europe and the Mediterranean, 1300–1800*, ed. by Jeff Fynn-Paul (Leiden and Boston: Brill, 2014), pp. 170–192 (pp. 191–192). See also Peter H. Wilson, 'The German "Soldier Trade" of the Seventeenth and Eighteenth Centuries: A Reassessment', *The International History Review* 4 (1996), 757–792 (pp. 775, 777–778).
11 Ingrao, *The Hessian Mercenary State*, pp. 22–44, 127.
12 Wilson, *War, State and Society*, p. 84.
13 *Svenska riksrådets protokoll*, vol. VI, 1636 (Stockholm: P.A. Norstedt & Söner, 1891), pp. 716–723.
14 Another exception is Sofia Gustafsson's excellent study of the effects of the building of the fortress Sveaborg off the southern coast of Finland in 1748–1756; Sofia Gustafsson, *Leverantörer och profitörer: Olika geografiska områdens och sociala gruppers handel med fästningsbygget Sveaborg under den första byggnadsperioden 1748–1756* (Helsinki: Societas Scientiarum Fennica, 2015).

The aim of the present chapter

Anders Nordencrantz's claim to the effect that a state which accepts subsidies is likely to become drugged and dependent, with only a few individuals profiting from them, is worthy of a serious examination. Turned into research questions, these would be: Who on the receiving side – Sweden – benefited from the subsidies? How did subsidies affect Swedish society? And, finally, what can be said about Swedish dependency on subsidies – did Sweden go wherever France led?

Through a detailed study of three periods – 1632, 1675–1677, and 1727–1729 – the wider effects of subsidies on Swedish society as well as the nature of dependency between Sweden and France is discussed. The study is primarily based on accounts of how the Swedish government spent subsidies during the aforementioned periods, as well as on records of discussions within the Council of the Realm. While the sources used for this study can only provide information about who may have gained from receiving part of the subsidies in the most tangible form – money – the aim is to take the analysis further and discuss who benefited from the subsidy system in a broader sense. In the background, there is another question, a much larger one, which has to do with state building. 'Our rise has come through war', Queen Christina (1626–1689) said in 1652, thus in a sense preceding Charles Tilly's well-known assertion that war, or the preparation for war, built states.[15] If resources – such as subsidies – were prerequisites for war, what was the significance of subsidies in relation to state building? There are arguments for the assumption that subsidies played a great role in terms of state building; one would be that major players such as France, Spain, or Britain needed the armies and allies they received through subsidies. Without subsidies, there would have been no armies, no wars, and no war preparations to make these major powers as strong as warfare made them. Another argument supporting the assumption that subsidies built states is that minor players such as Sweden, Denmark, or Brandenburg needed the money to safeguard their territories or partake in warfare. Subsidies not only paid for

---

15 Michael Roberts, *The Swedish Imperial Experience, 1560–1718* (Cambridge: Cambridge University Press, 1979), p. 22; Charles Tilly, *Coercion, Capital, and European States, AD 990–1990* (Oxford: Blackwell, 1990), pp. 14–15, 19–28.

soldiers but also contributed to the need for building an administration to handle war supplies, training of military personnel, transport, and foreign affairs.

Subsidies, state revenue, and war costs

For much of the time from the early seventeenth century to the end of the eighteenth century, Sweden was partially dependent on foreign money in order to play a role in European politics, and even maintain its own security.[16] A way to estimate dependency is by calculating how much of the war finances or state revenue came from French subsidies. Calculations for 1632 show that French subsidies covered about 15 per cent of the war cost. A calculation for the years 1630–1634 indicates that 15 per cent of the cost of war, amounting to 9 per cent of the state revenue, was covered by subsidies – regardless of giver – during the same time.[17] Calculations for the eighteenth century show that French subsidies amounted to at least between 5 and 15 per cent of the state revenue between 1747 and 1776, reaching 20 per cent and above in exceptional years. For the years 1727–1729, the Franco-British subsidies to Sweden amounted to 18 and 19 per cent of the state revenue. As research has shown, these figures are likely to be low; but exactly how low is very difficult to estimate.[18]

The 5 to 20 per cent that the subsidies were worth means that, without these, the resources would have had to be raised in other

---

16 See, for example, *Sveriges riksråds protokoll*, vol. V (Stockholm: P.A. Norstedts & Söners förlag, 1888), pp. 383–385 (17 December 1635); Stockholm, Riksarkivet (RA, the Swedish National Archive), Det odelade kansliet: Rådsprotokoll, vol. 37b (5 November 1662), 59a (21 February 1672), 63 (22 March 1674 and undated); Utrikesexpeditionen: Rådsprotokoll över utrikes ärenden för 1734 från 18 maj (6 August 1734); RA, Utrikesexpeditionen: Rådsprotokoll över utrikes ärenden 1740–1743 (5 August 1740).

17 Kersten Krüger, 'Dänische und schwedische Kriegsfinanzierung im Dreißigjährigen Krieg bis 1635', in *Krieg und Politik 1618–1648: Europäische Probleme und Perspektiven*, ed. by Konrad Repgen (Munich: R. Oldenbourg Verlag, 1988), pp. 275–299 (p. 288); Sven Lundkvist, 'Svensk krigsfinansiering 1630–1635', *Historisk Tidskrift* 2 (1966), 377–417 (p. 387). Lars Ekholm estimates that, in 1631, subsidies from France and the Netherlands together with favourable contracts for buying grain from Russia represented 45 per cent of the cost of war; see Lars Ekholm, *Svensk krigsfinansiering 1630–31* (Uppsala: Acta Universitatis Upsaliensis, 1974), p. 11.

18 Karl Åmark, *Sveriges statsfinanser 1719–1809*, parts I–III (Stockholm: Norstedt, 1961), pp. 151, 585–589.

ways, through taxation, contributions, loans, or higher tariffs on trade – or there would have been corresponding cuts or reductions in public spending. The latter is the most likely alternative, given the poor condition of Swedish finances during all the three periods studied here.[19] The importance of foreign financial support becomes evident from the point where Karl XI, in the early 1680s, decided to go his way without it. In order to finance a desperately needed reorganization of the army and expansion of the fleet with domestic funds only, the choice fell on forcing a reduction of land from the nobility – a decision with enormous financial and political implications.[20] Whether receiving 5 to 20 per cent of its state revenue from abroad made Sweden slightly or very dependent on France may also be measured by how the need for subsidies was discussed among Swedish politicians.

An argument frequently used by Swedish politicians in order to motivate why Sweden needed subsidies was that Sweden 'måste gripas under armarna' by France. The Swedish expression literally means that Sweden needed 'to be seized under the arms' in order to avoid falling to the ground.[21] This and similar expressions were used both within the Council of the Realm in closed debates and, seemingly openly, in discussions with French diplomats.[22] It reflects a feeling that Sweden was in dire need of support while referring to Sweden's financial inability to defend the country or to partake in war. In contacts with French officials, at times when Sweden either sought subsidies or was waiting for delayed subsidies to be paid, one can see the same kind of outspoken

---

19 For the 1630s, see Lundkvist, 'Svensk krigsfinansiering 1630–1635', pp. 383–384, 415–417; for the 1670s, see Göran Rystad, *Karl XI: En biografi* (Lund: Historiska media, 2001), pp. 27–28, 59, 62–63, 168–169; for the 1720s, see Åmark, *Sveriges statsfinanser*, pp. 129–144.
20 For a more developed description of the background of this decision, see Sven A. Nilsson, *På väg mot reduktionen: Studier i svenskt 1600-tal* (Stockholm: Natur och kultur, 1964), pp. 114–123.
21 See note 16.
22 Axel Oxenstierna to Cardinal Richelieu 24 September 1634, 11 May 1635. Also in instruction for Hugo Grotius 10 September 1635. See *Rikskanslern Axel Oxenstiernas skrifter och brevväxling*, 1:12. *Brev 1634, juni–dec* (Stockholm: Almqvist & Wiksell International, 1977), pp. 488–490; and *Rikskanslern Axel Oxenstiernas skrifter och brevväxling*, 1:13. *Brev 1635, jan–aug* (Stockholm: P.A. Norstedt & Söners förlag, 1949), pp. 250–251; and *Rikskanslern Axel Oxenstiernas skrifter och brevväxling*, 1:14. *Brev sept–dec* (Stockholm: P.A. Norstedt & Söner, 1950), pp. 24–26.

desperation.²³ It appears to be a paradox that, at the same time as Swedish diplomats and politicians quite unreservedly asked France for help, they were sensitive to how France would respond. Signs of French haughtiness were not well received, and members of the Council of the Realm discussed how to avoid Sweden's being seen as a mercenary.²⁴ One issue was that diplomats from less friendly courts visiting Stockholm sent dispatches to Vienna or Copenhagen reporting on Swedish eagerness to obtain subsidies, preferably from France.²⁵ French observers also viewed Sweden as impecunious and in need of help from allies, especially in the aftermath of the Great Northern War (1700–1721).²⁶

From a broader perspective, I suggest that one may analyse how individuals or groups employed the rhetoric of 'dependency' on the basis of how different individuals or groups hoped for, or were accused of gaining from, subsidies. For example, young officers expressed disappointment when the French ambassador in 1650 failed to deliver money that was needed for a Swedish regiment; there was a similar case in 1669, when Spanish money was not paid.²⁷

---

23 For example, Stockholm, RA, Det odelade kansliet: Rådsprotokoll, vol. 45 (3 December 1666), vol. 47 (24 September 1667).

24 For example, when discussing a possible treaty with the emperor, the Council of the Realm did not want to give the impression that Sweden would enter into such a treaty because of the money. Stockholm, RA, Det odelade kansliet: Rådsprotokoll, vol. 59b (4 December 1672). The French ambassador Terlon had implied that Sweden would do anything for France if the latter offered money. 'They are mistaken', says Magnus Gabriel De la Gardie, 'if they think so. They cannot treat us like the Swiss.' Stockholm, RA, Det odelade kansliet: Rådsprotokoll, vol. 63 (27 February 1674).

25 Wratislaus von Sternberg, 'Memorial on the Situation in Sweden, May 1674' in *Handlingar rörande Sverges historia ur utrikes arkiver samlade och utgifna af And. Fryxell, tredje delen*, ed. by Anders Fryxell (Stockholm: L.J. Hjerta, 1839), pp. 94–148 (pp. 123, 144); 'Utdrag och afskrifter ur Danska ministern Jens Juels bref till kungen af Danmark 1664 och följande år', in *Handlingar rörande Sverges historia ur utrikes arkiver samlade och utgifna af And. Fryxell, första delen*, ed. by Anders Fryxell (Stockholm: L.J. Hjerta, 1836), pp. 106–210 (p. 156).

26 La Courneuve, Archives diplomatiques (AD), Memoires et documents Suède 4 (discours by ambassador Pomponne 1668), and Memoires et documents Suède 9 (instruction for ambassador Lanmary October 1741).

27 *Johan Ekeblads bref. 1: Från Kristinas och Cromwells hof*, ed. by Nils Sjöberg (Stockholm: P.A. Norstedt & Söners förlag, 1911), p. 48; Jens Juel, 'Utdrag och afskrifter ur Danska ministern Jens Juels bref till kungen af Danmark 1664 och följande år', in *Handlingar rörande Sverges historia ur utrikes arkiver samlade och utgifna af And. Fryxell, första delen*, ed. by Anders Fryxell, pp. 106–210 (pp. 198, 248).

The uses of French subsidies in Sweden

For these young officers, war was a source of income that supported their social climbing. Thus, the English ambassador in Stockholm in 1653–1654 reported that Swedish officers hoped that the war between the Netherlands and Britain would continue, so that they would have the opportunity to join on Britain's side. However, the ambassador had been told that since the most powerful politicians in the country, chancellor Axel Oxenstierna and his sons, were so rich, Sweden would stay at peace. According to this reasoning, Oxenstierna and his immediate family had little personal interest in going to war – they did well without the extra money and did not need to raise their status – to the disappointment of the officers.[28]

The Thirty Years' War and the Swedish intervention

When Sweden entered the war in Germany in the summer of 1630 to fight for the Lutheran cause against the Holy Roman Emperor, the promise of French subsidies, which materialized with the treaty of Bärwalde in January 1631, was vital. The treaty is quite straightforward in what was expected from Sweden in return for the subsidies: thirty thousand infantry soldiers and six thousand cavalry were to fight in Germany. In return, Sweden would receive 400,000 *riksdaler* annually for five years.[29] Sweden would also receive a smaller sum as back payment for parts of 1630. On the death of King Gustav II Adolf in November 1632, the treaty expired since it was an agreement between kings, not between states; but it was in all essential aspects renewed in 1633. Apart from the obvious point that Sweden promised to provide an exact specified number of soldiers, neither of the treaties (1631 or 1633) goes into detail as to how the money was expected to be used, nor for whom it was supposed to be used.[30] France obviously expected to benefit from this deal by getting the Swedish king and his armies to fight the emperor on its behalf. The question here, however, is where the French money went and who else besides the French king managed to benefit from it. As French statesmen accepted Swedish control over the subsidies once they had been paid, it is necessary to examine

---

28 Bulstrode Whitelocke, *A Journal of the Swedish Embassy in the years 1653 and 1654* (London: Longman, 1855), vol. ii, pp. 34–35.
29 *Sverges traktater med främmande magter: jemte andra dit hörande handlingar: 5:1 1572–1632*, ed. by O.S. Rydberg and C. Hallendorff (Stockholm: P.A. Norstedt & Söners förlag, 1903), pp. 438–442.
30 See note 28 and *Sverges traktater med främmande magter: jemte andra dit hörande handlingar: 5:2 1632–1645*, ed. by C. Hallendorff (Stockholm: P.A. Norstedt & Söners förlag, 1909), pp. 12–18.

what Swedish statesmen used the subsidies for in order to determine their understanding of their fiscal situation.

Expenses 1632

One of the earliest accounts in the Royal Treasury of subsidy expenditure from the war is dated 1632 and shows the allocation of funds, 136,796 *riksdaler*, for the November term of that year.[31] By November 1632, Sweden had been at war in Germany for more than two years. The people listed in the account are all men and, not surprisingly, many of those were military commanders. The account lists most of the recipients by name, with only a few remaining anonymously hidden behind titles. By far the biggest share of the money was allocated to individuals, not to collectives or institutions. At the top of the list was Duke Wilhelm of Saxe-Weimar (1598–1662) who received 20,000 *riksdaler*, some 15 per cent of the total amount. Duke Wilhelm, brother of the more famous general Bernhard of Saxe-Weimar, sided with Gustav II Adolf in the German war but was sidestepped by Axel Oxenstierna after the death of the Swedish king in November 1632. The source does not specify for what purpose Duke Wilhelm received the money, so one can only speculate that it was intended for maintaining troops and/or recruiting soldiers. The Swedish army at the time was full of hired foreign officers fighting on the same side as the Swedish king and raising armies for him.[32] Others mentioned in the account included Donald Mackay, first Lord Reay (1591–1649), a Scotsman, and the German baron Dodo zu Innhausen und Knyphausen (1583–1636), who was third in command at the battle of Lützen where the Swedish king died and who became a Swedish field marshal in 1633. Both Mackay and Knyphausen received relatively small sums, but it was not stated for what purposes. Two officers, Lammermont and Hamilton, were paid substantial sums for army supplies, a total cost of 18,298 *riksdaler*. 'Hamilton' could refer to just about any of the sixty-five Scottish Hamiltons serving in the Swedish armies under King Gustav II Adolf.[33]

---

31 Stockholm, RA, Kammarkollegiet: Kansliet och kontorsarkiv, F3/1.
32 In 1631, around 80 per cent of the troops fighting for Sweden were hired, which gives us an idea of the importance of foreign officers. Lundkvist, 'Svensk krigsfinansiering 1630–1635', p. 384.
33 Hamilton, släkt, urn:sbl:12476, *Svenskt biografiskt lexikon*, accessed 10 July 2017.

The uses of French subsidies in Sweden

Although many who were paid from the subsidies were not Swedish, there were also Swedish noblemen and burghers on the receiving end. Some of them got what seem to be reimbursements, in total 67,141 *riksdaler* (49 per cent of the grand total). One of the recipients of such reimbursements was Baron Sten Bielke (1598–1638), who at the time was stationed in Stralsund and Pomerania in order to find resources and buy supplies for the Swedish army.[34] Bielke belonged to the group of noblemen and merchants who were asked to advance money towards French subsidies.[35] Others included the nobleman Klas Horn, most probably the Klas Horn (1583–1632) who at the time of his death was in charge of Stralsund, and Peter Grönberg (1579–1632).[36] Grönberg was a Swedish businessman and war financier who had earned the trust of Axel Oxenstierna. In 1631, he was raised to the nobility and at the same time stationed in Hamburg to buy weapons and gunpowder, to pay for the recruitment of soldiers and also to pay off creditors.[37]

Other Swedish recipients of money included Melchior Falkenberg (1597–1651), who was in the Netherlands to manage the copper trade, and Johan Leuhusen (1597–1641), who was used as an envoy by Axel Oxenstierna and who went on a diplomatic mission to Paris in 1631, together with Axel's cousin Bengt Oxenstierna. An entry for money that had been spent in France for travel and gifts – not specifying any details – can be referred to this diplomatic mission to Paris in 1631.

Even though details are missing from many of the entries, it is fair to say that by far the largest proportion of the funds from the third term of French subsidies in 1632 was used for supporting the military actions in Germany, as specified in the treaty. Most of the money was seemingly used for recruiting and maintaining troops or for buying supplies for troops, while only a minor share, some 4 per cent, was spent on diplomacy and an even smaller share covered the costs of managing the subsidies (approximately 1.5 per cent).

---

34 Sten Svantesson Bielke, urn:sbl:34575, *Svenskt biografiskt lexikon* (article by B. Boëthius), accessed 10 July 2017.
35 Axel Oxenstierna to Sten Bielke 9 May 1633 in *Rikskanslern Axel Oxenstiernas skrifter och brevväxling, 1:8. Brev 1633, Jan–maj* (Stockholm: P.A. Norstedt & Söners förlag, 1942), pp. 605–606.
36 Horn, släkt, urn:sbl:13802, *Svenskt biografiskt lexikon*, accessed 10 July 2017.
37 Peter Grönenberg (Gröneberg), urn:sbl:13267, *Svenskt biografiskt lexikon* (article by Birgitta Lager), accessed 10 July 2017.

As far as it is possible to trace what the money was spent on, most resources seem to have been spent outside Sweden. During this period, the subsidies never reached Sweden. They were spent in Europe and were to a large extent also used for paying non-Swedes for services rendered to the Swedish crown. Rather than being an independent agent, one could say that, as far as subsidies were concerned, the Swedish state merely acted as a distributor of French resources between France and the army commanders and suppliers to the armies engaged in the war in Germany. To what degree any of the people on the list actually profited personally from getting a share of the subsidies, or if they spent it all on paying salaries or buying supplies, is difficult to say. A possible profit may have arisen from being hired and given an opportunity to make a career and advance socially. Indirectly, however, people in Europe who supplied the Swedish armies would probably benefit from the subsidies.

The treaty of 1672 stipulated that Sweden would receive 400,000 *riksdaler* annually for three years in peacetime and 600,000 annually if war broke out.[38] In return, Sweden would keep sixteen thousand soldiers in Germany, with an exception for 1672 when the number had to be only six thousand. The treaty was renewed on 15 April 1675.[39] The treaties of 1672 and 1675 did not explicitly prohibit Sweden from using the money for purposes other than keeping armed forces in Germany.

Expenses 1675–1677

The situation in Sweden in the 1670s was different from that of forty years earlier. By 1630, Gustav II Adolf had ruled his country for many years and proved himself to be a capable commander of arms. He had also sought and managed to work together with the Swedish aristocracy with the aim of building an efficient civil service. Even though Sweden was a relatively poor country with a small population, the administration's increasing efficiency in retrieving

---

38 Traité d'alliance 14 April 1672, accessed 27 June 2017 at http://basedoc.diplomatie.gouv.fr/exl-php/cadcgp.php?CMD=CHERCHE&QUERY=1&MODELE=vues/mae_internet___traites/home.html&VUE=mae_internet___traites&NOM=cadic__anonyme&FROM_LOGIN=1.
39 Traité d'alliance 25 April 1675, accessed 27 June 2017 at: http://basedoc.diplomatie.gouv.fr/exl-php/cadcgp.php?CMD=CHERCHE&QUERY=1&MODELE=vues/mae_internet___traites/home.html&VUE=mae_internet___traites&NOM=cadic__anonyme&FROM_LOGIN=1.

The uses of French subsidies in Sweden

resources, and the increasing export of copper and iron, enabled the state to build a strong military. When Sweden agreed to a new treaty with France in 1672, it had been ruled by a government led by aristocrats since 1660 during the minority reign of Karl XI (1655–1697). There was strong criticism voiced against the government for mismanaging the state finances. The young king eventually decided to seek the advice of men outside the aristocratic circle that had ruled the country during his minority reign. He gradually excluded people such as the once-mighty chancellor Magnus Gabriel De la Gardie from his inner circle.[40]

The accounts from the 1670s are more detailed than the ones from 1632 and hence provide more in-depth knowledge of what the subsidies were used for.[41] The focal point here has been the years 1675–1677, during which Sweden was at war with Brandenburg and Denmark.

Unlike in 1632, the money actually arrived in Sweden and was apparently to a large extent also spent in Sweden. Again unlike the situation in 1632, most recipients were active in Sweden, including both women – albeit a small number – and men. As in the accounts from 1632, much of the money was distributed among individuals, but with the difference that what they had delivered in return, or were supposed to deliver, is also described in much greater detail.[42]

Of the total of 4,400,000 *daler silvermynt* (*ds*), which was the same as 2,400,000 *reichsthaler*, around 5.4 per cent was used for diplomacy and 8.9 per cent for the court. Most of the money allocated for the court was used for purchasing goods in Paris for the king's coronation, which took place on 28 September 1675. Other court expenses included liveries for courtiers and an unspecified sum used for the queen dowager.[43] Adding minor costs for the civil administration

---

40 Rystad, *Karl XI*, pp. 120–122, 128–135.
41 With regard to 1675, it is also possible to double-check the subsidy accounts with Rikshuvudboken (the general account of the state) for accuracy: Stockholm, RA, Kammarkollegiet, Generalbokhållaren: Rikshuvudböcker, vol. 129 (1675).
42 It is of course difficult to separate military and non-military purposes in a country so heavily militarized as Sweden was at the time. In this case, I have classified expenses for diplomacy and the royal court as non-military.
43 Spending subsidy money on the court was not unique for the period of 1675–1677; it had also been done in the previous period, 1672–1674. See Stockholm, RA, Det odelade kansliet: Rådsprotokoll, vol. 59b (4 December 1672).

and the percentage given to Johan Adlercrona for managing the subsidies – about 0.5 per cent altogether – approximately 15 per cent of the subsidies over the three years 1675–1677 was used for purposes other than purely military ones.[44]

Of the military costs, the single highest entry went to the army in Pomerania (1,295,000 ds). This was followed by costs for debts (367,000), the navy (364 000), the regiments in Skåne (253,000), and troops in Bremen (189,000). Other entries with high figures, although lower than those mentioned, include garrisons, ammunition, powder, and recruitment. Other expenses were far lower than any of these.[45]

The treaty with France stated that Sweden was paid subsidies to keep troops in Germany. According to the list of expenditures, keeping an army in Pomerania amounted to about 29.5 per cent of all subsidies, whereas the cost of troops in Bremen amounted to 4.2 per cent – altogether 33.7 per cent. As the headings for Pomerania and Bremen do not specify whether these figures covered all costs, such as supplies and transport, it is possible that one has to add a number of costs that may be found under other headings, such as buying supplies and recruiting soldiers. By excluding costs not intended for troops in Germany (costs for the navy, regiments in Skåne, and some of the debts that were obviously not connected to Germany), and treating all other expenses as costs pertaining to German troops, nearly 70 per cent of the subsidies were used for the purpose stated in the treaty. This is likely to be a generous calculation. The lowest figure, on the other hand, would be 33.7 per cent. In either case, a substantial part of the subsidies, at least 30 per cent, was used for purposes other than those stated in the treaty.

So far, we have looked only at what the money was used for; however, another issue is the question with whom the resources ended up. The group that received the largest sums for supplying the Swedish navy or army with goods included merchants, manufacturers, or members of the new nobility, who often also served as civil servants. Many of these were newcomers in Sweden or in Swedish service, much like the officers who were paid from the French subsidies in the early 1630s. Some were sons of immigrants

---

44 Stockholm, RA, Kammarkollegiet, Kansliet och kontorsarkiv, Generalstatskontoret 1653–1680.

45 For example, payment for tin copper (186 ds) or 22 barrels of rye (176 ds), both for the navy. See Stockholm, RA, Kammarkollegiet, Kansliet och kontorsarkiv, Generalstatskontoret 1653–1680.

who had arrived in Sweden during the Thirty Years' War. What the two generations had in common seems to be that their relocation to Sweden was an effect of Swedish involvement in European politics. Unlike the officers in the earlier period, though, people like Jakob Sneckensköld and Henrik Cronstierna (both of Livonian descent), Johan Adlercrona (of French descent), Abraham Boneauschöld (from France), Gerdt Störning (from Germany), Daniel Leijonankar (from Scotland), and the brothers Abraham and Jakob Reenstierna (from the Netherlands) lived in Sweden and had most of their business in Sweden. Altogether, this group of merchants, manufacturers, and lower civil servants were paid nearly 600,000 ds for clothes, fish, cheese, grain (rye), flour, cannons, tin, copper, ships, gunpowder, and other supplies. Others, like the newly ennobled Joel (Ekman) Gripenstierna, were reimbursed for having advanced money to the crown.

Moving away from the people who made a lot of money, there were also entries with smaller amounts, implying that there were others who may have benefited: a widow who had manufactured ensigns, the baker's office for providing bread, various (anonymous) skippers for transporting soldiers, the painter Baltsar Friedrich, a group of poor petitioners, the book-keeper Johan Mattsson, and others. The 4,000 ds used for constructing a stable must have resulted in a need for supplies and somebody to build it; the 1,000 ds called 'tobacco money for the queen dowager' means that somebody importing and selling tobacco might have profited.

Even though much of the subsidies was spent in Sweden, a substantial portion went back to France. The largest sum spent in France was spent on goods for the king's coronation: 207,000 ds. But that was not all: the gift for the French diplomat de la Picquetière, worth 3,500 ds, was taken from the subsidy money. The Swedish ambassador to Paris and the Swedish diplomat Nils Eosander Lillieroot, also in Paris, were both paid using the subsidy money, and it is fair to guess that a certain amount of that was spent in Paris.[46]

1727–1729: in the aftermath of the Great Northern War

Subsidies paid by France and Great Britain in 1727–1729 were a result of Sweden's joining the Hanoverian alliance that France, Great Britain, and Prussia had entered in 1725. The treaty of Hanover

---

46 This means that at least 6 per cent of the subsidies for 1675–1677 was spent in France.

was a response to the treaty of Vienna, which brought Spain, Austria, and Russia together. When Sweden became affiliated to the Hanoverian alliance in 1727, the secret articles stated that France and Britain would pay £50,000 sterling per annum in return for seven thousannd infantry soldiers and three thousand cavalry to be used if needed.[47] As with earlier treaties, there is no mention in detail how the Swedish government could allocate the money once it had reached Sweden. During the period 1727–1729, the subsidies from France and Britain made up 18–19 per cent of the annual state revenue.[48]

Expenses 1727–1729

The Great Northern War (1700–1721) had been extremely costly measured in both loss of lives and loss of land, and it put a financial strain on Sweden for a long time.[49] After the death of Karl XII (1682–1718) in November 1718 and the short reign, 1719–1720, of his sister Queen Ulrika Eleonora (1688–1741), the Swedish throne passed to her husband Landgrave Friedrich of Hesse-Cassel (1676–1751), who consequently became King Fredrik I of Sweden. As a reaction against the absolute rule of Karl XII, the monarchy was stripped of much of its power, the Parliament instead ending up being the strongest political institution throughout what has been labelled Sweden's 'Age of Freedom', beginning in the 1720s and ending only with the coup d'état in 1772, which once again gave the monarchy a stronger political position.

When joining the Hanoverian alliance in 1727, Sweden renewed its tradition of accepting financial support, this time from both France and Great Britain. With a few exceptions, Sweden had not received any French subsidies since the beginning of the 1680s.[50] Of the total of 3,690,000 *ds* Sweden received over the three years 1727–1729, slightly more than 20 per cent was used for non-military purposes. A large part of this was used to cover already incurred costs for the coronation in 1720 (150,000). Some expenses covered

---

47 Stockholm, RA, Originaltraktater med främmande makter. 14 mars 1727. Separata artiklar och sekret artikel till Litt. A.
48 Åmark, *Sveriges statsfinanser*, pp. 151, 585.
49 Sweden lost Bremen-Verden to Great Britain, parts of Pomerania to Prussia, and the Baltic provinces and part of Finland to Russia. The loss of the Baltic provinces in particular represented a tough blow for the Swedish economy.
50 In fact, the three-year subsidy treaty agreed between France and Sweden in 1715 is the only exception.

The uses of French subsidies in Sweden

historical agreements: Stanisław I Leszczyński of Poland, the deposed and exiled Swedish puppet king who ruled Poland in 1704–1709, was paid a yearly allowance taken out of the French subsidies. Another, though minor, part was used to pay off debts to Ottoman merchants to whom Sweden owed money for services rendered in the 1710s.[51]

Subsidies were also used to fill up the queen's private purse (15,000 *ds*), but the largest single amount (400,000) was used for covering the king's journeys back and forth to Hesse-Cassel. Besides these costs for the court, resources were also allocated for diplomacy such as the Swedish presence at the peace congress in Soissons, which amounted to 111,010, and gifts to foreign envoys in the amount of 43,000.

As in previous periods, by far the largest proportion of the subsidies was used for military purposes. Interestingly, though, of the 3,061,000 *ds* spent on the military, 38 per cent was spent on building or repairing fortresses, building new houses for the navy, or building warehouses. Nearly a third of the total amount of subsidies was used for the navy.

With the treaty stating that Sweden would, in return for subsidies, keep seven thousand infantry and three thousand cavalry, the spending of the subsidies – even what was spent on the military – seems to point in another direction from what was intended. The use of subsidies in the 1720s to a great extent mirrors the situation at the time. There was a lack of resources, which meant that some had to be allocated to pay for historical expenses such as the coronation and debts to Ottoman merchants. There was peace, and Sweden had allied itself with the enemies of its powerful neighbour Russia, which explains the investment in building for the future.

Unlike in 1632 and 1675, only a few names are named on the expense list for 1727–1729. These include a member of the Grill family, the wealthiest merchant family in Stockholm at the time, and the merchant Hans Lenman (1683–1739). Lenman, who had made a fortune from trading in salt and grain, was in charge of delivering English money to the Swedish crown in the early 1720s.[52] By the 1720s, Hans Lenman was active in all kinds of manufacturing and trading. He supplied the navy with hemp and canvas for sails,

---

51 Stockholm, RA, Statskontorets arkiv: Kammarkontoret G2, Q:5, Angående 1727, 1728 och 1729 Åhrs Franska och Engelska Subsidier.
52 Stockholm, RA, Betänkanden och memorial, utrikes ärenden, 27. Undated. (9 October 1719, 10 October 1719, 9 March 1721).

while also being contracted to build warships for the state. The latter circumstance is the reason why he was paid 50,000 *ds* in 1727.[53]

Swedish dependency

There is a difference between what the subsidy treaties stated and what the Swedish government actually used the subsidies for. This is more obvious in the 1670s and 1720s than in 1632, as not only were 15–20 per cent of the subsidies used for non-military purposes in these two later periods but a substantial share of the remainder was used for military purposes not mentioned in the treaties. Could this simply be a matter of book-keeping? That is unlikely. It is quite clear that the Swedish state, especially in the periods where the discrepancy is at its largest, treated subsidies as separate from other state income and expenditure. Still, it is quite puzzling that in spite of the claims of Swedish politicians that the country was dependent on subsidies, and despite Sweden's image – both in France and elsewhere – as a country that frequently and eagerly accepted subsidies, it seems that, once Sweden had received the money, it could manage these funds more or less any way it deemed fit. In that sense, Sweden's independence was seemingly respected or at least accepted by the payer.

There were attempts from the French side to monitor the Swedish use of subsidies, but by all accounts these attempts were fended off by the Swedes. In 1726, when Swedish councillors debated whether Sweden should accept subsidies from France, some raised the point that, in the 1670s, France had requested that how the subsidies were used would be controlled by France.[54] Nothing came of that request; but, in a council debate in 1680, information was given that Jean-Baptiste Colbert, in charge of French finances, had allegedly said that new subsidies would be paid to Sweden only if France could keep an envoy in Sweden who would monitor the use of the money.[55] Earlier, in 1662, when the French had refused to ratify the Fontainebleau treaty, the French ambassador Hugues Terlon

---

53 Hans Lenman, urn:sbl:11223, *Svenskt biografiskt lexikon* (article by Rune Kiellander), accessed 19 July 2017.
54 Stockholm, RA, Utrikesexpeditionen, riksrådsprotokoll i utrikesärenden 1724–27 (15 February 1726).
55 Stockholm, RA, Det odelade kansliet: Rådsprotokoll, vol. 72 (26 February 1680).

The uses of French subsidies in Sweden

was instructed that – if necessary – he should tell the Swedish government that they were to blame for the breakdown of the treaty owing to the misuse of subsidies. From the context, it appears that the French only wanted to use this as an excuse rather than as a serious accusation. The real reason for the refusal to ratify the treaty was changing conditions in Poland, which meant that France had less of a need for Sweden.[56]

Even though France unsurprisingly had an interest in keeping an eye on the use of subsidies given to Sweden, it seems that there were reasons why they could not force Sweden to accept being monitored. The Swedish attitude towards who had the last say in the use of subsidies is perhaps revealed by the councillor Sten Bielke in February 1672, when he simply stated in the council that Sweden might not have to keep the promised number of troops in Bremen, since it would be impossible for France to check.[57] Another example is when the Swedish council in early 1680 was debating whether it could demand subsidies that had not been paid by France even though Sweden had failed to live up to the conditions in the subsidy treaty from 1672, as Sweden had not kept the promised number of troops in Bremen. One reason, some of the councillors argued, for Sweden to demand subsidies in spite of the breach of the agreement was that Bremen had suffered badly because of French warfare.[58] It was decided that France should be approached with caution to see if it might be possible to obtain the subsidies. The use of subsidies for non-military purposes, or purposes that were not mentioned in the treaties, was rarely openly debated within the Swedish council. It is remarkable that when Sweden had broken the agreement from 1672 by not providing the number of troops agreed upon – and obviously spent the money on things other than that which was intended in the treaties – that was not in itself an issue in the council discussion.

There may have been a change in French policy from the 1730s onwards. In 1734, the Swedish ambassador to Paris, Niclas Peter von Gedda, reported that Cardinal Fleury wanted the subsidy treaty that was being negotiated to be very precise in specifying the uses for which the Swedes would be allowed to use subsidies. This was

---

56 Birger Fahlborg, *Sveriges yttre politik 1660–1664* (Stockholm: P.A. Norstedt & Söner, 1932), pp. 278–279.
57 Stockholm, RA, Det odelade kansliet: Rådsprotokoll, vol. 59a (21 February 1672).
58 Stockholm, RA, Det odelade kansliet: Rådsprotokoll, vol. 33c.

strongly rejected by his Swedish counterpart, president of the chancellery Arvid Horn. Horn's stern remark was that it was none of France's business.[59] Horn had spoken to the French ambassador in Stockholm and promised him that the subsidies would be used only for what had been agreed upon, and he felt that his word ought to be enough. Similar expressions of the French government becoming more interested in the Swedish use of subsidies can be found in a report from the French ambassador to Stockholm in 1746, where he suggests a more restrictive policy under which France would pay more attention to what it paid for. A stricter monitoring of the use of subsidies is also mentioned as part of the instructions for the new ambassador to Stockholm in 1774.[60]

For the periods 1675–1677 and 1727–1729, the Swedish government was able to reallocate subsidy funds and use them for investments beyond what had been agreed upon. Whether this was due to an overpayment of subsidies – intended or unintended – is not possible to say without carrying out a much more in-depth study. The French government's indulgence towards Swedish spending may partly be explained by its interest in building the Swedish state, an interest articulated in internal diplomatic correspondence. France sought a northern ally that could play a role in Germany and, in the eighteenth century, also act as a buffer against Russia. As long as Sweden built its military strength by modernizing its navy and fortresses, especially in Finland, that would be in the interest of France.[61] This is also how the Swedish Council of the Realm saw it.[62] Another aspect that helps explain France's attitude was the Swedish sensitivity – well-known in France – about appearing as lacking in dignity. Swedish governments were keen to protect the

---

59 Stockholm, RA, Utrikesexpeditionen, riksrådsprotokoll i utrikes ärenden 1733–1735 (21 April 1735).

60 La Courneuve, AD, Memoires et documents Sùede 22 (Sur l'etat ou se trouve la Suède a l'ouverture de Diette, report from ambassador Lanmary, November 1746); and MD Suède 25 (Instructions for ambassador d'Usson, 3 September 1774).

61 The wish to build Sweden is, for instance, reflected in a memorial by ambassador Pomponne (1668) and the instructions for ambassadors Lanmary (1741) and d'Usson (1774). The latter two refer back to how building the weak Swedish nation had been crucial for France. See La Courneuve, AD, MD Suède 4, 9, 25.

62 Stockholm, RA, Det odelade kansliet. Rådsprotokoll, vol. 59a (5 March 1672); Utrikesexpeditionen. Riksrådsprotokoll i utrikesärenden 1733–35 (14 January 1734).

crown's independence, which forced France to tread carefully if it wanted to keep this ally.[63]

Resources in motion

In basic terms, the subsidy system transferred resources from Catholic French tax-payers to soldiers in the Swedish armies, in order for the latter to kill and die for the Protestant cause on battlefields in northern Europe. The price for the system was mostly paid by peasants at both ends. Along the way from the French tax-paying farmer to the soldier in Swedish service on the battlefield, however, there were people who profited from the system.

As a result of the subsidy system, resources moved from wealthier states to Sweden. Like smaller German states that accepted subsidies as a way of acquiring allies and becoming part of European politics, Sweden too was brought into European big politics through – first and foremost – French subsidies. This, in turn, contributed to a movement not only of material resources but also of knowledge and expertise through the geographical and social movement of people. In the first line of people who stood to benefit from the system were the officers and merchants who not only received a share of the subsidies directly but also benefited socially and financially from the wars that the subsidy system paved the way for. The increasing demand for officers in the seventeenth century could not, as before, be met by the Swedish nobility, thus opening up for recruitment among non-nobles who had the opportunity to rise socially. A considerable number of the officers were recruited from abroad; and, while Sweden took subsidies during the Thirty Years' War, the Swedish armies became a training institution for officers and soldiers from around Europe, not least since the armies under the command of Gustav II Adolf provided a modern way of strategic warfare, which had been developed from Dutch models and later became a model for other armies.[64] Of the many officers from Scotland or Germany who fought in the Swedish armies during the wars in the seventeenth century, some stayed in Sweden and enjoyed remarkable careers. They became part of Swedish society, were

---

63 For example, La Courneuve, AD, MD Suède 4 (Histoire des Traités entre la France et la Suède depuis 1569 jusqu'en 1680, 10 October 1716); MD Suède 22 (Instructions for ambassador Lanmary, 3 October 1741).
64 Sverker Olofsson, *Gustav II Adolf* (Stockholm: Atlantis, 2007), pp. 174–175, 240, 317–318. For instance, Olofsson mentions Bernhard of Saxe-Weimar.

ennobled and gained distinction not only as officers but also in politics.[65] Among the many newly ennobled people were also merchants who were first- or second-generation immigrants and who can be found on account lists: Jean de Flon (ennobled Adlercrona), Daniel Young (ennobled Leijonanker), Esaias Pufendorfer (ennobled von Pufendorf), Abraham and Jacob Momma (both ennobled Reenstierna), Jakob Snäck (ennobled Sneckensköld), Abraham Boneau (ennobled Boneauschöld). There were also a large number of Swedish merchants who gained socially and financially from resources coming in.[66]

The number of new nobles rose sharply, and more so than in other European countries, as a result of the wars in the seventeenth century. The expansion of the civil administration, which was a result of the Swedish state activities, also contributed to the social climbing and ennoblement of educated men who were sons of burghers or clergymen. In the year 1700, the number of adult men within nobility had increased fivefold since 1600, and in 1750 the number had risen to about three thousand.[67] Being part of the wars made it necessary for Sweden to build an efficient state administration. Even though a very small share of the subsidies was used directly for administrative purposes, the development of new administrative units dealing with conquered provinces, handling resource revenues, or the increasing need for keeping in contact with foreign powers, was an effect of Swedish war policy fuelled by subsidies. As an indirect effect of the subsidy system, the many administrators who filled the Swedish bureaucracy were beneficiaries of a system offering career opportunities on a scale not seen before for men originating from a social layer below the nobility.

---

65 For example, Germans like Ascheberg, Königsmarck, or Wittenberg, or Scots like Lichton, Sinclair, Hamilton, or Douglas. Between 1633 and 1654, twenty-six Scottish-born individuals were ennobled, mostly officers. See Alexia Grosjean, *An Unofficial Alliance: Scotland and Sweden 1569–1654* (Leiden: Brill, 2003), pp. 148–149.

66 For example, Vilhelm Böös (ennobled Drakenhielm), Peter Grönberg (ennobled Grönberg), Johan Barckman (baron Leijonberg), Nils Eosander (baron Lillieroot) and Joel Ekman (ennobled Gripenstierna).

67 Ingvar Elmroth, *För kung och fosterland: Studier i den svenska adelns demografi och offentliga funktioner 1600–1900* (Lund: Bibliotheca Historica Lundensis, 1981), pp. 40–43; Björn Asker, *Hur riket styrdes: Förvaltning, politik och arkiv 1520–1920* (Stockholm: Skrifter utgivna av Riksarkivet, 2007), pp. 89–92; David Gaunt, *Utbildning till statens tjänst: En kollektivbiografi av stormaktstidens hovrättsauskultanter* (Uppsala: Almqvist och Wiksell, 1975), pp. 39–40, 107.

The uses of French subsidies in Sweden 115

These are all examples of social and sometimes geographical circulation and some of it also included the movement of knowledge and expertise. In peacetime, too, warfare and the alliances led to an increasing interaction with other states and, not least, to an increase in the need for experts not only in how to fight, supply armies, or administer a war but also in how to handle the transfer of large amounts of money. Thus, people like Jean Hoeufft in the first half of the seventeenth century, Jean de Flon (Adlercrona) in the second half and Hans Lenman in the first half of the eighteenth century, all with commercial networks in Europe and beyond, became invaluable for the Swedish state as experts on moving money. Throughout the seventeenth century, experts on trade and manufacturing were drawn to the promising opportunities offered by the growing Swedish economy.

Some of the long-term effects that came as a result of warfare were unlikely to have been planned, such as social levelling, while other actions were intended to be long-term investments. From the 1670s onward and especially in the 1720s, subsidies were used for long-term investments in building and repairing fortresses. In the 1670s, resources were used for building projects in Livonia, Wismar, Bremen, and Sweden, and in the 1720s for Finland, Pomerania, and Sweden.[68] In a council discussion in March 1672, before signing the 1672 treaty with France, Chancellor Magnus Gabriel De la Gardie rhetorically asked where Sweden would find the money for restoring fortresses, especially in Wismar, if there were no subsidies.[69] In both the 1670s and the 1720s, it would have been in the interest not only of the Swedish state but also of France that fortifications were up-to-date, so that Sweden would be strong enough to act as a buffer against the enemies of France.

The building projects provided work for master builders, craftsmen, and manual labourers, some of whom benefited from subsidies, although not all of them did. How such investments could have much further effects than what was possible to foresee is shown by the example of Sveaborg, one of the world's largest sea fortresses, which was built off the south-western coast of Finland in the mid-eighteenth century with the help of French subsidies. Sofia Gustafsson has shown how fortress-building spread knowledge of new technology and led to investments in infrastructure. The many soldiers involved in building had to be educated in the relevant crafts by experts

---

68 Stockholm, RA, Kammarkollegiet, Kansliet och kontorsarkiv F3/1.
69 Stockholm, RA, Det odelade kansliet: rådsprotokoll, vol. 59a (5 March 1672).

brought in from other parts of Sweden. Shipbuilders from the north of Finland moved south and gave rise to a shipbuilding industry near Helsinki, and, when there was no longer a need for soldiers who had learned how to lay bricks, they moved on and became part of a boom in house-building in Finland.[70] One may assume that similar effects were achieved when other fortresses were built with the support of subsidies: there was a need for supplies such as timber, nails, rope, glass, tar, stone, brick, cannons, and whatever else might be needed when new buildings for military purposes were erected.

Conclusion

For long periods during both the seventeenth and eighteenth centuries, Sweden was dependent on foreign subsidies: in 1631–1680, it needed financial support to uphold its armies in occupied territories in northern Europe; and from the 1720s onwards, it needed subsidies to secure its own territory as well. In the 1630s, subsidies were used to enable Sweden to enter the war in Germany as France's ally, thus being a part of European politics. In the 1670s, subsidies were used to preserve Sweden's and France's position in Germany, while in the 1720s, in the aftermath of the catastrophic Great Northern War, most subsidies were employed in order to secure Sweden's own territory and the small remaining parts of Germany it still held, at the same time as Swedes maintained some hope that Sweden would once again be able to reconquer lost provinces.

Receiving subsidies over a long period of time put Sweden in a position that might be interpreted as subordinate to France. It seems as if one way for both parties to handle this sensitive situation without losing prestige was to ensure that, once the subsidies had been paid, it was up to the Swedish state to use them properly. Most often, but not always, Sweden complied with the agreements it had made, after which it allocated the surplus as it pleased. It was only in the second half of the eighteenth century that France finally decided that paying Sweden cost too much and that the gain from doing so was too small. Until then, France sometimes

---

70 Sofia Gustafsson, *Leverantörer och profitörer*, pp. 56–57, 118, 146–150, 221–225; Sofia Gustafsson, 'Rörlig kunskap och flyttbara färdigheter: skolad arbetskraft vid fästningsbygget Sveaborg på 1750-talet', *Sjuttonhundratal: Nordic Yearbook for Eighteenth-century Studies 2016*, 31–53 (pp. 35–38, 42–45).

complained about the Swedish use of subsidies, and there was the occasional delay in paying with the justification that Sweden had to keep its part of the deal. The French wish to keep Sweden as an agent in Germany and as a buffer against Russia was enough to keep paying and not risk losing a long-time ally because of notions of prestige.

Besides moving financial resources, subsidies contributed to moving people geographically as well as socially. On an individual and collective level, there were a number of people who were directly on the receiving end of subsidies: army and naval officers, politicians, entrepreneurs managing the subsidies, diplomats, merchants, and manufacturers. They all had a potential interest in Sweden becoming or continuing to be a recipient of subsidies. For them subsidies offered opportunities for career and social climbing, as well as financial profit. Indirectly, there were many others who, without even knowing it, profited from the resources that flowed in with the subsidies.

Subsidies alone did not build the Swedish state, but it is safe to say that they exerted a considerable influence on the Swedish state and society. They were part of a wider resource mobilization which included various kinds of financing. Loans, taxation, customs, voluntary and forced contributions, looting, export, and trade could all, just like subsidies, lubricate the machinery of war in different ways. With subsidies periodically amounting to from 5 to over 20 per cent of state revenue, in a country with very limited resources otherwise, they enabled investments in fortresses and ships as well as in supplies for the army and the navy, the hiring of soldiers, and the administering of the planning and realization of warfare on a scale that would otherwise have been impossible. Subsidies were important for the Swedish economy during long periods. What sets subsidies apart from many of the other ways of gathering resources is that they brought together two or more states as allies which, at least officially, worked together towards a common goal as well as forcing the creation of a counterpart. France as the main supplier of subsidies thus promoted Swedish state formation during the seventeenth century and helped maintain the Swedish state during parts of the first half of the eighteenth century. It is also clear that despite the asymmetric relationship between giver and recipient, both parties were in fact dependent on the system to work.

5
The problems with receiving subsidies: Sweden and the lesser powers in the long eighteenth century

Erik Bodensten

Introduction: Why the lesser powers sought subsidies

During the long eighteenth century, subsidies constituted a necessary, albeit insufficient, method for lesser powers to achieve political and dynastic objectives. In the context of imperial and European politics, these subsidies were crucial for the ability of minor German states to defend themselves and act more proactively and offensively, in spite of their otherwise significantly limited financial, political, and military resources. According to Peter Wilson, 'only by capitalising on the military potential of their territory could the lesser princes hope to escape from their subordinate role in the grand drama of European politics'.[1] At this point, research on lesser powers within the Holy Roman Empire receiving subsidies is quite extensive.[2]

The research for this chapter has received support from the Crafoord Foundation. I would also like to extend a warm thank you to Svante Norrhem for all his generous help during both the application and the research process.

1 Peter H. Wilson, *War, State and Society in Württemberg, 1677–1793* (Cambridge: Cambridge University Press, 1995), p. 77.
2 See, for instance, Peter Claus Hartmann, *Geld als Instrument europäischer Machtpolitik im Zeitalter des Merkantilismus* (Munich: Kommission für Bayerische Landesgeschichte, 1978); Alois Schmid, *Max III: Joseph und die europäischen Mächte: Die Außenpolitik des Kurfürstentums Bayern von 1745–1765* (Munich: Oldenbourg, 1987); Charles W. Ingrao, *The Hessian Mercenary State: Ideas, Institutions, and Reform under Frederick II, 1760–1785* (Cambridge: Cambridge University Press, 1987), ch. 5; Jeremy Black, 'The Problem of the Small State: Bavaria and Britain in the Second Quarter of the Eighteenth Century', *European History Quarterly* 19 (1989), 5–36; Wilson, *War*; Peter H. Wilson, *German Armies: War and*

However, subsidies were also strategically crucial for other lesser powers throughout Europe. For the lesser signatory powers, the interstate subsidy treaties represented a political and dynastic means and should be seen as an aspect of international politics, rather than as a commercial enterprise.[3] The revenues stipulated and generated by the agreements were important; however, it was only rarely – such as in the case of Hesse-Cassel – that the subsidies covered the costs and resulted in a financial net profit.[4] Typically, the subsidy payments only covered a small portion of the costs; they were severely delayed, and they were given only after the receiver had carried out a costly mobilization. Often, the subsidies were reduced retroactively or cancelled altogether.[5]

Nevertheless, the subsidies constituted a means for the recipient to manage the rapidly increasing costs related to waging and preparing for war. The cost increase had to do with several different and interconnected factors. Suffice it to say that the long eighteenth century brought land and naval warfare on a new scale, which led to the fiscal-military state facing enormous challenges. This was particularly true for the smaller states, which were not in the same position as the great powers in terms of being able to extract ever more resources, either through borrowing or through territorial,

---

German Politics 1648–1806 (London: UCL Press, 1998); Peter H. Wilson, 'Prussia as a Fiscal-Military State, 1640–1806', in *The Fiscal-military State in Eighteenth-century Europe: Essays in honour of P.G.M. Dickson*, ed. by Christopher Storrs (Farnham: Ashgate, 2009), pp. 95–124; Andrea Thiele, 'The Prince as Military Entrepreneur? Why Smaller Saxon Territories Sent "Holländische Regimenter" (Dutch Regiments) to the Dutch Republic', in *War, Entrepreneurs, and the State in Europe and the Mediterranean, 1300–1800*, ed. by Jeff Fynn-Paul (Brill: Leiden, 2014), pp. 170–192; as well as Andreas Flurschütz da Cruz, Chapter 7 below. For a very useful overview, see Peter H. Wilson, 'The German "Soldier Trade" of the Seventeenth and Eighteenth Centuries: A Reassessment', *The International History Review* XVIII.4 (November 1996), 757–792.

3 This relationship is clarified in Wilson, 'The German'.

4 Ingrao, *The Hessian Mercenary State*, pp. 127–128; Wilson, *War*, pp. 77–84, 89.

5 Christopher Storrs, *War, Diplomacy and the Rise of Savoy, 1690–1720* (Cambridge: Cambridge University Press, 2007), pp. 103–118; Wilson, 'The German', 771–773; Christopher Storrs, 'The Savoyard Fiscal-Military State in the Long Eighteenth Century', in *The Fiscal-military State in Eighteenth-century Europe: Essays in honour of P.G.M. Dickson*, ed. by Christopher Storrs (Farnham: Ashgate, 2009), pp. 215–216.

commercial, or colonial expansion.⁶ Thus, the subsidies offered the lesser states and princes an opportunity – for many the only opportunity – to compensate for scarce fiscal resources and, albeit temporarily and on a shaky foundation, maintain large, standing, well-equipped, and well-disciplined troops ready for both defensive and aggressive action. As expressed by Christopher Storrs, the subsidies helped the princes bridge 'the gap between what their own states could support (economically and politically) and what successful war required'.⁷ Without these external resources, the lesser powers would have been forced to assume the entire cost of the military, which would have necessitated cutbacks and in many cases drastic arms reductions. Some lesser powers, including Savoy-Piedmont and Brandenburg-Prussia, successfully exploited favourable developments in international politics and enticed the great powers to provide them with significant subsidies. This, in turn, enabled an increased military capability and territorial expansion at the expense of their neighbours.⁸

However, one cannot simply reduce the reception of subsidies by the lesser powers to a mere question of financial-military assistance. The political-diplomatic assistance in exchange for military service was just as important. This explains why the lesser powers did not exclusively court the highest bidder offering the most money, but also why some subsidizers – France in particular – were frequently forced to offer higher subsidies than others. Within the framework of the Holy Roman Empire, for example, many prospective subsidy recipients gravitated toward the emperor, who was typically in a better position than other actors when it came to assisting them in their political and dynastic ambitions. In the broader context, where money served as a means and not as an end in itself, the fact that the emperor regularly offered lower subsidies, was often late in his payments, and was more inclined to break agreements was less important.⁹

---

6 With regard to the increase in military costs and the fiscal-military state during this period, see, for example, *War, State and Development: Fiscal-military States in the Eighteenth Century*, ed. by Rafael Torres Sánchez (Pamplona: Eunsa, 2007); *The Fiscal-military State in Eighteenth-century Europe*, ed. by Christopher Storrs; *The British Fiscal-military States, 1660–c. 1783*, ed. by Aaron Graham and Patrick Walsh (London: Routledge, 2016).
7 Storrs, *War*, p. 119.
8 See, for instance, Wilson, 'Prussia'; Storrs, 'The Savoyard'.
9 Wilson, *War*, pp. 87–88; Wilson, 'The German', 774–787, 791–792; Wilson, *German Armies*, pp. 97–100.

The problems with receiving subsidies

During the latter part of the seventeenth century, for example, Brandenburg provided troops for the emperor in the wars against France and the Ottoman Empire in exchange for subsidies, but also in exchange for various forms of political, diplomatic, and legal assistance. To crown it all, so to speak, in November 1700, just before the outbreak of the War of the Spanish Succession (1701–1714), the electoral prince Friedrich I (1657–1713) concluded a subsidy agreement with the Habsburg emperor Leopold I (1640–1705), which in exchange for eight thousand troops provided him with a large yearly sum and, more importantly, the royal title of King in Prussia.[10] A similar dynamic may be observed outside the empire, as in the example of Savoy-Piedmont. Through shifting subsidy alliances with France, Great Britain, Spain, and the United Provinces during the period of 1690–1713, Vittorio Amedeo II (1666–1732) managed to break out of his diplomatic isolation and establish close contacts with a large number of royal courts around Europe. This corresponded with the duke's aim to raise his status and secure his dynastic ambitions, which he successfully achieved in the context of the peace negotiations in Utrecht 1712–1713 when he was elevated to king of Sicily.[11]

Political and diplomatic assistance, which quite frequently took the route of a subsidy alliance, almost always constituted a prerequisite for territorial expansion, in particular for the lesser powers. In the Holy Roman Empire, the emperor was in a position to settle territorial disputes and divisions of estates.[12] Even outside of this legal structure, however, actors frequently needed to ensure that they had the recognition and support of someone else, which was rarely afforded without any form of compensation. For a lesser power, a subsidy alliance with a politically and diplomatically influential great power frequently represented the crucial difference between being able to annex a painstakingly conquered piece of territory and reluctantly being forced to return it. In his peace with France in 1679, for example, the increasingly diplomatically isolated elector of Brandenburg, Friedrich Wilhelm (1620–1688), was forced to return almost all the German lands taken from Sweden, an ally

---

10 Wilson, 'Prussia', pp. 114–115.
11 Geoffrey Symcox, 'Britain and Victor Amadeus II: Or, The Use and Abuse of Allies', in *England's Rise to Greatness, 1660–1763*, ed. by Stephen B. Baxter (Berkeley: University of California Press, 1983), pp. 151–184; Storrs, *War*, pp. 122–170.
12 Wilson, 'The German', 774–787, 791–792.

of France. For Sweden, on the other hand, the political and diplomatic support from France in the extended peace process that ended the northern sideshow of the Dutch War (1672–1678) was probably more important than the significant French subsidies during these years.[13] An unusual, yet illustrative, example of how generously a powerful subsidizer might reward a loyal and useful junior partner is the aforementioned acquisition of Sicily by Vittorio Amedeo. This Spanish island was to all intents and purposes beyond the power and reach of Savoy-Piedmont and could have been conquered and secured only by means of British naval power.[14] Hence, there were good strategic reasons for the lesser powers to conclude subsidy agreements with more powerful states.

However, receiving subsidies was not risk-free. On the contrary, it included a variety of strategic problems, dilemmas, and challenges, which the lesser receiving powers – Hesse-Cassel, Denmark, Württemberg, Bavaria, Portugal, Brandenburg-Prussia, and Savoy-Piedmont among others – struggled to address. At the same time, these difficulties seem to have increased throughout the eighteenth century.[15]

This chapter explores the strategic challenges facing the lesser powers during the long eighteenth century. It also examines to what extent the emergence of a new European states system, the novel scale and intensity of warfare, and the growing strength of the fiscal-military state over time rendered the role of the lesser states as subsidy recipients more problematic, not only in the Holy Roman Empire but also in a more general European sense. This allows us to acquire a deeper understanding of the conditions under which the lesser powers acted, as well as of the reasons why the international system increasingly came to be dominated by the great powers.

Our point of departure is Sweden, one of the lesser powers receiving subsidies that have been studied to a relatively small extent in this regard, and we particularly focus on the fifty-year period following the major Swedish defeat in the Great Northern War

---

13 Georg Landberg, *Den svenska utrikespolitikens historia, I:3 1648–1697* (Stockholm: Norstedts, 1952), pp. 200–203; Derek McKay, 'Small-power Diplomacy in the Age of Louis XIV: The Foreign Policy of the Great Elector during the 1660's and 1670's', in *Royal and Republican Sovereignty in Early Modern Europe: Essays in Memory of Ragnhild Hatton*, ed. by Robert Oresko, G.C. Gibbs, and H.M. Scott (Cambridge: Cambridge University Press, 1997), pp. 209–213.
14 Symcox, 'Britain and Victor Amadeus II', pp. 166–171; Storrs, *War*, p. 4.
15 Wilson, 'The German'; Wilson, *German Armies*, ch. 7.

(1700–21).¹⁶ The Swedish case is interesting in that it differs from many of the smaller, not least German, states whose receipt of subsidies has been in focus in previous research. First, Sweden was a territorially vast kingdom at the periphery of Europe and found itself in a very different geostrategic position compared to the lesser continental powers. Second, Sweden belonged to a part of Europe which was perhaps the most affected by the fundamental alterations in the states system during this period, primarily as a result of Russia and Prussia appearing as new great powers alongside France, Austria, and Great Britain.¹⁷ Third, in spite of its lost Baltic provinces and serious military-fiscal problems, Sweden had a significant military capability, which included a standing army of about 45,000 men, several major fortresses, some twenty ships of the line – a force often underestimated by historians – and a large oared navy. In Sweden, too, unlike the situation in the majority of the other recipients, a considerable portion of the subsidies was also allocated towards these capital-intensive naval forces.¹⁸ Fourth, and perhaps most importantly, during the period we focus on, Sweden was a

---

16 However, see Michael Roberts, *The Age of Liberty: Sweden 1719–1772* (Cambridge: Cambridge University Press, 1986), ch. 1; Patrik Winton, 'Denmark and Sweden in the European Great Power System, 1720–1765', *Revue d'histoire Nordique – Nordic Historical Review* 14.1 (2012), 39–62; Patrik Winton, 'Sweden and the Seven Years War, 1757–1762: War, Debt and Politics', *War in History* 19.1 (2012), 5–31; Peter Lindström and Svante Norrhem, *Flattering Alliances: Scandinavia, Diplomacy, and the Austrian–French Balance of Power, 1646–1740* (Lund: Nordic Academic Press, 2013); Erik Bodensten, 'Political Knowledge in Public Circulation: The Case of Subsidies in Eighteenth-century Sweden', in *Circulation of Knowledge: Explorations into the History of Knowledge*, ed. by Johan Östling, Erling Sandmo, David Larsson Heidenblad, Anna Nilsson Hammar, and Kari Nordberg (Lund: Nordic Academic Press, 2018), pp. 82–104, as well as Svante Norrhem, Chapter 4 above.
17 Hamish M. Scott, *The Emergence of the Eastern Powers, 1756–1775* (Cambridge: Cambridge University Press, 2001).
18 Jean Häggman, *Studier i frihetstidens försvarspolitik: Ett bidrag till Sveriges inre historia 1721–1727* (Stockholm: Uppsala universitet, 1922); Oscar Nikula, *Svenska skärgårdsflottan 1756–1791* (Helsingfors: K.F. Puromies boktryckeri, 1933); Leif Dannert, *Svensk försvarspolitik 1743–1757: I dess utrikespolitiska och inrikespolitiska sammanhang* (Uppsala: Appelberg, 1943); Gunnar Artéus, *Krigsmakt och samhälle i frihetstidens Sverige* (Stockholm: Militärhistoriska förlaget, 1982); Jan Glete, 'Den svenska linjeflottan 1721–1860: En översikt av dess struktur och storlek samt några synpunkter på behovet av ytterligare forskning', *Forum navale* 45 (1990), 9–68; Jan Glete, *Navies and Nations:*

constitutional monarchy, where the political decision-making process was entirely in the hands of the Council of the Realm and the Diet. This represents a clear difference compared to the other states receiving subsidies, states ruled by absolute monarchs. Among other things, this meant that increasing state revenues by means of extracting more resources became more or less politically impossible. Instead, Sweden was to an unusually high degree obliged to rely on foreign subsidies.[19]

The very fact that Sweden set itself apart in these respects provides us with a good opportunity for complementing our view of this phenomenon, but perhaps also to distinguish and understand the relevant set of problems generically: what strategic problems, dilemmas, and challenges united the lesser powers seeking and receiving subsidies from the major powers during this period?

The asymmetric Franco-Swedish subsidy alliance

Coming out of the Great Northern War, Sweden desperately needed the support of foreign subsidies. The strategy of avoiding subsidy alliances and treaty obligations, as they risked dragging Sweden into war – a strategy which had been in effect since around 1680 – was now considered a failure. In 1715, Sweden successfully concluded a three-year subsidy agreement with France. However, this treaty collapsed almost immediately as a result of a French policy reversal and an Anglo-French alliance.[20] New and growing tensions between the great powers following the War of the Spanish Succession offered Sweden the opportunity of joining the western power bloc. Having done so, Sweden received significant British and French subsidies in 1727–1729, as well as much-needed security

---

Warships, Navies and State Building in Europe and America, 1500–1860, vols I–II (Stockholm: Stockholms Universitet, 1993), vol. I, pp. 297–305; Jan Glete, 'Navies and Power Struggle in Northern and Eastern Europe, 1721–1814', in *Navies in Northern Waters, 1721–2000*, ed. by Rolf Hobson and Tom Kristiansen (London: Frank Cass, 2004), pp. 66–93.

19 Roberts, *The Age*, pp. 20–21.
20 Jerker Rosén, *Den svenska utrikespolitikens historia, II:1 1697–1721* (Stockholm: Norstedts, 1952), pp. 132, 137–138. In the final years of the war, Sweden also briefly came to receive some British subsidies, as well as a couple of smaller French payments; see Karl Åmark, *Sveriges statsfinanser 1719–1809*, parts I–III (Stockholm: Norstedts, 1961), pp. 571–572.

guarantees and British navy demonstrations in the Baltic Sea aimed at Russia.[21] Nevertheless, the Anglo-French detente of 1716 and the Alliance of Hanover in 1725 did not constitute a long-term basis for Swedish foreign policy. By the early 1730s, it was clear that the previous sharing of interests between France and Great Britain no longer existed. After a long period of recovery and diplomatic restraint, France was now able to start regaining its position as the leading power in Europe. From a Swedish perspective, this new strategic situation included several historically familiar elements. It was once again possible to discern the outlines of a states system whereby France alone was confronted by a broad alliance under Austrian leadership. In this context, Sweden could assume its former role as a junior subsidy partner to France and one of the cornerstones of France's eastern system, no longer tasked with directly confronting the emperor but rather weakening and preventing Russia from assisting Austria and meddling in continental matters.[22]

Leaving important domestic and dynastic motives aside, Sweden had two major strategic ambitions related to Russia: on the one hand, territorial expansion and a revision of power; on the other, preserving the peace and maintaining Sweden's fragile security. These two ambitions were clearly difficult to reconcile. However, this duality was in no way unique to Sweden; it may be seen elsewhere as well, for example in Savoy-Piedmont and Bavaria. Both of these powers were squeezed tightly between neighbouring great powers and thus accustomed to living in fear and minimizing risk. Nevertheless, they were also always ready to play for high stakes and exploit opportunities for expansion. The decision to accept subsidies from a great power, directed against another, was

---

21 Bertil Boëthius, *Sveriges traktater med främmande magter: Jemte andra dit hörande handlingar, Åttonde delen 1723–1771* (Stockholm: Kungl. Boktryckeriet, P.A. Norstedt & Söner, 1922), pp. 69–83; Olof Jägerskiöld, *Den svenska utrikespolitikens historia, II:2 1721–1792* (Stockholm: Norstedts, 1957), pp. 66–82; Åmark, *Sveriges statsfinanser*, pp. 572, 587; Roberts, *The Age*, pp. 33–34.
22 Arthur M. Wilson, *French Foreign Policy during the Administration of Cardinal Fleury 1726–1743* (Cambridge, MA: Harvard University Press, 1936), *passim*; Jägerskiöld, *Den svenska utrikespolitikens historia*, pp. 92–99; Roberts, *The Age*, pp. 20, 34; Jeremy Black, *European International Relations, 1648–1815* (Basingstoke: Palgrave, 2002), pp. 145–157.

never easy, and it was typically preceded by considerable doubts and difficult discussions. The example of Bavaria illustrates the consequences of making an error of judgement: before the War of the Spanish Succession, France sought to restore its network of subsidy alliances within the Holy Roman Empire. Here, the Bavarian Wittelsbachs played a key role. In 1701, Elector Maximilian Emanuel II (1662–1726) accepted a secret Franco-Bavarian subsidy alliance, after repeatedly having failed to gain the support of the emperor for his ambitious political and dynastic objectives. Before the final and reluctant break with the emperor the following year, Maximilian Emanuel received a clear promise that significant French forces were to join him on the Upper Danube, which also materialized. After some great successes – followed by generous offers to defect to the Grand Alliance – his fate was none the less sealed when the Franco-Bavarian forces suffered a crushing military defeat in 1704. It would take more than ten years, and only after the war was over, before Maximilian Emanuel was able to return to a financially ruined and politically and militarily marginalized Bavaria. New Bavarian attempts were made in the 1730s and 1740s, with the same catastrophic result, after which France finally withdrew its support.[23] Savoy-Piedmont, in turn, abandoned its old strategy of joining forces with Bourbon France at about the same time. To a large extent as a result of Vittorio Amedeo's successful use of mainly British subsidies, the duke succeeded in the feat of simultaneously freeing his state from its powerful neighbour – without becoming dependent on Austria – as well as expanding its territory.[24]

As far as Sweden was concerned, a Franco-Swedish subsidy alliance was seen as the only viable option capable of assisting Sweden in both its offensive and its defensive ambitions. Pro-French debaters in Sweden liked to emphasize that France was the only power with an interest in strengthening Sweden that simultaneously possessed the means necessary for doing so and was prepared to prioritize and pay for this task. Subsequently, from a Swedish perspective,

---

23 Wilson, *French*; Peter C. Hartmann, 'Die Subsidien- und Finanzpolitik Kurfürst Max Emanuels von Bayern im Spanischen Erbfolgekrieg', *Zeitschrift für Bayerische Landesgeschichte* 32.1 (1969), 238–289; Reginald de Schryver, *Max II: Emanuel von Bayern und das spanische Erbe: Die europäischen Ambitionen des Hauses Wittelsbach 1665–1715* (Mainz: Verlag Philipp von Zabern, 1996); Wilson, *German Armies*, pp. 107, 113–119, 250–258.
24 Symcox, 'Britain and Victor Amadeus II'; Storrs, *War*.

The problems with receiving subsidies

France's recovered strength and re-established policy in northern Europe naturally constituted a most welcome development. Swedish decision-makers in the Council of the Realm and the Diet disagreed on how best to use France and the instrument of subsidies for achieving the Swedish objectives, as well as when this should occur, whereas it is hard to detect any type of fundamental disagreement. The fact that Sweden needed large subsidies for its underfunded army and navy was evident to every informed analyst. Refraining from accepting French subsidies was in other words tantamount to giving up on at least Sweden's offensive ambition. Before the Swedish defeat in the war against Russia in 1741–1743, few Swedish politicians were prepared to do so.[25]

The fact that it was not until 1738 that a Franco-Swedish subsidy alliance was finally concluded was mainly a result of France, at the time, not having a need for a Swedish intervention in northern Europe. France instead prioritized theatres of war in Germany and Italy where – in spite of its name – the War of the Polish Succession (1733–1735/39) was mainly fought. In June 1735, however, a Franco-Swedish subsidy agreement was concluded. Nevertheless, as the war came to an end shortly thereafter, France's interest in Sweden vanished and Versailles subsequently refused to ratify the treaty and pay out the money. This incident ended up becoming exceedingly important in Swedish domestic politics, representing a sobering reminder for those who might have forgotten that the interests of Sweden and France only partly coincided and that the relationship was highly asymmetrical.[26] The French 'betrayal' in 1735 – as well as in earlier similar incidents in 1633–1634, 1661–1662, and 1716–1717 – would assume a prominent place in the Swedish debate concerning the Franco-Swedish subsidy alliance and its value during the following decades. The same must be said about the arrogant behaviour of Louis XIV (1638–1715) in the 1679 peace negotiations, which was neither forgotten nor forgiven. As mentioned above, France had secured the recovery of Sweden's lost provinces; but the insult – one of many – of paying one of the

---

25 Roberts, *The Age*, pp. 16–26, 114; Oskar Sjöström, 'Sekreta bihangen 1741 och deras idépolitiska bakgrund', *Sjuttonhundratal* (2008), pp. 5–24; Bodensten, 'Political Knowledge'.
26 Boëthius, *Sveriges traktater*, pp. 203–212; Jägerskiöld, *Den svenska utrikespolitikens historia*, pp. 99–123; Erik Bodensten, *Politikens drivfjäder: Frihetstidens partiberättelser och den moralpolitiska logiken* (Lund: Lunds universitet, 2016), pp. 162–164.

Swedish commanders directly, thereby circumventing the Swedish king, deeply offended the Swedes.[27] Less than a year after the 1738 subsidy treaty – where France agreed to assist Sweden with an amount corresponding to 900,000 *ds* annually for three years – the time had come for yet another such betrayal.[28] Emboldened by the Franco-Swedish subsidy alliance, the Swedish government transferred a fairly large troop contingent to Finland in order to negotiate, *armata manu*, with Russia concerning a revision of the last peace treaty and prepare for a Swedish attack. The Swedes hoped that the partial mobilization would also serve to strengthen the Swedish subsidy negotiations simultaneously taking place at several European courts. This endeavour proved to be an utter failure. The Swedish threat unintentionally contributed to the Ottoman Empire concluding a peace treaty with both Russia and Austria, thus ending a war which had been going on since 1736–1737 and which had been a fundamental element of the Swedish policy. Furthermore, it turned out that France had been the driving force in the negotiations – thus inflicting a harsh peace

---

27 See, for instance, *En Swensk Mans Tankar Om Dess Fädernes-lands Tilstånd, År 1675. Öfwersättning ifrån Latin. Med korta Anmärkningar, lämpade til närwarande tid* (Stockholm: Tryckt hos Carl Stolpe, 1769); Kungliga biblioteket (KB), Historia, D 351:8, *Samtal emellan Bonus och Cordatus*; KB, Historia, D 351:9, *Hyperborei Swar uppå Sin vän Austrasii bref*; D 351:9, *Reflexioner öfver Krigsdeclarationen år 1741*; KB, Historia, D 901, *Herr Gallipilei Bref till sin wän Severus*; *Partiers Ursprung och Wärkan I Swerige* (Stockholm: Tryckt i Kongl. Finska Boktryckeriet, hos Johan Arvid Carlbohm, 1769); 'Partistriden wid 1738–1739 års riksdag och dess orsaker', *Riksrådet grefve Gustaf Bonde: Anteckningar om Bonde-släkten*, vol. 3, Carl Trolle-Bonde (Lund: Gleerup, 1897–1899); *Swar, Uti Bref til Aristarchus, På Dess 12:te Nummer den 13 April 1769* (Stockholm: Tryckt i Kongl. Finska Boktryckeriet, 1769); *Sweriges Rikes Naturliga och Sanskyldiga Interesse uti Förbund med Kronan Frankrike, Granskat Uti Bref Ifrån En Wän i Stockholm til des Correspondent I anledning Af hans Swar På Des förra betydeliga Bref* (Stockholm: Tryckt i Kongl. Finska Boktryckeriet; Hos Johan Arvid Carlbohm, 1769); Uppsala universitetsbibliotek (UUB), Sveriges historia, F 275, *Bref til förswar af den med Ryssland förnyade Alliancen 1735*. For the 1679 incident in particular, see Ingemar Carlsson, *Olof Dalin och den politiska propagandan inför 'lilla ofreden': Sagan Om Hästen och Wår-Wisa i samtidspolitisk belysning* (Lund: CWK Gleerup, 1966), pp. 41–42; A.F. Upton, *Charles XI and Swedish Absolutism* (Cambridge: Cambridge University Press, 1998), pp. 27–28; Göran Rystad, *Karl XI: En biografi* (Lund: Historiska Media, 2001), pp. 116–118.

28 Boëthius, *Sveriges traktater*, pp. 270–276; Åmark, *Sveriges statsfinanser*, p. 573.

The problems with receiving subsidies

on the Habsburgs – apparently deceiving its northern ally for its own purposes. Now that Russia enjoyed peace and France had made it clear that it currently had no wish to see a Swedish attack, it was unthinkable for the Swedish government to proceed. Nor was it possible to withdraw its troops. Notwithstanding the political costs, this was out of the question from a military perspective, as Russia moved increasing numbers of troops to the border area. Needless to say, the detractors of the Franco-Swedish subsidy alliance had a field day.[29]

This event illustrates a general fact sooner or later experienced by every lesser recipient of subsidies: Whereas a subsidy alliance often served to create the *conditions* for more active and expansionist policies, it was far from certain that such policies could also be *realized*. The subsidy recipient had to take the interests and intentions of the giver into account, and, when a conflict of interest arose, the receiver generally had to stand down, at least if the subsidy alliance was to last, which these policies depended on. The support from the subsidizer came with conditions and the subsidies could always be withdrawn, reduced, or deliberately delayed. In 1684, for instance, Louis XIV made the limits for his support clear to his subsidy partner the Danish King Kristian V (1646–1699). French subsidies and diplomatic support had enabled the Danes to take possession over the duchy of Holstein-Gottorp, which was closely linked to Sweden. While the Danes were now preparing themselves for a direct attack on Sweden, the French king used his influence as subsidizer, forcing Denmark to back down and preventing a war he had no interest in.[30] Then again in 1743, Denmark was forced to abort its imminent invasion of Sweden, partly as a result of France holding back its subsidies, deemed essential to the Danish war-making capability.[31]

Defying the subsidizing great power in such situations represented significant risks for the lesser subsidized power. For instance, having

---

29 Wilson, *French*, pp. 318–326; Jägerskiöld, *Den svenska utrikespolitikens historia*, pp. 129–136. For the domestic political consequences, see Bodensten, *Politikens drivfjäder*, pp. 222–226.
30 Lars Christensen, 'I Solkongens Skygge: Dansk-franske relationer 1661–1693' (unpublished doctoral thesis, Syddansk Universitet, 2003), pp. 199–208; Lindström and Norrhem, *Flattering Alliances*, pp. 72–73.
31 Knud J.V. Jespersen and Ole Feldbæk, *Revanche og neutralitet, 1648–1814: Dansk udenrigspolitiks historie*, 2 (Copenhagen: Gyldendal, 2002), pp. 288–289.

failed to win the support of France and Austria for peace negotiations between Sweden and Prussia, the Swedish government none the less decided to proceed and unilaterally initiate negotiations. This resulted in a separate peace in May 1762, *status quo ante bellum*, which concluded Sweden's participation in the Seven Years' War (1756–1763). France answered by recalling its ambassador and largely suspending its subsidy payments. This aggravated the already serious fiscal and monetary crisis in Sweden but also served to discredit the Swedish government domestically in the eyes of the electorate. During the difficult negotiations in the following years, France clearly communicated its dissatisfaction with its subsidy client but also emphasized the extent to which the Swedish government was politically dependent on a good relationship with France. In April 1764, the increasingly strained Swedish government once again tried to obtain the withheld subsidy payments, without success. It was not until November that same year that both parties were able to agree on a compromise – the estates were to meet in January 1765 and France had no interest in seeing the government fall, just to be replaced by one more orientated towards Great Britain.[32]

In spite of the renewed subsidy alliance, however, this was exactly what happened. In February 1766, the new government signed a friendship treaty with Great Britain but failed in its efforts to secure subsidies and defence guarantees. France now referred to the provisions in the Franco-Swedish treaty which stipulated that the parties were required to obtain the consent of the other party in all negotiations with third parties, and, as this had not been the case, France declared that the treaty was now null and void. In the autumn of that same year, France also formally broke off its relationship with Sweden and cancelled all subsidy payments.[33] The situation to a large extent resembled the failed attempts of the Swedish government in 1735 to conclude a Franco-Swedish subsidy alliance, while at the same time seeking to avoid becoming too dependent on France and being reduced to a French satellite. Simultaneously with these

---

32 Boëthius, *Sveriges traktater*, pp. 886–893; Jägerskiöld, *Den svenska utrikespolitikens historia*, pp. 212–216, 221–224; Åmark, *Sveriges statsfinanser*, pp. 574, 588, 592; Michael F. Metcalf, *Russia, England and Swedish Party Politics 1762–1766: The Interplay between Great Power Diplomacy and Domestic Politics during Sweden's Age of Liberty* (Stockholm: Stockholm University, 1977); Michael Roberts, *British Diplomacy and Swedish Politics, 1758–1773* (Minneapolis: University of Minnesota Press, 1980).

33 Jägerskiöld, *Den svenska utrikespolitikens historia*, pp. 224–227; Åmark, *Sveriges statsfinanser*, p. 588, 592; Metcalf, *Russia*; Roberts, *British*.

negotiations, in 1735, the Swedish government decided to renew a previous twelve-year defence alliance with Russia, which was about to expire, without first consulting France as stipulated in the treaty. As Versailles had not yet had time to ratify the subsidy alliance, it was able to use this loophole as a pretext for terminating the treaty, as mentioned earlier.[34] In both 1735 and 1766, France had good reasons for breaking off relations with Sweden. One was obviously not having to pay out extensive subsidies to an ally that did not appear to be particularly useful at the time. Another reason, however, was the opportunity to clarify the true nature of the relationship: France could hardly be seen as accepting its junior subsidy partner freeing itself and disloyally approaching France's antagonists without suffering some consequences.

The subsidy agreements were generally formulated as agreements between equal partners, as in this case between the French king and the Swedish king. It was, for instance, understood that the above-mentioned obligation to consult one's partner before entering into new agreements with third parties only concerned the subsidy recipient.[35] The complex and rapidly changing European cabinet politics resulted in major difficulties for the lesser subsidy-receiving powers when the great powers suddenly and unilaterally changed their priorities. A particularly dramatic example in this regard was the 1756 Franco-Austrian and Anglo-Prussian rapprochement that turned the entire European system of alliances on its head and placed states such as Hesse-Cassel in a very difficult position. By 1755, Landgrave Wilhelm VIII (1682–1760) had yet again concluded an Anglo-Hessian subsidy treaty. In the light of Great Britain's long-standing and close relationship with the Habsburgs – also a traditional British subsidy ally – and with a similarly good relationship with Prussia, this agreement seemed relatively risk-free. In the event of a new major war in Europe, Hesse-Cassel could just as previously be expected to confront France along the Rhine as a junior ally and subsidy partner of Great Britain and Austria. The diplomatic revolution – as it became known – completely changed the strategic position of Hesse-Cassel, which now instead found itself in a very exposed

---

34 Jägerskiöld, *Den svenska utrikespolitikens historia*, pp. 99–123. The Swedish and French motives have been the subject of some debate; see Göran Nilzén, *Studier i 1730-talets partiväsende* (Stockholm: Stockholms universitet, 1971), pp. 133–134, 160–164, and the literature cited there. See also Lindström and Norrhem, *Flattering Alliances*, pp. 152–161.
35 Roberts, *The Age*, pp. 26–27.

position and open to primarily French attacks, which it could not possibly face on its own regardless of how many subsidies it received.[36] Unlike in 1735, the French reversal in 1739 did not result in Sweden losing its subsidies; however, as discussed above, it put the Swedish government in a precarious situation. In order to break the unsustainable deadlock, the Swedish government decided to convene the estates in August 1740. Before the Diet could assemble, however, the Habsburg Emperor Karl VI (1685–1740) passed away, shortly followed by the Russian ruler, Empress Anna Ioannovna (1693–1740). Faced with the prospect of a new major war of succession, France was once again willing to support a Swedish attack on Russia. In February 1741, the former Franco-Swedish subsidy treaty was renewed for another three years. As soon as the following month, the subsidies were increased somewhat in the event of Sweden attacking Russia, which it did in August.[37] Once again, it had become clear to what extent France, in its capacity as a great power and a subsidizer, laid out the framework for Swedish actions on the international scene.

Viable options and geostrategic realities

One indication of how well lesser powers managed to use the instrument of subsidies for achieving their political and dynastic objectives was the extent to which they possessed the strategic elements needed for being able to play off different givers against one another. Savoy-Piedmont, Denmark, and Brandenburg-Prussia belonged to the group of lesser powers that managed to establish themselves as attractive subsidy partners to many of the great powers in Europe. These powers regularly changed allies based on the promise of better conditions. Some princes, most notably Vittorio Amedeo and Friedrich Wilhelm, became known for their opportunism.[38]

---

36 Ingrao, *The Hessian Mercenary State*, p. 128; Wilson, *German Armies*, p. 266; Franz A.J. Szabo, *The Seven Years War in Europe, 1756–1763* (Harlow: Pearson, 2008), pp. 179–180, *passim*.
37 Wilson, *French*, pp. 330–338; Jägerskiöld, *Den svenska utrikespolitikens historia*, pp. 137–143; Åmark, *Sveriges statsfinanser*, p. 573; Bodensten, *Politikens drivfjäder*, pp. 222–227.
38 Symcox, 'Britain and Victor Amadeus II'; Storrs, *War*, pp. 122–170; McKay, 'Small-power Diplomacy'; Wilson, *German Armies*; Jespersen and Feldbæk, *Revanche og neutralitet*, pp. 102, 106, 114, 125, 159, 168, 267, 273–277, 282–296; Wilson, 'Prussia', pp. 114–115; Winton, 'Denmark', pp. 43–46, 50–52, 55–56, 59–61; Lindström and Norrhem, *Flattering Alliances*, pp. 68–69, 150–152.

The problems with receiving subsidies

However, success did not require such drastic reversals. For instance, Hesse-Cassel, which had great success as a recipient of subsidies, was very consistent in its subsidy alliance with Great Britain.[39] Instead, what was essential was that the lesser power – in addition to possessing military resources in demand – could make a prospective subsidy giver believe that it could also turn to another interested power, preferably one antagonistic to the former. This not only enabled the lesser power to obtain better conditions than would have been possible otherwise; it also strengthened the recipient's negotiating position once a subsidy treaty had been concluded, a position which might otherwise have been dangerously weak. The existence of alternative subsidy givers forced the dominant party to fulfil its commitments and also look after the interests of the junior party if the latter were to remain in the alliance and have it renewed once it expired.[40]

However, most of the lesser powers were unable to deal with the great powers in such a manner. In such a case, one alternative could be to turn to other lesser powers. For instance, the Republic of Venice was a significant giver of subsidies up until 1719; and, throughout the entire period, the United Provinces paid out large subsidies in peacetime as well as, in particular to the German states, providing them with troops. The lesser subsidizers represented lesser political risks. At the same time, however, the crucial political leverage that made subsidy treaties with the great powers attractive in the first place did not materialize. In these cases, subsidy agreements really turned into pure transactions, where the giver purchased military services in exchange for money. At any rate, this option ended up becoming less and less available throughout the period.[41]

It also became increasingly hard for the lesser powers to play off the great powers against one another. This was largely due to changes in the European states system during the period. Protracted conflicts between states such as France and Spain, and France and the United Provinces, ceased; these were conflicts which quite a few lesser powers had been able to exploit. The two new great powers of Prussia and Russia were both poor but had large military capabilities of their own. They themselves received subsidies, rather than offering them to others. From around 1760, Great Britain – arguably

---

39 Rodney Atwood, *The Hessians: Mercenaries from Hessen-Kassel in the American Revolution* (Cambridge: Cambridge University Press, 1980); Ingrao, *The Hessian Mercenary State*, ch. 5.
40 See, for instance, Storrs, *War*, pp. 122–170.
41 Wilson, 'The German', 782–787.

the largest subsidizer in the long eighteenth century – started to retreat from continental affairs and its previously very active involvement in imperial politics. The continental struggle with France and Spain came to the forefront, whereas the Hanoverian interest was played down. In the second half of the 1770s, several minor German states received British subsidies in exchange for assisting Great Britain in fighting the American rebellion; but it was only in the 1790s that Great Britain returned as a major subsidizer and participant in the continental power struggle.[42] Most importantly, however, the struggle between France and Austria – as well as the more general struggle between the Bourbons and the Habsburgs, which had dominated international relations in Europe for a long time – was put aside in the middle of the eighteenth century. For instance, following the mid-century Franco-Austrian rapprochement, and after Bourbon Spain had consolidated its position in Italy at about the same time, the strategic basis for Savoy-Piedmont's activist subsidy policy more or less evaporated.[43]

This became particularly evident with respect to the lesser German powers.[44] The difficulties of Hesse-Cassel during the Seven Years' War have already been mentioned. Another useful example is Württemberg, which at the same time failed to obtain good subsidy terms from the Franco-Austrian alliance in the absence of a credible alternative. The Württemberg duke Carl Eugen (1728–1793) vainly tried to strengthen his position, primarily in relation to the Habsburgs,

---

42 John M. Sherwig, *Guineas and Gunpowder: British Foreign Aid in the Wars with France, 1793–1815* (Cambridge, Mass.: Harvard University Press, 1969); Michael Roberts, *Splendid Isolation, 1763–1780: The Stenton Lecture 1969* (Reading: University of Reading, 1970); Ingrao, *The Hessian Mercenary State*, pp. 135–162; Jeremy Black, *A System of Ambition? British Foreign Policy 1660–1793* (Harlow: Longman, 1991), pp. 204ff; Wilson, 'The German', 786–787; Wilson, *German Armies*, pp. 311–312, 326; Scott, *The Birth*, pp. 146–147. Sweden received very substantial British subsidies in 1805–1816; Åmark, *Sveriges statsfinanser*, pp. 594, 852–856; Sherwig, *Guineas and Gunpowder*, pp. 366–368, *passim*; Jan Glete, 'The Swedish Fiscal-Military State in Transition and Decline, 1650–1815', in *War, State and Development: Fiscal-Military States in the Eighteenth Century*, ed. by Rafael Torres Sánchez (Pamplona: Eunsa, 2007), p. 108.
43 Storrs, 'The Savoyard', p. 203; Scott, *The Birth*, pp. 73–74, 81–92; Christopher Storrs, '"Große Erwartungen": Britische Subsidienzahlungen an Savoyen im 18. Jahrhundert', in *Das 'Blut des Staatskörpers': Forschungen zur Finanzgeschichte der Frühen Neuzeit*, ed. by Peter Rauscher, Andrea Serles, and Thomas Winkelbauer (Munich: Oldenbourg Verlag, 2012), pp. 87–126.
44 Wilson, 'The German', 778, 780–781, 786–787, 791–792.

The problems with receiving subsidies

by creating and providing very large forces, far larger than what was actually required in the subsidy agreements and far larger than his state finances allowed. In previous wars, Württemberg had been able to play off France and Austria against each other and even receive subsidies for remaining neutral. Now, however, Württemberg's interests were not looked after, despite its large troop contingent and despite the fact that Austria was engaged in a desperate military struggle and suffered from a chronic shortage of troops. The duke's politics contained an element of *sunk cost fallacy*, which was not unusual for subsidy recipients at this time: the more wholeheartedly he committed himself to the subsidy relationship and the larger his debts, the more difficult it was to cut his losses and give up the leverage he had worked so hard to attain, a leverage which might help him realize his territorial claims in a future peace negotiation. Well aware of this situation, the allies were in a position to make even more extensive demands.[45]

Württemberg's difficult position might have been avoided had it decided to limit its participation and withdrawn from the war at the first opportunity, or had it claimed to be neutral already from the outset. First, however, such a policy would not have resulted in any benefits for Württemberg. In relative terms, it would instead have weakened Württemberg's position in relation to its antagonistic neighbours, which chose to assist the allies. Second, a more cautious policy could very well have resulted in punishments, which happened to other German princes who tried to remain neutral at the same time. The Austro-Prussian dualism – which had increasingly come to characterize imperial politics – made it increasingly difficult for the German lesser powers to avoid having to take a clear side. The decision in 1761–1762 to finally start demobilizing and take Württemberg – now deeply in debt – out of the war was not unexpectedly followed by numerous unfavourable verdicts in the imperial courts.[46]

The Bavarian Wittelsbachs were faced with the same problem. Bavaria did not receive any subsidies between 1759 and 1800; this was not due to a lack of ambition, however, but rather to a lack of options. Just as in the case of Württemberg, the geostrategic location of Bavaria was the significant factor. Bavaria enjoyed few natural protective barriers and only had a few strong fortresses. In relation to the struggle between the Habsburgs and the Bourbons, this territory played a key strategic role; for both France and Austria,

---

45 Wilson, *War*, pp. 209–239.
46 Wilson, *War*, pp. 209–239; Schmid, *Max III*.

it constituted a defensive buffer zone as well as an offensive staging area. Bavaria thus represented an attractive subsidy partner for both of these great powers; but, as already mentioned, such alliances were also associated with great risks. Accepting subsidies from another power, directed at both Austria and France, was out of the question. At the outbreak of the Seven Years' War, Great Britain offered Bavaria subsidies in exchange for declaring itself neutral, which Bavaria reluctantly had to decline.[47]

The geostrategic position of the states in southern Germany may be contrasted with that of the states in the north, which generally faced a smaller risk of retaliation in their attempts to capitalize on the Franco-Austrian conflict. This also opened up for other possibilities in terms of alternative subsidizers, in particular the United Provinces and Great Britain. The position of Münster, for example, was very well suited to supplying the former with subsidy troops. The powers in southern Germany, on the other hand, and in particular those along the Rhine, were in a better position to offer direct access to strategic territories. The subsidizer's own troops could, for instance, be granted safe passage and the opportunity to receive supplies – winter quarters were particularly important in this regard. These military resources could be just as important as troops and explain why states such as Cologne, Trier, and Mainz, whose forces were small but which held several strategically important fortresses, were able to obtain subsidies.[48]

Sweden belonged to the group of lesser powers whose geostrategic position did not enable direct military co-operation with the forces of the subsidizer – at least not primarily – but could on the other hand be used for extending the latter's power projection far beyond what was possible in a direct sense. As part of the French eastern system, Sweden alone was able to directly threaten the exposed capital of Russia. That option was activated by France in 1741 by supporting the aforementioned Swedish attack on St Petersburg, which effectively deprived the Habsburgs of a potential ally during the War of the Austrian Succession (1740–1748).[49] Previously, the Swedish bridgehead in northern Germany had also indirectly extended

---

47 Black, 'The Problem', pp. 7, 24; Wilson, 'The German', 778.
48 Wilson, *War*, pp. 85–87; Wilson, 'The German', 779, 782–783; Wilson, *German Armies*, pp. 211–212.
49 Reed Browning, *The War of the Austrian Succession* (New York: St Martin's Griffin, 1993), pp. 65–66; M.S. Anderson, *The War of the Austrian Succession, 1740–1748* (London: Longman, 1995), pp. 79–80.

The problems with receiving subsidies 137

French power to this part of the empire and enabled France to attack the emperor and his allies here as well. The Austro-Prussian conflict, in combination with the Franco-Austrian alliance, once again made the remaining Swedish provinces in Germany strategically interesting and possible to capitalize on. Sweden could now side with both France and Austria and in exchange for subsidies attack Prussia from its exposed northern flank, which the two allies were unable to do by themselves.[50]

With the promise that major French subsidies would be forthcoming and that Sweden would regain its territories lost to Prussia 1720 in the coming peace negotiations, Sweden joined the strong anti-Prussian coalition in September 1757.[51] The Swedish intervention in the war has often been described as a military, political, and fiscal fiasco.[52] This is true in many ways. However, it should be noted that the Swedish generals were not trying to achieve a decisive military victory over the Prussians. Also, the subsidies represented a means rather than an end, and the actors knew that they would not cover the costs – the French subsidies to Sweden were significant, but still only covered around 20 per cent of all extraordinary wartime revenues.[53] Hence, they were close in size – in relative, not absolute, terms – to the extensive wartime subsidies received by Vittorio Amedeo, and fully comparable with the substantial British subsidies received by Friedrich II of Prussia (1712–1786) during the war.[54] Sweden's attack on Prussia in many ways represented a typical subsidiary war, where the lesser subsidized power hoped to make future political or diplomatic gains by providing assistance to the great power. Obviously, we do not know what these gains would have looked like; but there are good reasons for believing that the Swedish government, just as it had done in the subsidy

---

50 This strategic bridgehead also secured British subsidies during the Napoleonic Wars; see Sherwig, *Guineas and Gunpowder*, pp. 161–164.
51 Boëthius, *Sveriges traktater*, pp. 694–735; Jägerskiöld, *Den svenska utrikespolitikens historia*, pp. 199–208; Winton, 'Sweden', pp. 14–16.
52 Sten Carlsson and Jerker Rosén, *Svensk historia: II: Tiden efter 1718* (Stockholm: Svenska bokförlaget, 1961), pp. 156–167; Roberts, *The Age*, pp. 19–21, 43–45; Szabo, *The Seven Years War*, pp. 294–299, *passim*.
53 Winton, 'Sweden'.
54 Åmark, *Sveriges statsfinanser*, pp. 573–574, 588; Storrs, *War*, pp. 103–118; Hamish Scott, 'The Fiscal-military State and International Rivalry during the Long Eighteenth Century', in *The Fiscal-military State in Eighteenth-century Europe*, ed. by Christopher Storrs, p. 49; Storrs, 'The Savoyard', pp. 215–216; Winton, 'Sweden', pp. 22–24.

negotiations prior to the war, was particularly set on demanding territorial expansion in Pomerania. In the end, what was to solve the Swedish war equation was this type of traditional territorial expansion, at the expense of the neighbouring state, and not the French subsidies.[55] The risk taken by the Swedish government was primarily that, in the future peace settlement, France would not be able to or would not want to push for Swedish compensation. In 1757, however, this did not appear all that likely, as Prussia was confronted by a very strong and determined enemy coalition. Also, Sweden had been a loyal subsidy partner of France for a long time. A stronger Sweden in Germany, which was in a better position to counteract Prussia, was also in the interests of Austria and Russia. It was only after several years of very costly warfare, and when it was abundantly clear that France neither could nor had any desire to keep its earlier promise, that Sweden, just like Württemberg, chose to cut its losses.

From a Swedish perspective, the diplomatic revolution resulted in an unexpected and short-lived opportunity for expansion in the empire. However, throughout the entire period, Sweden had another primary interest, namely expansion and security vis-à-vis Russia. In this respect, Sweden belonged to the group of lesser powers that had difficulties in appealing to more than one potential subsidizer. Great Britain – Sweden's only real viable option apart from France – certainly wanted to see a restriction of Russian influence in the Baltic region, which is why it offered very active support to Sweden in the 1720s. Nevertheless, following a certain time lag, it became increasingly clear that British and Russian interests coincided in many respects, which resulted in a gradual improvement in Anglo-Russian relations. Above all, both states belonged to the anti-French camp, and they ended up becoming increasingly economically dependent on each other – a development which called the value

---

55 Cf. Winton, 'Sweden', p. 31. See also Sherwig, *Guineas and Gunpowder*, pp. 275–276, 284–286, 312, regarding the similar Swedish attempt in 1813–1814 to secure British subsidies and, more importantly, allied recognition of planned territorial acquisitions, this time in Norway.

56 Stewart P. Oakley, 'Trade, Peace and the Balance of Power: Britain and the Baltic, 1603–1802', in *In Quest of Trade and Security: The Baltic in Power Politics 1500–1990: Volume 1, 1500–1890*, ed. by Göran Rystad, Klaus-R. Böhme and Wilhelm M. Carlgren (Lund: Lund University Press, 1994), pp. 239ff.

of a potential Anglo-Swedish subsidy alliance into question.[56] In any case, compared to France, Great Britain had a significantly more restrictive approach with regard to subsidies. That approach more or less excluded peacetime subsidies, essentially a Swedish requirement.[57]

The fundamental problem facing Sweden was that France was really the only power that valued the military, geostrategic, and political resources Sweden could offer, a fact of which the French counterpart was certainly not unaware.[58] Conversely, Denmark – the other Scandinavian power – was frequently in a position to successfully play Great Britain, Austria, and France off against one another and even obtain subsidies simply by promising to remain neutral. Not least, Denmark was able to exploit its proximity to Hanover and provide subsidy troops either to protect or to threaten the Electorate, united in a personal union with Great Britain since 1714.[59] In this regard, Sweden's strategic position more resembled that of Portugal, which in its ambitions to counteract Bourbon Spain had no other option than to turn to its subsidy ally Great Britain, on which it grew increasingly dependent.[60]

Swedish attempts at playing France and Great Britain off against each other consistently failed.[61] Britain's interest in an Anglo-Swedish

---

57 C.W. Eldon, *England's Subsidy Policy towards the Continent during the Seven Years' War* (Philadelphia: University of Pennsylvania, 1938); Roberts, *British*, ch. 8; P.G.M. Dickson, *Finance and Government under Maria Theresia 1740–1780: Volume II, Finance and Credit* (Oxford: Clarendon Press, 1987), pp. 158–160; Jeremy Black, 'Parliament and Foreign Policy in the Age of Walpole: The Case of the Hessians', in *Knights Errant and True Englishmen: British Foreign Policy, 1660–1800*, ed. by Jeremy Black (Edinburgh: John Donald Publishers, 1989), pp. 41–54; Scott, 'The Fiscal-military', p. 49.
58 Cf. Winton, 'Denmark', pp. 45–46, 61–62, who does not consider the Swedish navy or geostrategic position – but only its army – as being an important asset in the subsidy negotiations.
59 See, for instance, Roberts, *British*, pp. 20, 28–29; Jespersen and Feldbæk, *Revanche og neutralitet*, pp. 102, 106, 114, 125, 159, 168, 267, 273–277, 282–296; Szabo, *The Seven Years War*, p. 132; Winton, 'Denmark', pp. 43–46, 50–52, 55–56, 59–61; Lindström and Norrhem, *Flattering Alliances*, pp. 68–69, 150–152.
60 David Francis, *The First Peninsular War, 1702–1713* (London and Tonbridge: Ernest Benn Limited, 1975); L.M.E. Shaw, *The Anglo-Portuguese Alliance and the English Merchants in Portugal, 1654–1810* (Aldershot: Ashgate, 1998).
61 See, for instance, Metcalf, *Russia*, pp. 18–19, 222–223.

subsidy alliance was always secondary at best, primarily focused on challenging its main opponent, France. This deprived France of an important ally, or at any rate created distrust between the two allies; strengthened Sweden's negotiating position, thus forcing France to increase its subsidies; and prevented a Swedish (and perhaps also a Danish) squadron from uniting with the French navy at a critical stage.[62]

The lack of other options than France constitutes an important reason why Sweden remained a French subsidy ally for so long and ended up being highly dependent on France. This became particularly evident during the fifteen-year period starting in the late 1740s, when Anglo-Swedish relations were very poor. However, it should be noted that Swedish behaviour on the international scene was never determined by France. For instance, the Swedish government *wanted* to attack Russia in 1741 and had sought to create favourable conditions for such an attack for a long time. This attack, just like the attack on Prussia, was not the result of an ultimatum from the subsidizer.[63]

Nor was Sweden in such a bad negotiating position that France looked likely to stop paying out very large sums of money. The 1738 subsidy treaty marked the beginning of an almost unbroken period of large French subsidy payments, which did not end until the mid-1790s.[64] These mainly peacetime subsidies enabled the Swedish government to compensate for its scarce fiscal resources, as well as to maintain and even strengthen its military capabilities. The importance of this factor is difficult to overestimate. This became particularly clear in the late 1740s, when France with a major effort, both diplomatically and financially, helped Sweden free itself from Russian dependency following the defeat in 1741–1743, while at the same time preventing Russia from interfering in the final phase of the War of the Austrian Succession.[65] The Franco-Swedish subsidy agreements concluded in 1747–1749 enabled a substantial expansion of both Swedish naval forces and fortresses. In the peak year of

---

62 Roberts, *British*, pp. xiii–xxv.
63 Roberts, *The Age*, pp. 26–27; Glete, 'The Swedish', p. 107. Cf. Winton, 'Denmark', pp. 50, 61–62.
64 Åmark, *Sveriges statsfinanser*, pp. 573–575, 585–586, 588, 591–594, 597.
65 Jägerskiöld, *Den svenska utrikespolitikens historia*, pp. 161–181; Jeremy Black, *From Louis XIV to Napoleon: The Fate of a Great Power* (London: UCL Press, 1999), pp. 96–100.

1750, the French subsidies amounted to approximately 17 per cent of the total Swedish state revenue.[66]

Concluding remarks: A new states system and falling demand for subsidy troops

By the end of the Seven Years' War, the European states system had become increasingly multipolar as a result of France's declining power, and Prussia's and Russia's assumption of the status of great powers. Instead of the previous balance of power between two nearly equally powerful blocs, the system disintegrated into a western and an eastern part, outside of which none of the five great powers retained much influence. Together, however, they came to dominate the system in a qualitatively new way. The role of the lesser powers was significantly reduced as a result. In particular, the last war – with warfare on a new scale and with a new intensity – had demonstrated the rather marginal relative fiscal-military importance of the lesser powers. These changes made it increasingly difficult for the lesser powers to form alliances with the great powers and to secure subsidies. As the demand for subsidy troops and lesser allies decreased – the Habsburg emperor, for instance, abandoned the instrument in the 1770s and 1780s – the lesser powers increasingly had to fall back on their own ever more limited financial, political, and military resources.[67]

For Sweden – located in the eastern part of the European states system and increasingly dependent on external financial and diplomatic support – this was a particularly disturbing development. The new strategic situation became evident in 1772 as the three eastern great powers were allowed to partition Poland without the two western great powers being able to prevent this from happening – a situation that may serve as an illustrative contrast to the powerful intervention of France and Great Britain in the Baltic region in the

---

66 Boëthius, *Sveriges traktater*, pp. 476–480, 507–512; Dannert, *Svensk försvarspolitik 1743–1757*, ch. 5–6; Nikula, *Svenska skärgårdsflottan*, pp. 21–25; Åmark, *Sveriges statsfinanser*, pp. 573, 588, 591; Patrik Winton, 'Parlimentary Control, Public Discussions and Royal Autonomy: Sweden, 1750–1780', *Histoire & Mesure* XXX.2 (2015), 59–60. See also Dickson, *Finance and Government*, pp. 394–396.
67 Wilson, 'The German', 784–787; Wilson, *German Armies*, ch. 7; Scott, *The Birth*, pp. 5–6, 35–38, 117–121, 143–150, *passim*; Hamish Scott, 'The Seven Years War and Europe's *Ancien Régime*', *War in History* 18.4 (2011), 435–437.

1720s. At the same time, the Swedish ambition to achieve a revision of power in the Baltic region and counteract Russia was being discarded, a process that had been ongoing ever since at least the 1740s. Instead, the ambition to secure peace led to more people putting their faith in Great Britain, a policy that in practice meant joining forces with Russia. In the view of an increasing number of Swedish decision-makers and opinion leaders, subsidies in general, and the Franco-Swedish subsidy alliance in particular, were seen as an overly risky and costly strategy. However, it should be pointed out that contemporaries found it hard to grasp just how much France's military, diplomatic, and financial influence and prestige had actually declined since the Seven Years' War and more or less evaporated in eastern Europe.[68]

Perhaps the most obvious expression of French weakness was its great difficulties in terms of living up to its subsidy commitments. For Sweden, this in many ways constituted a new experience, as France had always paid on time and frequently even in advance. The French payment problems not only affected Sweden; for instance, it was not until 1769 that Austria received its last wartime subsidies from France.[69] Following the Seven Years' War, all warring states were confronted with unprecedented financial difficulties, which in turn resulted in a period of international detente, as the great powers tried to avoid war and regain their strength. The same dynamics had previously appeared in the period following the War of the Spanish Succession and would once again become particularly clear following the Napoleonic Wars.[70] In these situations, the lesser powers experienced a significant weakening of their negotiating position, both with regard to obtaining new subsidies and with regard to receiving the ones already promised.[71] The very real inability to pay on the part of the subsidy givers here interacted with their much-reduced need to pay for allies.

Out of all the major subsidizers, it seems as if the war affected the French state finances the most; at the end of the 1760s, the

---

68 Roberts, *The Age*, pp. 48–58; Black, *From Louis*, pp. 114–127; Scott, *The Birth*, pp. 144–145; Bodensten, 'Political Knowledge', pp. 98–99.
69 Åmark, *Sveriges statsfinanser*, p. 574; Szabo, *The Seven Years War*, pp. 132–133, 299, *et passim*; Scott, 'The Fiscal-military', p. 49; Winton, 'Sweden', 22–24.
70 Scott, 'The Fiscal-military', pp. 38–40; Scott, 'The Seven', pp. 430–435.
71 See, for example, Ingrao, *The Hessian Mercenary State*, p. 128; Wilson, 'The German', 786–787; Wilson, *War*, p. 150.

money spent on interest represented almost two-thirds of governmental annual revenues.[72] This situation forced France to abandon, or at least suspend, its previous and generous subsidy policy. The French subsidies became smaller, were paid out to fewer receivers, and were more or less paid only in wartime. In this respect, France followed the British example.[73] However, this shift also reflected the altered strategic priorities of France. The colonial and naval struggle with Great Britain moved to centre stage, whereas the previous continental ambitions were downplayed. Nevertheless, it was only gradually and reluctantly that France was forced to abandon its influence, recognizing that many of its long-standing subsidy allies were no longer essential.[74]

The slowness with which France reluctantly carried out its strategic realignment seems to have saved Sweden from a very vulnerable position which it could otherwise have expected to find itself in, a position in which Poland and the Ottoman Empire – the two other powers that together with Sweden had formed the French *barrière de l'est* – increasingly found themselves. In 1771–1773, the new Swedish king, Gustav III (1746–1792), succeeded in reforging Sweden's ties with France and concluding a new Franco-Swedish subsidy alliance which enabled another extensive military expansion and modernization during the 1770s and 1780s, in particular with regard to the Swedish navy and oared flotilla.[75] There were good military and strategic reasons for the expansion of the Swedish

---

72 James C. Riley, *The Seven Years War and the Old Regime in France: The Economic and Financial Toll* (Princeton: Princeton University Press, 1986); James C. Riley, 'French Finances, 1727–1768', *Journal of Modern History* LIX (1987), 209–243; T.J.A. Le Goff, 'How to Finance an Eighteenth-century War', in *Crises, Revolutions and Self-sustained Growth: Essays in European Fiscal History, 1130–1830*, ed. by W.M. Ormrod, Margaret Bonney, and Richard Bonney (Stamford: Shaun Tyas, 1999), pp. 377–413; Scott, 'The Seven', pp. 432–434, 447–448.
73 Dickson, *Finance and Government*, pp. 180–183; Daniel A. Baugh, 'Withdrawing from Europe: Anglo-French Maritime Geopolitics, 1750–1800', *The International History Review* 20.1 (1998), 8–9; Wilson, *German Armies*, pp. 290–291; Scott, 'The Fiscal-military', p. 49.
74 Baugh, 'Withdrawing from Europe'; Scott, *The Birth*, pp. 143–146, 214–222. For Sweden, see Helle Stiegung, *Ludvig XV:s hemliga diplomati och Sverige 1752–1774* (Lund: CWK Gleerup, 1961); Metcalf, *Russia*; Roberts, *British*; Roberts, *The Age*, pp. 46–47.
75 Nikula, *Svenska skärgårdsflottan*, pp. 88–103; Jägerskiöld, *Den svenska utrikespolitikens historia*, pp. 237–238, 260–267; Åmark, *Sveriges statsfinanser*, pp. 574–575, 588, 593, 597; Glete, 'Den svenska', pp. 27–31, 36.

navy, even though this focus was also rational from a perspective of subsidy policy. In the naval arms race which involved Great Britain on the one hand and France and Spain on the other, and which became increasingly important in the decades following the Seven Years' War, relatively small auxiliary naval forces could turn the scales. Strengthening the navy, something both France and Great Britain valued the most at this time and something France encouraged its allies to do, thus strengthened Sweden's negotiating position, not least in relation to the other subsidy-seeking powers which did not possess this military resource.[76]

This was important, as Sweden's previously stellar military credibility had been increasingly challenged. Both in the war against Russia in 1741–1743 and in that against Prussia in 1757–1762, the Swedish army had tied down significant numbers of enemy troops but also exhibited a strikingly cautious behaviour. At least in the latter case, it was obvious that Sweden, for political reasons, had been very reluctant to risk its troops in battle and entirely prioritized the maintenance of these troops.[77]

The Swedish behaviour was understandable and not uncommon among subsidy recipients. Württemberg, for example, made the same call during the Seven Years' War, knowing full well that its negotiating position in relation to the subsidizer would collapse in the event of the loss of its army.[78] This behaviour, however, was fundamentally problematic in that the value of the subsidy receiver as an ally was based not only on its military capabilities but on its willingness to loyally deploy these. As shown by Patrik Winton in an illuminating analysis, the conflict between saving the troops of the subsidized power and providing military assistance to the subsidizer as agreed upon may explain the performance of the Swedish army during the war, characterized by recurring marches and countermarches into Prussian territory – seemingly offensive but without ever seriously facing the enemy on the battlefield. The Swedish behaviour was rational, as the Swedes never intended to recapture Pomerania – lost to Prussia in 1720 – on the battlefield

---

76 Baugh, 'Withdrawing from Europe', pp. 10, 14, 19.
77 Roberts, *The Age*, pp. 21–24; Szabo, *The Seven Years War*, pp. 158–159, 171–173, 224–225, 294–299, 332–333, 361–363; Winton, 'Sweden', pp. 14–16; Winton, 'Denmark', p. 58. This militarily cautious and politically shrewd behaviour was successfully repeated by Sweden in 1813–1814; see Sherwig, *Guineas and Gunpowder*, pp. 292, 312.
78 Wilson, *War*, pp. 216, 225.

The problems with receiving subsidies

but rather to regain it at the negotiating table. This is also reflected in the exceedingly vague instructions from the Swedish government to its generals in the field.[79] In practice, Sweden addressed this conflict by trying to keep its army active on Prussian territory and in full numbers, as agreed upon, while at the same time as far as possible reducing costs and risks while waiting for the great-power struggle to come to a conclusion. Just as in the case of Württemberg, however, the subsidizer ended up becoming increasingly dissatisfied over time. Not only did this undermine Sweden's prospects in a future peace negotiation, it also risked the value of Sweden as a subsidy ally in the longer term.

Following the Seven Years' War, it seems as if Sweden found itself in the same kind of 'vicious circle' as Württemberg, outlined by Peter Wilson: 'Without such an established [military] reputation, it was difficult to attract adequate subsidies, but without these it was difficult to provide first-rate troops.'[80] After each military failure, it became increasingly hard to obtain subsidies and equip, train, and pay larger forces.[81] During the 1760s, the Swedish government, deprived of previous subsidies, was forced to implement extensive military cutbacks.[82] Unable to take military risks and behave aggressively during long campaigns and against a strong opponent as a result of fiscal-military factors, it proved difficult for the lesser powers to avoid such a dynamic in the long run.

---

79 Winton, 'Sweden', 15–21.
80 Wilson, *War*, p. 84.
81 Ibid., pp. 226–238.
82 Carlsson and Rosén, *Svensk historia*, p. 179.

6
Pensions in Switzerland: practices, conflicts, and impact in the sixteenth century

Philippe Rogger

The development of Swiss power politics around 1500 was remarkable, albeit short-lived. During the Burgundian Wars (1474–1477), Swiss cantons under Bernese leadership skilfully exploited the anti-Burgundian constellation on the European stage to expand their sphere of influence westwards, while in the Milanese Wars (1494–1516) they extended their territory to the south, into Lombardy.[1] Victory over Burgundy in the Battles of Murten (1476), Grandson (1476), and Nancy (1477) and over the French in the Pavia Campaign (1512) and at Novara (1513) established the Old Swiss Confederacy as a military power. Its great power politics came to an abrupt end in 1515, however, as the Confederacy was defeated by the young French King François I in the Battle of Marignano.[2] In the period spanning roughly thirty years between the Burgundian and Milanese Wars, the loose alliance of petty states and microstates in the heart of Europe proved unable to cope with the political, military, and financial demands of great-power politics in a sustainable

---

1 Bernhard Stettler, *Die Eidgenossenschaft im 15. Jahrhundert* (Menziken: Markus Widmer-Dean, 2004), pp. 233–256; Walter Schaufelberger, 'Spätmittelalter', *Handbuch der Schweizer Geschichte*, vol. 1 (Zurich: Berichthaus, 1972), pp. 239–388 (pp. 336–358).

2 Walter Schaufelberger, *Marignano: Strukturelle Grenzen eidgenössischer Militärmacht zwischen Mittelalter und Neuzeit*, Schriftenreihe der Gesellschaft für militärhistorische Studienreisen, 11 (Frauenfeld: Huber, 1993); Regula Schmid, 'Gemein Eitgnossen hattend nie vil gewunnen, über den Gothart zu reisen: Ziele und Zwänge des eidgenössischen Ausgriffs in die Lombardei vor 1516', in *Marignano 1515: la svolta*, Atti del congresso internazionale, Milano, 13 settembre 2014, ed. by Marino Viganò (Milan: Fondazione Trivulzio, 2015), pp. 17–32.

fashion. But although its infantry's short phase of tactical superiority in the European theatres of war ended at Marignano, as a market for mercenaries and as a guardian of Alpine passes the *Corpus Helveticum* remained a power factor as Spain and France jostled for the predominant position in Europe.³ Hence, the victorious French king sought to form a military alliance with his Swiss enemies as swiftly as possible. And even when he did not initially succeed, he offered his adversaries an Eternal Peace (1516), which he made extremely attractive as a result of generous financial and trade incentives.⁴ His expensive investments and his persistence would pay off within a few years when the mercenary alliance of 1521 was established. Regularly renewed, this alliance tied its unequal partners together throughout the entire sixteenth, seventeenth, and well into the eighteenth century.⁵

Unusual conventions in diplomatic dealings with foreign powers developed owing to the weakness of the Confederacy's petty states, the lack of a power centre, the coexistence of different constitutions and (following the Reformation) confessions, and the relations of different cantons with other cantons and foreign powers.⁶ In the

---

3 André Holenstein, *Mitten in Europa: Verflechtung und Abgrenzung in der Schweizer Geschichte*, 2nd ed. (Baden: Hier und Jetzt, 2015; first published in 2014), pp. 112–124.
4 See *Après Marignan: La paix perpétuelle entre la France et la Suisse, 1516–2016*, ed. by Alexandre Dafflon, Lionel Dorthe, and Claire Gantet, Mémoires et Documents 4e série, vol. 14 (Fribourg: Société d'Histoire de la Suisse romande/Archives de l'État de Fribourg, 2018).
5 Andreas Würgler, 'Symbiose ungleicher Partner: Die französisch-eidgenössische Allianz 1516–1798/1815', *Jahrbuch für Europäische Geschichte* 12 (2011), 53–75; Ernst Wüthrich, *Die Vereinigung zwischen Franz I. und 12 eidgen: Orten und deren Zugewandten vom Jahre 1521* (Zurich, 1911).
6 There were five 'democratic' rural cantons (cantonal assemblies), four city cantons with patrician constitutions, and three city cantons with guild constitutions. One canton had both a rural and democratic and a city constitution. Two cantons were divided into two half-cantons. As for confession, after the Reformation, seven cantons remained Catholic, four were Reformed and two were mixed or bi-confessional. The *Corpus Helveticum* comprised the thirteen cantons with full rights involved in the administration of the subject territories (common bailiwicks), as well as allied principalities (the prince-bishopric of Basel, the princely abbey of St Gall, the principality of Neuchâtel), cities (Biel, Rottweil, Mulhouse, St Gall) and republics (Geneva, Valais, Grisons). See Andreas Würgler, '"The League of the Discordant Members" or How the Old Swiss Confederation Operated and How It Managed to Survive for So Long', in *The Republican Alternative:*

sixteenth century, for instance, Confederate embassies at foreign courts were a rarity, and there was no permanent representation by agents or residents.[7] However, foreign royal diplomats abounded in the *Corpus Helveticum* from the last quarter of the fifteenth century onwards, advancing the interests of their respective courts as Spain, Milan, Savoy, or the pope all sought alliances. Obtaining access to the Confederate mercenary markets was the principal aim of these powers. The pensions (payments into official accounts and to individuals) created by princes and kings to this end demonstrate the asymmetry in political relations between the Confederate cantons and their allies from the late fifteenth century onwards.[8]

To support this theory, the present chapter takes a closer look at the pension practices and the friction caused by this flow of money on various levels by focusing on the example of France: conflicts abounded over distribution due to French pensions during the Milanese War, and the relations between the cantons and their western ally were at times severely tested during the French Wars of Religion (1562–1598) because of outstanding pensions. Both

---

The Netherlands and Switzerland Compared, ed. by André Holenstein, Thomas Maissen, and Maarten Prak (Amsterdam: Amsterdam University Press, 2008), pp. 29–50 (pp. 29–35). Up to 1798, one can talk of two spheres of foreign policy: there was internal foreign policy pertaining to relations between the allied cantons and external foreign policy concerning the relations of individual cantons, or all of the cantons, with foreign powers. See Georg Kreis, 'Außenpolitik', *Historisches Lexikon der Schweiz*, www.hls.dhs.dss.ch/textes/d/D26455.php, accessed 18 September 2017.

7 See Nadir Weber and Philippe Rogger, 'Unbekannte inmitten Europas? Zur außenpolitischen Kultur der frühneuzeitlichen Eidgenossenschaft', in *Beobachten, Vernetzen, Verhandeln: Diplomatische Akteure und politische Kulturen in der frühneuzeitlichen Eidgenossenschaft*, ed. by Philippe Rogger and Nadir Weber, Itinera – Beihefte zur Schweizerischen Gesellschaft für Geschichte, 45 (Basel: Schwabe, 2018), pp. 9–44.

8 On the issue of asymmetrical foreign relations, see *Protegierte und Protektoren: Asymmetrische politische Beziehungen zwischen Partnerschaft und Dominanz (16. bis frühes 20. Jahrhundert)*, ed. by Tilman Haug, Nadir Weber, and Christian Windler, Externa, 9: Geschichte der Außenbeziehungen in neuen Perspektiven (Cologne: Böhlau, 2016), pp. 9–27; Andreas Affolter, *Verhandeln mit Republiken: Die französisch-eidgenössischen Beziehungen im frühen 18. Jahrhundert*, Externa, 11: Geschichte der Außenbeziehungen in neuen Perspektiven (Cologne: Böhlau, 2017); Tilman Haug, *Ungleiche Außenbeziehungen und grenzüberschreitende Patronage. Die französische Krone und die geistlichen Kurfürsten (1648–1679)*, Externa, 6 (Cologne: Böhlau, 2015); and Würgler, 'Symbiose'.

examples provide insights into the balance of power and dependencies that developed between the allies following the nascence of the pension system around 1500, dependencies which would be consolidated during the course of the sixteenth century. First, however, we must explain what the term 'pension' actually means in the context of the Old Swiss Confederacy.

Pensions, mercenary dealings, and foreign relations

From the late fifteenth century onwards, a great deal of money poured into the Confederacy from royal treasuries. Unlike German studies, for example, Swiss research literature only very rarely uses the term *subsidies* to denote these payments. The *Historisches Lexikon der Schweiz (HLS)* contains no entries for the word. In the *Enzyklopädie der Neuzeit*, on the other hand, a specific article defines subsidies as 'moneys of aid or support' paid to one power by another by contract, while also noting that the payment of subsidies was a 'common means of financing wars in the early modern period'.[9] Although the same reference work also contains an entry on pensions and rightly points out the ambiguity of the term, there is no substantial consideration of the significance of pensions as a form of transnational royal money transfer.[10] This lacuna is remarkable, since such pension payments are also documented for the Holy Roman Empire and other territories.[11] This contradiction, the lack of uniform terminology for cross-border money transfers, and the dominance of the term 'subsidies' in the German research literature thus demand an explanation of the term 'pensions'. On which basis were these payments made, what did they achieve, and what was

---

9 Michael Busch, 'Subsidien', *Enzyklopädie der Neuzeit Online*, ed. by Friedrich Jaeger, http://dx.doi.org/10.1163/2352-0248_edn_a4205000, accessed 6 September 2017.

10 Josef Ehmer, 'Pension', *Enzyklopädie der Neuzeit Online*, ed. by Friedrich Jaeger, http://dx.doi.org/10.1163/2352-0248_edn_a3186000, accessed 6 September 2017.

11 See Haug, *Ungleiche Außenbeziehungen, passim*; Friedrich Edelmayer, *Söldner und Pensionäre: Das Netzwerk Philipps II. im Heiligen Römischen Reich*, Studien zur Geschichte und Kultur der iberischen und iberoamerikanischen Länder, 7 (Vienna: Verlag für Geschichte und Politik, 2002), pp. 27–29; and Fritz Redlich, *The German Military Enterpriser and His Work Force: A Study in European Economic and Social History*, Vierteljahrschrift für Sozial- und Wirtschaftsgeschichte, Beihefte 47/48, 2 vols (Wiesbaden: Franz Steiner, 1964–65), vol. 1, pp. 327–330.

their significance for the political economy of the cantons of the Confederacy? Pensions first appear as royal payments in the Old Swiss Confederacy in connection to the anti-Burgundian alliances in the last third of the fifteenth century.[12] As noted by historian Valentin Groebner in the *HLS*, they 'aimed, both as public pensions paid into official accounts and as secret pensions paid to individuals, to influence political decisions and to secure foreign warlords access to the coveted Swiss mercenaries'.[13] The generosity of the European warlords was due, on the one hand, to the Confederacy's special geopolitical location in the heart of Europe and, on the other hand, to the potency of its markets of violence. The Confederacy bordered on the Free County of Burgundy to the west and the duchy of Milan to the south. Hence, it was positioned in both the Spanish and French spheres of interest, in terms of both geostrategy and trade policy.[14] This special geopolitical position, caught between the might of the Spanish and the French, took on further virulence due to the cantons' trade in mercenaries. From the late fifteenth century onwards, the Confederacy developed into a prosperous mercenary farm, becoming an important recruitment market. Large sections of the ruling elites made economic and political use of this situation. The leading political and military families enjoyed large profits and prestige as military entrepreneurs and recipients of pensions.[15] While the political-military elite secured and expanded

---

12 *Fremde Gelder: Pensionen in der Alten Eidgenossenschaft*, ed. by Maud Harivel, Florian Schmitz, and Simona Slanicka (Zurich: Chronos, forthcoming).
13 Valentin Groebner, 'Pensionen', *Historisches Lexikon der Schweiz*, www.hls.dhs.dss.ch/textes/d/D10241.php, accessed 6 September 2017. See also Valentin Groebner, *Gefährliche Geschenke: Ritual, Politik und die Sprache der Korruption in der Eidgenossenschaft im späten Mittelalter und am Beginn der Neuzeit*, Konflikte und Kultur – Historische Perspektiven, 4 (Constance: UVK Universitätsverlag Konstanz, 2000), pp. 159–163, and the same author's *Liquid Assets, Dangerous Gifts: Presents and Politics at the End of the Middle Ages* (Philadelphia: University of Pennsylvania Press, 2002).
14 Holenstein, *Mitten in Europa*, p. 113.
15 See the ongoing project of the Swiss National Science Foundation (SNF) led by Prof. André Holenstein at the University of Bern: Militärunternehmertum und Verflechtung. Strukturen, Interessenlagen und Handlungsräume in den transnationalen Beziehungen des Corpus Helveticum in der frühen Neuzeit. Projekt A: Philippe Rogger: Eidgenössisches Militärunternehmertum in der frühen Neuzeit – Strukturen, Handlungsräume und Familieninteressen (1550–1750), www.hist.unibe.ch/forschung/forschungsprojekte/militaerunternehmertum_amp_verflechtung/index_ger.html, accessed 6 September 2017.

local power via mercenary service, the risks for the ordinary soldiers were much greater. Nevertheless, these subjects also saw mercenary life as an opportunity and entered the service of foreign masters as military migrant workers for uncertain pay.[16] It is estimated that in the sixteenth century alone, around four hundred thousand Swiss mercenaries went to war for foreign powers.[17] Close to the theatres of war in Italy or France, the Swiss mercenaries had the advantage of rapid availability. 'The rival powers of Spain and France sought to bind this strategically sensitive space as closely as possible to themselves or to take it from their adversary. The aim was to secure the right to march their own troops through [the territory] and over the Alps, to keep the Swiss mercenary market open and to prevent their rival from gaining a dominant position in the Confederacy.'[18] As the *HLS* definition cited above also indicates, pensions entailed both public and private payments. It is important to make this distinction if we are to outline the conflicts caused by these pensions.

We first encounter pensions as public payments agreed by contract in the treaty of alliance with France of 1474. An annual payment of 20,000 francs was to be divided evenly between the then eight cantons of Zurich, Bern, Lucerne, Uri, Schwyz, Unterwalden, Zug, and Glarus and Freiburg and Solothurn.[19] After military conflict in

---

16 Philippe Rogger and Benjamin Hitz, 'Söldnerlandschaften – räumliche Logiken und Gewaltmärkte in historisch-vergleichender Perspektive: Eine Einführung', *Söldnerlandschaften: Frühneuzeitliche Gewaltmärkte im Vergleich*, ed. by Philippe Rogger and Benjamin Hitz, Zeitschrift für Historische Forschung, Beiheft 49 (Berlin: Duncker & Humblot, 2014), 9–43; Philippe Rogger, *Geld, Krieg und Macht: Pensionsherren, Söldner und eidgenössische Politik in den Mailänderkriegen 1494–1516* (Baden: Hier und Jetzt, 2015); Benjamin Hitz, *Kämpfen um Sold: Eine Alltags- und Sozialgeschichte schweizerischer Söldner in der Frühen Neuzeit* (Cologne: Böhlau, 2015).
17 Hans Conrad Peyer, 'Die wirtschaftliche Bedeutung der fremden Dienste in der Schweiz vom 15. bis zum 18. Jahrhundert', in Hans Conrad Peyer, *Könige, Stadt und Kapital: Aufsätze zur Wirtschafts- und Sozialgeschichte des Mittelalters*, ed. by Ludwig Schmugge, Roger Sablonier, and Konrad Wanner (Zurich: Verlag Neue Zürcher Zeitung, 1982), pp. 219–231 (p. 222); *Fighting for a Living: A Comparative History of Military Labour 1500–2000*, ed. by Erik-Jan Zürcher, Work Around the Globe, 1 (Amsterdam: Amsterdam University Press, 2013); Rogger and Hitz, 'Söldnerlandschaften'; André Holenstein, Patrick Kury, and Kristina Schulz, *Schweizer Migrationsgeschichte: Von den Anfängen bis zur Gegenwart* (Baden: Hier und Jetzt, 2018), pp. 47–59.
18 Holenstein, *Mitten in Europa*, pp. 113–114.
19 Rudolf Thommen, 'Friedensverträge und Bünde der Eidgenossenschaft mit Frankreich, 1444–1777', *Basler Zeitschrift für Geschichte und*

northern Italy, France renewed its agreement to pay the cantons enjoying full entitlement 2,000 francs in pensions (or peace payments) in the Eternal Peace of 1516.[20] François I increased the pensions to 3,000 francs in the mercenary alliance of 1521.[21] The king paid this amount, according to the wording of the treaty of 1521, 'in clear and open recognition of the men, the Confederates concerned [and] the deep love, liberality, obligingness, and fondness of said most Christian king towards Us'.[22] The king of Spain also promised the annual payment of 1,500 crowns to the Catholic cantons (excluding Solothurn) in the mercenary alliance in order to win favour. Felipe II paid the money 'out of especially graceful good will' for the purpose of 'better maintenance of mercenary friendship and alliance'.[23] Thus, the contractually agreed payments were not motivated by the warlords' tangible interests in recruitment licences; rather, they were a symbol of royal affection and friendship towards their partners in the alliance. Indeed, the two alliances between the cantons and France and Spain combine elements of friendly and military treaties of alliance.[24] Even if the rhetoric of friendship suggests an equal footing, the two parties are anything but equal, as we shall see below.[25]

Altertumskunde 15 (1916), 117–214 (p. 144). There were also provisions for pensions in the treaties of 1495 and 1499. *Ibid.*, 153–160.

20 *Die Eidgenössischen Abschiede aus dem Zeitraume von 1500 bis 1520*, ed. by Anton Philipp Segesser, Amtliche Sammlung der ältern Eidgenössischen Abschiede, vol. 3.2 (Lucerne: Meyer'sche Buchdruckerei, 1869), p. 1409.

21 *Die Eidgenössischen Abschiede aus dem Zeitraume von 1521 bis 1528*, ed. by Johannes Strickler, Amtliche Sammlung der ältern Eidgenössischen Abschiede, vol. 4.1a (Brugg: Fisch, Wild und Comp., 1873), p. 1498.

22 *Abschiede*, vol. 4.1a, p. 1498.

23 *Die Eidgenössischen Abschiede aus dem Zeitraume von 1587 bis 1617*, ed. by Josef Karl Krütli and Jakob Kaiser, Amtliche Sammlung der ältern Eidgenössischen Abschiede, vol. 5.1 (Bern: Wyß'sche Buchdruckerei, 1872), p. 1838; Rudolf Bolzern, *Spanien, Mailand und die katholische Eidgenossenschaft: Militärische, wirtschaftliche und politische Beziehungen zur Zeit des Gesandten Alfonso Casati (1594–1621)*, Luzerner Historische Veröffentlichungen, 16 (Lucerne: Rex 1982), p. 150.

24 Andreas Würgler, 'Freunde, *amis, amici*: Freundschaft in Politik und Diplomatie der frühneuzeitlichen Eidgenossenschaft', in *Freundschaft oder 'amitié': Ein politisch-soziales Konzept der Vormoderne im zwischensprachlichen Vergleich (15.–17. Jahrhundert)*, ed. by Klaus Oschema, Zeitschrift für Historische Forschung, Beiheft 40 (Berlin: Duncker & Humblot, 2007), 191–210 (p. 195).

25 Tilman Haug, Nadir Weber, and Christian Windler, 'Einleitung', pp. 9–27 (p. 12).

Although the articles on pensions contain no mention of the recruitment of mercenaries, the pension payments were motivated not by emotions but by power politics. The contracts provided for mutual military aid in the event of conflicts or the passage of troops and, above all, granted the French or Spanish king the right to recruit mercenaries to defend their territories.[26] While the military alliances with France of 1474, 1495, or 1499 did not stipulate how many soldiers were to be recruited, the treaty of 1521 prescribed a minimum of six thousand and a maximum of sixteen thousand.[27] The 1587 agreement with Spain stipulated a minimum of four thousand and a maximum of thirteen thousand mercenaries.[28] If the pensions were not paid on time, article 16 of the Spanish alliance allowed the cantons to annul the contract.[29] The annulment clause, testifying to the cantons' bad experiences with their allies, demonstrates the essentially commercial nature of these alliances: the deal was mercenaries for pensions.[30] For the cantons – and the Catholic cantons had a special interest in such services – the contractually agreed trade in mercenaries represented an extremely profitable business. From 1510 to 1610, in the Catholic city cantons of Fribourg, Lucerne, and Solothurn, the pensions amounted to 66.5 per cent, 41.2 per cent, and 36.9 per cent of the respective regular income. The figures were somewhat lower in the Reformed city cantons of Zurich (15.2 per cent), Basel (15.7 per cent), and Schaffhausen (32.1 per cent).[31] In the rural cantons, pensions may well have been much more important to state budgets than in the Catholic cantons owing to the weak structure of their economies: in Appenzell, pensions accounted for around 80 per cent in 1582–1583.[32] The alliances,

---

26 On the Spanish alliance, see *Abschiede*, vol. 5.1, pp. 1832–1833; Bolzern, *Spanien*, pp. 73–108.
27 Thommen, 'Friedensverträge und Bünde', pp. 144, 154, 158; *Abschiede*, vol. 4.1a, p. 1494.
28 Ibid., vol. 5.1, p. 1839.
29 Ibid., vol. 5.1, p. 1834.
30 Nathalie Büsser, 'Militärunternehmertum, Außenbeziehungen und fremdes Geld', in *Geschichte des Kantons Schwyz*, vol. 3, ed. by Historischer Verein des Kantons Schwyz (Zurich: Chronos, 2012), pp. 69–127 (p. 102).
31 Martin H. Körner, *Solidarités financières suisses au seizième siècle*, Bibliothèque historique vaudoise, 66 (Lausanne: Édition Payot, 1980), p. 112.
32 Christian Windler, '"Ohne Geld keine Schweizer": Pensionen und Söldnerrekrutierung auf den eidgenössischen Patronagemärkten', in *Nähe in der Ferne: Personale Verflechtung in den Außenbeziehungen der Frühen Neuzeit*, ed. by Hillard von Thiessen and Christian Windler, Zeitschrift für Historische

especially the close involvement with France in 1516–1521, brought the Confederates not only financial but also trade-related advantages (customs privileges, unrestricted access to trade fairs in Lyon, salt imports, etc.).[33] In terms of security policy, the cantons also profited from the opportunity to recall troops in the event of war, as first established in the provisions of the French alliance of 1521, and later in the Savoy alliance of 1577 and the Spanish military alliance of 1587.[34] A consequence of the recall clause was that the cantons could manage without an expensive standing army and were thus able to keep direct taxation low. As argued by Christian Windler, the 'successful Confederate model of Early Modernity, "state-building without direct taxation and a standing army", was only possible thanks to the intensity of external involvement and the extent of the resources that created'.[35] In contrast to the Spanish alliance or the Catholic cantons' treaties with Savoy in 1560 (renewed in 1577 and 1581) and the pope in 1565, the French alliance included all faiths and united both Catholic and Reformed cantons. The alliance formed with King Henri II in 1549 included the cantons Lucerne, Uri, Schwyz, Unterwalden, Zug, Glarus, Basel, Freiburg, Solothurn, Schaffhausen, and Appenzell and the allied cantons of the Abbey and City of St Gall, Grisons, Valais, and Mulhouse.[36] Despite the absence of Zurich in 1521 and the temporary withdrawal from the alliance by Bern in 1529 on account of reformatory opposition to pensions, the alliance with France played an important role in holding together the loose confederacy, since it balanced the tensions between the confessional blocs. It was renewed in the sixteenth century in 1549, 1564, and 1582, each time only with minimal changes, although France finally succeeded in expanding the alliance to include Bern in 1582–1583 and Zurich in 1614.[37] The installation of a permanent embassy in the Confederacy in 1522 and the role of the ambassadors as mediators in internal conflicts underline France's eminent interest

---

Forschung, Beiheft 36 (Berlin: Duncker & Humblot, 2005), 105–133 (pp. 105–106); Holenstein, *Mitten in Europa*, pp. 145–146.

33 Würgler, 'Symbiose', 69–72; Dafflon, Dorthe, and Gantet, *Mémoires et Documents*.

34 *Abschiede*, vol. 4.1a, pp. 1494–1495, vol. 5.1, p. 1835, and *Die Eidgenössischen Abschiede aus dem Zeitraume von 1556 bis 1586*, ed. by Joseph Karl Krütli, Amtliche Sammlung der ältern Eidgenössischen Abschiede, vol. 4.2 (Bern: C. Rätzer'sche Buchdruckerei, 1861), p. 1545.

35 Windler, '"Ohne Geld keine Schweizer"', p. 107.

36 Thommen, 'Friedensverträge und Bünde', p. 180.

37 Würgler, 'Symbiose', 124–133.

in maintaining good relations with the cantons or a smooth supply of mercenaries from as many cantons as possible.[38] From 1530 onwards, they had a permanent residence in Solothurn, from where they organized the recruitment of mercenaries and advanced the formation of mercenary alliances and capitulations.[39]

Since there was no centre of power comparable to a royal court, the regular Federal Diet (*Tagsatzung*) played only a co-ordinating role in foreign policy, which meant that the Confederacy presented the French, Spanish, and Savoy diplomats with difficulties.[40] Foreign policy was an affair for the sovereign cantons. They alone were responsible for forming alliances, with many decision-makers involved in the political process, be it the councillors in the city cantons or the countryfolk with voting and electoral rights in the rural cantons (*Landsgemeinden*). Occasionally, in city cantons such as Bern, even the subjects were consulted by the authorities on questions of alliances in the form of surveys (*Ämteranfragen*).[41] Given the decentralized political structure and the complex political setting in the polyarchies of the Confederacy, the diplomatic representatives of the European powers relied on personal connections and various communication channels to push their political interests. That was both very time-consuming and very expensive; they corresponded with many actors from different cantons, travelled to diets and conferences, met contacts in the cantons in person, or received them in their places of residence.[42] Drawing on recent insights into the history of diplomacy

---

38 Würgler, 'The League', p. 36.
39 Holenstein, *Mitten in Europa*, p. 134; Alexandre Dafflon, *Die Ambassadoren des Königs und Solothurn: Ein 'vierzehnter Kanton' am Ufer der Aare, 16. bis 18. Jahrhundert* (Solothurn: Zentralbibliothek Solothurn, 2014). For Spanish diplomacy, see Bolzern, *Spanien*, and Andreas Behr, *Diplomatie als Familiengeschäft: Die Casati als spanisch-mailändische Gesandte in Luzern und Chur (1660–1700)* (Zurich: Chronos, 2015).
40 Holenstein, *Mitten in Europa*, pp. 133–141; Andreas Würgler, *Die Tagsatzung der Eidgenossen: Politik, Kommunikation und Symbolik einer repräsentativen Institution im europäischen Kontext (1470–1798)*, Frühneuzeit-Forschungen, 19 (Epfendorf: Bibliotheca Academia, 2013), pp. 477–484; Weber and Rogger, 'Unbekannte'. On the functioning of the Federal Diet, see Würgler, *Tagsatzung*, and Michael Jucker, *Gesandte, Schreiber, Akten. Politische Kommunikation auf eidgenössischen Tagsatzungen im Spätmittelalter* (Zurich: Chronos, 2004).
41 Sarah Rindlisbacher, 'Zwischen Evangelium und Realpolitik: Der Entscheidungsprozess um die Annahme der französischen Soldallianz in Bern 1564/65 und 1582', *Berner Zeitschrift für Geschichte* 75 (2013), 3–39.
42 Würgler, *Tagsatzung*.

inspired by social and cultural history, we know that the Confederacy's transnational connections in the early modern period were achieved via personal networks composed of many different actors, each of whom pursued their own interests and whose loyalty to the polity was occasionally rather weak.[43]

These informal networks were usually formed by the establishment of patron–client relationships.[44] This policy made use of bribes in the form of all kinds of patronage (pensions, captain's ranks, aristocratic titles, etc.), secret payments to select politicians, military entrepreneurs, and trusted individuals playing a very important role. Indeed, towards the end of the sixteenth century, a much larger number of pensions were covertly paid to private individuals from state treasuries. Taking Lucerne as an example, while France in 1475 paid around half (45 per cent) of its pensions to private individuals, about a hundred years later, around 1580, the figure stood at roughly three-quarters. Spain, too, spent 4,000 *scudi* in private pensions per canton and year in 1587, while public pensions, as outlined above, amounted to only 1,500 *scudi*.[45] In the course of the sixteenth century, however, private pensions became more nuanced, with different categories distinguishing between purpose, mode of distribution, and the people dispensing them.[46] Individual

---

43 *Akteure der Außenbeziehungen: Netzwerke und Interkulturalität im historischen Wandel*, ed. by Hillard von Thiessen and Christian Windler, Externa, 1 (Cologne: Böhlau 2010); *Nähe in der Ferne*, ed. by Hillard von Thiessen and Christian Windler.

44 Ulrich Pfister, 'Politischer Klientelismus in der frühneuzeitlichen Schweiz', *Schweizerische Zeitschrift für Geschichte* 42 (1992), 28–68; Windler, '"Ohne Geld keine Schweizer"', pp. 105-133; *Soldgeschäfte, Klientelismus, Korruption in der Frühen Neuzeit: Zum Soldunternehmertum der Familie Zurlauben im schweizerischen und europäischen Kontext*, ed. by Kaspar von Greyerz, André Holenstein, and Andreas Würgler, *Herrschaft und soziale Systeme in der Frühen Neuzeit*, 25 (Göttingen: V & R unipress, 2018); for research on patronage in general, see Birgit Emich, Nicole Reinhardt, Hillard von Thiessen, and Christian Wieland, 'Stand und Perspektiven der Patronageforschung', *Zeitschrift für Historische Forschung* 32 (2005), 233–265.

45 Bolzern, *Spanien*, p. 150; Leonhard Haas, 'Die spanischen Jahrgelder von 1588 und die politischen Faktionen in der Innerschweiz zur Zeit Ludwig Pfyffers', *Zeitschrift für Schweizerische Kirchengeschichte* 45 (1952), 81–108, 161–189 (pp. 83–94); Windler, '"Ohne Geld keine Schweizer"', p. 110; Rogger, *Geld*, pp. 328–329.

46 Haas, 'Die spanischen Jahrgelder', p. 82; Büsser, 'Militärunternehmertum', pp. 90–93; Urs Kälin, 'Salz, Sold und Pensionen: Zum Einfluss Frankreichs auf die politische Struktur der innerschweizerischen Landsgemeindedemokratien im 18. Jahrhundert', *Der Geschichtsfreund* 149 (1996), 105-124

pensions, as a resource of patronage, influenced the political culture in the cantons.[47] Regular pensions were used by the French or Spanish king to reward clients for their service in furthering their patron's political goals, procuring mercenaries or supplying important information.[48] The dispensers of pensions, who acted as brokers by organizing the exchange of resources between the patron and his clients, were surrounded by pro-French, pro-Spanish, or pro-Savoy factions jostling for influence on behalf of their patrons.[49] Although we do not claim that there was a simple automatic connection between money and political power, the boundaries of entwinement were determined by the availability – or indeed shortage – of patronage resources.[50] Furthermore, the development and maintenance of these informal networks were determined not only by political culture but also by confessional circumstances. For instance, Spanish Milan had limited access to Reformed patronage markets.[51] With regard to transfers of resources in connection with mercenary service and pensions, client networks were of inestimable importance for the formation of political elites in the cantons.[52] Hence, it is not surprising

---

(pp. 114–119); Gustav Allemann, 'Söldnerwerbungen im Kanton Solothurn von 1600–1723, I. Teil', *Jahrbuch für Solothurnische Geschichte* 18 (1945), 1–122 (pp. 31–41).

47 See, for instance, U. Pfister, U. Kälin, C. Windler, and P. Rogger, 'Mit Fürsten und Königen befreundet – Akteure, Praktiken und Konfliktpotential der zentralschweizerischen Pensionennetzwerke um 1500', *Der Geschichtsfreund* 165 (2012), 223–254.

48 Pfister, 'Politischer Klientelismus', pp. 29–40; Simon Teuscher, *Bekannte – Klienten – Verwandte: Soziabilität und Politik in der Stadt Bern um 1500*, Norm und Struktur. Studien zum sozialen Wandel in Mittelalter und Früher Neuzeit, 9 (Cologne: Böhlau, 1998), pp. 135–138; Ulrich Vonrufs, *Die politische Führungsgruppe Zürichs zur Zeit von Hans Waldmann (1450–1489): Struktur, politische Networks und die sozialen Beziehungstypen Verwandtschaft, Freundschaft und Patron-Klient-Beziehung*, Geist und Werk der Zeiten, 94 (Zurich: Peter Lang, 2002), pp. 188–190.

49 Haas, 'Die spanischen Jahrgelder', pp. 81–108, 161–189; Windler, '"Ohne Geld keine Schweizer"', p. 115; Kälin, 'Salz, Sold und Pensionen', p. 109; Andreas Würgler, 'Factions and Parties in Early Modern Swiss Conflicts', in *Factional Struggles: Divided Elites in European Cities & Courts (1400–1750)*, ed. by Mathieu Caesar, Rulers & Elites, 10 (Leiden: Brill, 2017), pp. 196–215.

50 Behr, *Diplomatie als Familiengeschäft*, pp. 261–318, 322; Windler, '"Ohne Geld keine Schweizer"', p. 113.

51 Behr, *Diplomatie als Familiengeschäft*, pp. 263–291, 296.

52 See, for instance, Kurt Messmer and Peter Hoppe, *Luzerner Patriziat: Sozial- und wirtschaftsgeschichtliche Studien zur Entstehung und Entwicklung im 16. und 17. Jahrhundert*, Luzerner Historische Veröffentlichungen,

that, given this opaque flow of resources and the complex mesh of contacts, there was no shortage of contemporary criticism of the pension system. In the sixteenth century, money and gifts were part of the political discourse, and the line between legitimate practice and bribery was hotly debated.[53] As early as 1503, the entire Confederacy reached an agreement forbidding private pensions (the Pensions Letter). Nevertheless, this consensus lasted only until 1508, and it was the work of the Zurich reformer Zwingli – a harsh critic of mercenary service and pensions – that led to private pensions being forbidden in the Reformed city cantons.[54] However, such bans could easily be circumvented, as is shown by the example of Bern where, for a time, salt concessions were instead used as a patronage resource.[55] This criticism of private pensions is the subject of the first case study illustrating how the asymmetry in political relations between powers awarding and powers receiving pensions manifested itself.

Pensions as a patronage resource: cross-border practices of political influence during the Milanese Wars

The asymmetrical nature of the cantons' foreign relations becomes especially clear when the continental great powers sought to obtain licences to recruit Swiss mercenaries. France, Milan, and the pope regarded the cantons of the Confederacy as patronage markets in which recruitment largely depended on the attractiveness of their offers (pensions, pay, etc.).[56] This was also the case when the cantons began to pursue their own power politics in northern Italy in the early sixteenth century.

---

5 (Lucerne: Rex-Verlag, 1976), pp. 77–93; Philippe Rogger, 'Familiale Machtpolitik und Militärunternehmertum im katholischen Vorort: Die Pfyffer von Luzern im Umfeld des Dreissigjährigen Krieges', *Berner Zeitschrift für Geschichte* 77 (2015), 122–138; Rogger, *Geld*, pp. 323–343; Büsser, 'Militärunternehmertum', pp. 69–127.

53 Groebner, *Geschenke*; von Greyerz, Holenstein, and Würgler, *Herrschaft und soziale Systeme*; Andreas Suter, 'Korruption oder Patronage? Aussenbeziehungen zwischen Frankreich und der Alten Eidgenossenschaft als Beispiel (16.–18. Jahrhundert)', in *Korruption: Historische Annäherungen an eine Grundfigur politischer Kommunikation*, ed. by Niels Grüne and Simona Slanicka (Göttingen: Vandenhoeck & Ruprecht, 2010), pp. 167–203.

54 Groebner, *Geschenke*, pp. 178, 208, 239, 241–246.

55 Windler, '"Ohne Geld keine Schweizer"', pp. 126–133.

56 *Ibid.*, p. 113.

In the last decade of the fifteenth century, Italy became the focus of French and Spanish expansionism. Both countries had already achieved a high degree of monarchic concentration at this time, and dominion over Italy promised the wealth of its trade hubs as well as agricultural production in the north and centre. It would also mean securing a position as the dominant force in the Mediterranean and represented the key to European hegemony. In 1494, the French monarchy had achieved sufficient internal consolidation for Charles VIII to embark on a campaign to Naples. The aim was to realise Angiovinian claims to the rule of the House of Anjou over Naples by military means. Following the conflict between the Valois and the Habsburgs over the Burgundian Succession (1477–1493), the antagonism between the two houses continued on the Apennine peninsula, causing the swift collapse of the fragile Italian state system. The years between the 1494 Naples campaign of Charles VIII and the victory of King François I in Marignano in 1515 were characterized by several military campaigns and shifting coalitions and alliances between the power blocs involved. With the help of the Confederacy's cantons, France conquered the duchy of Milan in 1499 and occupied it in the ensuing years.[57] Indeed, the cantons supplied the French king with the mercenaries he urgently needed for his Italian campaigns until 1509. Between 1509 and 1511, however, the Confederacy split with France when the Swiss did not renew the mercenary alliance of 1499 after it expired in 1509. Instead, an alliance was formed with the pope in 1510 and rapprochement was sought with the Holy Roman Emperor (the Hereditary Agreement of 1511).

The Pavia campaign of 1512, pursuing the Confederacy's own designs for power, led to the capitulation of Cremona, Pavia, and Milan. When France was driven out of Lombardy, the conflict over the duchy escalated markedly.[58] On 29 December 1512, the Confederacy made Massimiliano Sforza, the son of Ludovico Sforza and the formal feudal overlord of Milan, duke of the city without considering the interests of the Holy Roman Emperor. Milan thus

---

57 Alfred Kohler, *Expansion und Hegemonie: Internationale Beziehungen 1450–1559*, Handbuch der Geschichte der Internationalen Beziehungen, 1 (Paderborn: Ferdinand Schöningh, 2008), pp. 6–7, 327–341; Heinrich Lutz, 'Italien vom Frieden von Lodi bis zum Spanischen Erbfolgekrieg (1454–1700)', in *Handbuch der europäischen Geschichte*, vol. 3, ed. by Theodor Schieder (Stuttgart: Klett-Cotta, 1971), pp. 851–901 (pp. 864–871).
58 Schaufelberger, 'Spätmittelalter', pp. 348–358.

became a tributary protectorate of the Confederacy.[59] But the French King Louis XII was by no means inclined to accept the loss of a duchy to which he had declared hereditary claims. It seems as if immediate attempts to reconquer the territory were out of the question following France's bitter defeat. Instead, Louis used diplomatic channels to approach his former allies, turned enemies, in order to regain control over this rich and geopolitically vital duchy, requesting peace negotiations.

Hence, a phase of intensified diplomatic activity in the individual cantons and at the Federal Diet began. From July 1512 onwards, various dynasties offered to serve as mediators between the Confederacy and the French king. Pope Julius II, the greatest beneficiary of the summer of 1512, had no interest in such a development and sternly warned the Confederacy against taking up the offers of Savoy or Lorraine.[60] Outside of official communications, France paved the way for peace talks via informal channels in the hope of gaining access to the Swiss mercenary markets as soon as possible. This explosive political constellation initially required that France proceed covertly. In order to provide safe passage for a French legation, Simon de Courbouson, *Hofmeister* to Philiberta of Luxembourg, was sent as the representative of French interests. To distribute the French pensions, Courbouson relied on a network of various intermediaries in the cantons who had local connections, were familiar with the political situation, and knew who was worth investing in and who was not. In Bern, for example, the innkeeper and member of the *Grossrat* Michel Glaser served as a broker, secretly distributing 1,500 crowns (out of a total of 2,100 crowns) to over 160 individuals without instructions from France. He was rewarded for his risky services with 600 crowns of the French pension payments; 665 crowns went into the pockets of seventeen members of the *Kleinrat*. Thus, over half of the twenty-seven members of the *Kleinrat*, the city-state's most important political body, had secretly received French pensions from Glaser. The remaining money (835 crowns) was primarily distributed between members of the *Grossrat*, mercenary leaders, and guildsmen. The sum of 2,100 crowns was a substantial one – it was the equivalent of roughly half of Bern's state budget. Glaser performed these secret payments

---

59 Ernst Gagliardi, *Novara und Dijon: Höhepunkt und Verfall der schweizerischen Grossmacht im 16. Jahrhundert* (Zurich: Leemann, 1907), p. 19; Schaufelberger, 'Spätmittelalter', p. 353.
60 *Abschiede*, vol. 3.2, pp. 647, 651.

partly in person at his inn and partly via third parties. He received assistance from another member of the *Grossrat* and intermediaries in the town's guilds. In Zurich, on the other hand, a member of the *Kleinrat*, a knight, and a member of the Constaffel circle acted as brokers, secretly distributing French pensions (to the tune of 1,000 crowns) with the assistance of twelve sub-brokers to approximately eighty people, many of whom belonged to the diets and guild rooms that held great political influence in the city.[61] Hence, politics often took place outside of the diets intended for that purpose. Indeed, inns, for example, played an important role in the establishment of informal 'pension networks'. As observed by Simon Teuscher, in 'terms of its suitability as a place where political groups could form, the inn can well be termed the counterpart of the town hall, with partially complementary functions'.[62]

Split by political orientations, the urban inns were frequented by pro- or anti-French factions. Around 1500, the pope's supporters met in the Schlüssel tavern, whereas the clients of the French king met for their evening drinks in Gasthaus Sonne, run by the above-mentioned Glaser.[63] Despite the fact that the clients could not stipulate the size of their pensions themselves, the local connection of the pension business provided the elites with a lot of room for manoeuvre. The clamour for the favour of foreign potentates was not so much a matter of political loyalty; the authorities' actions were often

---

61 Rogger, *Geld*, pp. 209–232, 255–272. See also Gagliardi, *Novara und Dijon*, pp. 19–38; Teuscher, *Bekannte – Klienten – Verwandte*, pp. 147, 184, 196–197, 199; and Hans Braun, 'Heimliche Pensionen und verbotener Reislauf: Die Prozesse vom Sommer 1513 im Spiegel von Verhörprotokollen aus dem Berner Staatsarchiv', in *Personen der Geschichte – Geschichte der Personen. Studien zur Kreuzzugs-, Sozial- und Bildungsgeschichte: Festschrift für Rainer Christoph Schwinges zum 60. Geburtstag*, ed. by Christian Hesse, Beat Immenhauser, Oliver Landolt, and Barbara Studer (Basel: Schwabe, 2003), pp. 25–41.
62 Teuscher, *Bekannte – Klienten – Verwandte*, p. 200; see also Pfister, 'Politischer Klientelismus', pp. 32–39; Beat Kümin, *Drinking Matters: Public Houses and Social Exchange in Early Modern Central Europe* (Basingstoke: Palgrave Macmillan, 2007), pp. 83, 126, 130; and Philippe Rogger, 'Solvente Kriegsherren, vernetzte Wirte, empfängliche Politiker: Interessenpolitik auf den eidgenössischen Gewaltmärkten um 1500', *Lobbying: Die Vorräume der Macht*, ed. by Gisela Hürlimann, André Mach, Anja Rathmann-Lutz, and Janick Marina Schaufelbuehl, Schweizerisches Jahrbuch für Wirtschafts- und Sozialgeschichte 31 (Zurich: Chronos, 2016), 49–60 (pp. 54–57).
63 Teuscher, *Bekannte – Klienten – Verwandte*, p. 148.

dominated by self-serving motives. The lists of pensions documented in Swiss and foreign archives demonstrate that the diets maintained political contacts with several powers at the same time. Consequently, many Bernese clients were awarded pensions by more than one patron. Regardless of the provenance of these lists, be they from Milan, France, or the Holy Roman Empire, the same names are often encountered. These multiple loyalties on the part of the Confederacy's elites were clearly something their wealthy benefactors were prepared to overlook in the case of influential clients. For the Holy Roman Emperor, merely neutralizing or silencing a supporter of France could be a worthwhile investment.[64]

Such practices, only the subject of rumour, and the fact that France had secretly recruited Swiss mercenaries proved a severe test of political unity in the Confederacy.[65] The legitimacy of the great-power interests in the Confederacy's markets of violence was precarious, as the secret pensions represented more than a whiff of corruptibility and venality.[66] In the summer of 1513, there were violent protests against the pension system undertaken by subjects in the city cantons of Bern, Lucerne, Solothurn, and – two years after a similar incident related to the Battle of Marignano – in Zurich. In the course of these protests, some recipients of pensions were deposed, fined, or sentenced to hand over their French money to the city treasury. Pardons, however, were forthcoming as soon as the riots had ended. The receipt of private pensions was forbidden (with the exception of Solothurn), which had no effect on the clandestine continuation of this lucrative practice.[67] However, the Bernese subjects also demanded an institutionalized say concerning alliance policy. With the exception of Zurich, the cantons upheld the time-honoured rights of their subjects.[68] The real peak of the riots in Bern was the performance of the city's clerk, who took it upon himself to stand before the angry subjects and read out loud the names of everyone who had received secret payments from the French broker Michel Glaser (who was sentenced to death). By theatrically reading out the names and the sums of money they had received, the clerk turned the suspicions concerning individual members of the Diet that had been circulating prior to the riots into certainties. For the audience of rebelling subjects, the links between the Bernese elite

---

64 Rogger, *Geld*, pp. 142–151.
65 Braun, 'Heimliche Pensionen', pp. 29, 36–41.
66 Groebner, *Geschenke*, pp. 155–226.
67 Rogger, *Geld*, pp. 55–116.
68 *Ibid.*, pp. 106–112.

and the French king took on the character of a tight network of transnational connections.[69] The secret transactions were a cause of growing dissatisfaction among the subjects of the city state of Bern, partly because they had come to symbolize immoral politics and partly because they raised the question of who profited the most from the trade in mercenaries and pensions.[70] In Bern, for instance, the subjects, consulted by the authorities on important issues such as the formation of alliances, complained that, as captains, the city elites permanently led 'our flesh and blood' from the land.[71] The rural districts were thus confronted with an increased, uncontrolled exodus of men who were fit for work whenever war was brewing. Given the subjects' great enthusiasm for mercenary service in the early sixteenth century, it can be assumed that especially housefathers (i.e. the rural notables) in their role as farm owners or master craftsmen had a lot to lose financially from the uncontrolled military economic migration. The temporary absence, potential disabling, or death of a mercenary in Italy represented an economic burden for the running of a farm or a trade, quite apart from the emotional drama for his social sphere.[72] The social explosiveness of this setting becomes clear if we consider that only one in three returned unharmed from the battles of 1500.[73] Unlike the simple mercenaries who risked life and limb for uncertain pay in Italy, the city aldermen had nothing to fear in this regard. Far removed from the physical dangers of the battlefield, they determined the political framework of mercenary service and were rewarded with high pensions. The fact that private pensions were forbidden during the pension riots, and that demands were made in Bern in 1514 to the effect that if an alliance was formed part of the pensions should go to the subjects, suggests that the secret payments collided with the popular ideas of appropriate financial dealings – of a moral economy.[74]

---

69 Ibid., pp. 69, 215–232.
70 Groebner, *Geschenke*, p. 190.
71 Catherine Schorer, 'Berner Ämterbefragungen: Untertanenrepräsentation und -mentalität im ausgehenden Mittelalter', *Berner Zeitschrift für Geschichte und Heimatkunde* 51 (1989), 217–253 (p. 237).
72 Rogger, *Geld*, pp. 323–343.
73 Peyer, *Könige, Stadt und Kapital*, p. 221.
74 Schorer, 'Berner Ämterbefragungen', p. 233; see also Kälin, 'Salz, Sold und Pensionen', p. 115, and Daniel Schläppi, 'Das Staatswesen als kollektives Gut: Gemeinbesitz als Grundlage der politischen Kultur in der frühneuzeitlichen Eidgenossenschaft', *Historische Sozialforschung* 32 (2007), 169–202 (p. 179).

Pensions as promises: France's debt policy during the French Wars of Religion

In 1597, Renward Cysat, the Lucerne city clerk and an outstanding observer of the political situation of his time, wrote a commentary on the transformation in the Lucerne treasury over the course of the previous fourteen years.[75] His remarks in 1574 on the Confederacy's relations with France following the accession of King Henri III are particularly harsh. He accuses the latter of a general inability to keep order in his kingdom and in matters of war, while expressing unveiled criticism of the king's financial policy: where money should have been saved, it was wasted, and where it should have been invested, it was saved.[76] The Swiss also suffered from this policy (especially the Catholic cantons), Cysat asserts, since they always dependably supplied mercenary troops, who were now in a pitiful situation under Henri III. The king's ill-advised policy was not only due to his incompetence, Cysat claims, but was also a political strategy. He deliberately 'introduced all kinds of harmful innovation, discoveries and finances to the detriment of the Confederates'.[77] What is behind this accusation?

In the second half of the sixteenth century, the French crown was undoubtedly confronted by fundamental political challenges. At the same time, the financial situation was extremely tense. Military expenditure during the Wars of Religion caused huge deficits.[78] A debt of 101 million *livres* in 1576 had reached 133 million by 1588.[79] At the end of the century, the state budget was in a desolate state: 'The debts of nearly four decades of war meant that by 1598 the crown was in debt to the tune of 300 million *livres*'.[80] The

---

75 Renward Cysat, 'Über die Beziehungen der Schweiz zu Frankreich in der Zeit Heinrichs III.', ed. by Theodor von Liebenau, *Anzeiger für schweizerische Geschichte* new series 8 (1898–1901), 457–460; also see Fritz Glauser, 'Cysat, Renward', in *Historisches Lexikon der Schweiz*, www.hls-dhs-dss.ch/textes/d/D11751.php, accessed 6 September 2017.
76 '[W]here they should save they have spent, and where they should delve into their pockets they have saved'; Cysat, 'Über die Beziehungen', p. 458.
77 Cysat, 'Über die Beziehungen', 458.
78 James B. Wood, *The King's Army: Warfare, Soldiers, and Society during the Wars of Religion in France, 1562–1576* (Cambridge: Cambridge University Press, 1996), pp. 275–300; Arlette Jouanna, *La France du XVIe siècle, 1483–1598* (Paris: Presses Universitaires de France, 1996), pp. 566–568.
79 Jouanna, *La France du XVIe siècle*, p. 593.
80 Mack P. Holt, *The French Wars of Religion, 1562–1629*, 2nd ed. (Cambridge: Cambridge University Press, 2005; first published in 1995), p. 217.

Confederacy's allies were also affected by France's empty coffers; the annual costs of Swiss pensions amounted to 200,000 *livres* between around 1560 and 1574 – almost 4 per cent of the total royal army expenditure in peacetime.[81] And, although the Swiss mercenary contingent was better paid than the French soldiers and generally received preferential treatment, their demands during the Wars of Religion went unmet for months and years.[82] In 1570, for instance, the king owed the Pfyffer and Schiesser regiments alone 800,000 *livres*.[83] Indeed, the Swiss regiments were a comparatively large burden for the French budget. The monthly costs of a Swiss mercenary contingent with twenty companies, or six thousand men, stood at around 73,000 *livres*. A single ten-company regiment of French infantry cost only about 20,000 *livres* per month.[84] It is no surprise that the crown could only partially fulfil its obligations given the deficits that grew each year. Cysat reported that outstanding payments to Swiss creditors had reached such a high level under Henri III 'that they cannot be calculated or estimated'.[85] At the Federal Diet in late November 1586, the French debts, consisting of peace payments, pensions, loans, and payment of mercenaries, were declared to amount to 2.5 million crowns, including outstanding interest.[86] In the ensuing years, the figures grew from bad to worse. Around 1600, the outstanding peace payments, public and private pensions, mercenary arrears, loans, and interest are believed to have amounted to 36 million *livres*.[87] It is thus hardly surprising that the outstanding credits in France were permanently on the agenda when the Swiss delegates met.[88] This is well illustrated by the eleven years between 1575 and 1585. During this period, the congresses, which were sometimes divided by confession, tabled the subject of French

---

81 Wood, *The King's Army*, p. 282 (tab. 11.1).
82 *Ibid.*, pp. 235, 279.
83 Theodor Müller-Wolfer, 'Der Staatsmann Ludwig Pfyffer und die Hugenottenkriege', *Zeitschrift für Schweizerische Geschichte* 8 (1928), 1–63, 113–148, 241–320 (p. 15).
84 Wood, *The King's Army*, p. 283.
85 Cysat, 'Über die Beziehungen', 459.
86 *Abschiede*, vol. 4.2, p. 965.
87 Walter Schmid, *Der Beitritt Zürichs zum französischen Soldbündnis 1614* (Zurich: Gebr. Leemann & Co., 1943), p. 66 (and note 7); Allemann, 'Söldnerwerbungen', p. 111.
88 On the thematic activities of the Federal Diet in the spheres of foreign policy, the administration of the common bailiwicks and internal affairs, see Würgler, *Tagsatzung*, pp. 207–221.

debt around ninety times, as documented by the minutes of the Federal Diet.[89] These records concisely demonstrate the extent of the problem.[90] Yet it would be a mistake to believe that the diplomatic discord between the cantons and France began with the accession of Henri III in late May 1574, as might be inferred from the report of the Lucerne clerk. As a matter of fact, outstanding pensions and mercenary pay had been a bone of contention since the beginning of the Franco-Confederate alliances in the fifteenth century.[91] The problem of debts was already entrenched before Henri III and was thus mentioned immediately after he ascended to the throne, when the French ambassador appeared before the Federal Diet on 20 June 1574. After he had ended his address and handed over a letter from Catherine de Médicis (of 10 June) to the nine cantons allied with France, the response of these cantons expressed sorrow concerning the death of Charles IX and wished his successor Henri III good fortune. But they also did not miss the opportunity to inform the new king that they expected France to honour its promises regarding the pensions.[92] Just two months later, on 20 August 1574, the French ambassador called a conference of the Catholic cantons in which he related the king's regret that the Catholic cantons had been forced to endure so much stalling regarding pension payments and that some cantons consequently had supplied mercenaries to the king of Spain.[93] To avoid further excursions to other rulers, he would henceforth attempt to 'show his good intentions in every way and even surpass his predecessors in so doing'.[94] But, as Cysat correctly observed, French payment practices did not improve under the new king. As early as June 1575, the cantons allied with France complained

---

89 Between 1575 and 1585, the Swiss delegates met on average 25 times per year. The subject of payments is mentioned after the register entries and the list of departures in *Abschiede*, vol. 4.2. On the problem of the regests in the minutes of the Federal Diet, see Würgler, *Tagsatzung*, pp. 63–80, and Jucker, *Gesandte, Schreiber, Akten*, pp. 33–60.
90 See also Allemann, 'Söldnerwerbungen', pp. 107–122; Büsser, 'Militärunternehmertum', pp. 105–107; and Hitz, *Kämpfen um Sold*, pp. 199–211, 247–304.
91 On this point, see the indexes to the following volumes of *Abschiede*.
92 *Abschiede*, vol. 4.2, pp. 541–542. On the presence of the European powers at the Federal Diet and the significance of this institution for diplomacy, see Würgler, *Tagsatzung*, pp. 113–122, 150–160, 347–363.
93 *Abschiede*, vol. 4.2, pp. 548–549, 542.
94 *Ibid.*, vol. 4.2, p. 548.

to the ambassador about two lapsed pensions, and in 1579 the court was in arrears with four pensions.[95] Consequently, promises were made and deadlines were adhered to.[96] The ambassador was repeatedly asked to take the Swiss issues to the king (which he promised to do), to remind him of the outstanding mercenary payments and pensions, and to see that the money was received as soon as possible.[97] But it was of little use. The ambassador and other French representatives mostly endeavoured to apologize to the Swiss for outstanding payments, make uncertain agreements, gain their confidence and calm them down, or explain why the debts could not be paid this time.[98] In February 1580, for instance, the French ambassador appeared before the Federal Diet once again. His apologetic explanations for the failure to honour the pensions and other promises were not greeted with much sympathy, and the Diet's response was stern. No payments had been received for four years, neither pensions nor other debts. The interest was constantly growing. The Diet wished to know when the peace payments, pensions, etc. would be paid. The ambassador was left with few alternatives but to admit that the king was simply unable to raise such a large sum within a year. Nor was he able to specify a time when the payments would be made. Nevertheless, he promised that he would do everything he could about the matter.[99] It would appear that France proved either unable or unwilling to pay its growing debts, although it repeatedly made substantial partial payments.[100] Occasionally, the king felt the need to act in person and write a letter of apology.[101] The issue of debt sometimes became so urgent that special sessions of the Federal Diet took place.[102] And in order to increase pressure in the negotiations, the cantons repeatedly sought conflict with the king by sending letters containing direct demands – bypassing the ambassador – or, if all else failed, sending costly envoys to the Paris court.[103]

---

95 *Ibid.*, vol. 4.2, pp. 567, 688.
96 *Ibid.*, vol. 4.2, pp. 603, 652, 710–711, 721, 724, 732, 735, 737, 743, 745, 810.
97 *Ibid.*, vol. 4.2, pp. 548, 569–570, 574, 575, 581, 584, 590, 688, 904.
98 *Ibid.*, vol. 4.2, pp. 798, 849, 902, 904, 949–950, 959.
99 *Ibid.*, vol. 4.2, p. 707.
100 Müller-Wolfer, 'Der Staatsmann Ludwig Pfyffer', 15–16; Allemann, 'Söldnerwerbungen', p. 111.
101 *Abschiede*, vol. 4.2, p. 599.
102 *Ibid.*, vol. 4.2, pp. 710, 743, 756, 859.
103 *Ibid.*, vol. 4.2, pp. 613, 753–754, 952.

Despite these conflicts with France and Henri III over outstanding debts, it is remarkable that the Swiss exercised a certain measure of restraint and made the supply of mercenaries conditional upon partial payments and wages, but did not withdraw from the alliance owing to the arrears despite their threat to do so.[104] On the contrary, the alliance with Henri III was renewed with great ceremony in 1582. This is even more astonishing given that not only the king's debt but also his role in the conflict over Geneva, whose protection had been guaranteed between France, Bern, and Solothurn by the Treaty of Solothurn since 1579, had met with firm resistance in the Catholic cantons. This was due to the fact that when Duke Carlo Emanuele I of Savoy took over government affairs following the death of his father Emanuele Filiberto, there was a noticeable intensification of the conflict that had been smouldering between Savoy and Bern concerning the city on the Rhône. Carlo Emanuele left France and the Swiss in no doubt regarding his claim to the economically and politically important centre in the Lake Geneva basin. He was also prepared to use military means to get what he wanted. The Reformed city of Bern had a deep geopolitical interest in Geneva's independence under its own protection, as it served as a western gate to the Confederacy. The Catholic cantons, however, were prepared to offer military support (alliance with Savoy in 1577) if the duke attempted to conquer the site of Calvin's work. A few days after the alliance was ceremonially renewed in Paris on 2 December 1582, various representatives of the Catholic cantons tried to persuade the king himself to relinquish his erstwhile policy concerning Geneva. They demanded an immediate end to French protection for the city. Henri III rejected this demand, partly because Bern's return to the alliance was all but sealed at that point.[105] While the internal tensions between the Swiss confessional blocs intensified (with an alliance between Bern, Zurich, and Geneva in 1584, a special union of the Catholic cantons in the Golden Alliance in 1586), meanwhile the conflict with their French ally escalated when

---

104 *Ibid.*, vol. 4.2, pp. 588, 600, 719.
105 Peter Stadler, 'Das Zeitalter der Gegenreformation', in *Handbuch der Schweizer Geschichte*, vol. 1 (Zurich: Berichthaus, 1972), pp. 571–672 (pp. 593–595, 601–602); Peter Stadler, *Genf, die grossen Mächte und die eidgenössischen Glaubensparteien 1571–1584*, Zürcher Beiträge zur Geschichtswissenschaft, 15 (Affoltern am Albis: J. Weiss, 1952); Rindlisbacher, 'Zwischen Evangelium und Realpolitik', pp. 28–32; Müller-Wolfer, 'Der Staatsmann Ludwig Pfyffer', 46–56.

Catholic contingents fought for the Holy League against Henri III in 1585.[106] One might ask why the Catholic cantons did not split with France completely, at least after forming the Spanish mercenary alliance of 1587. It was not just for religious reasons that Spain was a reliable and potent military partner guaranteeing the Catholic special alliance of 1586; the alliance (excluding Solothurn) with King Felipe II also promised lucrative trade in mercenaries and pensions.[107] Quite apart from that, the Catholic cantons (excluding Solothurn) had maintained profitable business relations with Savoy in the military sphere since 1577.[108] Although there were prospects of at least partially compensating for leaving the alliance with France with Spanish and Savoy pensions, the outstanding credits prevented a break with France – on the contrary, they served to bind the cantons to Henri III. Hence, it is not too far-fetched to argue that the French policy of empty coffers was a useful tool for keeping the Swiss creditors close even during phases of political differences. Cysat, who as a committed Catholic reformer was critical of French policy anyway, appears to have seen through this logic. According to Cysat's report, the French ambassador from 1566 to 1571, Pomponne de Bellièvre, advised Henri III upon entering office to remain heavily in debt to the Swiss. This way, Cysat continued, Henri attempted to 'keep them on a string and in his grip, so if he wanted anything from them, he could force them to do his bidding with their own money, which he still owed them, however little money he had'.[109] Leaving the alliance would undoubtedly have meant losing the outstanding credits. And the Swiss creditors could not afford or indeed want

---

106 Stadler, 'Zeitalter', pp. 602–604; Müller-Wolfer, 'Der Staatsmann Ludwig Pfyffer', 114–128; Hitz, *Kämpfen um Sold*, p. 45; *Abschiede*, vol. 4.2, pp. 882–883, 885.
107 Bolzern, *Spanien*, pp. 109–188. The Spanish pensions were, in fact, never paid on time. No payments were made at all for some individual years after 1597. *Ibid.*, pp. 169–188.
108 See the mercenary alliance treaty of 1577 in *Abschiede*, vol. 4.2, pp. 1541–1551. The annual pensions of 300 gold guilders per canton, however, were considerably less than the French or Spanish pensions. *Ibid.*, p. 1550.
109 Cysat, 'Über die Beziehungen', 459. The same conclusion was drawn by the papal nuncio Ladislao d'Aquino (1546–1621) in his official report to Rome in 1612. See [Ladislao d'Aquino,] 'Die päpstliche Nuntiatur in der Schweiz 1612: Information des Cardinals d'Aquino für seinen Amtsnachfolger. Uebersetzt von Prof. Jak. Burkhardt', *Taschenbuch für Geschichte und Alterthum in Süddeutschland* 5 (1846), 223–256 (p. 242).

that, despite the significant differences between the two parties. By remaining loyal to the alliance, they kept alive the chance of one day being paid. In this respect, one might conclude that pensions were an extremely effective instrument of power; withholding payment enabled Henri III to consolidate his position. France's high mercenary and pension debts thus did not have the centrifugal effect one might assume because of the diplomatic tensions they caused; rather, the faltering payments played a large role in stabilizing Franco-Swiss relations in the long term.

Conclusion

This assessment takes us back to our initial thesis that pensions implied asymmetrical political relations between the Confederacy and its allies. Both conflicts outlined above, brought about by transnational patronage practices and a policy of empty coffers, would seem to support this theory. There was significant dependence on France as a patron power with respect to both private and public pensions. The above-mentioned conflicts concerning the distribution of funds around 1500 document the growing political importance of external involvement and the resources thereby negotiated. They make it clear that the elites with informal connections to France benefited personally from foreign-policy relations. Pensions, captain's ranks, titles, and other patronage resources were fundamental to the accumulation of political power of the ruling elites. The reciprocity of the ruling class's transnational connections and the formation of elites is quite evident.[110] Foreign involvement was thus something of an obligation which no political actor could avoid. However, relations with the French king were of a clientelist nature, meaning that the exchange of resources took place between a socioeconomically superior patron and a client of lower status. The patron's dominant position can be explained, among other things, by the exclusivity of the goods at his disposal and the opportunity to replace his client with another at any time. The patron had his Swiss clients more or less in his pocket.

Similarly, the significance of public pensions for the state treasuries meant that ending the alliance with France was not a realistic option for the cantons of the old Swiss Confederacy, as pensions were not legally recoverable – their payment or non-payment was solely at

---

110 See Windler, '"Ohne Geld keine Schweizer"', pp. 126–133.

the discretion of the French king. The fact that they never received the full amount they were owed meant that the relationship with France could not be terminated.[111] The picture of pensions painted by the treaties as a sign of royal affection, and the equality suggested by the friendly rhetoric of the military alliances, thus constituted an unconvincing attempt to conceal the asymmetry in Franco-Swiss political relations.

---

111 See the general reflections on the economy of social relationships in *Die Ökonomie sozialer Beziehungen: Ressourcenbewirtschaftung als Geben, Nehmen, Investieren, Verschwenden, Haushalten, Horten, Vererben, Schulden*, ed. by Gabriele Jancke and Daniel Schläppi (Stuttgart: Franz Steiner Verlag, 2015).

7
Subsidy treaties in early modern times: the example of the German principality of Waldeck

Andreas Flurschütz da Cruz

Subsidy treaties: definitions and contents

During the early modern period, German princes collectively received more subsidies for their troops than any other single state received at the same time.[1] But of course there were variations over time, as well as variations between the German princes, who were not the only players in this business: there were also other states in Europe on the receiving end, such as Denmark and Savoy. This chapter deals with one of the smallest among them, the German principality of Waldeck.

The present discussion focuses on troop-leasing contracts as a specific form of subsidy treaty. It seeks to identify the key players and their motives for either hiring or leasing large contingents of soldiers, often entire regiments, from/to other states (the second section of the chapter). Focusing on the case of the German principality of Waldeck (the third section), it sets out to exemplify the assumptions presented in the second section. The concluding section intends to clarify whether the frequently criticized 'soldier trade' ('Soldatenhandel') between German princes and foreign powers was just a way for lower-ranking rulers to make money or whether these projects had other aims as well.[2]

---

1 Peter Keir Taylor, *The Household's Most Expendable People: The Draft and Peasant Society in 18th Century Hessen-Kassel* (Ann Arbor: Michigan University, 1987), p. 56.
2 Friedrich Kapp, *Der Soldatenhandel deutscher Fürsten nach Amerika (1775–1783)* (Berlin: Verlag von Franz Duncker, 1864. Reprint Munich 1986).

It is possible to adapt the example of Waldeck to older scholarship, showing that renting out soldiers was not just an instrument for making money but that it could be a quite expensive activity, even for the receiver of subsidies. Furthermore, it shows that not only large German territories like Prussia and Hanover took part in the business but also, sooner or later, nearly every German prince. The chapter suggests that other forms of 'profit', such as international relations and contacts, sometimes even linked to dynastic benefits, could be much more important for the smaller German princes than for the major ones, as the former had to take active measures to be recognized in Europe's early modern community of states.

Royal subsidizers and princely German troop providers

Taking a closer look at the two parties involved in subsidy treaties allows us to identify interesting similarities, both on the side of the subsidizing states and on that of the subsidized territories which provided mercenary troops and their princes. On the side of the powers that paid subsidies, we find governments paying huge amounts of money in order to hire troops from their allies.[3] A major player was England/Great Britain,[4] which was dynastically and religiously linked to the Netherlands from the final third of the seventeenth century onwards. After setting aside their commercial rivalries, which had caused three Anglo-Dutch wars between 1652 and 1674, these two powers co-financed a considerable number of subsidy projects with minor German princes. A third important actor in this field of international military relations was the *Serenissima*, the Republic of Venice. From 1645 until 1719, it was a major subsidizer of a number of German princes, hiring their armies for defending its lands in the eastern Mediterranean against Ottoman forces – a giant military subsidy project, which, in the end, proved unsuccessful.[5]

---

3 For example, Peter Taylor counted 22 million florins paid as subsidies by different countries to Hesse-Cassel between 1677 and 1815 for the raising and renting out of more or less 238,400 soldiers: *The Household's Most Expendable People*, p. 56.

4 Dwyryd Wyn Jones, *War and Economy in the Age of William III and Marlborough* (Oxford: Basil Blackwell, 1988); John Brewer, *The Sinews of Power: War, Money and the English State, 1688–1783* (New York: Alfred A. Knopf, 1989).

5 Venice, Archivio di Stato di Venezia (ASVe), Senato, Deliberazioni, Corti, Registri, 63, and other holdings; Benjamin Arbel, 'Venice's Maritime Empire in the Early Modern Period', in *A Companion to Venetian History, 1400–1797*,

Those three powers are politically characterized by their corporate structure and mixed monarchical or republican constitution. Their oligarchic regimes favoured a 'classical republican' ideology, according to which standing armies were regarded as harmful to the preservation of political liberty. England had already experienced a lapse into military dictatorship when Oliver Cromwell took charge of the troops to usurp the rule of Britain in 1653.[6] Regarding the political organization of those states, one may find clear resemblances in their military needs and political priorities. Great Britain became known as the guarantor of the balance of powers in Europe in the eighteenth century, whereas Venice and the Dutch Republic arguably pursued similar interests, at least on a regional scale. While Venice sought to halt the expansion of the Ottoman Empire, the Netherlands had to defend itself against the hegemonic ambitions of France.

On the other side, we find those rulers who lent their troops to these limited monarchies and republics. Most of them were princes of the Holy Roman Empire and were traditionally, or had recently become, 'armed states'. This status had many advantages in the seventeenth-century Holy Roman Empire, as the emperor in his wars against the France of Louis XIV imposed a heavy burden on unarmed princes by quartering his and his allies' troops on their land. For a German ruler, the maintenance of the troops of other princes was quite expensive but entailed neither glory nor honour. While the leaders of great battles were usually promoted and rewarded with titles and goods – most famous amongst them were Albrecht von Wallenstein and Prince Eugene of Savoy – nobody remembered those who became poor by quartering the troops of other powers. Hence, being an unarmed principality became decidedly unattractive at least by the time of the French wars between 1667 and 1697.

Nevertheless, there were enormous advantages involved in outsourcing the costs of large numbers of troops by providing them

---

ed. by Eric R. Dursteler (Leiden and Boston: Brill, 2014), pp. 125–253 (p. 203); Guido Amoretti, *La Serenissima Repubblica in Grecia: XII–XVIII secolo. Dalle tavole del Capitano Antonio Paravia e dagli archivi di Venezia* (Turin: Omega Edizioni, 2006); Stephan Karl Sander-Faes, 'Die Soldaten der Serenissima: Militär und Mobilität im frühneuzeitlichen Stato da mar', in *Militärische Migration vom Altertum bis zur Gegenwart* (Paderborn: Studien zur Historischen Migrationsforschung, vol. 30, 2016), pp. 111–126.

6 Wolfgang Reinhard, 'Staat und Heer in England im Zeitalter der Revolutionen', in *Staatsverfassung und Heeresverfassung in der europäischen Geschichte der frühen Neuzeit*, ed. by Johannes Kunisch and Barbara Stollberg-Rilinger (Berlin: Historische Forschungen, vol. 28, 1986), pp. 173–212.

to foreign kings. The most obvious motive was money. German princes seeking to circumvent the budgetary approval of their estates, above all on military investments, urgently needed money. Foreign subsidy payments for rented troops enabled the prince to become more independent of his estates (*Landstände*), who at the same time tried to limit princely power and extend their influence over public decisions. However, recent research has shown that, for seventeenth- and eighteenth-century princely war entrepreneurs, the financial motivation for leasing their armies to other powers might have been overestimated. Providing large numbers of equipped soldiers was not only lucrative but also entailed financial obligations,[7] and no one could be sure if the payments agreed upon by the contracting parties in the subsidy treaties would actually materialize. At least initially, the raising and provisioning of armies was a losing business. In 1702, Landgrave Carl of Hesse-Cassel (1654–1730) insisted on an advance payment of at least half of the contracted sum of a total of 400,000 florins to raise six thousand soldiers for the English king and the Dutch Republic, because of 'the high expenditure the troops' raising had already caused him'.[8] Sometimes, expenses for levy and equipment eventually exceeded the income that the contracting parties had agreed upon, and additional money had to be raised to fill the gap.[9] A Waldeckian officer ensured the States-General in 1767 that the Prince of Waldeck had incurred a loss from the last treaty and that he had to add 16,000 florins each year to the expenses for the troops instead of becoming rich by renting them out.[10] Often, such losses even resulted in legal proceedings related to the amount and terms of the payments.

---

7 Peter H. Wilson, 'The German "Soldier Trade" of the Seventeenth and Eighteenth Centuries: A Reassessment', *The International History Review* XVIII.4 (1996), 757–792 (p. 758); Johannes Burkhardt, 'Vollendung und Neuorientierung des frühmodernen Reiches 1648–1763', in *Gebhardt Handbuch der deutschen Geschichte*, vol. 11 (Stuttgart: Klett-Cotta, 2006), p. 135.
8 Marburg, Staatsarchiv Marburg (HStAM), 4 h, no. 3975, instruction Kassel 1702, 26 March. Copy of the subsidy treaty in HStAM, 118 a, no. 652: 'les grosses depenses que ce Corps Luy a deyá coûté à mettre sur pied'. All translations are by the author unless otherwise stated.
9 HStAM, 118 a, 967 I, fols 15r–16r.
10 HStAM, 118 a, no. 665/17, H.C. von Kalm to the States General, The Hague, 14 August 1767: 'daß der Fürst aljährl. 16000 fl. zugeschoßen, welches ich allein in der Absicht anführe, daß er sich damit nicht bereichert, sondern vielmehr persöhnlichen Verlust gehabt'.

Prestige and other advantages that came along with these interstate contracts may have been far more important than money.[11] In spite of the mostly unequal relations between the money-offering (subsidizer) and the troop-providing (subsidy recipient) partner, the agreements resulted in interdependencies: the party offering money did so because it lacked sufficient troops and needed to acquire the military force necessary to participate in certain conflicts. The soldier-providing 'client', on the other hand, depended on the financial resources of his 'patron' to maintain his standing army and increase his independence of the estates of his territory. As a result of those circumstances, even 'a relatively insignificant prince of the empire' could become 'the ally of the principal powers of the world'.[12]

German sovereigns held a princely but by no means a royal standing. When Elizabeth Stuart prepared to get married to Elector-Palatine Friedrich V in 1613, there were great doubts regarding the spouse's status. After the Thirty Years' War, the German dynasties sought to make their princely rank unambiguous.[13] Therefore, their apparent main task regarding the military subsidy projects was simply to 'get in touch' with foreign rulers, whatever the cost might be, and regardless of whether the contracts they entered into would bear fruit or even cause debts. In spite of its asymmetry, striking a deal with a foreign power laid the foundation for a partnership, and the ruler's partner also got some of the former's prestige out of it. In fact, during the early modern period, some of the most important German princes providing troops to foreign governments managed to achieve royal dignity and European thrones for themselves, such as the dukes of Brunswick/Hanover in Great Britain (1714–1901) and the electors of Saxony in Poland (1697–1763). The example

---

11 Johannes Kunisch, 'La guerre – c'est moi! Zum Problem der Staatenkonflikte im Zeitalter des Absolutismus', in *Fürst – Gesellschaft – Krieg: Studien zur bellizistischen Disposition des absoluten Fürstenstaates*, ed. by Johannes Kunisch (Cologne: Böhlau, 1992), pp. 1–41.

12 Carl Brinkmann, 'Charles II and the Bishop of Münster in the Anglo-Dutch War of 1665-6', *The English Historical Review* 21 (1906), 686–698 (p. 686); cf. Tilman Haug, Nadir Weber, and Christian Windler, 'Einleitung', in *Protegierte und Protektoren: Asymmetrische politische Beziehungen zwischen Partnerschaft und Dominanz (16. bis frühes 20. Jahrhundert)*, ed. by Tilman Haug, Nadir Weber, and Christian Windler (Cologne: Böhlau, 2016), pp. 9–27.

13 Cf. Barbara Stollberg-Rilinger, *Des Kaisers alte Kleider: Verfassungsgeschichte und Symbolsprache des Alten Reiches* (Munich: C.H. Beck, 2008), p. 150.

of the Landgrave of Hesse-Cassel is also interesting: through being a subsidy receiver, he had risen to become sufficiently important to be a consort of a Swedish princess and, in a second step, to reach the Swedish throne (1720–1751). Thus, military subsidy treaties could be coupled with inter-dynastic marriage projects.[14] Even though not every troop-providing German prince was rewarded with a European crown, dealing with foreign rulers seemed a promising strategy to stabilize one's position within the German and European noble hierarchy and lay the foundations for the international career of this prince and his lineage. The German principality of Waldeck is a good example with regard to proving this thesis.

Waldeck: the princely tradition of military entrepreneurship

Early international military projects (seventeenth century)

Although German princes and nobles were engaged in subsidy treaties before 1648, the Peace of Westphalia, which specified the *ius armorum* and the *ius foederis* as landmarks of sovereignty, redefined the legal position of German princes: they were enabled to negotiate and form alliances with foreign powers – as long as these did not turn against the empire itself – and became subjects of international law.[15] The princes of Waldeck had played an important role in the arena of

---

14 Philip Haas, *Fürstenehe und Interessen: Die dynastische Ehe der Frühen Neuzeit in zeitgenössischer Traktatliteratur und politischer Praxis am Beispiel Hessen-Kassels* (Darmstadt and Marburg: Quellen und Forschungen zur Hessischen Geschichte, 177, 2017), pp. 53–56.

15 Heinz Schilling, *Höfe und Allianzen: Deutschland 1648–1763*, Das Reich und die Deutschen, 5 (Berlin: Siedler, 1989), p. 32; Ronald G. Asch, 'The *ius foederis* Re-examined: The Peace of Westphalia and the Constitution of the Holy Roman Empire', in *Peace Treaties and International Law in European History: From the Late Middle Ages to World War One*, ed. by Randall Lesaffer (Cambridge: Cambridge University Press, 2004), pp. 319–337; Karl Otmar von Aretin, *Das Alte Reich 1648–1806, vol. 1: Föderalistische oder hierarchische Ordnung (1648–1684)* (Stuttgart: Klett-Cotta, 1993), p. 19; Ernst-Wolfgang Böckenförde, 'Der Westfälische Frieden und das Bündnisrecht der Reichsstände', *Der Staat* 8.4 (1969), 449–478; Heinhard Steiger, 'Die Träger des ius belli ac pacis 1648–1806', in *Staat und Krieg: Vom Mittelalter bis zur Moderne*, ed. by Werner Rösener (Göttingen: Vandenhoeck & Ruprecht, 2000), pp. 115–135; Kyle M. Ballard, 'The Privatization of Military Affairs: A Historical Look into the Evolution of the Private Military Industry', in *Private Military and Security Companies: Chances, Problems, Pitfalls and*

interstate military collaborations ever since subsidy treaties became a relevant instrument of co-operation between European countries. Count Josias II of Waldeck (1636–1669) was a central figure in the final phase of the war of the Republic of Venice against the Ottomans between 1645 and 1669. As the archives of Waldeck have been only partially inventoried and the existing Venetian material mentions him only briefly, we do not know very much about the actual dimensions and background of his commitment to sending troops to Venice. Together with various members of the noble family von Degenfeld, he seems to have been one of the first German noblemen to raise troops and lease them to a foreign power.[16] He was no ruling prince, however, and his conscriptions apparently did not have a specific political motivation, instead being a vehicle to get him personally into Venetian service, which subsequently became a family tradition: when his nephew, Count Heinrich Wolrad of Waldeck (1665–1688), died at Negroponte in 1688, the *Serenissima* immediately turned to the brothers and cousins of the deceased to nominate a successor from their ranks to continue the 'condotta'; in other words, to continue recruiting troops for the Republic.[17] The candidate who was finally selected for the task was Heinrich Wolrad's younger brother, Count Carl (1672–1694). For the extremely young nobleman, the Venetian employment clearly served to lay the groundwork for his military career and improve his position within the aristocratic hierarchy of the empire; that is, 'to qualify himself so much the better'.[18] The House of Waldeck supplied the Republic of Venice with troops until the Peace of Passarowitz in 1718, which marked the end of the Ottoman conflict.[19] It used these

---

Prospects, ed. by Thomas Jäger and Gerhard Kümmel (Wiesbaden: VS Verlag für Sozialwissenschaften, 2007), pp. 37–53 (p. 38); Bernhard R. Kroener, 'Kriegswesen, Herrschaft und Gesellschaft 1300–1800', *Enzyklopädie Deutscher Geschichte*, 92 (Munich: Oldenbourg, 2013), pp. 38–39.

16 ASVe, Senato, Deliberazioni, Mar, Registri, 135.
17 HStAM, 117, no. 1329, Venice 1688, 26 November.
18 HStAM, 117, no. 1329, Venice 1689, 21 January: 'damit Er sich desto beßer qualificiren könne'.
19 A copy of the peace treaty can be found in: Deputazione Veneta di Storia Patria (ed.), *I Libri Commemorali della Repubblica di Venezia, Regesti vol. VIII* (Monumenti Storici, Serie Prima, Documenti, vol. XVII), Venice, 1914, pp. 125–127; cf. also Egidio Ivetic, 'The Peace of Passarowitz in Venice's Balkan Policy', in *The Peace of Passarowitz, 1718*, ed. by Charles Ingrao, Nikola Samardžić, and Jovan Pešalj (West Lafayette, IN: Purdue University Press, 2008), pp. 63–72.

military contracts mainly to establish its first-born sons as military commanders within the ranks of international aristocratic society.[20] Several other German territories, such as Brunswick, Limpurg, the Elector of Saxony from the Albertine branch of the house of Wettin, and even some of the smaller Ernestine Saxon territories, imitated Waldeck's subsidy strategy with varying degrees of success.[21]

Brokering subsidy treaties: negotiations with the Netherlands and Great Britain

Count Georg Friedrich von Waldeck (1620–1692), a cousin of Josias, Heinrich Wolrad, and Carl, was promoted to Prince of the Empire by Emperor Leopold I in 1682 as a reward for his military success.[22] He was the one who had arranged the first among many subsidy agreements with the Republic of the Netherlands for his patron and feudal lord, Landgrave Carl of Hesse-Cassel,[23] and he may also have initiated a treaty for his own principality: in 1688, Georg Friedrich and William of Orange hammered out a plan to place 'the Venetian regiments' into the service of the latter once they returned from the Levant.[24] This project probably concerned Waldeckian troops. William needed large numbers of soldiers in the Dutch Republic's conflict with France, and he had the necessary funds at his disposal to afford them. Georg Friedrich was an influential counsellor in Cassel, as well as at the courts of Vienna and The

---

20 HStAM, 118 a, no. 1054.
21 ASVe, Senato, Deliberazioni, Mar, Registri, 153 and 154; Collegio, Lettere Principi, 7; Oliver Heyn, *Das Militär des Fürstentums Sachsen-Hildburghausen 1680–1806* (Veröffentlichungen der Historischen Kommission für Thüringen, Kleine Reihe, vol. 47) (Cologne: Böhlau, 2015), p. 135; Bastian Hallbauer and Jan Schlürmann, 'Das schleswig-holsteinisch-gottorfische Militär 1623–1773', in *Handbuch zur Nordelbischen Militärgeschichte: Heere und Kriege in Schleswig, Holstein, Lauenburg, Eutin und Lübeck, 1623–1863/67*, ed. by Eva Susanne Fiebig and Jan Schlürmann (Husum: Husum Druck- und Verlagsgesellschaft, 2010), pp. 61–92; Andrea Thiele, 'The Prince as Military Entrepreneur? Why Smaller Saxon Territories Sent "Holländische Regimenter" (Dutch Regiments) to the Dutch Republic', in *War, Entrepreneurs, and the State in Europe and the Mediterranean, 1300–1800*, ed. by Jeff Fynn-Paul (Leiden and Boston: Brill, 2014), pp. 170–192.
22 On him and his career, see Gerhard Menk, *Georg Friedrich von Waldeck (1620–1692): Eine biographische Skizze*, Waldeckische Historische Hefte, 3 (Arolsen: Waldeckischer Geschichtsverein, 1992).
23 HStAM. 117, no. 1358, Kassel, 17 September 1688.
24 HStAM, 117, no. 1346, 1688.

Hague; and he laid the foundations for continuous military co-operation between the Landgraves and Waldeck, on the one hand, and the Netherlands, on the other, which for many decades also included Great Britain.

Given his role as middleman for Hesse-Cassel, Georg Friedrich can thus be seen as a broker of military subsidy treaties. Moreover, he arranged such contracts not only for his own house and the Hessian Landgrave but also for other sovereigns of the empire. In 1688, for example, he assisted the duke of Württemberg with his treaty with Willem III of Orange.[25] Soon, Duke Friedrich Carl hired the first thousand cavalry soldiers. This marked the beginning of another German prince's long-lasting military co-operation not only with the Netherlands, but with various foreign rulers.[26] In the same year, which seems to have played a crucial role in the history of this subject, several thousand soldiers from Brandenburg regiments also entered Willem's (William's) service.[27]

When Waldeck signed its first own major troop agreement with the British King George II (r. 1727–1760) in 1742,[28] the principality had already established a tradition of military interstate co-operation. Since 1614, Waldeck had been linked by feudal ties to the dukes of Brunswick-Lüneburg, who became Electors of Hanover in 1692 and occupied the British throne after 1714.[29] The regiments provided to the British had, as a matter of fact, not been created specifically for this purpose, at least not all of them. In fact, the Waldeckian

---

25 HStAM, 117, no. 1440, Stuttgart, 28 March 1688.
26 ASVe, Senato, Deliberazioni, Mar, Registri, 154; Peter H. Wilson, *War, State and Society in Württemberg, 1677–1793* (Cambridge: Cambridge University Press, 1995), p. 91. At the same time, 1688, Württemberg started another military project together with Venice: Rudolf von Andler, 'Die württembergischen Regimenter in Griechenland 1687–89', *Württembergische Vierteljahreshefte für Landesgeschichte* new series 31 (1922–1924), 217–279; John Childs, *Armies and Warfare in Europe, 1648–1789* (Manchester: Manchester University Press, 1982), pp. 47–48.
27 HStAM, 117, no. 1459, 1688.
28 HStAM, 118 a, no. 729; Benno von Canstein, *Der Waldeckisch-Englische Subsidienvertrag von 1776 – Zustandekommen, Ausgestaltung und Erfüllung: Eine rechtsgeschichtliche Untersuchung zur Darstellung von Rechts- und Verwaltungspraxis in einem deutschen Territorialstaate des ausgehenden 18. Jahrhunderts unter besonderer Berücksichtigung wehrrechtlicher Aspekte* (Cologne: Universität zu Köln, 1987).
29 HStAM, 118 a, no. 1196; Johann Jacob Moser, *Einleitung in das Chur=Fürst=und Herzoglich Braunschweig=Lüneburgische Staats=Recht* (Frankfurt and Leipzig, 1755), p. 673.

regiments, which comprised approximately two thousand recruits, had already existed for decades, serving such different powers as Venice (1716–1718) and the Holy Roman Emperor (1740).[30] On April 20, 1776, Prince Friedrich Carl August von Waldeck (1743–1812) signed a subsidy treaty with Great Britain in which he agreed to send 660 infantrymen to America.[31] Waldeck was one of seven German territories to support the British in the American War of Independence by sending troops to their rebellious North American colonies: the others were Anhalt-Zerbst, Ansbach-Bayreuth,[32] and the Wolfenbüttel and Lüneburg branches of Brunswick, as well as Hesse-Cassel[33] and Hesse-Hanau.

Finances, patronage, networking, and international prestige

Three-quarters of the money paid by Great Britain to Waldeck served to cover the costs for the troops; the actual 'subsidy' for the private use of the Prince of Waldeck came only to a quarter of the payments (approximately £6,000 a year).[34] This sum was paid from 1776 to 1784 and amounted to a total of £52,146 – a tiny sum in comparison with Waldeck's debts, which reached several million florins in this period.[35] The subsidies thus brought a slight relief to the disastrous financial situation of the principality but did not solve the problem at all.

These figures show that money was neither the only nor the main consideration for the princes of Waldeck when it came to supporting

---

30 HStAM, 118 a, no. 1054 and 1102.
31 HStAM, 118 a, no. 949.
32 Erhard Städtler, *Die Ansbach-Bayreuther Truppen im Amerikanischen Unabhängigkeitskrieg 1777–1783: Forschungen zur Kulturgeschichte und Familienkunde* (Nuremberg: 1956).
33 *Die 'Hessians' im Amerikanischen Unabhängigkeitskrieg (1776–1783): Neue Quellen, neue Medien, neue Forschungen*, Veröffentlichungen der Historischen Kommission für Hessen, 80, ed. by Holger Th. Gräf, Andreas Hedwig, and Annegret Wenz-Haubfleisch (Marburg: Historische Kommission für Hessen, 2014); Holger Th. Gräf, 'Die "Fremden Dienste" in der Landgrafschaft Hessen-Kassel (1677–1815): Ein Beispiel militärischer Unternehmertätigkeit eines Reichsfürsten', in *Schweizer Solddienst: Neue Arbeiten. Neue Aspekte. Service Étranger Suisse. Nouvelles Études. Nouveaux Aspects*, ed. by Rudolf Jaun, Pierre Streit, and Hervé de Weck (Birmensdorf: Schweizerische Vereinigung für Militärgeschichte und Militärwissenschaft, 2010), pp. 83–103.
34 HStAM, 118 a, no. 966 and no 949, subsidy treaty 20 April 1776, §13.
35 HStAM, 118 a, no. 967 I, fols 32v–33r.

their foreign allies with troops for decades or even centuries, although the pecuniary element seems to have become more important in the second half of the eighteenth century.[36] Of particular relevance, though, were the additional possibilities offered by the treaties in a society fundamentally based on a system of patron–client relationships.[37] The subsidy business was a 'machine of patronage' pointing in several directions: it served as a vehicle for the princes of the empire not only to join the retinue of foreign rulers but also to build up (or expand) their own clientele by promoting and benefiting favoured courtiers applying for positions in the military hierarchy of Waldeckian regiments. A large number of such requests have been preserved.[38] The military projects did not just help the princes define and improve their standing within imperial and international aristocratic society; they also represented an opportunity to get in touch with their own peer group. When the Prince of Waldeck signed the American contract with the British king in 1776, he knew right from the beginning that it would not be possible to recruit enough men from his own principality. Immediately, Prince Friedrich Carl August sent confidential letters to the other princely houses in the region to ask them for permission to recruit soldiers in their countries. As a next step, he presented his request to the Free Imperial Cities of the empire to fulfil his obligations to the British.[39] Several nobles rejected his request as they themselves had similar projects in mind and as their countries were already full of recruiting officers from different nations. Others accepted the request and hoped to profit from the agreements.[40] Military projects thus generated a significant job market involving different social layers among the population.[41]

---

36 HStAM, 118 a, no. 665.
37 Heiko Droste, 'Patronage in der Frühen Neuzeit – Institution und Kulturform', *Zeitschrift für Historische Forschung* 30 (2003), 555–590; Birgit Emich, 'Staatsbildung und Klientel – politische Integration und Patronage in der Frühen Neuzeit', in *Integration. Legitimation. Korruption: Politische Patronage in Früher Neuzeit und Moderne*, ed. by Ronald G. Asch, Birgit Emich, and Jens Ivo Engels (Frankfurt am Main: Peter Lang, 2011), pp. 33–49.
38 HStAM, 118 a, no. 721.
39 HStAM, 118 a, no. 1009.
40 HStAM, 118 a, no. 1013.
41 Matthias Asche, 'Krieg, Militär und Migration in der Frühen Neuzeit: Einleitende Beobachtungen zum Verhältnis von horizontaler und vertikaler Mobilität in der kriegsgeprägten Gesellschaft Alteuropas im 17. Jahrhundert', in *Krieg, Militär und Migration in der Frühen Neuzeit*, ed. by Matthias

Not only lords but also civil servants, who functioned as intermediaries and providers of goods, money, contacts, and favours, could make their fortune within the machinery of subsidies.[42] The Waldeckian Secret Secretary August (von) Frensdorff, for example, seems to have been one of the chief architects of the 1776 treaty, while the diplomat Ludwig von Thun took care of the prince's affairs and interests in The Hague. Both were specialists, and their importance can hardly be overestimated. When Thun, who had been in charge of the Prince of Waldeck's negotiations with the Netherlands since 1742, died in 1752, his wife took over this task for the next two decades before passing it on to her nephew – a very interesting case demonstrating the relevance of women in this business, a topic which merits further investigation in its turn.[43] The business thus remained within this 'civil-servant dynasty' for at least sixty-two years (1742–1804).

Another crucial position was that of the commissioners and 'solliciteurs-militairs', who were in charge of the financial dealings linked to carrying out the terms of the treaties. They arranged transfers from the tax receivers to the soldiers. Especially Jewish court factors and military contractors, like the brothers Jacob and Philip Marc, who had significant financial scope and credit, played an important role in this field, as they were part of far-flung international financial and economic networks.[44]

Asche, Michael Herrmann, Ulrike Ludwig, and Anton Schindling, Herrschaft und soziale Systeme in der Frühen Neuzeit vol. 9 (Berlin: Lit, 2008), pp. 11–36 (p. 14).

42 Marika Keblusek, 'Introduction: Profiling the Early Modern Agent', in *Your Humble Servant: Agents in Early Modern Europe*, ed. by Hans Cools, Marika Keblusek, and Badeloch Noldus (Hilversum: Uitgeverij Verloren, 2006), pp. 9–15.

43 HStAM, 118 a, no. 900; cf. Nathalie Büsser, 'Die "Frau Hauptmann" als Schaltstelle für Rekrutenwerbungen, Geldtransfer und Informationsaustausch: Geschäftliche Tätigkeiten weiblicher Angehöriger der Zuger Zurlauben im familieneigenen Solddienstunternehmen um 1700', in *Schweizer Solddienst*, ed. by Rudolf Jaun, Pierre Streit, and Hervé de Weck, pp. 105–114; John A. Lynn, *Women, Armies, and Warfare in Early Modern Europe* (Cambridge: Cambridge University Press, 2008).

44 HStAM, 118 a, nos 948, 981 and 993–995; Mark Häberlein and Michaela Schmölz-Häberlein, 'Revolutionäre Aussichten: Die transatlantischen Aktivitäten der Gebrüder Mark im Zeitalter der Amerikanischen Revolution', *Jahrbuch für Europäische Überseegeschichte* 15 (2015), 29–90. Cf. Pepijn Brandon, 'Finding Solid Ground for Soldiers' Payment: "Military soliciting" as Brokerage Practice in the Dutch Republic (c. 1600–1795)', in *The*

At the same time, the princes often took a personal interest in the negotiation of subsidy treaties and regarded them as an appropriate medium for entering into discussions with their peers. The Stadholder of the United Provinces, Willem IV, himself wrote to the Prince of Waldeck in 1749 to negotiate the future employment of the latter's troops.[45] In 1756, Willem's widow consulted with her so-called 'cousin' Friedrich Carl August regarding this question and even smoothed the way for his negotiations with the States-General.[46] In 1776, King George III personally thanked his Waldeckian 'cousin' for his troop offer;[47] and as late as 1806, when the future of the Waldeckian regiments in Dutch service was anything but certain, Friedrich Carl August sent a handwritten letter to King Louis of Holland (1778–1846, r. 1806–1810), one of Napoléon's brothers, to entrust the matter to him.[48]

Military subsidy projects: a key instrument of early modern state and dynastic politics?

Subsidy treaties faced public followed by legal opposition more or less simultaneously with the end of the Holy Roman Empire. The forced recruitment of soldiers in many German territories for foreign military service drew increasing criticism from proponents of the Enlightenment; and several disastrous subsidy projects discredited the practice, which was outlawed at the Congress of Vienna in 1814.[49] The military arrangements between German princes and

---

Spending of States: Military Expenditure during the Long Eighteenth Century: Patterns, Organisation, and Consequences, 1650–1815, ed. by Stephen Conway and Rafael Torres (Saarbrücken: VDM Verlag Dr. Müller, 2011), pp. 51–82.

45 HStAM, 118 a, no. 652/54: William IV of Orange to Prince Waldeck, 25 April 1749.
46 HStAM, 118 a, no. 652/78: Anne to Prince Waldeck, The Hague, 13 December 1756.
47 HStAM, 118 a, no. 949, fol. 8: George III to Waldeck, St James, 2 January 1776.
48 HStAM. 118 a, no. 3712/69: Waldeck to King Louis Napoléon of Holland, Arolsen, 6 October 1806, and King Louis Napoléon of Holland to Waldeck, Wesel royal quarters, 23 October 1806.
49 Preparing the British-American troop project in 1776, the Waldeckian administration, which had difficulties hiring enough soldiers, pretended that the men hired for Great Britain would most probably not be sent to the American colonies: 'daß wenn sie auch wieder eine mehr als gewiße

foreign powers thus came to an end, as did the constitutional structure of the Holy Roman Empire.

One of the central questions raised in this chapter has concerned the motives of German princes for entering into agreements with foreign powers. Quite a few explanations (or rather: justifications) for this practice are given in the analysed sources. Political (e.g. patriotic) reasons are listed along with ideological and religious motives: Waldeck's support in the Dutch war against France (1672–1678)[50] was important not just for the affairs of these countries but also for the German territories. Supporting the enemies of the French, the German princes also expected 'good effects on the conservation of German liberty', a liberty which had been threatened by Louis XIV.[51] Especially in supporting this conflict, German Protestant

---

Erwartung nach America geschickt werden sollten, sie in ein clima wie das hiesige Land, und wo es sehr wohlfeil leben ist, kommen und mithin einen untrieglichen Weg ihr Glück reichlich zu machen erhalten würden'. HStAM, 118 a, no. 971/4, fol. 6r, §6. Discussions regarding the recruitment of foreigners and the preference to locals (HStAM, 118 a, no. 665 and 1013), as well as regarding volunteers (who should get 'special advantages'; HStAM, 118 a, no. 971/2) and the prohibition of forced recruitment (HStAM, 118 a, no. 971/4). HStAM, 118 a, no. 971, fols 1r-1v: 'die Unglückliche Überschiffung der Hannoveraner, einen so starcken Eindruck auf die Gemüther gemachet'; Frederic Groß, 'Einzigartig? – Der Subsidienvertrag von 1786 über die Aufstellung des "Kapregiments" zwischen Herzog Karl Eugen von Württemberg und der Niederländischen Ostindienkompanie', in *Militärische Migration vom Altertum bis zur Gegenwart*, ed. by Christoph Rass (Paderborn: Studien zur Historischen Migrationsforschung, vol. 30, 2016), pp. 143–164; Lothar Höbelt, 'Vom militärischen saisonnier zum miles perpetuus: Staatsbildung und Kriegsführung im ancien régime', in *Krieg und Gesellschaft*, vol. 2, ed. by Thomas Kolnberger and Ilja Steffelbauer (Vienna: Mandelbaum, 2010), pp. 59–79; Hans-Martin Maurer, 'Das württembergische Kapregiment: Söldner im Dienste früher Kolonialpolitik (1787–1808)', *Zeitschrift für Württembergische Landesgeschichte* 47 (1988), 291–307. HStAM, 118 a, no. 660: Secret Secretary August Frensdorff, Promemoria, 28 February 1814, §1: 'Ist die Frage: ob es einem Reichsfürsten überall erlaubt seyn werde, Truppen in fremden Sold zu geben?'

50 HStAM, 117, no. 1329/6, Giovanni Matteo Alberti to Georg Friedrich von Waldeck, Venice, 21 January 1689: 'in dem Eß *toto mundo politico* nuzen solte, wann diesem Höffertigem Hanen Könnte der Kam[m] recht geschoren werden'.

51 HStAM, 117, no. 1436/1, Dutch resident in Berlin, Ham, to Georg Friedrich von Waldeck, 23 October 1688: 'des bons effects pour la conservation de la liberté de l'Allemagne', HStAM, Landgrave Carl of Hesse-Cassel to Georg Friedrich von Waldeck, Kassel, 17 September 1688: 'daß die leüte fortkommen und des publici dienst darunter nicht ferner gehemmet werde'.

princes – last but not least – also saw an important measure for preserving religious liberty in the Holy Roman Empire. At least, that is what they argued.[52] We do not know, however, whether these were genuine motives or rather pretexts to conceal other intentions. Regarding the relationship between the monetary aspects of interstate military subsidy treaties and less tangible immaterial factors, such as reputation and prestige, it appears as if money played an important role; however, the raising of troops might also require high investments, and payment by the subsidizing power might be uncertain. Opportunities for communicating and consulting with influential and prestigious foreign powers, and thus enhancing one's own reputation within the arena of interstate relationships, seemed far more important than actual financial gains, which more or less balanced each other out and did not significantly affect the state's budget. This is why we cannot even be certain if the German-Venetian agent Dr Giovanni Matteo Alberti, alias Johann Matthäus Albrecht, referred to material or immaterial 'profit' when informing Georg Friedrich von Waldeck about the latest military events and needs of the Republic in 1689, assuring him that Waldeck's co-operation 'will conduce to its great profit'.[53] In the long run, the treaties' effect on the reputation of a princely house could be much more beneficial – even from a financial perspective – compared to substantial but unique or short-lived subsidy payments.

Waldeck's experience with military subsidy contracts from the mid-seventeenth century to the late eighteenth century is just one example of many from early modern Germany. To assess the importance of those projects as a key instrument of state and dynastic politics, it is essential to adopt a comparative perspective including other territories: to discover the unifying principles in subsidy affairs as well as temporary shifts, but also to understand the diversity inherent in them. In such a synchronic as well as diachronic comparison, similarities and differences could be shown with regard to political, constitutional, and political factors: secular states as troop-offering countries (such as Hesse-Cassel or Waldeck) probably pursued motives other than those of ecclesiastical territories like Münster, Würzburg, or Bamberg, dynastic kingdoms as subsidizers

---

52 HStAM, 117, no. 1440/2: Duke Friedrich Carl von Württemberg to Erffa, Stuttgart, 28 March 1688: 'fur daß vatterlandt und die Religionsfreyheit'.
53 HStAM, 117, no. 1329/6, Giovanni Matteo Alberti to Georg Friedrich von Waldeck, Venice, 21 January 1689: 'weil ich gewiß bin d(ass) solcheß nicht werden abschlagen in dem eß zu ihrem Großen prouit dienet'.

had another scope than republics; and it might even be important to integrate confessional positions and interests into a concept of German subsidy receivers.

In order to understand subsidy troop contracts, they should not merely be studied individually. On the one hand, interstate subsidy treaties were joint projects and referred to one another: the princely houses were in constant contact, and they exchanged information whenever preparations were made for new contracts.[54] On the other hand, both the states providing troops and those offering subsidies were engaged in competition, depending on the current political situation as well as on the conditions of supply and demand.[55] Economic rivalry as well as political factions could create opposition: some princes of the empire would not let the troops of their princely peers pass through their territories in order to prevent their co-operation with antagonistic foreign powers. In the Holy Roman Empire, this especially applied to the allies and clients of France.[56]

Whilst Waldeck's rise to the status of a hereditary principality went hand in hand with its early military efforts, other dynastic ambitions did not play such an important role, as the princely house of Waldeck was among the smallest in the Holy Roman Empire and marriage projects with foreign royal partners (as in the case of Hesse-Cassel and Sweden) were out of reach. None the less, the military deals with Venice, the Netherlands, and Great Britain served to secure Waldeck's precarious position within the structure of the Holy Roman Empire until its very end, as well as to strengthen its place within the noble hierarchy of Europe.

---

54 Copy of the Dutch–Hessian treaty of 1701 in the Waldeckian Archive: HStAM, 118 a, 652: 'Auf folgende punkte ist zu refletiren, wann man ein Regiment oder Bataillon in Holländische Dienste übergeben will.' Cf. also HStAM, 118 a, 665.
55 HStAM, 118 a, no. 652: Secret Councillor von Grass to Waldeck, The Hague, 30 March 1742: 'da hingegen die offertes von anderen herrn wegen ihrer trouppen bis noch refusiert seind'.
56 The Prince of Waldeck's problems with the prince-bishops of Münster, Padernborn, and Cologne; HStAM, 117, no. 1358: 'daß derselbe keine Regimenter so vor die Holländer /: wie die formalia gelautet:/ geworben, durchs Münsterische laßen würde, so embarrasiret mich solches nicht wenig'; discussion regarding an alternative route: 'welcher so viel beschwerlicher sein wird, weil Er durchs Cöllnische fallen und daselbst noch mehr opposition haben dürffte'.

8

Small powers and great designs: diplomacy, cross-border patronage, and the negotiation of subsidy alliances in the north-western part of the Holy Roman Empire (late seventeenth century)

Tilman Haug

In his study of mercenaries in north-western Germany in the early modern period, Peter Burschel stated that the end of the Thirty Years' War with the Peace of Westphalia did not mark a significant decrease in demand in the regional mercenary markets, which remained at a fairly constant level throughout the entire seventeenth century.[1] Even at a superficial glance at the political and military landscape in the north-western periphery of the Holy Roman Empire, this region may provide an example of the intense and prolonged susceptibility of the European order to military conflicts and their consequences, as it was particularly close to the main theatres of the Dutch conflicts with Spain, the Thirty Years' War and the major wars waged by Louis XIV against his European rivals.[2] Owing to the failure in negotiations between France and the Spanish monarchy in Münster, this military struggle continued up until the Peace of

---

1 Peter Burschel, *Söldner im Nordwestdeutschland des 16. und 17. Jahrhunderts: Sozialgeschichtliche Studien* (Göttingen: Vandenhoeck & Ruprecht, 1994), p. 113.
2 See, for instance, Andreas Rutz, 'Der Westen des Reiches als Kriegsschauplatz und Erfahrungsraum im langen 17. Jahrhundert', in *Krieg und Kriegserfahrung im Westen des Reiches 1568–1714*, ed. by Andreas Rutz and Marlene Tomczyk (Göttingen: Vandenhoeck & Ruprecht, 2016), pp. 11–30. For the Rhine region in particular, see Max Braubach, 'Vom Westfälischen Frieden bis zum Wiener Kongress (1648–1815)', in *Rheinische Geschichte*, 3 vols, ed. by Georg Droege (Düsseldorf: Schwann, 1980), vol. 2, pp. 219–365 (pp. 240–265). For the structural proneness to warlike conflict in Europe, see Johannes Burkhardt, 'Die Friedlosigkeit der Frühen Neuzeit: Grundlegung einer Theorie der Bellizität Europas', *Zeitschrift für Historische Forschung* 24 (1997), 509–574.

the Pyrenees in 1659 and gravely affected the territories on the left bank of the Rhine. Other minor, mostly low-intensity, military conflicts in Europe following 1648 included the war between Sweden and Denmark, which again was part of a major conflict in northern Europe, two military confrontations between Sweden and the Hanseatic city of Bremen, the punitive action of Bishop Christoph Bernhard von Galen against his own city of Münster and its council's ambition to become a free city (alongside his many other military adventures), and territorial struggles such as the 'Kuhkrieg' (cow war), named after the capture of a significant amount of livestock during its course, between the duke of Neuburg and the elector of Brandenburg.[3] This was followed by the more aggressive and expansionist posture of Louis XIV's foreign policy and the onset of a series of French wars of aggression, the attack on Spanish territories in 1667 marking the beginning of a period that has been dubbed the 'second Thirty Years' War'.[4] Many of these conflicts, especially those on a larger scale from the 1660s onwards, involved subsidy treaties with German potentates in the region, where European diplomacy in relation to large and political conflicts in regional and local theatres often created interconnections and provided opportunities for some lesser estates of the Holy Roman Empire to engage in an elaborate form of military entrepreneurship undertaken by ruling princes.[5]

The eighth chapter in the Peace of Westphalia formally granted electors and princes of the empire the right to conclude *cum exteris foedera* with the soft and flexible provision stipulating that alliances should not be directed against the emperor and the empire.[6] This enabled the armament of princes in asymmetrical relations with foreign princes and could eventually enable them to obtain certain possibilities of immersing themselves in the European concert of powers, enhance their status on the political stage, and make territorial gains. Traditionally, the right to conclude foreign military

---

3 For the conflict and the expansionist plans of the Brandenburg elector, see Ernst Opgenoorth, *Friedrich Wilhelm: Der Große Kurfürst von Brandenburg*, 2 vols (Göttingen: Musterschmidt, 1971), vol. 1, pp. 211–216.
4 Burkhardt, 'Friedlosigkeit', p. 510.
5 See the classic account in Fritz Redlich, *The German Military Enterpriser and His Work Force: A Study in European Economic and Social History*, 2 vols (Wiesbaden: Franz Steiner, 1964–1965), vol. 2, pp. 5–11.
6 Antje Oschmann, *Die Friedensverträge mit Frankreich und Schweden, vol.1: Urkunden. Acta Pacis Westphalicae, Serie III Abt. B* (Münster: Aschendorff, 1998), p. 11.

alliances was regarded as a clear step towards sovereign power politics outside the empire.⁷ More recent research, however, has rather placed it in the context of regional defence and peacekeeping or a right of resistance assumed by imperial estates. Despite the pursuit of their own interests, electors and princes engaging in treaties with foreign powers continued to regard the empire and its various internal security alliances – which could include foreign allies and their subsidies – as a central point of reference.⁸

The present chapter focuses on the practices of diplomacy and various cross-border negotiations concerning the formation of foreign subsidy alliances on various levels in the north-western periphery of the Holy Roman Empire in the first decades after the Peace of Westphalia. This field of inquiry is explored in three case studies: first, the attempt of the duke of Neuburg to use subsidies to recruit and equip more substantial military forces and the career of Georg Christian von Hessen-Homburg as negotiator and struggling military entrepreneur; second, the case study of Münster's prince-bishop Christoph Bernhard von Galen and his English subsidy alliance in 1665–1666 directed against the Republic of the Netherlands, and, third, the involvement of German princes in the Dutch War of 1672 and Wilhelm von Fürstenberg's diplomatic role in the formation of a subsidy alliance.

On the one hand, this chapter examines the practices of diplomats and cross-border patronage networks in negotiating subsidy treaties between asymmetrical partners and maintaining communication, ensuring flows of financial resources, and enabling the recruitment of mercenary armies. It particularly focuses on the activity of networks, clients, and brokers in the service of foreign powers.⁹ On

---

7 See, for example, Ernst Wolfgang Böckenförde, 'Der Westfälische Frieden und das Bündnisrecht der Reichsstände', *Der Staat* 8 (1969), 449–478.

8 Karl Otmar von Aretin, 'Die Kreisassoziationen in der Politik der Mainzer Kurfürsten Johann Philipp und Lothar Franz von Schönborn 1648–1711', in Karl Otmar von Aretin, *Das Alte Reich: Friedensgarantie und europäisches Gleichgewicht* (Stuttgart: Klett, 1986), pp. 167–208; Ronald G. Asch, 'The ius foederis Re-examined: The Peace of Westphalia and the Constitution of the Holy Roman Empire', in *Peace Treaties and International Law in European History: From the Late Middle Ages to World War One*, ed. by Randall Lesaffer (Cambridge: Cambridge University Press, 2004), pp. 319–337.

9 For a comparative European perspective on these problems, see the contributions in *Nähe in der Ferne: Personale Verflechtung in den Außenbeziehungen der Frühen Neuzeit*, ed. by Hillard von Thiessen and Christian Windler (Berlin: Duncker & Humblot, 2005).

the other hand, the chapter addresses how princes negotiated and balanced their various roles as subsidy takers entitled to autonomous military action and ambitious de-facto warlords with their roles as members of the Holy Roman Empire. The latter mandated their loyalty to its head and obliged them to maintain peace following the norms of the Peace of Westphalia. How did these actors seek to reconcile their often problematic alliances with various, often conflicting, roles with regard to their political environment? What was the role of the Holy Roman Empire as a political framework in respect to foreign subsidy alliances?

Between European ambitions, regional security, and military entrepreneurship: projects concerning a French subsidy alliance involving Philipp Wilhelm von Neuburg

Duke Philipp Wilhelm of Palatinate-Neuburg was originally destined to be a dedicated Habsburg loyalist, yet found himself in collaboration with French politics in the Holy Roman Empire and was temporarily one of France's most significant supporters.[10] Following the untimely death of the Roman King Ferdinand IV in 1654, as a result of which the usually secure Habsburg succession on the imperial throne suddenly hung in the balance, the duke emerged as a serious contender for the throne. This made him one of the most important players in Mazarin's policy of installing a non-Habsburg candidate on the throne, even though Neuburg's successful candidacy seemed to become ever more unlikely the closer it came to the actual election after the death of Emperor Ferdinand III in April 1657.[11] Philipp Wilhelm's position was ambiguous. He never intended to break entirely with his house's traditionally close ties to the Austrian Habsburgs, but

---

10 For his earlier years and his 1650s political biography, see Hans Schmidt, *Philipp Wilhelm von Pfalz-Neuburg 1615–1690*, 2 vols (Düsseldorf: Schwann), vol. 1, 1973.
11 On the 1657/1658 imperial election, see Martin Göhring, 'Kaiserwahl und Rheinbund von 1658: Ein Höhepunkt des Kampfes zwischen Habsburg und Bourbon um die Beherrschung des Reiches', in *Geschichtliche Kräfte und Entscheidungen: Festschrift zum 65. Geburtstag von Otto Becker*, ed. by Martin Göhring and Alexander Scharff (Wiesbaden: F. Steiner, 1954), pp. 65–83; S.N.F. Gie, 'Die Kandidatur Ludwigs XIV. bei der Kaiserwahl vom Jahre 1658 mit besonderer Berücksichtigung der Vorgeschichte', *Abhandlungen zur mittleren und neueren Geschichte* 61 (1916), pp. 1–108; Alfred F. Pribram, 'Zur Wahl Leopolds I., 1654–1658', *Archiv für österreichische Geschichte* 73 (1888), 81–222.

he utilized French interest in co-operation as an asset in furthering his immediate political concerns as a *Landesherr*. Neuburg's involvement with the French and his subsequent attempts to obtain French subsidies for the formation of an army were not untypical of minor German princes in the region. Neuburg sought to obtain a certain degree of security for his territories scattered around the empire. His territories on the left bank of the Rhine were particularly affected by the ongoing Franco-Spanish conflict. In this situation, the French eventually guaranteed the integrity of his possessions in the north-west; France offered to mediate in relation to Neuburg's conflicts with Brandenburg, and offered to represent his interests in any peace negotiation with Spain.[12] Nevertheless, the duke's interests in co-operation with France went beyond profiting from the efforts of French diplomacy on his behalf. In 1656, Philipp Wilhelm considerably raised the stakes for his compliance with French policies and demanded a subsidy treaty that would allow him to raise a sizeable armed force of around twenty thousand men.[13] The projected military alliance would support all of Philipp Wilhelm's political roles and ambitions.

First, the alliance would have solidified the duke's position in a still volatile military conflict in the lower Rhine region and helped protect Neuburg's territories. The alliance would also have been instrumental in keeping at bay Neuburg's main rival, the prince elector of Brandenburg with whom he was involved in a series of territorial struggles and by whom he felt threatened.

Second, Neuburg underlined the mutual usefulness of this armament project and offered offensive as well as defensive alliances with the French, alliances that would allow him to contain the Spaniards on behalf of his French sponsors or, if required, directly engage them in offensive military action in the Spanish Netherlands. This was also in accordance with the duke's immediate interests as a territorial ruler, as he particularly struggled to end the long-term Spanish occupation of the town of Jülich.[14] Neuburg also pointed out that his army could be employed in the larger European arena

---

12 Schmidt, *Philipp Wilhelm*, pp. 101–102.
13 *Ibid.*, pp. 155–156.
14 For Jülich under Spanish occupation and the political ramifications, see Günter Bers, *Don Gabriel de la Torre: Ein spanischer Gubernator der Stadt und Festung Jülich (1641–1660). Zur Stadtgeschichte im Dreißigjährigen Krieg* (Jülich: Verlag der Joseph-Kuhl-Gesellschaft, 2013).

of conflict with the Habsburgs, even though the duke's plans for strategic movements and the necessary neglect of his more localized strategic interests seemed rather unrealistic.

Third, leading an army and being militarily and financially aligned with a major European power could also grant 'political capital' on both an instrumental and a symbolical level on the European stage for otherwise comparatively insignificant princes. Philipp Wilhelm was indeed preoccupied with an ambitious and lofty project on a large European scale: his desire to be elected king of Poland, thereby rising to a status in European social and political prestige above his rank as an otherwise relatively insignificant prince of the Holy Roman Empire.[15] Cardinal Mazarin showed some interest in the alliance but remained sceptical towards Neuburg's plans, while also suspecting that Neuburg's desire for French subsidies and the recruitment of a sizeable army were partly meant to impress the potential voters among the Polish nobles.[16]

While neither Neuburg's Polish ambitions nor his prospects as regards the imperial throne ever materialized (or were very promising to begin with), his ambitions were persistently supported by one particular actor in the French camp: Georg Christian of Hesse-Homburg, a converted Catholic German prince originally employed in the Spanish army, who had 'defected to the French side and who offered his services'.[17] Mazarin and his close collaborator in all foreign affairs, the former ambassador at the Peace of Westphalia, Abel Servien, formed a patron–client relationship and employed Homburg to broker French subsidies, pensions, and political concessions to German electors and princes in the run-up to the imperial election. They intended to capitalize on Homburg's various entanglements in the empire, which also included close relations with Neuburg.[18]

---

15 Schmidt, *Philipp Wilhelm*, pp. 156–159.
16 Archives diplomatiques du ministère des Affaires étrangères (AMAE), Correspondance Politique, Allemagne, vol. 133, fol. 164r, Servien to Mazarin, 14 July 1656.
17 His political biography is detailed in Margarethe Hintereicher, *Georg Christian von Hessen-Homburg (1626–1677): Offizier, Diplomat und Regent in den Jahrzehnten nach dem Dreissigjährigen Krieg* (Darmstadt: Hessische Historische Kommission, 1985).
18 Hintereicher, *Georg Christian*, pp. 89–133; Tilman Haug, *Ungleiche Außenbeziehungen und grenzüberschreitende Patronage: Frankreich und die geistlichen Kurfürsten 1648–1679* (Cologne: Böhlau, 2015), pp. 179–192.

A closer look at Homburg's employment as a client not only corrects the implicit image of informal local brokers and 'enablers' who merely paved the way for 'proper' French diplomats. Contemporary modes of formalization and officialization allowed Homburg to shift between informal and formal roles as a negotiator, doubling as a French diplomat with the 'proper' French envoy, Robert de Gravel, as his formal subordinate.[19] The case of Homburg's employment also reveals some risks and dysfunctionalities in conducting external affairs by local proxies. Not only were Homburg's diplomatic missions prone to end in embarrassing blunders, since he was less familiar with the empire's political culture than expected. His close ties to Neuburg also represented a liability with regard to the room for manoeuvre of French diplomacy in the empire. Homburg increasingly confounded his roles as French negotiator and as a de-facto client of Philipp Wilhelm. Apart from Philipp Wilhelm's candidacy to the imperial throne, Homburg actively promoted the latter's military ambitions.

Difficulties increased when Mazarin and Robert de Gravel began to knit closer ties to Johann Philipp von Schönborn, the elector of Mayence, who (albeit ambiguously and reluctantly at first) embraced the proposals for an alliance that resembled the later Alliance of the Rhine.[20] Homburg saw Neuburg's subsidies and armament as being in jeopardy and derailed Gravel's negotiations in dismissing Johann Philipp's projects concerning a security alliance as ill-conceived illusions. He insisted on the necessity of arming the duke of Neuburg, which initially succeeded in slowing down Gravel's rapprochement with Johann Philipp.[21]

However, not only Homburg's unconditional fidelity towards Philipp Wilhelm compromised his French services as a French client and negotiator. Insisting on French subsidies and an alliance treaty for Philipp Wilhelm coincided with his desire to establish himself as a military entrepreneur, for which he obtained a French commission and funds to recruit a regiment for the French army, which he hoped

---

19 This is explicitly stated in Homburg's Instruction, see AMAE, Correspondance Politique Allemagne, vol. 137, fol. 205v, Seconde Instruction de M. le Prince de Hombourg assisté du S. de Gravel, Paris, 27 April 1657.
20 For the rapprochement of France and Mayence, see Claude Badalo-Dulong, *Trente ans de diplomatie française en Allemagne: Louis XIV et l'Électeur de Mayence (1648–1678)* (Paris: Plon, 1956), pp. 23–26.
21 AMAE, Correspondance politique Allemagne, vol. 137, fol. 375r, Homburg to Servien, Frankfurt, 24 June 1657.

to lead into battle himself. Yet, Homburg not only proved to be rather inept in this task; he was now actively undermined by the French envoy Robert de Gravel, his colleague and bitter rival, who intervened to cut off and redirect Homburg's funds.[22] A French-funded army under Neuburg's command could also have profited the ambitious yet unfortunate Homburg as a would-be military entrepreneur. Despite being relegated to second rank concerning French political affairs of the empire, Neuburg still managed to obtain some degree of French subsidies to keep an armed force in his territories along the Rhine. With the final decision to join and contribute to the Alliance of the Rhine (after the failure of a non-Habsburg election) with a partially French-funded army corps in 1658, however, the French intended to cut back seriously on any individual armament for German princes. Instead of arming the duke of Neuburg, Mazarin initially proposed making him the supreme commander of the troops of the new defensive alliance.[23] Philipp Wilhelm von Neuburg joined the alliance, but in relations with the reluctant French *plenipotentiaires* he and his negotiators still insisted on further French payments to keep Neuburg's army in order to safeguard his territories.[24] One year later, in 1659, the Peace of the Pyrenees was concluded and Mazarin ostensibly negotiated the release of Jülich on Neuburg's behalf. Even though Neuburg remained a French sympathizer, Mazarin now felt free to reject further demands for French subsidies by the duke, let alone French financial support for any ambitious Polish projects.[25]

---

22 Hintereicher, *Georg Christian*, p. 154.
23 For the Alliance of the Rhine of 1658 and French participation, see Roman Schnur, *Der Rheinbund von 1658 in der deutschen Verfassungsgeschichte* (Bonn: Röhrscheid, 1955); Anuschka Tischer, 'Die Vorgeschichte des ersten Rheinbundes von 1658', in *Der Erste Rheinbund (1658)*, ed. by Martin Peters, historicum.net, www.historicum.net/themen/erster-rheinbund-1658/der-rheinbund-in-geschichte-und-gedaechtnis/die-vorgeschichte-des-ersten-rheinbundes-von-1658, retrieved 4 November 2017. For Mazarin's proposal, see: Mazarin to Robert de Gravel, Dijon, 19 November 1658, in *Lettres du Cardinal Mazarin pendant son Ministère*, ed. by Gustave d'Avenel/Adolphe Chéruel, 9 vols (Paris: Imprimerie Nationale, 1894–1906), vol. 9 (1906), p. 101.
24 AMAE, Correspondance politique, Allemagne, vol. 141, fol. 298v, Gramont and Lionne to Mazarin, Frankfurt, 18 August 1658. The idea of further French subsidies for Philipp Wilhelm von Neuburg does not seem to have vanished that easily, as suggested by Schmidt, *Philipp Wilhelm*, p. 279.
25 AMAE, Correspondance politique, Allemagne, vol. 146, fol. 112r–v, Mazarin to Robert de Gravel, St Jean de Luz, 12 September 1659.

England's unlikely continental sword: the challenges of Christoph Bernhard von Galen's subsidy alliance with the Stuart monarchy 1665–1666

Georg Christian von Homburg's severe setbacks in both the diplomatic and the military entrepreneurial arena did not cost him his political or military career. In 1665, he found himself being the official field commander at the head of an army invading the Dutch Republic.

Obtaining this post, however, was directly related to the military ambitions of another German prince, whose diplomacy had succeeded in co-opting a major European conflict to secure funding for a military operation that also benefited his local interests and ambitions. Christoph Bernhard von Galen, the prince-bishop of Münster, was known for his uncompromising political stance and military aggressiveness, highly unusual at the time for an ecclesiastical prince and a cleric.[26]

The most frequent objective of the bishop's military activity, and the driving force of his willing involvement as a provider of a military force subsidized by foreign powers, was attacking the Dutch Republic. A domineering political and economic actor in the regional power system, the Dutch had created a system of political dependencies and protections among the princes and prince electors of the empire, a system which included Dutch garrisons in Cleves curtailing the direct power of Friedrich Wilhelm of Brandenburg as the nominal overlord of the territory.[27] Dutch protections directly affected Christoph Bernhard's political ambition when his own city of Münster

---

26 Particularly for Christoph Bernhard's foreign and imperial policies, see Wilhelm Kohl, *Christoph Bernhard von Galen: Politische Geschichte des Fürstbistums Münster 1650–1678* (Münster: Regensberg, 1964); Ernst Marquardt, *Christoph Bernhard von Galen: Fürstbischof von Münster* (Münster: Aschendorff, 1951); Peter Berghaus, Gerhard Langemeyer, and Peter Ilisch, *Bommen Berend: Das Fürstbistum Münster unter Bischof Christoph Bernhard von Galen 1650–1678* (Greven: Cramer, 1972). For Christoph Bernhard's role conflicts, see Bettina Braun, *Princeps et episcopus: Studien zur Funktion und zum Selbstverständnis der nordwestdeutschen Fürstbischöfe nach dem Westfälischen Frieden* (Göttingen: Vandenhoeck & Ruprecht, 2013), pp. 323–342.

27 For the particular situation in the margraviat of Cleves, see Michael Kaiser, 'Temps de l'occupation – temps de la liberté: les territoires du duché de Clèves et du comté de la Marck sous l'occupation des Provinces-Unies', in *Les ressources des faibles: Neutralités, sauvegardes, accommodements en temps de guerre (XVIe–XVIIIe siècle)*, ed. by Jean-François Chanet and Christian Windler (Rennes: Presses universitaires de Rennes, 2009), pp. 241–260.

sought to establish itself as a free city and initially succeeded in obtaining Dutch support and protection. The city was eventually coerced back into submission by the pugnacious bishop by means of military force.[28]

In 1663, Christoph Bernhard came in even more direct conflict with the Dutch when his troops occupied entrenchments near Diel in eastern Frisia to collect debts from their ruling house – debts to which the bishop claimed he was entitled. His soldiers were forced to stand down by Dutch forces, who acted as protectors of the Frisian estates.[29] In response to this humiliating injury to his honour and a long-standing desire for territorial expansion, Christoph Bernhard offered himself as an ally and continental military arm of the English, who were about to enter the Anglo-Dutch War of 1665–1666.[30] Alongside alliances with Brandenburg and Philipp Wilhelm of Neuburg, it was a subsidy treaty with the Stuart monarchy that would provide Christoph Bernhard with considerable means for recruiting an army and conducting a punitive military action in the Netherlands which should be carried out in close co-operation with London. The campaign should also eventually secure the town and domain of Borkelo for Christoph Bernhard. In June 1665, his Lieutenant-Colonel Heinrich Alexander Wrede travelled to London to conclude the alliance, which granted £150,000 to the bishop of Münster to fund his armament.[31] This was very welcome and indeed necessary financial aid, as the prince-bishop still partly depended on the budgetary rights of his estates and had by far overstretched his financial capacities even before the Dutch campaign was planned.[32]

---

28 Alwin Hanschmidt, 'Zwischen bürgerlicher Stadtautonomie und fürstlicher Stadtherrschaft (1580–1661)', in *Geschichte der Stadt Münster*, 2 vols, ed. by Franz-Josef Jakobi (Münster: Aschendorff, 1994), vol. 1, pp. 249–299 (pp. 284–287).
29 Kohl, *Christoph Bernhard von Galen*, pp. 178–180.
30 For the genesis and the history of this particular alliance, see Carl Brinkmann, 'Charles II and the Bishop of Münster in the Anglo-Dutch War of 1665–6', *The English Historical Review* 21 (1906), 686–698; Kohl, *Christoph Bernhard*, pp. 197–199.
31 Offensiv- und Subsidienvertrag des Königs von Großbritannien mit dem Fürstbischof von Münster, London, 3 June 1665, in *Akten und Urkunden zur Außenpolitik Christoph Bernhards von Galen (1650–1678)*, 3 vols, ed. by Wilhelm Kohl (Münster: Aschendorff, 1980–1986), vol. 1 (1980), pp. 455–456.
32 For these sorts of difficulties, see Theodor Verspohl, *Das Heerwesen des münsterischen Fürstbischofs Christoph Bernhard von Galen 1650–1678* (Hildesheim: Lax, 1909), pp. 99–101.

This alliance between a major European power and what must from the Stuart perspective have been seen as a minor and distant principality not only was unlikely and asymmetric but also entailed a series of practical political challenges. To begin with, the diplomatic negotiations and political and military co-ordination of activities between the bishop and the Stuart king reveal the former's ability to mobilize diplomatic negotiators and 'transterritorial' networks in order to overcome the lack of formalized relations.

In the case of the 1665 alliance, the English Catholic exile community and its entanglements with the Catholic peerage provided a communication node between the unlikely allies, where more formalized diplomatic contacts were sporadic at best.[33] Following Christoph Bernhard's informal talks with William Temple in Münster, the bishop managed to send an English 'ex-patriate', Father Joseph Sherwood, a Benedictine monk of noble descent, to London for the detailed negotiations on the terms of the subsidy alliance.[34] Sherwood was 'available' for the services of a German prince-bishop in England, as his monastery in Lamspringe near Hildesheim had been re-established by English Catholic exiles and maintained close contacts with its noble benefactors in England, who donated resources for the reconstruction of the convent church.[35]

Sherwood's mission reflects the frequent use of hybrid social actors, in terms of ethnic and cultural affiliation, as negotiators – actors who were supposed to capitalize on their familiarity with the social and political culture on the ground as well as on their interpersonal relations in order to achieve success. Yet, while Sherwood seems to have been favourably perceived by his English interlocutors, and even after the negotiation demonstrated his abilities to gather political information on English affairs through various channels – he even managed to obtain a letter of recommendation from King Charles in 1673 – it is not easy to determine to what degree he mobilized any personal networks derived from 'social capital' through his closeness to the Catholic peerage or other

---

33 More generally on the English Catholic communities, see Geert H. Janssen, 'The Exile Experience', in *The Ashgate Research Companion to the Counter-Reformation* (London and New York: Routledge, 2013), pp. 73–90.
34 Kohl, *Christoph Bernhard*, p. 198.
35 For this monastery, see *Lamspringe: An English Abbey in Germany 1643–1803*, ed. by Anselm Cramer (Ampleforth: Ampleforth Abbey Trustees, 2004).

interpersonal relations for his negotiations on behalf of the bishop of Münster.[36]

When the flow of the much-needed subsidies began to stall, Sherwood was once again sent to London with an urgent mission to unblock the funds. Christoph Bernhard strongly suggested that he should exploit the very few contacts that von Galen himself had established with English diplomats in the empire, namely those with Temple and the brother of the Catholic Irish peer and ambassador to the imperial court in Vienna, the Earl of Carlingfort. For the same mission, Sherwood was also given substantial funds, 'to give a gratification … if the entire sum of the remaining one [i.e. the subsidy rate] could thus be unblocked'.[37] If necessary, in other words, Sherwood was instructed to bribe English officials to free up the remaining portions of the English subsidies – a practice requiring some local knowledge of the workings of a foreign court and administration, but not necessarily very close long-term personal relationships, on the part of the negotiator on the ground.

Later, the aforementioned Wrede, who seems to have shared some personal familiarity with Temple, was once again sent to England to urge that the remaining subsidies be paid out.[38] But, without additional favourable advocates for Christoph Bernhard's cause, Wrede was simply instructed to be persistent in his appeals to Arlington and other court officials.[39] Wrede's effort was unsuccessful. The flow of money remained insecure and, particularly after the emperor and Brandenburg launched attempts to mediate a peace, Christoph Bernhard's loyalty to the alliance increasingly appeared compromised.[40] Members of the prince-bishop's chapter, who opposed

---

36 See, for instance, VWA, Ass. L, 489, Nr. 3, Sherwood to Christoph Bernhard, Hildesheim, 29 November 1669; for the letter of recommendation: VWA, Ass. L. 489, Nr. 32, Charles II to Christoph Bernhard, Whitehall, 29 March 1673.
37 'daß die verehrung davon in memorial gemeldet, gegeben werden solle, wan dadurch die gehele summe des restants loß zu machen'; Nebenmemorial Christoph Bernhards für Pater Joseph Sherwood OSB zur Gesandtschaft nach England, Münster, 2 November 1665, in *Akten und Urkunden*, vol. 1, p. 532.
38 Temple to Wrede, Brussels, 10 May 1665, in *The Works of Sir William Temple*, 4 vols (London: S. Hamilton, 1814), vol. 1, pp. 220–224.
39 Christoph Bernhard to Wrede, Münster, 8 January 1666, in *Akten und Urkunden*, vol. 1, p. 521.
40 Wrede to Christoph Bernhard, Oxford, 7 January 1666, in *Akten und Urkunden*, vol. 1, p. 525.

the treaty, had anticipated such difficulties and warned him of the unreliability of their English partner – 'England virtually never kept its word to anyone' – and further suspected that communication and co-ordination with such a distant ally with complicated political structures would be difficult.[41]

These difficulties eventually affected the military success of the alliance. While von Galen quickly earned his nickname 'Bommen Berend' ('Bomber Bernd') for his troops' extensive use of mortar fire against fortified sites throughout the campaign, there was very little military co-ordination with the English, who suspended plans for an invasion even though Christoph Bernhard's army attempted to establish landing zones.[42] The frequent lack of English subsidies exposed the serious underfunding of the campaign and its complete dependence on contributions by the occupied, which were hard to come by as the invasion quickly began to stall. Desertions and the bribing of the scarcely paid officers and troops by the Dutch massively contributed to the dismantling of Christoph Bernhard's army.[43]

Even before Christoph Bernhard's army was on the march, a second difficulty had begun to emerge. Dutch networks and the political, social, and financial entanglements of neighbouring German princes and nobles within the United Provinces stymied Christoph Bernhard's attempts to spend his promised English funds in the region's mercenary markets, and particularly to enlist the units of the dukes of Brunswick, all of whom had recruited forces during an armed internal conflict between the various branches of the House of Brunswick. Von Galen enlisted the Brunswickian Colonel Johann Georg von Gorgas to undertake and co-ordinate recruitments in the north-western part of the empire; but, when he attempted to negotiate with the dukes of Brunswick over the transfer of a substantial part of these forces, Duke Georg Wilhelm had already committed his troops to the Dutch, apparently in exchange for a reduction of his debts in the Netherlands. His rival Duke Georg Friedrich right away rejected any co-operation with Münster's recruitment efforts.[44]

---

41 'Engelandt hette baldt niemanten wort gehalten'; Protokoll des Domkapitels, s.l., 18 September 1665, in *Akten und Urkunden*, vol. 1, p. 474.
42 For the fiscal-military rationale of this strategy for the collection of contributions, see Redlich, *German Military Enterpriser*, vol. 2, pp. 11–12.
43 Floris der Kinderen, *De Nederlandsche Republiek en Munster geburende de Jaren 1650–1666* (Leiden: Gebroeders van der Hoek, 1871), pp. 265–293.
44 *Akten und Urkunden*, vol. 1, pp. 458–459. For Gorgas's substantial contribution, see Georg Tessin, 'Beiträge zur Formationsgeschichte des Münsterischen

Dutch 'micro-politics' became even more visible when Christoph Bernhard failed to employ as his supreme commander the experienced military entrepreneur Count Georg Friedrich von Waldeck, who had also recruited troops for the confusing Brunswick conflict. Christoph Bernhard's efforts were to a large extent blocked as a result of Waldeck's affairs and dependencies in the Netherlands. Not only did he cite his friendship and kinship relations to the Dutch political and military establishment, notably to Maurice of Nassau; his estates in the Netherlands and other financial affairs also committed him to the Dutch camp.[45] Later, in 1672, Waldeck would assume supreme command of the Dutch army facing, among others, Christoph Bernhard's troops.[46]

When, in 1665, the general states began to realize the danger posed by von Galen's recruitments, they reinforced their troops and enlisted the Brunswickian units.[47] The dismayed prince-bishop in turn wrote angrily to Waldeck and expressed his disappointment that Waldeck had refused 'the general's rank in our imperial army'.[48] This rather odd reference to the Holy Roman Empire points to a third complicating and limiting factor in the asymmetrical alliance that Christoph Bernhard had entered. Even though a subsidy treaty with a major European power may have helped imperial princes assert a superior political and social status, the case of Christoph Bernhard demonstrates that a prince still had to reconcile the waging of a war supported by foreign subsidies with the overarching framework of the Holy Roman Empire and its internal alliances and mutual security guarantees, designed to stabilize the Peace of Westphalia and prevent foreign conflicts from spilling over to the empire.

The English offensive military alliance was clearly one of the main opposing factors, which is why the emperor and the imperial

---

Militärs', *Westfälische Forschungen* 32 (1982), 87–111 (p. 90). Christoph Bernhard to Franz Egon von Fürstenberg, Münster, 18 June 1665, in *Akten und Urkunden*, vol. 1, p. 457. Kohl, *Christoph Bernhard*, pp. 199–200.

45 Kohl, *Christoph Bernhard*, p. 200.
46 For Waldeck's career, see Gerhard Menk, *Georg Friedrich von Waldeck (1620–1692): Eine biographische Skizze* (Arolsen: Waldeckischer Geschichtsverein, 1992). For the counts of Waldeck as European military entrepreneurs, see Andreas Flurschütz da Cruz, Chapter 7 above.
47 For the Dutch efforts to recruit the Brunswick troops, see der Kinderen, *De Nederlandsche Republiek*, pp. 289–293.
48 'Das generalat über unsere Reichsarmee'; Christoph Bernhard to Georg Friedrich Graf von Waldeck, Borculo, 30 September 1665, in *Akten und Urkunden*, vol. I, p. 476.

estates assembled in Regensburg and why even Christoph Bernhard's initial allies Brandenburg and Neuburg universally rejected his war. The fact that the Stuart monarchy, as the deputies at the imperial Diet complained, had made inroads in the empire via Münster and used English money for establishing an 'armoury' (*rüßthaus*), where even a second-rate warmongering prince could procure a sizeable army and shatter a precarious peace, was regarded as a considerable security hazard.[49] Thus, Christoph Bernhard fashioned his own English-subsidized campaign so as to make it form part of a legitimate imperial war effort. Indeed, he claimed that he was reinstating territories of the empire occupied by the Dutch and thus acting not only on the basis of legitimate purposes as a *Landesherr* but ultimately in the shared interest and on behalf of all imperial estates as a defender of the empire.[50] However, this bold claim seems more than anything to have baffled and angered the assembled deputies and shattered any desperate hopes for obtaining additional funds or troops for the war effort.[51]

Being a member of the aforementioned Rhine alliance himself, Christoph Bernhard also attempted not only to overcome the stiff French opposition to the offensive alliance but also to present the Dutch conflict as a case of collective self-defence for all the members of the alliance. Success in this attempt would have granted him additional military and financial assistance in the face of dwindling English resources.[52] He also planned to persuade Sweden, as a fellow imperial estate and member of the alliance, to join the war against the Dutch.[53]

Regarding the empire and its estates, another factor entered the equation. Despite the bi-confessional alliance with England, the prince-bishop still had to shake off the impression of a religious

---

49 Basserode to Christoph Bernhard, Regensburg, 19 November 1665, in *Akten und Urkunden*, vol. 1, p. 497.
50 Basserode to Christoph Bernhard, Regensburg, 9 November 1665, in *Akten und Urkunden*, vol. 1, p. 493; Christoph Bernhard to Basserode, n.p., 15 October 1665, in *Akten und Urkunden*, vol. 1, p. 481.
51 Christoph Bernhard to Basserode, Regensburg, 10 December 1665, in *Akten und Urkunden*, vol. 1, p. 505; Basserode to Christoph Bernhard, Regensburg, 9 November 1665, in *Akten und Urkunden*, vol. 1, p. 493.
52 Christoph Bernhard to Louis XIV, Münster, 7 January 1666, in *Akten und Urkunden*, vol. 1, p. 519.
53 Instruktion des Fürstbischofs von Münster für Friedrich Korff-Schmising zur Gesandtschaft an den französischen Hof, n.p., August 1665, in *Akten und Urkunden*, vol. 1, p. 467.

war waged by a zealous ecclesiastical prince (which he blamed on defamation instigated by the Dutch and the faithless Waldeck).[54] Although von Galen was indeed a zealous and intolerant sponsor of Catholic reform in his own bishopric, there is a remarkable absence of professed religious motivation for the military actions in 1665–1666.[55] The pope, for example, was officially notified only well after the campaign had ended and was then given Christoph Bernhard's more secular justifications for the war.[56] Confronted with allegations of leading a war of religion by the negotiators of Brandenburg, von Galen actively stressed his otherwise problematic English alliance and claimed: 'one must not imagine that one could turn this war into a religious matter, since [von Galen] ... had joined forces with England'.[57] Obtaining subsidies from a foreign Protestant power could here conveniently be used as an argument to absolve von Galen from allegations of breaking the religious peace mandated by the treaties of 1648.

There was not very much denominational solidarity among fellow Catholic and ecclesiastical potentates with regard to Christoph Bernhard's aggressive stance either. Instead, the position of Cologne's elector and archbishop Max Heinrich and his principal collaborators, advisers and ministers, the two brothers Franz Egon and Wilhelm von Fürstenberg – who were both by far the most important clients and agents in the French diplomatic network in the empire – was highly ambiguous.[58] As French clients, they should have stridently opposed Christoph Bernhard's planned attack on the Dutch and

---

54 Christoph Bernhard to Basserode, St Ludgersburg, 18 September 1665, in *Akten und Urkunden*, vol. 1, p. 473.
55 For Christoph Bernhard's strong confessional stance in his own territory, see Manfred Becker-Huberti, *Die tridentinische Reform im Bistum Münster unter Fürstbischof Christoph Bernhard von Galen 1650–1678* (Münster: Aschendorff, 1978).
56 Christoph Bernhard von Galen to Pope Alexander VII., Münster, 2 July 1665, in *Die Korrespondenz des Münsterer Fürstbischofs Christoph Bernhard von Galen mit dem Heiligen Stuhl (1650–1678)*, ed. by Alois Schröer (Münster: Aschendorff, 1972), pp. 332–335.
57 'Man dürfe sich aber nicht einbilden, als wen man aus dieser kriegsunruhe ein religionswerck machen wollte, den er sich ja mit Engelandt ... verbunden hette'; Schöning to Frederick William of Brandenburg, Meppen, 5 November 1665, in *Akten und Urkunden*, vol. 1, p. 488.
58 Particularly with regard to Wilhelm von Fürstenberg, see Max Braubach, *Wilhelm Egon von Fürstenberg (1629–1704)* (Cologne: Röhrscheid, 1972); John T. O'Connor, 'William Egon von Fürstenberg, German Agent in the Service of Louis XIV', *French Historical Studies* 5 (1967), 119–145.

stopped any attempt at recruiting troops in his territories in its tracks, given the fact that Louis XIV resolutely opposed the war against the Dutch and vowed to protect the Republic.

Nevertheless, Christoph Bernhard was granted recruitment privileges on Cologne territory.[59] On the one hand, the Fürstenberg brothers tried to dissuade Christoph Bernhard from war on behalf of the English, whereas, on the other hand, it is likely that they banked on a military disaster and even occupation of the bishopric of Münster, in hopes that such a development would prompt Rome to unseat the belligerent prince-bishop.[60] This unholy speculation was driven by micropolitical interest and the scramble for the amassment of benefices by Archbishop Max Heinrich and the Fürstenbergs, who hoped to install their master in Christoph Bernhard's place and had also committed the French crown to assist them in their own quest for free episcopal sees in 1658.[61] By the start of Christoph Bernhard's campaign, Wilhelm von Fürstenberg tried to move his French patrons in this direction, even though no French request on that matter was ever presented in Rome.[62]

However, Louis XIV eventually acted upon his warnings to the prince-bishop and sent troops to terminate Christoph Bernhard's campaign, although these troops took no direct action but rather oversaw the increasing disintegration of Christoph Bernhard's army. When Friedrich Wilhelm of Brandenburg in this situation renewed his offers for mediation in peace talks (alongside a thinly veiled threat to otherwise join the war on the Dutch side), Christoph Bernhard von Galen suspended the military campaign and entered into negotiations that ultimately resulted in the Peace of Cleves in 1666 and Christoph Bernhard's temporary abandonment of territorial expansion at the expense of the United Provinces.[63] It was only then

---

59 Christoph Bernhard to Franz Egon von Fürstenberg, Münster, 18 June 1665, in *Akten und Urkunden*, vol. 1, p. 457.
60 Braubach, *Fürstenberg*, pp. 96–97.
61 Max Braubach, 'Der Pakt der Brüder Fürstenberg mit Frankreich', in Max Braubach, *Kurköln: Gestalten und Ereignisse aus zwei Jahrhunderten rheinischer Geschichte* (Münster: Aschendorff, 1949), pp. 19–42.
62 Wilhelm Egon von Fürstenberg an Lionne, Oberkirch, 16 September 1665, in *Akten und Urkunden*, vol. 1, p. 472.
63 Ernst Opgenoorth, *Friedrich Wilhelm: Der Große Kurfürst von Brandenburg: Eine politische Biographie*, 2 vols (Göttingen: Musterschmidt, 1978), pp. 89–93.

that the English government stepped in for a last-ditch effort to save their alliance, dispatching William Temple to Cleves and then to Münster to stop the treaty and its subsequent ratification and to provide some of the overdue subsidies with a view to keeping the bishop in line. Lamentably for his principals, Temple succeeded neither in persuading the prince-bishop to remain in their alliance nor in reversing the payment of English subsidies after Christoph Bernhard had signed the peace treaty.[64]

Gearing up for the 'grand dessein': German princes and the negotiation of French subsidy alliances for Louis XIV's Dutch War

By 1668, the strategic situation on the larger European scale had changed a good deal: the Netherlands gradually emerged as the principal enemy of Louis XIV, and he began to arrange French diplomacy in Europe as a tool to enable large-scale warfare against the Dutch. This constellation would ultimately commit the Fürstenberg brothers and Christoph Bernhard to the same political camp. Soon after the end of the War of Devolution (1667–1668), Wilhelm von Fürstenberg shifted into high gear as Louis XIV's principal negotiator in the empire to broker subsidy alliances with German princes – alliances that should, on the basis of his and foreign secretary Lionne's thinking, enable them to recruit armies that would participate in a French attack on the Netherlands.[65] As shown in Paul Sonnino's comprehensive study of the run-up to the Dutch War, these negotiations proved to be complicated and the French attack had to be delayed repeatedly; it is also evident that the military outlines for the campaign and the subsequent roles of the German allies frequently changed.[66]

Fürstenberg's negotiations in the Holy Roman Empire demonstrate particularly well how the French diplomatic effort to form subsidy alliances relied on French cross-border patronage relations as an

---

64 For this last episode, see William Temple to John Temple, Brussels, 10 May 1666, in *Works of Temple*, 4 vols, pp. 242–252.
65 Braubach, 'Der Pakt der Brüder Fürstenberg'; Hans Böhmer, 'Forschungen zur französischen Rheinpolitik im 17. Jahrhundert: Wilhelm Egon von Fürstenberg und die französische Diplomatie in Deutschland', *Rheinische Vierteljahrsblätter* 4 (1934), 225–259.
66 Paul Sonnino, *Louis XIV and the Origins of the Dutch War* (Cambridge: Cambridge University Press, 1988).

important tool of French diplomacy. Fürstenberg and other actors acted within a local French network of informants, political brokers, and (unofficial as well as official) negotiators. They were obligated to the crown in 'cross-border' patron–client relationships that resembled the networks of clients serving as channels for royal patronage to provincial elites in exchange for their compliance in organizing provincial politics, which contributed to the political integration of the kingdom's periphery.[67] As French clients, the two Fürstenberg brothers were not only indispensable pillars of French politics in the empire. As clients, the Fürstenbergs amassed multiple, often rivalling, loyalties – a very common phenomenon found in many patronage relations in the early modern period. They carefully balanced and played out their many roles as powerful counsellors, ministers, and diplomats to a prince elector, clients of the French crown, clergymen, and members of a traditionally pro-Habsburg noble house to their own advantage to improve their noble status, ecclesiastical careers, or revenues.[68]

Moreover, the negotiations for subsidy alliances reveal how Wilhelm von Fürstenberg imposed his family's respective 'micropolitical' interest on to the negotiations and the operational preparations for war. In his treaty with Cologne, Fürstenberg made sure that the alliance treaty with Archbishop Max Heinrich would not only secure the Dutch-occupied city of Rheinberg for his elector and principal but also guarantee the Fürstenbergs several rich Dutch-controlled manors.[69] Moreover, Wilhelm von Fürstenberg himself joined the ranks of German military entrepreneurs when, in the run-up to the war that his negotiations would eventually facilitate, he began recruiting a regiment on his own with French funds in 1669 and thus joined the ranks of German military entrepreneurs. But interestingly, Wilhelm insisted on posting his regiment under French command, not under that of Max Heinrich's army operating on the basis of French subsidies.[70] Considering Fürstenberg a client of the French crown does not mean that he simply served the interests of a unified governmental mind on a strictly local level.

---

67 Sharon Kettering, *Patrons, Brokers, and Clients in Seventeenth-century France* (New York: Oxford University Press, 1986).
68 For the workings of this clientele and the practices of the Fürstenberg brothers and other actors from the 1650s to the 1670s, see Haug, *Ungleiche Außenbeziehungen*.
69 Braubach, *Fürstenberg*, p. 220.
70 *Ibid.*, pp. 231–232.

The French stance on the vast system of subsidy alliances with German princes was subject to the interplay of ministerial and court-faction infights, which typically aligned themselves with conflicts over larger political issues. As the crown's client in the empire, Fürstenberg had close ties to the French foreign secretary Hugues de Lionne, who acted as a kind of patronage manager towards French clients abroad but with whom Fürstenberg also had a personal friendship, Lionne having been a French ambassador at the Frankfurt imperial election of 1657–1658.[71] As Lionne's confidant, Fürstenberg subsequently saw his project of alliances heavily contested by Lionne's bitter rival Louvois, the French minister of war, who sought a more exclusive role for the regular French troops throughout the campaign.[72]

As a client, Fürstenberg was not merely an instrument for French interests and brokerage in the empire; he had easy access to the court and the king and could play his own party in the faction rivalries. Still, Wilhelm's room for manoeuvre in terms of subsidy alliances became substantially curtailed with Lionne's death in 1671 when Louvois temporarily took over as foreign minister. Fürstenberg's negotiations for subsidy alliances were also riddled with other difficulties. Not only would it eventually prove too complicated to co-ordinate the complex interests and rivalries of the elector of Brandenburg, Philipp Wilhelm von Neuburg, or the dukes of Brunswick into an offensive alliance; Fürstenberg's leverage for the negotiation of military alliances was also dependent on French payments to the courts of larger European powers – for example costs associated with Sweden's abandonment of the Dutch, which at one point effectively defunded Fürstenberg's planned subsidy alliances.[73]

Finally, in 1672, Fürstenberg could muster two rather 'obvious' offensive subsidy alliances with Max Heinrich of Cologne, still firmly in the grip of the influence of both Fürstenberg brothers, and with Christoph Bernhard von Galen who got a chance to rekindle his infamous feud with the Dutch, now aided by French subsidies. While Max Heinrich as a particularly weak monarch was practically carried into the alliance by the Fürstenberg brothers, Christoph Bernhard von Galen's involvement was more proactive: he had already become a beneficiary of French subsidies in exchange for his neutrality during the War of Devolution in 1667 and immediately

---

71 *Ibid.*, p. 36.
72 Sonnino, *Dutch War*, pp. 140–141.
73 *Ibid.*, pp. 151–153.

invested the funds in a modest rearmament.[74] With the Peace of Aachen in 1668, this source of revenue was cut off abruptly. No payment of French subsidies to Münster in peacetimes was to be expected, as was pointed out by Friedrich Korff-Schmising, one of his negotiators, who was sent to Paris to collect these debts.[75] The preparations for a French war against the Dutch Republic were hence eagerly awaited by Christoph Bernhard, who needed little persuasion to insert himself into a coalition for a renewed attack on the Dutch for a highly paid subsidy alliance. Several delays and the preliminary offer of a less lucrative and merely defensive alliance, which effectively froze him out of what he called the 'grand dessein', apparently only rendered the prince-bishop nervous and angry.[76] Finally, in 1672, the bishop joined an alliance to go on the offensive against the Dutch with France and Cologne that secured him 13,000 écus, for which he had to provide nine thousand troops, while Max Heinrich committed a contingent of around eight thousand for 11,000 écus.[77] Münster and Cologne did not enter the war as distant proxies but operated closely together with the French army. Being in a subsidy alliance with France also meant that Münster was expected to provide supplies, mainly ammunition, for the entire coalition army.[78]

Christoph Bernhard von Galen's alliance was widely rejected in the empire. His own chapter would generally have approved of subsidies for an armed neutrality or defensive warfare, but it was staunchly opposed to an offensive campaign with the French that endangered the safety of the bishopric.[79] Dealing with his own chapter also led the bishop (in opposition to the earlier English

---

74 Kohl, *Christoph Bernhard*, pp. 255–256; Tessin, 'Formationsgeschichte', p. 93.
75 Korff-Schmising to Christoph Bernhard, Paris, 13 December 1669, in *Akten und Urkunden*, vol. 2, p. 181; Korff-Schmising to Christoph Bernhard, Paris, 13 December 1669, in *Akten und Urkunden*, vol. 2, p. 182.
76 Friedrich Korff-Schmising to Christoph Bernhard, Paris, 24 March 1670, in *Akten und Urkunden*, vol. 2, pp. 221–222; Verjus to Louis XIV, Bielefeld, 13 June 1671, in *Akten und Urkunden*, vol. 2, p. 289; Kohl, *Christoph Bernhard*, p. 334.
77 Kohl, *Christoph Bernhard*, p. 354; Braubach, *Fürstenberg*, pp. 219–222.
78 Französisch-münsterische Konvention, Ostendorf, 22 January 1672, in *Akten und Urkunden*, vol. 2, p. 357; Louvois to Christoph Bernhard, Rumigny en Thiérarche, 30 April 1672, in *Akten und Urkunden*, vol. 2, p. 397.
79 Protokoll des Domkapitels zu Münster, Münster, 8 March 1672, in *Akten und Urkunden*, vol. 2, p. 367; Protokoll des Domkapitels zu Münster, Münster, 12 March 1672, in *Akten und Urkunden*, vol. 2, p. 369.

Small powers and great designs

alliance) to emphasize more decidedly the confessional nature of the military action he was about to join.[80] Consulting his 'conscience counsellor', the Jesuit Theodor Körler, the bishop inquired if his duty, born out of an allegiance to the pope as a protector of church possessions, the opportunity of a triumphant victory over heresy, and his Christian conscience, compelled him to wage an aggressive war alongside the 'roi très chrétien' and a fellow ecclesiastical prince. Fashioning the Dutch War as a religious conflict in this respect also served more opportunistic purposes, as von Galen also inquired whether it was then permissible to completely ignore his chapter in the decision to enter the war.[81] While Pater Körler generally approved of guarding and eventually regaining Catholic territory, he found neither the imagined papal commission nor the conscience argument convincing.[82]

The chapter continued to disapprove of an offensive war in a French alliance. This could not be changed, either by religious justifications or by constructing a 'preventive war' against the Dutch who, allegedly, were about to attack the bishopric and other parts of the empire, which meant that stopping them in their tracks would be an act of patriotism and guarantee of peace towards the bishopric and the empire.[83] Likewise, Pope Clement X himself repudiated any military adventure in the Netherlands with regard to Christoph Bernhard.[84] All of this eventually caused Christoph Bernhard to send his army into the field without any further consultation.

There was also more fierce resistance to Christoph Bernhard's action, particularly by his fellow imperial estates and by Emperor Leopold I, who sent one of his generals and diplomats, the marquis de Grana, to the bishopric to formally reprimand von Galen for his offensive alliance.[85] With the gradual involvement of the emperor and

---

80 Christoph Bernhard explored a confessionally homogeneous subsidy alliance by the end of 1666, see Denkschrift 1666 [late 1666], in *Akten und Urkunden*, vol. 2, p. 41.
81 Braun, *Princeps*, p. 340.
82 Gewissensvotum des P. Körler, early 1672, in *Korrespondenz Christoph Bernhard*, pp. 453–456.
83 Christoph Bernhard to the Münster Chapter, St Ludgersburg, 30 March 1672, in *Akten und Urkunden*, vol. 2, p. 376.
84 Clement X to Christoph Bernhard, 30 April 1672, in *Korrespondenz Christoph Bernhard*, pp. 449–450.
85 Ferdinand von Fürstenberg to Christoph Bernhard, Neuhaus, 8 April 1672, in *Akten und Urkunden*, vol. 2, pp. 387–388; Marquis de Grana to Leopold I, Lennepp, 13 April 1672, in *Akten und Urkunden*, vol. 2, pp. 388–389.

an increasing number of imperial estates in the conflict following the initial phase of the Dutch War, the role of the political framework of the empire and its impact on patron–client relations and military entrepreneurship in foreign services changed. Such warlike subsidy alliances were now treated no longer as infractions of the Peace of Westphalia in a larger sense or as hazards in relation to territorial security and religious peace but increasingly as treason or breaches of fealty towards emperor and empire. With no unified procedures in place that could put the empire in a formal state of war, a *Reichskrieg* against France was cumulated through a subsequent combination of legal measures in 1673–1674.[86]

This development was accompanied by a series of violent acts which were ostensibly aimed at disrupting the peace negotiations under way in Cologne and included the singling out of Wilhelm von Fürstenberg as the main promoter of treasonous subsidy alliances and armaments.[87] Fürstenberg was eventually kidnapped and imprisoned by a band of imperial officers as a corrupt traitor and defector. Keeping his regiment in French service while allegedly ignoring an imperial mandate to withdraw to the empire weighed particularly heavily in these accusations[88] While Fürstenberg's own contradictory assemblage of identities between affiliations in France and the empire turned against him during the Dutch war, in effect this also blocked any penal consequences for Fürstenberg and made his eventual release an important *point d'honneur* for the French during the peace negotiations in Nijmegen.[89]

Not unlike Fürstenberg's treatment, an act of spectacular violence was also planned and approved by some officials in Vienna to counter Christoph Bernhard's collaboration with France. Even before the empire had started to enter the war, a young officer, Adam von der Kette, was dispatched to Münster to assassinate von Galen.[90] Even though these plans were revealed at an early stage, Christoph Bernhard appeared scared at the prospect of being treated as a rebel

---

86 See Christoph Kampmann, 'Reichstag und Reichskriegserklärung im Zeitalter Ludwigs XIV', *Historisches Jahrbuch* 113 (1993), pp. 41–59.
87 For the failure and Habsburg disruption of the peace talks in Cologne, see Marie-Felicia Renaudin, 'L'échec du congrès de Cologne: De la fête au drame', *Revue d'histoire diplomatique* 118 (2004), 223–249.
88 Käthe Spiegel, *Wilhelm Egon von Fürstenbergs Gefangenschaft und ihre Bedeutung für die Friedensfrage 1674–1679* (Bonn: Röhrscheid, 1936); Haug, *Ungleiche Außenbeziehungen*, pp. 430–450.
89 Paul Otto Höynck, *Frankreich und seine Gegner auf dem Nymwegener Friedenskongreß* (Bonn: Röhrscheid, 1960), pp. 21–22.

and an enemy by the emperor, and his resolve to fight in the French coalition began to crack. Yet, only after two disappointing campaigns in the Netherlands, von Galen decided to switch sides and join a ragtag coalition of imperial troops and allied princes. This decision was born not solely out of a strong desire for his own security or feelings of what might be called imperial patriotism but also out of the failure of his French allies to secure his territories against Dutch reprisals and, on a regular basis, provide the guaranteed subsidies for his large army.

Still acting as a minor prince turned military entrepreneur, Christoph Bernhard would not commit his troops to the imperial coalition in the German north-west without securing for himself an extraordinarily advantageous monthly rate of subsidies of 15,000 *reichstaler* (after an immediate payment of 40,000 *reichstaler*) and a very generous command over the army.[91] Nevertheless, Christoph Bernhard's stance toward subsidy alliances turned even more 'entrepreneurial' as the excruciating war dragged on and frequently led him to lend out his troops to, for instance, the king of Denmark, the countess of Frisia, and other members of the anti-French coalition.[92]

Conclusions

The cases presented in this chapter have shown that subsidy alliances not only provided major European powers with what would today be called boots on the ground and the necessary infrastructure for pursuing military campaigns; they also afforded minor princes the chance to promote their interests in territorial security or expansion, as well as possibly providing them with a military asset of symbolic value to enhance their status on the larger European stage. Brokering such alliances between asymmetrical partners was often undertaken with the help of cross-border networks or clients of

---

90 For a more comprehensive account of this attempt, see Eberhard Wiens, 'Beiträge zur Geschichte der Verschwörung des Adam von der Kette gegen das Land und Leben des Fürstbischofs von Münster, Christoph Bernhard von Galen', *Westfälische Zeitschrift* 4 (1841), 289–321; see also André Krischer, 'Eine grausame und gefehrliche Verräterey und Conjuration: Der versuchte Anschlag auf den Münsteraner Fürstbischof Christoph Bernhard von Galen 1673', in *Höllische Ingenieure – Attentate und Verschwörungen in kriminalitäts-, entscheidungs- und sicherheitsgeschichtlicher Perspektive*, ed. by Tilman Haug and André Krischer (Constance: UVK, forthcoming).
91 Kohl, *Christoph Bernhard*, pp. 409–416.
92 *Ibid.*, pp. 475–478.

foreign powers in the empire, who inserted their own interests and prospects for rewards into these negotiations. In other cases, such as the English alliance with Münster, the lack of functional 'lubricants' for communication and military coordination as well as a certain susceptibility to Dutch 'counter-patronage' significantly impaired the subsidy alliance.

While the political framework of the empire and its internal system of alliances explicitly allowed for external alliances for security and peacekeeping purposes, these factors also placed some constraints on subsidy alliances; examples include the ways in which the Rhine alliance put the duke of Neuburg's armament into question or presented offensive alliances as a danger to the contemporary order of peace. With the more active involvement and transformation of the empire into an actor of foreign power politics during the Dutch War, French subsidy alliances came close to treason, while other foreign subsidies remained crucial to keeping actors like Christoph Bernhard von Galen in the war. Thus, foreign subsidy alliances after the Peace of Westphalia provided new political opportunities for German potentates to impose themselves on the European stage; but their asymmetrical alliances not only reveal a multiform diplomatic game with multiple loyalties and ambiguous negotiators, they also show that the princes' affiliation to the empire as a political body remained a significant norm of reference with which they sought to align their alliances in one way or another.

9
The 'fiscal-military hub' of Amsterdam: intermediating the French subsidies to Sweden during the Thirty Years' War

Marianne Klerk

Much scholarly attention has been paid to early modern subsidy practices on an interstate level, as arrangements and transfers of military resources between states. Subsidies are often portrayed as financial tools of alliances by which a powerful state lured a weaker one into its sphere of influence with the promise of money, a much-needed resource in this period of increasing military conflict in Europe.[1] One of the most notorious examples is the French financial support to Sweden during the Thirty Years' War. It has been described as turning the Scandinavian monarchy into virtually 'a French Satellite' and forming a significant part of the Swedish state revenue, especially after the lucrative Prussian licences came to an end in 1635. At the Peace of Stuhmsdorf that year, Sweden was forced to return its recent conquests in Prussia to Poland, including the right to levy tolls on shipping to and from Prussian ports.[2] Influenced by the 'contractor state' debate, historians (as testified by Svante Norrhem and Erik Thomson in the Introduction, above) have recently pointed to the pivotal role of private contractors and agents who could transfer subsidies across the boundaries

---

1 See, for example, Peter Claus Hartmann, *Geld als Instrument europäischer Machtpolitik im Zeitalter des Merkantilismus* (Munich: Kommission für bayerische Landesgeschichte, 1978); *Flattering Alliances: Scandinavia, Diplomacy, and the Austrian–French Balance of Power, 1648–1740*, ed. by Peter Lindström and Svante Norrhem (Lund: Nordic Academic Press, 2013).

2 Sven-Erik Åström, 'The Swedish Economy and Sweden's Role as a Great Power 1632–1697', in *Sweden's Age of Greatness 1632–1718*, ed. by Michael Roberts (London: Macmillan, 1973), pp. 79–100 (p. 94).

of states through their contacts. However, such studies still focus on individual contractors supplying their 'own' domestic states. Following the Tilly thesis regarding war-making and state-making, a particular emphasis is thereby placed on the formative power of foreign subsidies in building up the modern, sovereign state and the European state system.

This chapter offers a different perspective on the study of subsidies by looking beyond the interstate level, adding a new dimension to our understanding of the development of the state system. Not only were subsidies arranged by state and non-state agents; this contribution argues that subsidies along with other war-making resources were organized in specific urban European centres, here referred to as 'fiscal-military hubs'. The growing scale of early modern military conflict in Europe launched a flourishing industry in war-organization across Europe. States became increasingly dependent on private entrepreneurs and their extensive European business networks to pay and/or cash their foreign subsidies, to supply them with human resources, weaponry, provisions, and transport, and to provide them with credit. In cities working as hubs within a wider fiscal-military system, merchants, bankers, financiers, and agents gathered to buy and sell military resources, ranging from credit to cannons and from soldiers to fully equipped ships. Neither the location nor the status of political capital defines a fiscal-military hub, but rather the presence of an elite of merchant-financiers with expertise and elaborate networks in the business of war. Whereas, for instance, the production of weaponry was decentralized – executed in small workshops spread over large, regional areas – the organization and distribution were centralized by these elites in the hubs to meet large-scale demand from states or contractors.[3] The three most important hubs were Amsterdam, Hamburg, and Genoa. Other centres with less centrifugal fiscal-military power included Paris, Vienna, and Danzig. The hubs were connected through the complex and strong business networks of private military entrepreneurs and together these constituted a 'fiscal-military system' in Europe. This system emerged parallel to the European state system, as the nascent states tapped into its resources from the 1560s onwards, and broke down in the 1860s when warfare had become nationalized. It may be seen as a paradox of history that early modern European conflict

---

3 David Parrott, *The Business of War: Military Enterprise and Military Revolution in Early Modern Europe* (Cambridge: Cambridge University Press, 2012), p. 214.

was possible only through co-operation between states and between state and non-state actors.[4] The fiscal-military hub of Amsterdam and how the hub transferred French subsidies to Sweden during the Thirty Years' War form the case study of this chapter. Both parties signed the Treaty of Bärwalde on 23 January 1631 guaranteeing the latter French sponsorship for five years (an annual 400,000 *taler*). In turn, Gustav II Adolf accepted Richelieu's conditions, in particular to conclude no separate peace with third parties.[5] The dominant themes in the existing literature on the French subsidies encompass the influence gained by France in relation to Swedish policy, the exact amounts of the payments and who administered these, the negotiations between Richelieu and Oxenstierna, and to what extent the payments were part of the actual war finances of Sweden.[6] Research on private entrepreneurs and how they transferred resources mainly focuses on particular financiers working for specific states, such as the banker Hans de Witte for the Austrian Habsburgs, the financier Philip Burlamachi for England, and the Amsterdam-based arms merchants Louis de Geer as well as Elias and Pieter Trip for Sweden, and Jean Hoeufft for France and the Dutch Republic.[7] An excellent study following international flows of resources was executed by Julia Zunckel, who uncovered the transnational networks of arms dealers from Genoa, Hamburg, and Amsterdam during the Thirty Years' War, an issue which was brought up by David Parrott in his brilliant

---

4 On the fiscal-military system, see Peter Wilson, Chapter 3 above.
5 'Traicté de Bervald entre le Roy de France et de Suede (…)', AE Suède 2 fols 2–5 and Swedish National Archive, ASRA OT Frankrike n° 2A.
6 On Franco-Swedish relations discussed in this manner, see Geoffrey Parker, *The Thirty Years' War* (London: Routledge, 1984); on the Swedish war finances, see Christoph Kampmann, *Europa und das Reich im Dreißigjährigen Krieg: Geschichte eines europäischen Konflikts* (Stuttgart: Kohlhammer, 2008), pp. 77–82; Sven Lundkvist, 'Svensk krigsfinansiering 1630–1635', *Historisk Tidskrift* 83 (1963), 1–38.
7 Anton Ernstberger, *Hans de Witte: Finanzmann Wallensteins*, Vierteljahrschrift für Sozial- und Wirtschaftsgeschichte, Beiheft 38 (Wiesbaden: Steiner, 1954); Arthur V. Judges, 'Philip Burlamachi: A Financier of the Thirty Years' War', *Economica* 6 (1926), 285–300; Erik Thomson, 'Jan Hoeufft and the Thirty Years War: An Essay on Diplomatic History's Limits', working paper presented at the Historical Department at Umeå University (16 March 2013); Regina Schulte, 'Rüstung, Zins und Frömmigkeit: Niederländische Calvinisten als Finanziers des Dreißigjährigen Krieges', *Bohemia: Zeitschrift für Geschichte und Kultur der böhmischen Länder* 35 (1994), 46–62.

book *The Business of War*.⁸ A reason why early modern financial transfers in particular attract little attention might be the absence of easily accessible private business sources. The financial trade, for example, was less controlled by the States-General in the Dutch Republic than the trade and production of weaponry. The export of arms was licensed and requests for export can be traced back in the state archives. On the whole, historians interested in the intersection between government and the private sector tend to rely on state sources. While identifying the individual agents and their correspondents is frequently not particularly challenging, reconstructing how their businesses actually operated and following the money represents a more difficult task.⁹

A useful source offering insight into the dealings of these businessmen, however, is the notarial records of Amsterdam, as we shall see in this chapter. When conflict arose between merchants over a specific deal, a payment, or other forms of transfers, a merchant could bring in a notary who would officially appeal to the accused merchant. Other merchants would mediate as a panel of judges in these disputes. Besides state sources, official correspondence, and fragments of private business archives, these records provide an entry point into the inner workings of the fiscal-military hub of Amsterdam while transferring the French subsidies to Sweden. The objective of this chapter is to explain the nature of the Amsterdam fiscal-military hub and how it functioned by looking into the Franco-Swedish subsidy transfers, as well as to emphasize the fundamentally interacting elements of the fiscal-military hub of Amsterdam: credit, commerce, and the highly transnational and elaborate connections of the Amsterdam-based military entrepreneurs.

---

8 Julia Zunckel, *Rüstungsgeschäfte im Dreißigjährigen Krieg: Unternehmerkräfte, Militärgüter und Marktstrategien im Handel zwischen Genua, Amsterdam and Hamburg* (Berlin: Duncker & Humblot, 1997); Parrott, *The Business of War*.

9 As stated by Richard Harding and Sergio Solbes Ferri, 'Introduction', in *The Contractor State and Its Implications, 1659–1815*, ed. by Richard Harding and Sergio Solbes Ferri (Las Palmas de Gran Canaria: Universidad de Las Palmas de Gran Canaria, 2012), pp. 9–19 (p. 12); and by Roger Knight and Martin Wilcox, 'War, Government and the Market: The Direction of the Debate on the British Contractor State', in *The Contractor State and Its Implications, 1659–1815*, ed. by Richard Harding and Sergio Solbes Ferri (Las Palmas de Gran Canaria: Universidad de Las Palmas de Gran Canaria, 2012), pp. 175–198 (pp. 175–176).

The Amsterdam market for murder: credit, commerce, and connections

The first payment of the French subsidies was personally transferred from Paris by the Swedish financial agent Erik Larsson von der Linde. He was commissioned by the Swedish king to co-ordinate the war subsidies in Amsterdam. The next payments were handled by his son Lorens.[10] Most of the subsidies were remitted through bills of exchange, a proportion of which was transferred in Amsterdam. The other Swedish agent in Amsterdam, Melchior von Falkenberg, wrote to Oxenstierna in January 1631 that he and Larsson needed help from the highly placed Amsterdam merchant-regent Samuel Blommaert to cash the bills of exchange: 'neither I nor Erik Larsson could get any money on bills of exchange without the assistance of his factor Samuel Blommaert, who has been the caution for all the letters of exchange I have drawn on Hamburg and Danzig until this point'.[11] Two things need to be highlighted here. First is the mention of the use of bills of exchange, which were orders (not legal promises) to pay and functioned both as instruments of credit and as instruments of remittance and currency conversion.[12] Together with other manners of loans and debts, bills of exchange were crucial financial instruments of the fiscal-military system, by which large sums of money could be transferred across Europe.[13] Second, Falkenberg draws a link between Amsterdam, Hamburg, and Danzig in his dealings with the French subsidies. The symbiotic relationship between these three fiscal-military hubs, as contended in this chapter, structured the payments of the French subsidies to Sweden during the Thirty Years' War.

Following the generic explanation of how bills of exchange were exchanged, we may argue that Larsson or Falkenberg served as the so-called 'deliverer' lending money from the 'taker', who in turn supplied the deliverer with a bill of exchange. The credit was denominated in the currency of the place of payment or in an international currency such as the florin. Blommaert was the 'taker' in Amsterdam, supposing that was what Falkenberg meant by 'assistance'. The bill of exchange was drawn on his particular

---

10 Thomson, 'Jan Hoeufft and the Thirty Years' War', p. 7.
11 Translated by Erik Thomson, *ibid.*, p. 7.
12 Pit Dehing, *Geld in Amsterdam: Wisselbank en wisselkoersen, 1650–1725* (Hilversum: Verloren, 2012), p. 198.
13 See Peter Wilson, Chapter 3 above.

correspondent in Hamburg or Danzig, also called the 'drawee' (payer). The latter paid in the specific currency or international coinage to the 'payee' or the Swedish agent of Larsson or Falkenberg in Hamburg or Danzig. This is certainly an oversimplified account of the transfer business of subsidy payments, but it may give a clearer image of the basic actions needed to transfer subsidies. The reality was far more complex. Besides the fact that a bill of exchange was a negotiable document (to be bought and sold to other parties), the actual transfer of subsidies involved numerous contacts as well as multiple bills drawn on various cities simultaneously or in sequence – first a bill was drawn on Amsterdam from which another was drawn on Hamburg, payments were delayed or not paid at all by the French crown, or simply spread out by the financier, whose remittances could also involve other transfer deals or portions of the subsidy payments.[14]

With this money, Sweden could finance its troops in the Holy Roman Empire, of which 70 per cent went to the army in the German lands, 8 per cent was spent on the embassy in Osnabrück, and 6 per cent on diplomats, residents, and correspondents.[15] The Swedes organized their military campaigns in the Empire from Hamburg, not only for its geographical position but as the city itself was a mighty fiscal-military hub and was outshone only by Amsterdam from the 1650s onwards.[16] Danzig was located on the eastern side from where the Swedish troops moved into the German lands. Additionally, the Baltic port city was a nodal point in the Hanseatic trade network and functioned as a fiscal-military hub in the Baltic region. This identifies the co-operation not only between state and private agents but also between fiscal-military hubs themselves. Hamburg dealers in fiscal-military resources needed their Amsterdam connections and vice versa. The Swedish agents in Hamburg and the French agents in Paris needed the assistance of the merchant-financiers in Amsterdam as well as their own representatives setting up shop in the Dutch city.

---

14 See Erik Thomson, Chapter 10 below.
15 Gottfrid Lorenz, 'Schweden und die französischen Hilfsgelder von 1638 bis 1649', in *Forschungen und Quellen zur Geschichte des Dreißigjährigen Krieges*, Schriftenreihe der Vereinigung zur Erforschung der Neueren Geschichte e.V., 12, ed. by Konrad Repgen (Münster: Aschendorff, 1981), pp. 98–148 (p. 99).
16 Hermann Kellenbenz, 'Hamburg und die französisch-schwedische Zusammenarbeit im 30jährigen Krieg', *Zeitschrift der Vereins für Hamburgische Geschichte* 49/50 (1964), 83–107.

The 'fiscal-military hub' of Amsterdam

This brings us to the core question of this chapter: why would the French and Swedish agents involved not simply transfer the subsidies through the fiscal-military hub of Hamburg alone? What could Amsterdam offer them that Hamburg could not? The answer lies in three interrelated aspects fundamental to the efficacy of the Amsterdam market for murder in the seventeenth century: first, the city was the financial centre of Europe; second, it was the continent's entrepôt; and, third, very importantly, it housed an elite of merchant-financiers with extensive, transnational networks and the utmost expertise in the fiscal-military business.

Financial centre

At the beginning of the seventeenth century, Amsterdam became the leading centre of financial exchange in Europe. Historians point to various causes behind this emergence, notably the migration of banking experts from the south of the Netherlands at the end of the sixteenth century fleeing the hardships of war and religious persecution by the Catholic Habsburgs. Antwerp had become the key centre for foreign exchange (parallel to its expansion into a commercial hub) in the early sixteenth century; however, in combination with this migration, the centre of gravity gradually moved to Amsterdam. The migrants took their capital, expertise, and European networks with them and introduced Antwerp practices of financing, banking, money-exchange, maritime insurance, and financial reporting. This was enhanced by financial institution-building, innovations such as the Bank of Exchange (1609), Bank of Credit (1609), the Stock Exchange (1602), set up by the East India Company to exchange its printed stocks, and the West India Company (1674). The Bank of Exchange secured, advanced, and enlarged (long-distance) transfers of money. A variety of instruments of credit and capital purchase, such as the issuing of shares, were developed for harmonizing money transfers. Amsterdam created an excellent reputation for the business of credit. The market of invested capital grew massively. Amsterdam-based financiers invested and participated in foreign enterprises, and international commercial networks were becoming more and more interconnected through Amsterdam credits. At the end of the century, Amsterdam had become the centre of a complex network of credit stretched out across Europe.[17]

---

17 Dehing, *Geld in Amsterdam*, pp. 199–200.

Above all, Amsterdam was the preferred city in Europe for borrowing funds. Most of the bills of exchange drawn in Amsterdam were from other cities in Europe rather than from Amsterdam itself. Many merchants involved in the international trade positioned their power base in Amsterdam, from which they could transfer money to their business partners (mostly relatives) abroad or lend them credit by offering to draw a bill on themselves. If a merchant-financier had no family relations in a certain city, he would make use of agents who mediated the transfers for him. An important reason why foreign merchants drew on Amsterdam was that it had the lowest real and relatively stable interest rates.[18] Knowledge of the money-transfer business was invaluable for the Amsterdam elite, as demonstrated by a 1662 textbook on trade, in possession of the family of the famous fiscal-military entrepreneur Louis de Geer. The examples seem to be taken from reality: 'I have to pay 4,000 *taler* to Liebert Wolters in Hamburg and since I have no money for that there, I accorded with Jacomo Roulandt here in Amsterdam, who has money there at Egidio Roulant, on whom he gives me an exchange that I have sent to Liebert Wouters to receive from the same Egedio Roulant 4,000 *taler*.'[19]

The use of bills of exchange greatly increased in the seventeenth century rather than the actual movement of coins. Newly instituted banks acted as clearing banks for the bills, harmonizing the issue of the quantity and quality of coinage and stabilizing the transfer market. The Amsterdam Bank of Exchange was the most important institution designed for this purpose. During the Thirty Years' War, Amsterdam became the centre of European merchant banking; and, as the war continued, an increasing amount of transfers not related to the Dutch Republic were exchanged through the Bank of Exchange. In 1635, the flow of money to Amsterdam had created a financial bubble that burst, which meant that the subsidies had to be transported in barrels of coins accompanied by a passport for export

---

18 Pit Dehing, 'Geld als Water? Amsterdam en de internationale kapitaalstromen (1600–1730)', in *De Republiek tussen zee en vasteland: buitenlandse invloeden op cultuur, economie en politiek in Nederland 1580–1800*, ed. by Karel Davids, Marjolein 't Hart, Henk Kleijer and Jan Lucassen (Leuven and Apeldoorn: Garant, 1995), pp. 229–249 (pp. 229–235).

19 Joan Römelingh (ed.), *Een rondgang langs Zweedse archieven: Een onderzoek naar archivalia inzake de betrekkingen tussen Nederland en Zweden 1520–1920* (The Hague: Martinus Nijhoff, 1986), p. 468.

granted by Louis XIII.[20] A similar bubble of bills of exchange drawn on Amsterdam burst during the War of the Spanish Succession.[21] Although many exchanges were still executed privately between merchants and agents, bills over 600 florins and payable in Amsterdam had to go through the bank. France made extensive use of the Amsterdam exchange business to pass money to its troops in foreign territories or to transfer subsidies across Europe. The French crown would contract bankers to remit the subsidy payments.[22]

In the case of the Swedish subsidies, France initially signed a contract with the financier Claude Charlot for the advancement and transfer of the subsidies. Charlot then commissioned the Swedish agent Erik Larsson in Amsterdam, from where he (together with his son Lorens and Samuel Blommaert operating with various other Dutch merchants) transmitted the money to Hamburg or Danzig. When Charlot went bankrupt, the French government contracted the arms dealer and merchant-financier Jean Hoeufft in 1633. From Paris, he arranged the transfer with his nephew in Amsterdam or directly to, for instance, the banker Lucas von Spreckselen in Hamburg, which was then cashed by the Swedish resident Johan Adler Salvius, a relative of von Spreckselen.[23] There was a lot of money to be made in the remittance of subsidies; but it was also a risky business, partly because payments might be delayed or not paid at all – as was often the case with the French subsidies – but also for other reasons than a mere lack of money. A fine example is the conflict between Salvius and the French resident Claude de Meulles, who withheld the bill of exchange of 240,000 *reichsthaler* in the summer of 1644 as France disagreed – to say the least – with the Swedish invasion of Denmark at that time. Salvius travelled to Münster to speed up the payment, but, as he had no luck in doing

---

20 Thomson, 'Jean Hoeufft and the Thirty Years' War', p. 12; Nationaal Archief (The Hague), 1.01.08 Staten Generaal, 12587–54. The passport explained: 'qu'a cause de l'Interruption du commerce les correspondances des negotiants ont cesse, De Lorre qu'il leur feroit tres difficille de tirer de ce Royaume par lettre de change le million de liures que nous leur avons payé, nou suppliant de permettre a Jean Heuft qui a ordre pour la remisse dud. Million en Hollande de faire transporter a diverses fois.' All translations are by the author unless otherwise stated.
21 Guy Rowlands, *Dangerous and Dishonest Men: The International Bankers of Louis XIV's France* (Basingstoke: Palgrave Macmillan, 2014), p. 144–165.
22 *Ibid.*, pp. 33–83.
23 Thomson, p. 253 below.

so, his wife travelled to Hamburg to advance the war payments to the Swedish troops from her own affluent funds.[24]

While diplomatic and other state sources reveal the contracts signed with financiers and describe the complications of certain transfers, reconstructing the exact remittance business is rather difficult, even elusive, as Erik Thomson argues.[25] There is the complexity of the business itself and the lack of private business sources pertaining to the key figures, such as Jean Hoeufft, as well as the misfortune of the absence of the ledgers of the Amsterdam Bank of Exchange prior to 1644 owing to a fire in the old city hall in 1652.[26] In particular, the difficulty with bills of exchange is that they are 'invisible transfers', as described by Leos Müller.[27] Snippets are sometimes found in books of accounts, as in those from Elbing, Danzig, and Hamburg on the years 1634–1636 accounting for the supplies of food and money by Pieter and Isaak Spiering to the Swedish troops in the Empire. The Dutch brothers Spiering thrived in the Baltic barley market, collecting the Livonian tolls for Sweden, and between 1637 and 1652 Pieter served as the Swedish ambassador to the Dutch Republic. Their ledgers mention four bills: a bill of exchange of 18,000 *taler* from Danzig commissioned by Isaac Spiering drawn on Mattheus Hoeufft in Amsterdam; a bill of 15,000 *taler* commissioned by Pieter and Isaac Spiering drawn on Jacques Verpoorten Adriansson in Hamburg; a bill (not naming the amounts) commissioned by Isaac Spiering drawn on Abraham Willemsen van Beijerlandt in Amsterdam and Jacques Verpoorten Adriansson in Hamburg; and a bill for Mattheus Hoeufft in Amsterdam to pay 5,000 *taler* to the Lord High Chancellor of Sweden Axel Oxenstierna. Thus, for the supplying of the Swedish troops, the Spiering brothers used the money transmitted through Hamburg as well as Amsterdam, the latter being used as an intermediate hub – perhaps for its favourable exchange rates – but it also seems as if the Swedish subsidies were cashed in Amsterdam. Why would the Spiering brothers – if

---

24 Kellenbenz, 'Hamburg und die französisch-schwedische Zusammenarbeit im 30jährigen Krieg', 96–97.
25 Thomson, p. 252 below.
26 Oscaer Gelderblom, *Zuid-Nederlandse kooplieden en de opkomst van de Amsterdamse stapelmarkt (1578–1630)* (Hilversum: Verloren, 2000), p. 268.
27 Leos Müller, 'The Dutch Entrepreneurial Networks and Sweden', in *Trade, Diplomacy and Cultural Exchange: Continuity and change in the North Sea area and the Baltic c. 1350–1750*, ed. by Hanno Brand (Hilversum: Verloren, 2005), p. 66.

they needed to supply the Swedish army in the German lands – cash bills of exchange in Amsterdam and not directly in Hamburg? The answer lies in the other element of the Amsterdam market for murder: its function as an international entrepôt.

Amsterdam entrepôt

Seventeenth-century Amsterdam was the commercial centre of Europe, a centre which developed in parallel to the volume and complexity of its financial business. These two features were of mutual importance for the efficiency of the fiscal-military hub, since finance and commerce were strongly linked to each other under the pressure of warfare. Historiography has emphasized how in the Dutch Republic trade was stimulated and, in some ways, even shaped by warfare, notably its own revolt against Habsburg Spain (1568–1648). The cutting-off of most of the Iberian trade connections, for instance, stimulated Dutch merchants to explore commercial possibilities overseas, which also meant seizing Iberian trading posts and colonies. The States-General assigned the Dutch East India Company (VOC) a war-making mission and a semi-sovereign authority: to declare war, form alliances and contracts, raise troops, and name governors and officers. The result was extremely lucrative 'rich trades' in high-value textiles and spices, and new ways of managing capital and credit flows, such as the establishment of the Stock Exchange by the VOC in 1609. However, historians have added that Dutch trade would probably have been even more prosperous without the hindrance of warfare, as would be shown in relation to the economic boom during the Twelve Years' Peace (1609–1621).[28] Yet another important side note is that war was particularly favourable for the merchant groups of Holland rather than the inland provinces and the rural communities of the Dutch Republic, not least because of the fact that the war against Spain was fought outside of Holland's territory from 1576, and for the influx of wealth, expertise, and connections. The economy and standards of living rose rapidly in Holland as trade and industries expanded and diversified to even higher levels

---

28 See, for instance, Geoffrey Parker, 'War and Economic Change: The Economic Costs of the Dutch Revolt', in *War and Economic Development*, ed. by Jay M. Winter (Cambridge: Cambridge University Press, 1975), pp. 49–71; Jonathan Israel, *Dutch Primacy in World Trade, 1585–1740* (Oxford: Clarendon Press, 1989), pp. 12–120; J. Leslie Price, *Dutch Culture in the Golden Age* (London: Reaktion Books, 2011), pp. 34–38.

than before the war. Moreover, new industries came into being during the war, such as the very prosperous arms industry. Rising demands from the army, navy, colonial companies stationing town soldiers, militias, fortifications, private men, and foreign buyers made this industry an essential part of the economy within two decades, making up at least 5 per cent of the Dutch GNP. [29]

A reason why the war subsidies were transferred and cashed in the Amsterdam hub relates to the arms business, one of the most flourishing trades of the city. Cash was needed for particular purchases, such as weaponry and munitions, and Amsterdam was a vital weapons arsenal in Europe, where foreign agents collected the military gear for wars fought far beyond the Dutch borders. Hamburg formed another key centre of the arms trade, interconnected by the interests of its arms dealers to those in Amsterdam. The Hanseatic and free imperial city was a significant supplier of war material to Spain, yet its merchants often purchased the weaponry in Amsterdam before delivering it to the Habsburgs. The Amsterdam weapons trade – excluding the cannon trade – was based on a growing, comprehensive arms industry in the Dutch Republic supplied by raw materials through the city's entrepôt. Additionally, Amsterdam arms dealers could rely on the Dutch army arsenals if they ran out of stock. Consequently, the arms market in Amsterdam offered foreign buyers flexibility and velocity. One of the most far-reaching innovations was the sale of package deals in which merchants acted as intermediaries between arms producers, sources of raw materials, and foreign buyers to provide a regiment with all the equipment needed.[30]

At the start of the Swedish war preparations, Dietrich von Falkenberg, the marshal of the royal court of the Swedish king, signed a contract with the wealthy arms dealer Elias Trip in Amsterdam on 17 May 1629. The size of the sold goods (package deal) and the promised delivery time exemplifies the adeptness of the

---

29 Marjolein 't Hart, *The Dutch Wars of Independence: Warfare and Commerce in the Netherlands 1570–1680* (London and New York: Routledge, 2014), p. 181.
30 Peter Wilson, 'War Finance, Policy and Strategy in the Thirty Years' War', in *Dynamik durch Gewalt? Der Dreißigjährige Krieg (1618–1648) als Faktor der Wandlungsprozesse des 17. Jahrhunderts*, ed. by Michael Rohrschneider and Anuschka Tischer (Münster: Aschendorff, 2018), pp. 229–250; Peter W. Klein, *De Trippen in de 17e eeuw: Een studie over het ondernemerschap op de Hollandse stapelmarkt* (Assen: Van Gorchum, 1965), pp. 205–208; 't Hart, *The Dutch Wars of Independence*, p. 184.

Amsterdam arms market: 40,602 muskets, 4,602 casques, 3,456 pieces of armour, 3,456 pikes, 72 drums; 100 halberds, 24 partisans, 500 cuirasses, 4,500 units of gunpowder, 4,500 fuses, 4,500 musket balls, and 8,058 rapiers. Within two weeks, almost half the material would be delivered and the rest within three weeks or one month after that. Von Falkenberg would order and commission an 'express man' in Amsterdam, a man to whom Trip delivered the arms and ammunition. Within nine days after delivery, von Falkenberg would pay Trip 190,000 guilders 'in banco' (banking money from the Bank of Exchange).[31] Six days after signing the contract, Sweden placed a request to the Dutch States General to export 8,000 pounds of gunpowder, 8,000 pounds of fuses, and weaponry for nine thousand men. The material would most probably be transported to the troops in the Holy Roman Empire instead of Sweden. At first, the request was granted on the precondition that Sweden would pay the usual duties; but, after the States-General ran into a conflict with von Falkenberg during the summer, a conflict concerning the Swedish recruitment of soldiers at the Dutch frontiers (and apparently also illegitimately by way of the Swedes' contractors in the Republic), the duties were lifted as a concession to Sweden.[32]

Another reason why the subsidies were transferred through Amsterdam is the intrinsic link between the financing of war and trade, between credit and commerce, which the city facilitated exceptionally well. Between 1628 and 1633, the Swedish crown commissioned Erik Larsson and Conrad Falkenberg (the brother of the other Swedish agent in Amsterdam, Melchior Falkenberg) to sell the Swedish copper and manage other financial operations, such as the sale of Swedish grain in Amsterdam. The Dutch merchant Samuel Blommaert brokered the sale of copper, parallel to intermediating in the transfer of the subsidies.[33] The copper trade made

---

31 Contract printed: 'Contract tusschen Elias Trip en Diderik van Vackenburgh, over de levering van wapenen aan Gustaaf Adolf. 17 mei 1629.', *Kroniek van het Historisch Genootschap* VI 31 (Utrecht, 1876), pp. 151–154.
32 See Resolutions 4, 23 May 1629 and for the conflict 1, 13 April 1629; 1, 31 May 1629; 3/5, 6 June 1629; 3, 7 June 1629; 3/21 12 June 1629, *Resolutiën Staten-Generaal 1626–1630*, ed. I.J.A. Nijenhuis, P.L.R. De Cauwer, W.M. Gijsbers, M. Hell, C.O. Van Der Meij, and J.E. Schonneveld-Oosterling, Huygens Instituut Online Publications, available at http:// resources.huygens.knaw.nl/.
33 Gerhard W. Kernkamp, 'Brieven van Samuel Blommaert aan den Zweedschen Rijkskanselier Axel Oxenstierna 1635–1641', *Bijdragen en Mededeelingen van het Historisch Genootschap* 29 (1908), 24–29, 67–131.

up a large part of the Swedish military finances, and Amsterdam was the main market for the sale of Swedish copper, which was often used as collateral for credit. Lübeck in particular used to be a major buyer of Swedish copper, and the city had an important copper industry. However, Sweden moved its copper business to the growing staple market of Amsterdam. In 1613, the Swedes negotiated with the States-General for credit that would be paid from the frequent copper shipments. Johannes van Dillen asserted that the amounts the States-General could collect were not substantial, although the credit had risen to more than 750,000 guilders by 1618.[34]

Since the credit business was profitable, Dutch entrepreneurs stepped in. One of them was Louis de Geer who had gained expertise in the French copper industry, was an arms dealer, and already had connections with Swedish entrepreneurs. In 1618, de Geer formed a consortium to provide King Gustav II Adolf with 250,000 guilders.[35] Although the king granted the entire transfer of copper to the States-General, Lübeck and Hamburg continued to be important trading-places for Swedish copper until 1627, when the remaining copper in these cities was shipped to Amsterdam. The firm of the Trip family received the commission to organize the Swedish copper business. In 1629, the relatives Dietrich and Conrad von Falkenberg signed a contract with two members of the Trip family to transfer the copper credit business from Pieter to his (distant) uncle Elias Trip – the latter being the brother-in-law of Louis de Geer. The advance payment by Pieter Trip to the Swedish crown had amounted to 566,411 guilders, 4 stuivers and 8 pennies. Because of the low copper price, an amount of 1,368 Swedish shipping pounds of raw copper and 2,389 Swedish shipping pounds of copper was not (yet) sold.[36] The second contract with Elias alone stated that Swedish copper was only to be transferred to the Trip merchant, who had to sell the copper 'for cash money and nothing else'; but the Swedish king was free to transport and sell cannons made from copper to

---

34 Johannes G. van Dillen, 'Amsterdamsche notarieele akten betreffende den koperhandel en de uitoefening van mijnbouw en metaalindustrie in Zweden', *Bijdragen en Mededeelingen van het Historisch Genootschap* 5 (1973), 211–301 (p. 214).
35 *Ibid.*, 215.
36 *Ibid.*, 233–235: 'Contract tusschen Diederick en Conrad von Falckenberg, gemachtigden van den koning van Zweden, en Pieter en Elias Trip. 1629 Mei 16, Not. Arch. 700. Not. J. Warnaertsz.'

whomever he preferred.[37] This contract ended in 1632, and by that time Louis de Geer had returned from his travels abroad and re-entered the copper trade. Together with Falkenberg, de Geer tried (but failed) to persuade Trip to transmit the deposited copper. In 1634, Trip seized a transport of copper to de Geer in Amsterdam. He argued that the shipment was his, since Sweden had not paid him its interest on time.[38]

The seizure of goods from the competition was a recurrent phenomenon. Private entrepreneurs also seized subsidy transfers in case of a commercial conflict with one of the states involved. Time and time again, Louis de Geer (as well as Trip) failed to be in agreement with the Swedish agents in Amsterdam. On 11 December 1632, a notarial appeal was sent to Louis de Geer on behalf of Conrad von Falkenberg.[39] He claimed that Louis de Geer had seized 40,000 *taler* of the transfer of Dutch subsidies to Sweden (a total of 60,000). The cunning merchant had settled two years of interest with the States-General that he still had to pay for the Swedish king based on a previously procured credit from the Republic to Sweden. Falkenberg was enraged. This old debt should not, he felt, be used to seize and stall the (rest of the) subsidy payment for over one year. Falkenberg thought de Geer should have paid the interest from the Swedish copper trade, although that trade suffered from low prices at the time, as copper had flooded the market in Amsterdam.[40] The Swedish agent bitterly described the consequences of the unpaid subsidies: 'His Majesty would suffer great hindrance and harm, because not only would he under protest have to withdraw several bills of exchange, but he would have to let various garrisons be not-provisioned and unsupplied.'[41] The conflict continued well into the spring of 1633, with notarial calls sent back and forth and de Geer defending his actions in a letter to Oxenstierna. De

---

37 Ibid., 235–238: 'Contract tusschen Diederick en Conrad von Falckenberg, gemachtigden van den koning van Zweden, en Elias Trip betreffende de beleening en verkoop van koper. 1629 Mei 19, *Not. Arch.* 700. *Not. J. Warnaertsz.*'
38 Ibid., 216–217; Klein, *De Trippen*, pp. 379–399.
39 Van Dillen, 'Amsterdamsche notarieele akten', 248–254: 'Notarieele aanzegging namens den vertegenwoordiger van den koning van Zweden aan Louis de Geer, benevens het antwoord van laatstgenoemde. 1623 December 11, *Not. Arch.* 406 f. 453. *Not. Nic. Jacobs.*'
40 Ibid., 218.
41 Ibid., 249.

Geer claimed that he had used the sums to stop the price drop of copper, which he had done in the interest of the Swedish crown.[42] His correspondence contains other instances of seizing the French subsidy transfers to Sweden in Amsterdam (or requesting to do so).[43] De Geer's wealth stemmed from his role as 'an intermediary between Amsterdam credit and staple markets and the Swedish Crown'.[44]

Networks and expertise

Amsterdam thus offered a wide variety of military resources to be bought, sold, drawn credit from, and exchanged within the city walls itself. Resource mobilization was built on a system of multiplied credit: to obtain credit in order to obtain even more credit and to pay off interest. Yet another important reason why Swedish and French agents exchanged the subsidies through Amsterdam was the presence of a fiscal-military elite. The city harboured an elite with an extremely high level of expertise in fiscal-military matters and transnational business networks, which is a specific element of a fiscal-military hub since various activities of resource mobilization clustered around such an elite.[45] It seems as if, in the early stages of the fiscal-military hub of Amsterdam, a considerable portion of the fiscal-military entrepreneurs came from a Flemish Calvinist background (notably from Antwerp and Liège) or was heavily intertwined in the Protestant diaspora in Europe. As mentioned before, the migration of many merchants from the south of the Netherlands to Amsterdam conveyed advanced financial instruments and expertise, while also furthering the Amsterdam commerce and connections to trade routes. Amsterdam developed into a financial centre in conjunction with an emerging staple market of global proportions, which attracted numerous foreign tradesmen, bankers as well as state agents and diplomats, who set up shop to organize

---

42 *Ibid.*, 254–255: 'Notarieele aanzegging namens den vertegenwoordiger van den koning van Zweden aan Louis de Geer. 1633 Januari 15. Not. Arch. 407 f. 29. Not Jac. Jacobs.'; *ibid.*, 256–262: 'Notarieele aanzegging names Louis de Geer aan de vertegenwoordiger van den koning van Zweden benevens diens antwoord. 1633 Februari 22, *Not. Arch. 407 f. 130. Not. Jac. Jacobs.*'
43 Gerhard W. Kernkamp, 'Brieven van Louis de Geer', *Bijdragen en Mededeelingen van het Historisch Genootschap* 29 (1908), 259–260, 265–267, 306–308, 308–309, 311–313.
44 Müller, 'The Dutch Entrepreneurial Networks and Sweden', p. 69.
45 Parrott, *The Business of War*, pp. 212–213.

their commerce and credit. The business of war represented a vital part of their dealings.[46] What were the requirements for becoming a successful war-entrepreneur? A relatively small group of merchant-financiers could enter the business of mediating subsidies between states. With some exceptions, such as the Amsterdam merchant-financier Philip Calandrini, many entrepreneurs possessed no specific financial-banking expertise. However, examples of Amsterdam-based financiers tell us that they had already gained extensive knowledge during commerce with the states involved in the subsidy business, as was the case with de Geer and Sweden and with Jean Hoeufft and his Franco-Dutch dealings. Access to the subsidy-transfer business could, in turn, consolidate into a firm foundation for taking up banking.[47] In particular, many Amsterdam-based merchant-financiers during the Thirty Years' War had dealt in arms and munition before engaging in the organization of war finance, such as the aforementioned Louis de Geer, the Trip family, and Jean and Mattheus Hoeufft, as well as the brothers Gabriel and Selius Marselis financing Denmark and Philip Calandrini transferring finances for England through his brother-in-law based in London, Philip Burlamachi.[48] During the 1620s, Jean Hoeufft specialised as a weapon merchant supplying France with artillery and naval vessels.[49] Together with his brother Dirck/Diederick (whose sons Mattheus and Jan Jr Hoeufft took over the business in Amsterdam after his death in 1634), Jean Hoeufft ordered the building (and arming) of a warship in Amsterdam in 1620, designed for Charles de Gonzaga, the duc de Nevers, and his private crusading order of the 'Christian Militia'.[50] The affairs

---

46 Schulte, 'Rüstung, Zins, und Frömmigkeit', 45–62; Ole Peter Grell, *Brethren in Christ: A Calvinist Network in Reformation Europe* (Cambridge: Cambridge University Press, 2011).
47 Michiel De Jong, '*Staat van oorlog.' Wapenbedrijf en militaire hervorming in de Republiek der Verenigde Nederlanden, 1585–1621* (Hilversum: Verloren, 2005), pp. 328–332.
48 Hans Vogel, 'Lijst van wapenhandelaren 1600–1650', in *Het arsenaal van de wereld: Nederlandse wapenhandel in de Gouden Eeuw*, ed. by Jan Piet Puype and Pien Van Der Hoeven (Amsterdam: Uitgeverij de Bataafsche Leeuw B.V., 1993), p. 76; Michael G. de Boer, 'Een Amsterdamsche "Lorrendraayer", Celio Marselis', *Jaarboek Amstelodamum* 38 (1941), 48–67.
49 Raphaël Morera, 'Du commerce aux finances: La fortune de Jean Hoeufft (1578–1651), entre la France et les Provinces-Unies', *Revue d'histoire moderne et contemporaine*, 63.1 (2016), 7–29. doi:10.3917/rhmc.631.0007.
50 Stadsarchief Amsterdam, not. S. Cornelisz (NA 5075, inv. 24–645), 24 Maart 1620; Thomson, 'Jean Hoeufft and the Thirty Years' War', pp. 5–6; Parrott, *The Business of War*, p. 38.

of the fiscal-military entrepreneurs ran through family connections with relatives based in most of the hubs across Europe (including Hamburg) and otherwise through their agents. These family connections secured the fundamental trust needed for transferring large sums of money. A subsequent requirement was high liquidity – which was often provided through arms trade (and banking) – in order to make advance payments. The list of the 250 richest people of the Dutch Golden Age (commissioned by the Dutch Rijksmuseum and the magazine *Quote*) includes various fiscal-military entrepreneurs, such as Louis de Geer with a fortune of 1,500,000 florins (number 3), Elias Trip with 1,000,000 florins (number 8), Mattheus Hoeufft with 1,000,000 florins (number 11) and Gabriel Marselis with 750,000 florins (number 29).[51]

Additionally, the entrepreneurs were closely connected to the government and some even held political office. Samuel Blommaert was the director of the Dutch West India Company from 1622 to 1629 and from 1636 to 1642, and Jean Hoeufft became the official representative of France in the Dutch Republic as well as the Dutch representative in France during the 1630s. The strong entanglement of the merchant elite and the magistracy is an important theme in the literature on the Dutch Republic.[52] Yet it must be stressed that the early private business of war was conducted in the open, instead of hiding in the shadows as the present-day private military sector does. It was a prestigious business, since warfare had been one of the essential tasks of the nobility. The mounting demand for resources from the sixteenth century and onwards now opened up new possibilities; financier-merchants could associate with the noble business of war, and they proudly did so. The house of the Trip family – built by order of the two sons of Elias – was the largest private residence in seventeenth-century Amsterdam and consisted of two houses hidden behind an impressive seven-window-wide facade embellished with cannons, cannonballs, and mortars as well as olive branches, since war brought peace. As argued by David Parrott, the business of war provided the fiscal-military entrepreneurs with social standing and cultural validation.[53]

---

51 Kees Zandvliet, *De 250 rijksten van de Gouden Eeuw: kapitaal, macht, familie en levensstijl* (Amsterdam: Rijksmuseum Publishing, 2006), p. XL.
52 See in particular Pepijn Brandon, *War, Capital, and the Dutch State (1588–1795)* (Leiden: Brill, 2015), pp. 41–82.
53 Parrott, *The Business of War*, pp. 249–259.

The presence of a fiscal-military elite and their specific expertise and connections influenced the choice of remittance location. In the Treaty of Bärwalde (1631), the French stipulated as a condition to the Swedes that the subsidies had to be remitted in Paris or Amsterdam while later treaties named Amsterdam and Hamburg. This might be related to the fact that France had already had subsidy payments running through Amsterdam for decades. As early as 1593, Dutch subsidies (a total of 1,600,000 guilders) flowed to France and ended in 1598. From then onwards, the subsidy flow reversed to the Republic until 1609, at the beginning of the Dutch Twelve Years' Truce with Spain, and restarted in 1621 at the resumption of the conflict. The first contractor for the advancement and transfer of the subsidies was Pieter van Beeck until 1626, when Gereard van Schoonhoven and Joost Brasser took over up until 1630, when Willem van Borselen and Cornelis Spiering arranged the transfers until 1631, after which Jean Hoeufft entered the transfer business until 1646. Michiel de Jong estimated that Jean and Mattheus transferred at least 14,170,000 guilders.[54] As Erik Thomson explains, with the signing of the Treaty of Bärwalde, Hoeufft seized the opportunity of handling the war subsidies to Sweden as well. In 1633, he was officially commissioned by the Swedish crown.[55] Thus, the existing infrastructure of the Dutch subsidies through Amsterdam was used and extended to transfer the Swedish subsidies. Herman Kellenbenz argues that Hamburg was not generally speaking of any great interest to France during the Thirty Years' War prior to the late 1630s, at which point the semi-neutral city of Hamburg came to form a perfect hub as a port city between the north of the Netherlands and the French harbours for the French operations along the Rhine.[56]

The importance of personal connections is also exemplified by the fall of Erik Larsson as a Swedish agent for the transfer of subsidies. King Gustav II Adolf suspected Larsson of misusing his office for personal profit and of being too closely and dangerously connected to the merchant elite of Amsterdam. His displacement, however, meant the loss of his networks and subsequently the favourable conditions resulting from these. The new agents had to

---

54 De Jong, *Staat van Oorlog*, pp. 327–328.
55 Thomson, p. 243 below.
56 Kellenbenz, 'Hamburg und die französisch-schwedische Zusammenarbeit im 30jährigen Krieg', 86–90.

co-ordinate the Swedish credit as well as to inspect Larsson's dealings, which, according to Erik Thomson, was an impossible task subsequently leading to a drop in Swedish financial credit.[57] This formed the larger context of de Geer seizing the Dutch subsidies to Sweden in Amsterdam in 1632.

Conclusions

Research into the early modern business of subsidy transfers faces many obstacles and limitations when seeking to 'follow the money'. For now, it is possible to make a few suggestions and conclusions. Further research is required before it can be assessed to what extent the subsidy business contributed to Amsterdam's overall economic development. However, by following the money through chains of negotiations and brokerage, we are able to identify those involved in the business, and by studying them we can calculate the proportion of these fiscal-military businessmen. In this way, their place in the wider economic activity of the city can be evaluated. Amsterdam attracted a variety of fiscal-military entrepreneurs seeking high profits and even social standing. Because of its elite of merchant-financiers and its highly developed financial and commercial markets, the fiscal-military hub of Amsterdam was a relatively safe bet to invest in. It seems as if money and agents remained in Amsterdam as well as even some material resources, only changing owners and value within the city walls. The function of a fiscal-military hub may be compared with that of a central airport or other transport facility from which most services operate, combined with that of a stock exchange facilitating the asset trade in continuous action from a central location (floor of exchange) and, in doing so, altering the value of the transacted assets. For this reason, the term 'hub' is an apt choice. In a way, one could argue that the hub itself – its agents, traders, shippers, bankers, financiers, etc. – arranged and transferred resources for the military campaigns. Additionally, while research on particular financiers brings us insight into the complex connections and activities of subsidy transfers, the focus on a particular person might lead to the danger of overstating the significance of such a fiscal-military entrepreneur. Their activities should be compared to others in a broader context; that is, these individuals not only had personal networks but were also tied within the European system

---

57 Thomson, 'Jean Hoeufft and the Thirty Years' War', p. 7.

of hubs containing numerous entrepreneurs who handled large sums of money and/or organized package deals. This chapter suggests shifting the focus from entrepreneurs to fiscal-military hubs in order to obtain further insights into resource mobilization, in particular the relationship between the business of war and European state formation.

10

Jean Hoeufft, French subsidies, and the Thirty Years' War

Erik Thomson

Historians of early modern Europe have emphasized the importance of entrepreneurs and private contractors to governance, ascribing particular importance to the merchants and bankers who lent money to crowns, organized chartered companies, and equipped and provisioned armies, as well as to the officers who recruited, armed, and led military units.[1] Although Guy Rowlands has charted some of the operations of international remittance bankers during the reign of Louis the XIV in a recent book, historians have generally neglected the role of bankers and merchants in diplomacy during the Thirty Years' War.[2] Yet bankers and merchants played crucial roles in early modern diplomacy, drawing upon contacts, financial techniques and institutions, and sources of coin and capital to make possible the payment of subsidies and other diplomatic gifts and expenditures that the chapters in this volume suggest were crucial to relations among sovereigns.[3]

---

1 David Parrott, *The Business of War: Military Enterprise and Military Revolution in Early Modern Europe* (Cambridge: Cambridge University Press, 2012); *The Contractor State and Its Implications, 1659–1815*, ed. by Richard Harding and Sergio Solbes Ferri (Las Palmas de Gran Canaria: Universidad de Las Palmas de Gran Canaria, 2012); and *War, Entrepreneurs and the State in Europe and the Mediterranean, 1300–1800*, ed. by Jeff Fynn-Paul (Leiden: Brill, 2014).
2 Guy Rowlands, *Dangerous and Dishonest Men: The International Bankers of Louis XIV's France* (Basingstoke: Palgrave Macmillan, 2015).
3 Immediately relevant exceptions include: Sune Lundgren, *Johan Adler Salvius: Problem kring freden, krigsekonomien och maktkampen* (Lund: Lindstedts, 1945); Claude Badalo-Dulong, *Banquier du Roi: Barthélémy Hervart, 1606–1676* (Paris: Ségur, 1951); and the same author's *Mazarin*

Cardinal Richelieu, in his *Testament politique*, praised Louis' actions in 'taking up the purse and not the sword' before 1635, when after a formal declaration of war the king of France would brandish his sword in one hand while dispensing funds from the purse in the other.[4] Subsidy payments involved complex transactions, as financial intermediaries were obliged by treaty to provide large sums of money in a specified currency, at a given date and location, while war strained European financial markets and bankers. During the sixteenth and early seventeenth centuries, emissaries often took on the payment of subsidies alongside their other tasks, sometimes in conjunction with merchants.[5] As early as 1626, Richelieu recognized the peculiar demands of subsidy payments when he noted that any anti-Spanish alliance would require that 'those who enter into it would each provide a solvent banker who would respond and oblige themselves'.[6] The French historians Jacques Bottin and Raphaël Morera have shed light on the until-recently obscure but absolutely crucial figure of Jean Hoeufft, by suggesting the importance of examining the relations between mercantile activity, financial

---

et l'argent: Banquiers et prête-noms (Paris: École des Chartes, 2002). The late, great harpsichordist Gustav Leonhardt's erudite *Het huis Bartolotti en zijn bewoners* (Amsterdam: Meulenhoff, 1979) is also excellent. Diplomatic historians often neglect the importance of financers, who do not appear, for example, in Madeleine Haehl, *Les affaires étrangères au temps de Richelieu: Le secréteriat d'État, les agents diplomatiques (1624–1642)* (Paris: Direction des Archives, Ministère des affaires étrangères, 2006).

4 'Si c'est un effet d'une prudence singulière d'avoir occupé dix ans durant toutes les forces des ennemis de vostre Estat par celles de vos alliez en mettant la main à la bourse et non aux armes.' *Testament politique*, ed. by Françoise Hildesheimer (Paris: Société de l'histoire de France, 1995), p. 74.

5 Thus Jacques Bongars uses his contacts with Nikolas Malapert, Caesar Calandrini, and Daniel van der Meulen to make payments; see Ruth Kohlndorfer-Fries, *Diplomatie und Gelehrtenrepublik: Die Kontakte des französischen Gesandten Jacques Bongars (1554–1612)* (Tübingen: Max Niemeyer, 2009). Benjamin Aubery du Maurier supervised subsidy payments to the Dutch; see *Mémoires de Benjamin Aubery du Maurier (1566–1636)*, ed. by Claire Martin (Geneva: Droz, 2010), pp. 132–135.

6 'Advis sur les affaires présentes qu'a le Roy en février 1626' in *Les papiers de Richelieu: Section politique Intérieure ...*, ed. by Pierre Grillon (Paris: Pedone, 1975–), vol. I, No. 41, p. 298, 'Quelque traicté qu'on fasse, il faut que ceux qui y entreront donnent chacun un banquier solvable qui responde et s'oblige de faire tenir en tous les lieux où sera l'armée les monstres de chaque prince.'

activity, and arms dealing drawing upon Hoeufft's Dutch kin.[7] Morera rightly notes that Hoeufft was essential to the foreign policies associated with Cardinals Richelieu and Mazarin by procuring weapons and naval vessels, and to French diplomacy by paying subsidies to the United Provinces. If anything, Morera understates Hoeufft's importance and the importance of subsidies to Hoeufft's business.[8] Hoeufft remitted subsidies not only to the United Provinces but also to many of France's other allies during most of the Thirty Years' War, including Sweden, Hesse-Cassel, and Transylvania.[9]

In this chapter, I focus on Hoeufft's role as the organizer of subsidy payments from the king of France to most of the French king's allies. I will touch upon other aspects of his career as a merchant of ships, grain, arms, and munitions, a banker engaged in royal finances, a committed Calvinist with distinct religious beliefs, a patron, and as an actor with an important role in diplomatic negotiations and information networks, only to the extent that is necessary in order to place his role with regard to subsidy payments in its appropriate context. This reflects not only the subject of this book but also the fact that subsidy payments were absolutely crucial

---

7 Raphaël Morera, 'Du commerce au finances: la fortune de Jean Hoeufft entre la France et les Provinces Unies', *Revue d'Histoire moderne et contemporaine* 63.1 (2016), 7–29, and *L'assèchement des marais en France au XVIIe siècle* (Rennes: Presses Universitaires de Rennes, 2011), pp. 114–122. See also the comparison between Hoeufft and Louis de Geer by Jacques Bottin and Pierre Jeannin, 'Entre conviction et réalisme: deux hommes d'affaires protestants du premier XVIIe siècle', in *D'un Rivage à l'Autre: Villes et Protestantisme dans l'Aire Atlantique (XVIe–XVIIe siècles)*, ed. by Guy Martinière, Didier Poton, and François Souty (Paris: Imprimerie nationale, 1999), p. 158. See also Eduard de Dienne, *Histoire du dessèchement des lacs et marais de France avant 1789* (Paris: Champion, 1891), and Fritz Redlich, *The German Military Enterpriser and His Workforce: A Study in European Economic and Social History* (Wiesbaden: Franz Steiner, 1964–1965), pp. 407–408.

8 I presented a working paper which set Hoeufft's work in a diplomatic context, 'Jean Hoeufft and the Thirty Years War: An Essay on Diplomatic History's Limits', at Umeå University, 16 May 2013, available at www.cedar.umu.se/digitalAssets/120/120438_joint-seminar-with-guest-researchers.pdf. accessed 14 October 2018. The current chapter draws on several summers of archival research to develop a small aspect of that earlier paper. I thank Svante Norrhem and the Winnipeg RH foundation for supporting this research.

9 The subsidies to Transylvania were remitted by way of Lyon and Venice, and thus through different networks from those described here. See Paris: Archives Diplomatiques (AD), Correspondance Politique (CP), Allemagne, 27, fol. 284, Mazarin to D'Avaux and Servien, and fol. 376.

to Hoeufft's success as an entrepreneur. Subsidies were vital to foreign and military affairs, and arguably even important to the early seventeenth-century macro-economy. As Marianne Klerk and Peter Wilson argue in Chapters 9 and 3 above, early modern warfare and diplomacy depended upon access to fiscal-military 'hubs', with financial institutions and markets for armaments, munitions, food, capital, and even armies. Hoeufft benefited from occupying what the social network theorist Ronald Burt has called a 'structural hole', profiting from his relations with kith and kin to bind together fiscal-military hubs and networks that otherwise had few connections, such as Richelieu's and Mazarin's creatures, French financiers, Dutch and Hamburg merchant groups, and members of the Dutch political elites of different factions.[10] Burt and others suggest that it is rare for an entrepreneur to be able to profit from such structural holes for long, as others usually offer themselves as alternative and cheaper ways of performing those functions of brokerage, unless political power protects the broker's status.[11] Obtaining the official position of remitter of subsidies, however, allowed Hoeufft and his network to profit from a version of what the Dutch economic historian P.W. Klein has called a 'monopoly game', and to reinforce his unique position as a broker between networks and add others to his networks, such as Swedish fiscal officials.[12] Rather than using ties to a crown to attempt to corner the market in copper or another commodity, as Klein argues was the intent of such major Amsterdam arms dealers as the Trip brothers and Louis de Geer, Hoeufft's role as the broker of subsidy payments gave him unique access to high-quality assignations from the French crown while giving him an unparalleled ability to extend

---

10 Ronald S. Burt, *Structural Holes: The Social Structure of Competition* (Cambridge, MA: Harvard University Press, 1992). See also Ray E. Reagans and Ezra Zuckerman, 'Why Knowledge Does Not Equal Power: The Network Redundancy Trade-off', *Industrial and Corporate Change* 17 (2008), 903–944, and their 'All in the Family: Reply to Burt, Podolny, and van de Rijt, Ban and Sarkar', *Industrial and Corporate Change* 17 (2008), 979–999.
11 Ronald S. Burt, 'Bridge Decay', *Social Networks* 24 (2002), 333–363, and Mark Granovetter, *Society and Economy: Framework and Principles* (Cambridge, MA: Harvard University Press, 2017), pp. 106–126.
12 P.W. Klein, 'A 17th Century Monopoly Game: The Swedish–Dutch Trade in Tar and Pitch', in *Wirtschaftskräfte in der europäischen Expansion* (Stuttgart: Klett-Cotta, 1978), pp. 459–471, and his classic *De Trippen in de 17e eeuw: een studie over het ondernemersgedrag op de Hollandse stapelmarkt* (Assen: Van Gorcum, 1965).

credit to a wide variety of merchants, bankers, generals, and diplomats throughout northern Europe.

Hoeufft's establishment as a merchant-banker

Jean Hoeufft's family was originally from Roermond, a town between Aachen and Eindhoven. His parents converted to Calvinism and fled to Liège, where Jean was born in 1578. Liège probably played a crucial part in his development, as wealthy merchants developed new ways of combining their capital with investment from Antwerp to fund the exploitation of mines, blast furnaces, and arms manufactories.[13] Hoeufft's youth coincided with a significant disruption to Liège's trade, for the closing of the Scheldt and weakening of Antwerp as a commercial centre caused many of these entrepreneurs to leave Liège. A striking number of these émigrés – Jean Curtius, Louis de Geer, and the Trip brothers, for a start – became central figures in the European arms trade.[14] It might be useful to think of the Liège diaspora who were central actors in the financing and arming of the French and Protestant coalition in the Thirty Years'

---

13 As Bas van Bavel notes, 'more recent in-depth studies on this interesting sector are lacking', *Manors and Markets: Economy and Society in the Low Countries, 500–1600* (Oxford: Oxford University Press, 2010), p. 252, n. 34. But see Jean LeJeune, *La formation du capitalisme moderne dans la principauté de Liége au XVIe siècle* (Paris: Les Belles Lettres, 1939); Myron P. Gutmann, *Toward the Modern Economy: Early Industry in Europe, 1500–1800* (Philadelphia: Temple University Press, 1988), pp. 48–83; and Brian G. Awty, 'The Development and Dissemination of the Walloon Method of Iron Working', *Technology and Culture* 48.4 (October 2007), 783–803.

14 Marjolein t'Hart, 'From the Eighty Years War to the Second World War: New Perspectives on the Economic Effects of War', *Tijdschrift voor Sociale en Economische Geschiedenis* 11 (2014), 261–279, and *The Dutch Wars of Independence: Warfare and Commerce in the Netherlands* (London and New York: Routledge, 2014), pp. 170–190; Pepijn Brandon, *War, Capital and the Dutch State (1588–1795)* (Leiden: Brill, 2015); Julia Zunckel, *Rüstungsgeschäfte im Dreißigjährigen Krieg: Unternehmerkräfte, Militärgüter und Marktstrategien im Handel zwischen Genua, Amsterdam und Hamburg* (Berlin: Duncker & Humblot, 1997); L.F.W. Andriaenssen, 'De Amsterdamse geschutgietereij: Over het Oorlogsindustriële ondernemingschap van de Stedelijke overheid', *Amstelodamum* 49 (2002), 44–89; *The Arsenal of the World: The Dutch Arms Trade in the Seventeenth Century*, ed. by Jan Piet Puype and Marco van der Hoeven (Amsterdam: Batavian Lion, 1996); and Regina Schulte, 'Rüstung, Zins und Frömmigkeit: Niederländische Calvinisten als Finanziers des Dreißigjährigen Krieges', *Bohemia: Jahrbuch des Collegium Carolinum* 35 (1994), 45–62.

War as forming a 'business group', in Mark Granovetter's term, whose members co-ordinate their activities while competing for individual pieces of business.[15]

While much of his kindred moved to the United Provinces, Hoeufft himself moved to Rouen in 1600 and received a letter of naturalization the next year.[16] He began to trade in a range of goods, to supply ships including those in the VOC (Verenigde Oostindische Compagnie, Dutch East India Company), and to invest in voyages to Brazil, Canada and Virginia.[17] At least annually from 1609 to 1615, Hoeufft in partnership with his brother Diederick and the merchant Pieter van Beeck began to charter roughly a dozen ships of an average of slightly less than 120 tonnes to carry salt from Brouage to Rouen and other French ports, presumably reflecting engagement with French finances.[18] He also began to engage in exchange transactions,

---

15 Mark Granovetter, 'Coase Revisited: Business Groups in the Modern Economy', *Industrial and Corporate Change* 4 (1995), 93–130.

16 Michel Mollat, *Le commerce maritime Normand à la fin du Moyen Age: Étude d'histoire économique et sociale* (Paris: Plon, 1952); H. Lapeyre, *Une famille de marchands: les Ruiz* (Paris: Armand Colin, 1955); Philip Benedict, 'Rouen's Foreign Trade during the Era of the Religious Wars (1560–1600)', *The Journal of European Economic History* 13 (1984), 29–74; and Gayle K. Brunelle, *The New World Merchants of Rouen, 1559–1630* (Kirksville, MO: Sixteenth Century Journal, 1984).

17 Jacques Bottin, 'Négoce et crises frumentaires: Rouen et ses marchands dans le commerce international des blés, milieu XVIe–début XVIIe siècle', *Revue d'histoire moderne et contemporaine* 45 (1998), 558–588 (pp. 579–585). He remained involved in foreign trade, sending a ship to Virginia in 1621; Amsterdam Stadsarchief, Not. Arch. 547, fol. 304, 16 November 1621. See also Cornelius Jaensen, 'Champlain and the Dutch', in *Champlain: The Birth of French America*, ed. by Raymonde Litalien and Denis Vaugeois (Montreal: Editions de Septentrion / McGill-Queen's University Press, 2004), p. 239.

18 For Van Beeck, see Amsterdam Stadsarchief, 30452: Archief van S. Hart: (gedeeltelijke) toegang op de notariële archieven, 91, 'Heuft'. For comparison, the 1640 fleet conveying salt under the so-called Gabelle monopoly was composed of 58 ships, mostly of 50–60 tons. See Marcel DelaFosse and Claude Laveau, *Le commerce du sel de Brouage aux XVIIe et XVIIe siècles* (Paris: Armand Colin, 1960), p. 90, and Daniel Dessert, *L'argent du sel: le sel de l'argent* (Paris: Fayard, 2012). If the surviving register is correct, Hoeufft's chartered ships represented 8.75 per cent of the total tonnage arriving in Rouen from 26 January to 11 December 1614. See Pierre Dardel, *Le traffic maritime de Rouen aux XVIIe et XVIII siècles: Essai statistique* (Rouen: Laine, 1946), p. 24.

with merchants of Antwerp among others.[19] Roughly at the time of the outbreak of the Bohemian revolt, and certainly by the expiry of the Twelve Years' Truce, Hoeufft began to deal in arms and munitions much more intensively, particularly with the French. He exported saltpetre from Lorraine to the Netherlands, and in 1629 shipped over one hundred shiploads of grain from France to the Netherlands at the behest of the States-General to ease a shortage caused by disruptions in the Baltic.[20] Above all, he provided large numbers of weapons and naval vessels to the French monarchy, drawing upon supplies from the Netherlands. Morera claims that Hoeufft was probably the single greatest provider of vessels to the French navy as well as the largest single supplier of artillery to the French crown. Other members of the Liège diaspora watched his progress, and considered their own commercial opportunities in relation to the French, with a hint of scepticism. When writing to his partner Pieter Trip to tell him to stop extending credit to the French in 1627, Louis de Geer commented, 'I know that French court all too well. Hoeufft hasn't got much from there. He would have made a lot, if the profits counted as they stand in the book, and not in the cassa.'[21]

Subsidies, risk, and assignations

On the face of it, taking on the role of remitter of subsidies should have increased Hoeufft's exposure to financial risks from the French

---

19 See Amsterdam, International Institute of Social History, Bijzondere collective van het Nederlandsch Economisch-Historisch Archief, No. 144, 'Franstalig journal van een wissel- en diamanthandelaar te Antwerpen over de period 1609–1613', entry for 12 February 1611.
20 See 27 September 1619, No. 1679, and 13 October 1620, No. 4103, in *Resolutiën der Staten-Generaal*, ed. by J.G. Smit and J. Roelerink (The Hague: Martinus Nijhoff, 1981), Nieuwe reeks, vol. 4, pp. 252 and 626. Hereafter *RSG*. *RSG* 29 May 1621, No. 1044, *RSG*, 5, p. 165, 21 June 1621, No. 1185, *RSG*, 5, p. 186, and 1 July 1621, No. 1274, *RSG*, 5, 200. For the grain, see Baugy to Richelieu (18 June 1629), Paris: Archives Diplomatiques, Correspondance politique, Hollande, 12, fol. 105, Brasset to Villiers Hotman (15 April 1630), fol. 373.
21 Minute of Louis de Geer to Pieter Trip (14/29 [April] 1627), in *Louis de Geers Brev och Affärshandlingar, 1614–1652*, ed. by E.W. Dahlgren (Stockholm: P.A. Norstedt, 1934), No. 72, 119, 'Ick kenne het fransche hof te wel. Heuft moet er noch al veel van hebben, heeft hij der veel bij gewonnen, die proffijten achte al int boeck staen, ende niet in cassa.' All translations are by the author unless otherwise stated.

crown. After Christian IV's defeat, those who remitted French subsidies to the Danish were not paid the money they advanced.[22] Hoeufft had difficulty trying to get paid for loans to the Dutch ambassador in Paris, Gideon van den Boetzelaer, heer von Langerak, in 1630.[23] His family had already begun to involve him more closely in affairs with and financing of other Protestant powers. Diederick Hoeufft, together with Gerhart Thijns (Gerdt Thiens) (unhappily) lent the landgrave of Hesse-Cassel 50,000 guilders in 1626.[24] Thiens was the brother-in-law of the *Bewindhebber* of the Dutch West India Company and great merchant Samuel Blommaert, who also shared kin relations to Hoeufft through the Coijmans.[25] In 1631 Jean Hoeufft entered into a contract to transfer the French subsidies to the United Provinces, in conjunction with his Amsterdam-based nephew Mattheus. They stepped into the role abandoned by a shifting consortium of financiers that had replaced his old partner Pieter van Beeck, who had repeatedly failed to have adequate funds to cover delays in payment.[26] Perhaps the previous contractors had been rattled by the liquidity problems of one of their counterparties, the financier Philip Burlamachi, which would lead to his bankruptcy a year and a half later.[27]

---

22 AD, CP Danemark, 1, fol. 146, lists debts in 1630. The ambassador Zobel complained to Richelieu that he had still not been paid on 1 August 1630, fol. 241. Zobel was engaged in French finances. See Paris: Archives Nationales (AN) MC ET/CV/444.

23 Den Haag, Nationaal Archief, Staten Generaal, 1.01.02. 6762, Jean Hoeufft to States General, 16 May 1630, 31 July 1630. The draft response, dated 4 October 1630, temporizes.

24 *RSG*, digital edition, 38/03/1626; 1, 21/03/1626, 14; 31/03/1626, 7; 23/03/31, 6 available at www.historici.nl/Onderzoek/Projecten/BesluitenStatengeneraal1626-1651/silva/sg/resoluties/ . . ., accessed 27 October 2017.

25 Klein, *De Trippen in de 17e eeuw*, pp. 326–327, n. 17.

26 Michiel de Jong, '*Staat van oorlog*': *Wapenbedrijf en militaire hervorming in de Republiek der Verenigde Nederlanden, 1585–1621* (Hilversum: Verloren, 2005), pp. 310–336, and 'Kooplieden en hun belangen in de Overheidsfinanciën van de Republiek: Bilaterale subsidies en leningen als "case-study", 1615–1630', in *Ondernemers & bestuurders: Economie en politiek in de Noordlijke Nederlanden in de Late Middeleeuwen en Vroegmoderne tijd*, ed. by Clé Lesger and Leo Noordegraaf (Amsterdam: NEHA, 1999), pp. 277–297.

27 A.V. Judges, 'Philip Burlamachi: A Financier of the Thirty Years War', *Economica* 18 (November 1926), 285–300, and Ole Peter Grell, *Brethren in Christ: A Calvinist Network in Reformation Europe* (Cambridge: Cambridge University Press, 2011), pp. 92–101.

Equally, the payment of French subsidies to the Swedes promised by the 1631 treaty of Bärwalde hardly went smoothly. In Paris, the subsidies were entrusted to the financier Claude Charlot, who would rapidly go bankrupt.[28] Charlot advanced the subsidies to the Swedish agent Erik Larsson (von der Linde), who in conjunction with his son Lorens and his factor Samuel Blommaert co-ordinated the actions of a group of merchants in Amsterdam. That group included the unfortunate Pieter van Beeck, who failed to remit money promptly to the Swedes, just as he had previously failed to do for the Dutch, and died without having paid the subsidies fully in the summer of 1631.[29] The Swedish King Gustav II Adolf grew suspicious that Larsson was in collusion with Dutch merchants and overly interested in his own profit. He attempted to replace him with new factors who were not as well connected in Amsterdam, and were given the impossible task of auditing Larsson's activities, separating the crown's obligations from merchants whom the king distrusted and maintaining the crown's credit (on these developments, see also Marianne Klerk, Chapter 9 above). Even before Gustav II Adolf's death at Lützen these disputes caused Swedish credit to plummet, and the Swedes complained repeatedly to the French about the delays in receiving the subsidy money.[30]

---

28 Charlot's bankrupcy was well advanced by 17 May 1634, when the Council ordered the seizure of all his papers. See Paris, Archives Nationales, E*117A, fol. 353. On Charlot's business, see Françoise Bayard, *Le monde des financiers au XVIIe siècle* (Paris: Flammarion, 1988), pp. 154–155, 160, 272, 275, 281, 284–287, 289, 326, 355, 367, and 372, and Dessert, *L'argent du sel*, pp. 34–42.

29 Instruction for Erik Larsson (16 January 1631), in *Arkiv till upplysning om svenska krigens och krigsinrättningarnes historia* (Stockholm: 1854–1861), vol. I, p. 305, Gustav II Adolf to Axel Oxenstierna (16 January 1631) in *Rikskanslern Axel Oxenstiernas skrifter och Brevväxling* [AOSB], vol. II, 1, No. 500, pp. 682–684, and Lars Ekholm, 'Kontributioner och krediter: Svensk krigsfinansiering 1630–1631', in *Det kontinentala krigets ekonomi: Studier i krigsfinansiering under svensk stormaktstid* (Uppsala: Scandinavian University Books, 1971), pp. 181–183. Melchior Falckenberg to Axel Oxenstierna (27 January 1631), Stockholm, Riksarkivet [RA], Oxenstiernska Samlingen, E 597b, 'här till haffwer hwarken iagh eller Erich Larßon kunnadt få penningar på wexell, uthan hans factors Samuel Blommaerts tillhielp, hwilken haffwer warit borgen för alla waxlar som båda Erich Larßon och iag haffwar dragit båda på Dansick och Hamborg allt här till.' Charnacé to Chavigny, 17 April 1631, AD, CP Suède, 2, fol. 50.

30 Georg Wittrock, *Svenska handelskompaniet och kopparhandeln under Gustaf II Adolf* (Uppsala: Almqvist & Wiksell, 1919), pp. 145–149; see also

Hoeufft tentatively began to approach the Swedish subsidies in 1631. Perhaps the French emissary Hercule de Charnacé suggested that Hoeufft might remit the Swedish subsidies as well, for he noted in his diary in 1631 that he had met 'Mr Hoeufft the Flemish merchant who resides at Paris' to talk of affairs shortly after refusing to receive a diamond-encrusted portrait of Gustav II Adolf from Erik Larsson.[31] Things grew even more pressing after the death of the Swedish king in November 1632. The Swedish Chancellor Axel Oxenstierna, directing Swedish affairs in the Holy Roman Empire, had to settle the finances of the German war.[32] Hoeufft began to correspond directly with Oxenstierna.[33] At the same time, he worked closely with French financial officials to obtain good assignations for the Swedish subsidy payments, as well as to lobby for a missed subsidy payment from before Gustav II Adolf's death.[34] On 28 May 1633, Oxenstierna gave Hoeufft the formal charge to collect the French subsidies to the Swedish army and provided a commission to present to Louis XIII.[35]

Ekholm, 'Kontributioner och krediter', p. 232, and Conrad Falkenberg to Axel Oxenstierna, 5/15 June 1632 and 6/16 October 1632, *AOSB*, vol. II, 11, Nos 32–33, 612–616.
31 AD, CP, Suède, 3 fol. 75v, Journal de Charnacé, 8 September 1631.
32 Roland Nordlund, 'Krig genom ombud: De svenska krigsfinanserna och Heilbronnförbundet 1633', in *Det kontinentala krigets ekonomi*, pp. 271–451. See also Peter H. Wilson, *The Thirty Years War: Europe's Tragedy* (London: Penguin, 2009), pp. 549–553. These problems are not dealt with by Gottfried Lorenz, 'Schweden und die Französischen Hilfsgelder von 1638 bis 1649: ein Beitrag zur Finanzierung des Krieges im 17. Jahrhundert', in *Forschungen und Quellen zur Geschichte des Dreißigjährigen Krieges*, Schriftenreihe der Vereinigung zur Erforschung der Neueren Geschichte e.V., 12, ed. by Konrad Repgen (Münster: Aschendorff, 1981), pp. 98–148.
33 RA, Oxen. Sam E 622a (29 April 1633, 17 April 1633, 10 June 1633).
34 Hoeufft's large correspondence with the Bouthilliers, extant in the eighteenth century, appears to have vanished. Jacques LeLong, *Bibliothèque historique de la France, contenant le Catalogue des Ouvrages, imprimés & manuscrits, qui traitent de l'Histoire de ce Royaume, ou qui y ont rapport; avec des notes Critiques et Historiques* (Paris: Jean-Thomas Herissant, 1769–1778), vol. III, p. 97, No. 30743, 'Ms. Lettres de M. Hoeufft, Banquier, employé par le Roi en Hollande, depuis le 15 Novembre 1635 jusqu'au 11 Octobre 1645. Ces quatre recueils [étoient] dans la Bibliothèque de M. Bouthillier, ancien Evêque de Troyes: le premier 0.4, le second, L. 4; le troisième, V.5; & le quatrième X.5'.
35 Axel Oxenstierna to Hoeufft (28 May 1633) and Louis XIII (same date), in *AOSB*, vol. I, 8, Nos 326–327, 731–733.

From 1633, Jean Hoeufft occupied a unique position as the financial intermediary formally responsible for assuring the punctual remittance of subsidies from France to its allies. His financial role also gave him a political role, where he lobbied French officials on behalf of the Dutch and Dutch statesmen on behalf of the French. Hoeufft was asked, for instance, by Cardinal Richelieu and Louis XIII himself to propose political and military actions to the prince of Orange and other notables in the United Provinces.[36] Hoeufft used this position to ensure that he would be paid punctually, representing his credit as essential to the functioning of the alliance, and his claim was often accepted by French statesmen. Hoeufft worked extremely closely with superintendent Claude de Bullion, who noted that 'I've done everything imaginable to persuade M. Euf [Hoeufft] to accept the assignations. He does not want to oblige himself to furnish money in Amsterdam if I don't give him cash in this town.'[37] This circumstance rested in part on close personal connections; Hoeufft took up residence in Paris on rue Mauconseil, a seven-minute walk from Bullion's palace on the other side of St Eustache. Bullion frequently notes in letters to Richelieu that Hoeufft had told him some news, or that Hoeufft was present.[38] As Bullion noted in a letter to Secretary of State Chavigny,

> I showed Monsieur Hoeufft that the assignations for the million given to him are good and payable within the year. He wanted some changes to some of them. I came to an agreement with him. And in order to advance the payment, I promised him some interest so that he will presently furnish My Lords of the States-General a notable sum on his credit.[39]

---

36 Den Haag, Nationaal Archief, Collectie Van Wijn, 1.13.20, bestanddeel 330, Jean Hoeufft to Frederik Hendrik, Prince of Orange, Paris, 23 June 1634.

37 AD, Mémoires et documents, France, 822, fol. 2. 'J'ay faict tout ce qui est imaginable pour persuader M Euf pour prendre des assignations. Et ne veult s'obliger a faire fournir l'argent dans Amsterdam si je ne luy donne content en cette ville.' See similar observations in David Parrott, *Richelieu's Army: War, Government and Society in France, 1624–1642* (Cambridge: Cambridge University Press, 2001), p. 263.

38 AD, Mémoires et documents, France, 822 (MDF) fol. 105. Bullion to Richelieu (23 October 1636): 'Je commenceray cette lettre par une bonne Nouvelle de M Euf qui m'asseure', AD, MDF, 826, fol. 87, Bullion to Richelieu, 30 January 1637, 'Pour satisfaire au commandement de VE j'ay parlé a M. Euf luy disant que je desirois parler a un anglois nommé Jaric ou Vanderlay', and Hoeufft reports finding him on fol. 103 (1 February 1637).

39 AD, MDF, 827, fol. 113, Bullion to Chavigny (16 June 1637), 'J'ai faict voir a Monsieur Euft que les assignations du million qui lu en esté donnees

Hoeufft did receive favourable assignations; shortly after Chavigny met him at Bullion's house at eight in the morning to straighten out some remittances to Hamburg, the Council issued an assignation that would automatically turn to a provision to receive coin directly from the treasury should the funds not otherwise be available.[40]

He occasionally faced problems with officials who did not treat him so scrupulously, and on those occasions Hoeufft might write to Richelieu, appeal to the Dutch ambassador, and even procure a letter from the States-General asking that he be paid for the good of the alliance.[41] Indeed, the 1639 treaty for 1,200,000 *livres* of additional subsidies prescribed, in the treaty's second article, that 'the French king would provide for the said money assignations which will be good, and to the contentment of him whom it would please the said Lords of the States-General to authorize in France'.[42] This right to judge the assignations would be repeated in subsequent treaties.[43] Nevertheless, on the payer's side of the bill of exchange Hoeufft was not simply given cash, but had to judge whether assignations and other assets would allow him to maintain his liquidity.

Contracts and cost of exchange

Although Hoeufft eventually received commissions both from the United Provinces and the Swedish crown to act as their financial

---

sont bonnes et payables dans cette annee. Il desire quelque changement de quelqu'unes d'eux. Je suis demeuré d'accord avec luy. Et affin d'avancer le payement je luy ay promis quelque interest affin qu'il fournisse a Messieurs les Estats pnt:mt une notable somme sur son credit.'

40 AD: MDF, 828, Chavigny to Richelieu (20 November 1637); the assignation is in the AN, E*114B, fol. 327, 26 Novembre 1637.
41 All these in AD, CP Hollande, 20, Hoeufft to Richelieu (10 Avril 1637), fol. 70; Guillaume de Lyere to Richelieu (18 April 1637), naming Hoeufft officially commissionaire, 29 May 1637, fol. 111; Charnacé informs Richelieu that the States-General sent a deputation to him (29 May 1637), fol. 113; States-General demand payment (29 May 1637); Richelieu's secretary Charpentier noted that the Cardinal has pledged that the assignations were good, and promised Hoeufft an additional 20,000 *livres* in interest, 'Du xxvii jan 1638', fol. 376.
42 Den Haag, Nationaal Archief, Staten Generaal, 1.01.02, 12587.71, treaty of 24 March 1639, signed for France by Bullion and Bouthillier, not coincidentally the two *surintendants de Finance*.
43 Den Haag, Nationaal Archief, Staten Generaal, 1.01.02, 12587–75, 14 February 1641, 1.01.02, 12587.79A, 8 March 1642, 1.01.02, 12587.85, 30 March 1643, and 1.01.02, 12587.91, 29 February 1644.

agent in France, he played a different role in each case because of the different stipulations about the payment of subsidies in treaties between France and these two powers. Treaties with both powers differed from those with the Swiss, for example, in that they did not specify – with the minor exception of 50,000 *livres* to be distributed to officers in the French regiment in the United Provinces at the discretion of the French ambassador – pay for individual officers, or the disposition or use of the subsidy money.[44]

The first article of the 1630 treaty between France and the United Provinces specified that France would pay 1,000,000 *livres* per year payable every six months as long as the war continued.[45] In the 1630 treaty no place of payment was specified, though Paris would be designated at a later date. The States-General formally received the subsidy from the king of France in Paris, and thus the States-General entered into a contract with Hoeufft for the costs of exchange and transfer of the money to the United Provinces. The States-General allowed costs of 2 per cent for 'provision and risk of the exchange', though they also made allowances for extraordinary costs.[46] Treasurers scrutinized Hoeufft's accounts and extra costs regularly.[47] In 1639, the States-General formed a committee to examine his accounts, which informally put the Hoeuffts' contract up for bidding.[48] Mattheus Hoeufft claimed that the States-General could not find any other merchants to take up their remittances on the same conditions as the Hoeuffts when a committee rejected other expenses in 1647.[49] Two per cent was a significant reduction

---

44 AN, K 114B, No. 44, the 'Estat de la recepte et depence' for the Swiss pensions.
45 I follow Den Haag, Nationaal Archief, Staten Generaal, 1.01.02.12587–42, treaty of 17 June 1630.
46 See Extracts from resolutions about Hoeufft's accounts in Den Haag, Nationaal Archief, Staten Generaal, 1.01.02. 12475.75.2; this one is from 3 July 1634.
47 Den Haag, Nationaal Archief, Staten Generaal, 1.01.02. 6762. Jean Hoeufft to Staten Generaal, 29 October 1632, 'heb ick gesonden aen Ewe Hoog: Moog: de Rekening van mine administratie der achthondert dry en sestich dusent vier hondert gulden so ick vant twede million, ent handen van min heer den Ambassad. Langerack ontfangen heb'.
48 Den Haag, Nationaal Archief, 1.01.02, 3198, registers van ordinaris resoluties van de Staten-Generaal, 1639. Committee formed, fol. 48v, 7 July, Hoeufft's accounts scrutinized, fol. 348, and again on 14 July, fols 364–365. Hoeufft complains about their examination on fol. 435v, 17 August, and fol. 612r, 10 November.
49 Den Haag, Nationaal Archief, 1.01.02, 6269, Matthieu Hoeufft to Staten Generaal, 29 January 1647.

in exchange costs over previous rates: Michiel de Jong estimates that rates on subsidy payments fell from 8 or 9 per cent to 6.25 per cent between 1595 and 1630, and Pit Dehing suggests that exchange rates from Amsterdam to Paris were above 4 per cent in the 1630s, though they fell below that in the 1640s.[50] One important unknown, then, is what the States-General actually allowed the Hoeuffts in 'extraordinary' costs.

The treaty of Bärwalde allowed the Swedes to choose whether the subsidies would be paid in Paris or Amsterdam, and specified 1,000,000 *livres tournois* or 400,000 *reichstaler*.[51] Later subsidy treaties allowed payment either in Amsterdam or in Hamburg. Thus, the French were responsible for the costs of the exchange and remittance of the funds. Hoeufft did not enter into a long-term contract with the French state for these transfers; but, since he had been given a commission by the Swedes, French officials could not negotiate with other bankers to make the exchange. In 1638, Bullion noted to Richelieu that

> [a]s soon as I received Your Eminence's order I sent for Monsieur [Hoeufft] who did not want to furnish the portion in Amsterdam except during next August … He demands for the charge of money, for the interest, and for the exchange on the order of 28 *livres* per hundred. I have not been able to get better conditions up to the present moment.[52]

Bullion's letter suggests that Hoeufft charged the French 28 per cent for the costs of exchange, significantly more than he charged the

---

50 De Jong, 'Staat van oorlog', p. 332; Pit Dehing, *Geld in Amsterdam: Wisselbank en wisselkoersen, 1650–1725* (Hilversum: Verloren, 2012), p. 370.
51 Traktat mellan konung Gustav II Adolf och konung Ludvig XIII af Frankrike om förbund för fem år, subsidier för Sveriges deltagande i tyska kriget, m. m. Bärwalde, 1631, januari 13, g. st., in *Sverges traktater med främmande magter: jämte andra dit hörande handlingar*, ed. by O.S. Rydberg and Carl Hallendorff (Stockholm: P.A. Norstedt & Söner, 1903), vol. V, I (1572–1632), p. 349, 'Rex Galliae quadringenta millia thalerorum Imperialium, id est millionem librarum Turonensium quotannis contribuito, eiusque summae mediam partem decimoquinto mensis Maji, alteram decimoquinto Novembris Lutetiae Parisiorum, uel Amstelodami in Batavia, prout Regi Sueciae commodius acciderit, deputatis ad id Regis Sueciae commodius acciderit, deputatis ad id Regis Sueciae ministris infallibiliter numerato ac tradito.'
52 AD, Bullion to Richelieu, MD France, 830, fol. 274. 'Aussi tost que j'ay receu l'ordre de VE envoyé querir Monsieur Euft lequel ne veult fournir la partie a Amsterdam que dans le mois d'Aoust … Il demande pour la taxe des monnoyes, pour l'interest et pour le change a raison de xxviii ll pour cent jusques a present je ne luy peu avoir a meilleure condition.'

States-General for similar transactions – from 2 to perhaps 5 per cent, allowing for extraordinary charges. While Bullion implies that these costs were high, other orders seem to suggest that they were not extraordinary, although surviving evidence is spotty. One order from later in the year directed the royal treasurer to pay Hoeufft 640,000 *livres* in cash for the first term of the Swedish subsidy, 140,000 *livres* or 18.75 per cent for the costs of exchange. Another allowed him 40 per cent (120,000 *livres*) to send another 300,000 *livres* of the Swedish subsidy to Hamburg, so that the extraordinary ambassador Claude de Mesmes, count of Avaux, in Hamburg would deliver it to the Swedish representative Johan Adler Salvius.[53] Both of these payments involved Hoeufft receiving cash in hand from the treasurer, so in this case there should not have been interest to cover time waiting for poor or tardy assignations. It seems likely that the difference between the costs paid by the States-General and the French for similar exchange transactions represented a profit for the Hoeuffts and their associates.

Banks and bills of exchange

Historians of banking and finance have called attention to the manner in which war finance fostered institutional developments in the first half of the seventeenth century such as the chartered companies and exchange banks, for instance the Amsterdam *Wisselbank*.[54] Merchants, including those who partially engaged in war finance, combined the use of these innovatory institutions with older forms of finance, such as the direct funding of mercantile activities and drawing bills of exchange.[55] The Hoeuffts were certainly familiar

---

53 AD: CP, Suède, 5, 'Ordonnance pour pension du Suède, 5 May 1637[8]', fol. 67, 'Ordonnance pour les suedois ___ nov 1638', fol. 108.

54 Lucien Gillard, *La Banque d'Amsterdam et le florin européen au temps de la République néerlandaise (1610–1820)* (Paris: Éditions de l'École des Hautes Études en Sciences Sociales, 2004); Pit Dehing, *Geld in Amsterdam*; Stephen Quinn and William Roberds, 'An Economic Explanation of the Early Bank of Amsterdam, Debasement, Bills of Exchange and the Emergence of the First Central Bank', in *The Origins and Development of Financial Markets and Institutions: From the Seventeenth Century to the Present*, ed. by Jeremy Atack and Larry Neal (Cambridge: Cambridge University Press, 2009), pp. 32–70, and the essays in *The Bank of Amsterdam: On the Origins of Central Banking*, ed. by Marius van Nieuwkerk (Amsterdam: Sonsbeek, 2009).

55 Oscar Gelderblom, Joost Jonker, and Clemens Kool, 'Direct Finance in the Dutch Golden Age', *Economic History Review* 69 (2016), 1178–1198.

with these developments. Jean Hoeufft, to judge from the inventory after his death, engaged in extensive banking in Paris, as well as in investments in *rentes* and other forms of government obligations; Mattheus Hoeufft was among the most active account holders in the Wisselbank, receiving and forwarding funds to clients who included most of the prominent arms dealers and financiers.[56]

Yet despite regulations that mandated that bills of exchange over 600 florins (and from 1643 over 300 florins) had to be settled in the Wisselbank, the Hoeuffts organized the payment of subsidies and other remittances using bills of exchange outside the Wisselbank. Apart from assignations and the risk of tardy payment by the French, the Hoeuffts' remittance network probably faced difficulties of payment stemming from the size of the subsidy payments, compounded by the monetary complications of wartime. The size of the payments might have strained the payment capacity of the Wisselbank. From 1633 to 1648, Hoeufft relayed 1,000,000 and eventually 1,200,000 *livres* of regular subsidies to the United Provinces, and another 1,000,000 and more to the Swedes. By most measures, this payment itself would be substantial. It was roughly the value of the foreign currency in the *Trésor* royal in March 1636, for instance.[57] To this could be added extraordinary subsidies, such as 1,000,000 *livres* for the siege of Breda in 1637, subsidy payments to Hesse, Weimar, and other allies, other payments for diplomatic expenses and armies in the Holy Roman Empire, and purchases of armaments, munitions, and naval vessels. Hoeufft also extended credit to other agents associated with the French crown, such as

---

56 Morera, 'Du commerce au finances', 23, and AN, MC/ET/XV, 148, Inventaire de Jean Hoeufft, lists roughly 183,000 *livres* of loans to over eighty different people. Mattheus Hoeufft's inventory contains no records of financial assets, as opposed to household possessions and real estate. See 'Inventaris van silverweerck ... naegelaten by den Heer Mattheus Hoeuft', Den Haag, Haags Gemeentearchief, Notarissen ter standplats 's-Gravenhage, 281, Martin Beeckman, fol. 351r–370v, 23 July 1669. Mattheus Hoeufft first appears in the index to the ledgers of the Wisselbank in 1631, with reference to two ledger pages. Stadsarchief Amsterdam, 5077, Archief van de Wisselbank, 2.4.2.1. Index op de grootboeken, 696 'DD'. In the next surviving index, he had 11 ledger pages (697, 'ZZ'). By the time of the first surviving ledger, in 1644, the index listed eight pages, from 1 February to the end of August (698). The same period the following year also required eleven pages (700).
57 Jérôme Jambu, *Tant d'or que d'argent: La monnaie en Basse Normandie à l'époque moderne (XVIe–XVIIe siècle)* (Rennes: Presses Universitaires de Rennes, 2013), p. 334.

Alphonse Lopez, when they were without other funds.[58] Without complete records of all his transactions, one can nevertheless safely conclude that from 1633 until 1648, they included the annual remittance from France to the Netherlands of a bare minimum of 3,000,000 *livres*, or roughly 2,000,000 Dutch guilders. This was a significant amount of money, more than half the total metal reserves of 3,474,527 guilders of the Amsterdam Wisselbank of Amsterdam in 1634; and although deposits in the Wisselbank grew to over 5,000,000 in the late 1630s and more than 8,000,000 in 1640 and 1641, the Hoeuffts' exchanges would always have involved significant proportions of the bank's liquidity.[59] Certainly Mattheus Hoeufft's Wisselbank account balance rarely exceeded 200,000 guilders. While this was a substantial sum, it would not have sufficed to make the subsidy payments, and transactions in the account rarely exceeded 20,000 guilders.[60]

Jean Hoeufft occasionally described how financial and monetary problems frustrated his activities. Louis XIII granted Hoeufft permission to export 400,000 *livres*' worth of foreign coins from France in June 1635, allegedly because the war had so perturbed the bill-of-exchange market that no one would accept bills for the subsidy.[61] Jean Hoeufft wrote to Chavigny in 1641 that though the subsidy money was ready in Amsterdam, 'there is no possibility of drawing letters of change from Amsterdam for Hamburg, as there is even less coin there, because Messieurs of the Bank of Amsterdam will not spend a single *reichsthaler* owing to the transport that the English do with them'.[62] The subsidies themselves may have

---

58 Paris: AD, CP, Hollande, 21, Lopez to Richelieu, Amsterdam 13 February 1640, fol. 458v. On Lopez, see Françoise Hildesheimer, 'Lopez (Alphonse)' in *Dictionnaire Richelieu*, ed. by Françoise Hildesheimer and Dénes Harai (Paris: Honoré Champion, 2015), pp. 221–222.
59 J.G. van Dillen, *Bronnen tot de geschiedenis der wisselbanken (Amsterdam, Middelberg, Delft, Rotterdam) 1603–1820* ('s-Gravenhage: Nijhoff, 1925), vol. II, p. 963.
60 There are lacunae in the books. See, for example, Stadsarchief Amsterdam, 5077, Archief van de Wisselbank, 2.4.2.1 Grotebocken, 50, februari-augustus 1644, 25.
61 Nationaal Archief, Den Haag, 1.01.08, Staten Generaal, 12587.54: 'Een copie authentijck van en paspoort voor Sr. Jan Heuft tot transport van 400000 lvr in vreemde specien van 10:e junij 1635'.
62 Paris: AD, CP, Hollande, 23, Hoeufft to Chavigny, Paris, 27 June 1641, fol. 182. On these shortages, see J.G. van Dillen, 'Oprichting en Functie der Amsterdamse Wisselbank in de zeventiende Eeuw, 1609–1686', in *Mensen*

contributed to the difficulties of the exchange market. Although figures for balances of trade are notoriously unreliable, by one estimate Hoeufft's subsidy payments would have been worth nearly half of the value of all Dutch imports from France.[63] Frank Spooner called attention to the way in which 'the brutal decline in the course of French exchange rates coincided with the inflation of circulation in the kingdom, and the volume of credit, which was determined in part by the financial operations of Richelieu and his politics of subsidies to allies, above all to Sweden: a flow of bills of exchange went the way of Amsterdam'.[64] As the Swedish economist Knut Wicksell argued, balance-of-payment surpluses in wartime often cause a disproportionate decline in exchange rates and interest rates.[65] Hoeufft's remittances were more than half Holland's and the Generality's annual debt purchases during the period.[66] It does not seem outside the realm of possibility that the French subsidy money contributed to the excess capital that caused low interest rates in the late 1630s and 1640s, leading to the increased deposits in the Wisselbank, sometimes dramatic increases in the price of assets such as tulips and housing, and Dutch merchants seeking to invest outside of the Netherlands, for instance Hoeufft's wetland drainage projects in Poitou.[67]

---

en achtergronden: Studies uitgegeven ter gelegenheid van de tachitigste jaardag van de schrijver (Groningen: J.B. Wolters, 1964), pp. 360–362; M.S. Polak, *Historiografie en economie van de 'muntchaos': de Muntproductie van de Republiek* (Amsterdam: NEHA, 1998), pp. 178–187, and Quinn and Roberds, 'An Economic Explanation', pp. 56–59.

63 See S. Groenveld and H.L.Ph. Leeuwenberg, *De bruid in de schuit: De consolidatie van de Republiek, 1609–1650* (Zutphen: De Walburg Pers, 1985), pp. 160–161.

64 Frank C. Spooner, *L'Économie mondiale et les frappes monétaires en France 1493–1680* (Paris: Armand Colin, 1956), p. 311. For quoted exchange rates, see Markus A. Denzel, *Handbook of World Exchange Rates, 1590–1914* (Farnham: Ashgate, 2010), p. 65.

65 Knut Wiksell, 'Växelkursernas gåta', *Ekonomisk tidskrift* 21.4 (1919), 87–103. On the use of this, see Magnus Andersson, *Den europeiska varu- och kreditmarknaden under 1700-talet: Handel och sjöfart med Göteborg som utgångspunkt* (Gothenburg: Gidlunds förlag, 2016), p. 17.

66 Jan de Vries and Ad van der Woude, *The First Modern Economy: Success, Failure and Perseverance of the Dutch Economy, 1500–1818* (Cambridge: Cambridge University Press, 1997), pp. 116–117.

67 See the monetarist explanation of the Tulipmania, for example, in Doug French, 'The Dutch Monetary Environment during Tulipmania', *Quarterly Journal of Austrian Economics* 9 (2006), 3–34, and James E. McClure and

Jean Hoeufft often insisted that it took considerable time to prepare the remittance of money, which suggests that the matter was not as simple as writing a letter of exchange. I believe that Hoeufft attempted to spread out the payments – both in time, by turning some of the bills of exchange for longer periods, and by forming a payment consortium to spread the capital demands out to some extent. The Hoeuffts had previously organized large syndicates of people to lend money to potentially risky borrowers. The 'Staet van de geaccepteerde Wisselen' of 1630 detailed how Mattheus Hoeufft, on behalf of Jean, arranged the debts of the Dutch Ambassador Gideon van den Boetzelaer, heer von Langerak, in 1630.[68] In total, Langerak owed 40,424 '*Croonen*', divided into thirty-seven bills of exchange from Amsterdam, fourteen from Rotterdam, four from Delft, two from Dordrecht, and seven from Middelburg. Seven of the bills for roughly 15 per cent of the total debt were drawn on Mattheus. Such techniques reduced the risk from default or delay in payment.[69]

Although the evidence remains incomplete, the remittance of subsidies and other moneys involved a smaller group of people. One Colbert[70] who was dispatched to Hamburg in order to act as a treasurer for the French emissary Melchior Mitte de Miolans, the marquis de Saint-Chamond, prepared accounts of his receipts and expenses for the king's service in 1637. In total he received 1,906,526

David Chandler Thomas, 'Explaining the Timing of Tulipmania's Boom and Bust: Historical Context, Sequestered Capital and Market Signals', *Financial History Review* 24.2 (2017), 121–141. The price of housing in Amsterdam rose, through a few severe plague outbreaks, until shortly after the signing of the Peace of Westphalia. Clé Lesger, *Huur en conjunctuur: de woningmarkt in Amsterdam, 1550–1850* (Amsterdam: Historisch Seminarium van de Universiteit van Amsterdam, 1986), pp. 46–47, and Piet M.A. Eichholtz, 'A Long Run House Price Index: The *Herengracht* Index, 1628–1973', *Real Estate Economics* 25 (1997), 175–192.

68 Den Haag, Nationaal Archief, Staten Generaal, 1.01.02. 6762. Elias Trip and Tallemant also appear on the list, as does Jean Hoeufft's brother Diederick from Dordrecht.

69 Oscar Gelderblom, Joost Jonker, and Clemens Kool, 'Direct Finance in the Dutch Golden Age', *Economic History Review* 69.4 (2016), 1178–1198.

70 I agree with Anja Victorine Hartmann that this is either Jean Baptiste-Colbert (1590–1663) or his son Nicolas. See *Les papiers de Richelieu: Section politique extérieure: Correspondance et papiers d'État: Empire Allemand*, ed. by Anja Victorine Hartmann (Paris: Pedone, 1999), vol. III, p. 106, n. 7.

livres.[71] He was first given a bill of exchange for 305,860 *livres* from Jean Hoeufft for Pieter Spierinck, the Swedish resident in The Hague. This money was intended for a portion of the subsidy payment from 1632 that the French had not delivered after Gustav II Adolf's death and other moneys to be paid after the ratification of the Treaty of Wismar.[72] Two letters of change were drawn on one M. Sarin and on one M. Delf in Amsterdam, worth 200,000 *livres* in total.[73] Another letter of change for 166,666 *livres* was written by 'Messieurs Lumague', a family of Parisian bankers, on Guillaume Bartolotti of Amsterdam. Four letters of exchange were drawn by Jean Hoeufft on Mattheus Hoeufft, totalling 630,000 *livres*. One letter for 500,000 *livres* was drawn by Jean Hoeufft on Lukas van Sprekelsen of Hamburg. The final letter for 100,000 *livres* was drawn by Jean Hoeufft on either Mattheus Hoeufft or van Sprekelsen. In other words, in 1637, Jean Hoeufft and his nephew handled the remittance of at least a third of the French money. This money was principally used to pay 1,250,000 *livres* to the Swedes, and 540,000 *livres* to the landgrave Wilhelm of Hesse-Cassel; other uses included French agents' salaries and travel costs, diplomatic gifts, and additional exchange charges of 1,557 *livres* to Mattheus Hoeufft for costs of an extra bill of exchange from Amsterdam to Hamburg.

These transactions reveal not only the credit available to the Hoeuffts but also how much these transactions reflected a 'reinforced' structural hole, not just Hoeufft's 'natural' position in kinship networks. The Hoeufft family had a long history of business with the Lumagues and Bartolotti, who probably also had the capital and contacts required to take on the Hoeuffts' role as remitter of subsidies. Hoeufft's connection to Pieter Spierinck, however, was a consciously cultivated tie. Spierinck came from a famous tapestry-weaving family in Delft who had, as a result of an inheritance dispute, come to Sweden early in Gustav II Adolf's reign in order to seek assistance in forcing Danzig's town council to provide

---

71 'Estat du maniment faict par le Sieur Colbert des deniers qui luy ont esté mis entre les mains pour les affaires d'Allemagne en l'année mil six cens trente sept', AD, CP Allemagne, 14, fols 422–428.
72 Sverker Arnoldsson, *Svensk-fransk krigs- och fredspolitik i Tyskland* (Gothenburg: Erlanders, 1937), p. 7 *et passim*, and Tor Berg, 'En fransk subsidieutbetalning till Axel Oxenstierna 1636', *Historisk Tidskrift* 74 (1954), 64–68.
73 I could not identify these two.

satisfaction. In the 1620s, Pieter Spierinck and his brother took on the administration of the war tolls or 'licences' that the Swedish crown levied on shipping into Danzig and other harbours on the coasts of Prussia and Livonia. The Swedish Chancellor Axel Oxenstierna came to depend upon Spierinck's financial acumen; Spierinck retained control over the Swedish and Livonian sea tolls, Sweden's other major reliable source of international currency, when he was appointed resident to the Netherlands.[74] In early 1635 Peter Spierinck travelled to France, where he met Hoeufft to assure the reliable payment of French subsidies, leaving his book-keeper Peter Heltscher, who would subsequently become chief Livonian toll-administrator, in Paris to establish relationships.[75] (The new Swedish ambassador Hugo Grotius had to ask the Superintendent of Finances Claude Bouthillier to release Spierinck from jail in Calais, where he had been incarcerated when trying to leave for Holland; Grotius noted that Spierinck, 'knowing he had enemies, which those who administer finances never lack, had found it advisable to travel incognito through Germany and while crossing France'.)[76]

Swedish connections helped Hoeufft broaden his contacts in Hamburg, allowing him not only to remit subsidies but also to pay French armies operating in northern Germany.[77] While serving as Swedish resident in Hamburg in the period immediately after Gustav II Adolf's death, Johan Adler Salvius had formed close connections with Hamburg's merchants. Indeed, he threatened the Swedish

---

74 See Badeloch Noldus, 'An "unvergleichbarer Liebhaber": Peter Spierinck, the Art-dealing Diplomat', *Scandinavian Journal of History* 31 (2006), 173–185. This article neglects the financial side of Spierinck's activity, for which see Einar Wendt, *Det svenska licentväsendet i Preussen* (Uppsala: Almqvist & Wiksell, 1933).
75 Spieringk to Axel Oxenstierna from Delft (1/11 March 1635), RA: Oxen. Sam. E727, Peter Heltscher to Axel Oxenstierna, 11 March 1636, RA: Oxen. Sam. E697, and Spieringk to A.O. (28 January 7 February 1635), 5/15 March and 2_/3_ [May] 1635), RA: Oxen Sam. E727.
76 Grotius to Claude Bouthillier (25 February 1635), *Briefwisseling van Hugo Grotius*, vol. V, No. 189, 329, 'sçachant qu'il a des enemies, qui ne manquent jamais à ceux qui administrent les finances, avoit trouvé bon de passer incognu par l'Allemagne et traversant la France s'embarquer à Calais'. See also Axel Oxenstierna to Paul Strassburg (10 March 1635), *AOSB*, vol. I, 13, Nos 70, 182.
77 Stephan Michael Schröder, 'Hamburg und Schweden im 30-jährigen Krieg – vom potentiellen Bündnispartner zum Zentrum der Kriegsfinanzierung', *Vierteljahrschrift für Sozial- und Wirtschaftsgeschichte* 76.3 (1989), 305–331.

minority government that need was driving him out of crown service, and 'to provide for myself in private as a merchant'.[78] Hoeufft's correspondent Lukas van Sprekelsen was related to Johan Adler Salvius.[79] Even if Jean and Mattheus Hoeufft's own correspondence with Axel Oxenstierna could not be characterized as warm, being able to maintain good relations with the Hoeuffts was viewed as meritorious by other Swedish statesmen. For example, a young Swedish emissary in Amsterdam, Harald Appelboom, who openly voiced hopes of succeeding Pieter Spierinck as ambassador in Sweden, wrote in some detail to Adler Salvius – at this point one of the Swedish plenipotentiaries at the Westphalian peace – who had instructed him to meet Mattheus Hoeufft and ask about remittance of the subsidy to Hamburg. Appelboom described to Salvius how Hoeufft had told him that the letters were just being sealed, whereupon Hoeufft had observed that he would be pleased to pay Appelboom any salary that was assigned to him and offered to intercede with Salvius so that Appelboom would be paid 3,000 *reichsthaler* of back pay which he was owed.[80] Rather than merely profiting from a naturally occurring spot between networks, the Hoeuffts actively cultivated connections, using the opportunity that the subsidy payments presented.

Conclusion

The Hoeuffts' ability to profit from being the payer of French subsidies to the monarch's allies in the United Provinces and Sweden, and to princes of the Holy Roman Empire, existed only as long as the French monarch had funds and allies which France was obliged to pay as long as it maintained an army in the field. In 1648, these two factors ceased to exist. For the first time, Hoeufft agreed to lend money for subsidy payments; his heirs would claim – and Jean Baptiste Colbert would accept – that Hoeufft had never been repaid these advances of more than 3,600,000 *livres* for letters of exchange

---

78 Lundgren, *Johan Adler Salvius*, pp. 72–73, 'Nöden driver mig ur tjänsten och till att på köpmansvis livnära mig in privato.'
79 Heiko Droste, 'Johan Adler Salvius i Hamburg: Ett nätverksbygge i 1600-talets Sverige', in *Mare Nostrum: Om Westfaliska freden och Östersjön som ett svenskt maktcentrum* (Stockholm: Riksarkivet, 1999), pp. 243–256.
80 Appelboom to Salvius, Amsterdam, 22 April 1645. RA: Johan Adler Salvius och hans sekreterare Georg Kellers samling, vol. 12. I would like to thank Heiko Droste, who brought this reference to my attention.

for the service of the king in foreign countries.[81] After the representatives of the United Provinces signed the Peace of Münster, merchants began to doubt that those involved in the French financial networks would still maintain their credit. Doubts principally focused on Jeremie Calandrini, who had begun to participate in the consortia of people who remitted the French subsidies to the Swedes. In early June, the Amsterdam banker Julien Lansson confronted Calandrini, asking him whether he intended to honour an obligation for 26,000 guilders which he entered into on behalf of Abel Servien, one of the French plenipotentiaries at the Westphalian peace contract.[82] The acting French resident in the Hague, Henri Brasset, wrote to Servien noting that Mattheus Hoeufft could not persuade people in Amsterdam or Hamburg to honour Calandrini's credit, observing that 'all the bankers are in a confusion, and the cause of this is the things going on in Paris, God willing there will be a prompt resolution to those affairs'.[83] As a result, the French agent Claude de Meulles, who had replaced Colbert in Hamburg, had trouble collecting part of the Swedish subsidies because of Calandrini's bankruptcy.[84]

Jean Hoeufft had perhaps already gained what he hoped for. In 1648, in response to a letter telling about his move to the new

---

81 'Mémoire des héritiers du sieur Hoeft, hollandais, à l'ambassadeur de Hollande …', Paris: Bibliothèque nationale de France, Mélanges de Colbert 119–119bis, fol. 966v. They thank Colbert for a favourable response in the 'Mémoire présenté à l'ambassadeur de Hollande en France', Paris: BNF, Mélanges de Colbert 120–120bis, fols 173–174v.

82 Stadsarchief Amsterdam, 1648 Juli 16: Nots. Arch 1690/1221 Nots Pieter de Bary. Merchants holding the obligation included Julien Lanson en Zoonen, Jan Daniel de Haz, Jan Daniel Rosa, Advocaat Cloeck, Nots. Tielmans, and Dirck de Keijser. See Hermann Kellenbenz, 'Hamburg und die Französisch-Schwedische Zusammenarbeit im 30-jährigen Krieg', Zeitschrift des Vereins für hamburgische Geschichte 49/50 (1964), 102–103.

83 Brasset to Servien, 6 July 1648, fol. 209v. 'C'est que aujourd'huy les banquiers sont tous en confusions es en ala a cause de ce qui se se passe a Paris. Dieu veut qu'il y est bien tost une prompte composition des affairs la'. For Hoeufft's inability to save Calandrini, see 17 August 1648, fol. 299. Paris: AD, CP Hollande, 47.

84 Paris: AD, CP Hambourg, 2, Meulles to Salvius, 16 April 1648, fol. 139v, Meulles to 'Monseigneur' [Avaux?] (28 August 1648): 'le principal que je puisse dire a present est que nostre banquier de cette ville ma dit que ces messieurs d'Amsterdam qui doivent fournir la premiere moitié du subside ont remis si peu de chose que cella ne veut pas le parler', Copy of Meulles's protest to Calandrini, 9 October 1648, fol. 215, and more discussion of it 13 November 1648, fol. 224.

Academy at Breda, Hoeufft thanked the Huguenot theologian André Rivet for telling him of the States-General's plans to banish 'popery and idolatry' from Breda, the siege of which in 1637 he had extended his credit to fund. He hoped that 'God would unite and bless [the members of the States-General], if they continue to take his cause into their consideration, without which our hopes are all vain'. He recounted victories of the 'confederates' from Bavaria to Brazil, anticipating a final victory over the Spanish. Hoeufft closed his letter by thanking Rivet for moving to Breda to teach, noting that '[y]ou will be contented in your old age nourishing young plants to serve the Church of God in edification'.[85] He did not seem to take a very active role in the Fronde – on either side – and died in the autumn of 1651. Mattheus Hoeufft lived until 1669, but he withdrew from banking and, seemingly, from the world of diplomacy, notifying the French in early 1652 that he intended to move from Amsterdam to The Hague, and that the man he was leaving to see to his affairs would not accept even a letter without payment in advance.[86]

Even if it were possible to calculate the costs and profits from the remittance work, the Hoeuffts' work on the subsidies should not be seen in isolation. The connections they established could be exploited for monetary gain; Jean Hoeufft proposed that Louis de Geer should partner with him to exploit a concession to mint copper coin in France, only to abandon it, explaining that 'cabals and oppositions have formed against the licence'.[87] Morera was entirely right to say that French foreign policy would not have functioned without Jean Hoeufft, who provided the French monarchy with

---

85 Leiden, Leiden University Library, Special Collections, Letters, BPL. 2211. Jean Hoeufft to André Rivet, Paris, 18 July 1648. 'J'espere que Dieu les unira et benira, s'ils continuent d'avoir sa Cause en Recommendation sans quoy touz nos esperances sont vaines ... Au rest, j'ay este resjouy lors que j'entendiz que vo:s allez vous employer dans l'academie de Breda. Vo:s au:e ce Contentem:t de nourrir des jeunes plantes dans v:re veillesse po:r servir a l'Eglise de Dieu en edification.'
86 BNF, Clairambault, 438, fol. 4. Les heritiers de Jean Hoeufft to Brienne, 2 March 1652.
87 Stockholm: Riksarkivet, Leufsta Arkivet, Jean Hoeufft to Louis de Geer, from Paris, 30 November 1641, and Jean Hoeufft to Louis de Geer, from Paris, 21 December 1641, 'Il c'est [*sic*] forme des oppositions et aultres brigues et comme vous cognoissez les mutations et variété du monde, c'est pourquoy je suis d'advis ... vous ne fassiez rien jusques a autre de mes advis et ordre.'

connections enabling France to procure the metal, cannons, muskets, saltpetre, and naval vessels necessary to wage war that lay at the heart of the cardinals' policies. So too Hoeufft managed to be the banker that Richelieu thought was a necessary part of alliances, and he managed the fiscal side of the alliances with only small flaws for the best part of two decades. Yet it is also true that the cardinals' foreign policy, and particularly the payment of subsidies, enabled Hoeufft's entrepreneurial strategy, allowing his family to profit from occupying a unique position in European commerce and politics.

Select bibliography

Abbenhuis, Maartje. *An Age of Neutrals: Great Power Politics 1815–1914* (Cambridge: Cambridge University Press, 2015)
Affolter, Andreas. *Verhandeln mit Republiken: Die französisch-eidgenössischen Beziehungen im frühen 18. Jahrhundert*, Externa: Geschichte der Außenbeziehungen in neuen Perspektiven, 11 (Cologne: Böhlau, 2017)
Albrecht, Dieter. 'Zur Finanzierung des Dreißigjährigen Krieges: Die Subsidien der Kurie für den Kaiser und Liga 1618–1635', *Zeitschrift für bayerische Landesgeschichte* 19 (1956), 534–567
Åmark, Karl. *Sveriges statsfinanser 1719–1809*, parts I–III (Stockholm: Norstedt, 1961)
Amoretti, Guido. *La Serenissima Repubblica in Grecia. XII–XVIII secolo: Dalle tavole del Capitano Antonio Paravia e dagli archivi di Venezia* (Turin: Omega Edizioni, 2006)
Anderson, Matthew Smith. *The Origins of the Modern European State System, 1494–1618* (London: Longman, 1998)
Anderson, Matthew Smith. *The War of the Austrian Succession, 1740–1748* (London: Longman, 1995)
Andersson, Magnus. *Den europeiska varu- och kreditmarknaden under 1700-talet: Handel och sjöfart med Göteborg som utgångspunkt* (Gothenburg: Gidlunds förlag, 2016)
Artéus, Gunnar. *Krigsmakt och samhälle i frihetstidens Sverige* (Stockholm: Militärhistoriska förlaget, 1982)
Asker, Björn. *Hur riket styrdes: Förvaltning, politik och arkiv 1520–1920* (Stockholm: Skrifter utgivna av Riksarkivet, 2007)
Atwood, Rodney. *The Hessians: Mercenaries from Hessen-Kassel in the American Revolution* (Cambridge: Cambridge University Press, 1980)
Babel, Rainer. *Garde et protection: Der Königsschutz in der französischen Außenpolitik vom 15. bis zum 17. Jahrhundert*, Beihefte der Francia, 72 (Ostfildern: Thorbecke Verlag, 2014)

Badalo-Dulong, Claude. *Banquier du Roi: Barthélémey Hervart, 1606–1676* (Paris: Ségur, 1951)
Badalo-Dulong, Claude. *Mazarin et l'argent: Banquiers et prête-noms* (Paris: École des Chartes, 2002)
Barthas, Jérémie. *L'argent n'est pas le nerf de la guerre: Essai sur une prétendue erreur de Machiavel* (Rome: École Française de Rome, 2012)
Baugh, Daniel A. 'Withdrawing from Europe: Anglo-French Maritime Geopolitics, 1750–1800', *The International History Review* 20.1 (1998), 1–32
Baumann, Reinhard. *Landsknechte* (Munich: C.H. Beck, 1994)
Behr, Andreas. *Diplomatie als Familiengeschäft: Die Casati als spanisch-mailändische Gesandte in Luzern und Chur (1660–1700)* (Zurich: Chronos, 2015)
Bély, Lucien. *L'art de la paix en Europe: Naissance de la diplomatie moderne XVIe–XVIIIe siècle* (Paris: Presses Universitaires de France, 2007)
Bély, Lucien. *La société des princes, XVIe–XVIIIe siècle* (Paris: Fayard, 1999)
Bers, Günter. *Don Gabriel de la Torre: Ein spanischer Gubernator der Stadt und Festung Jülich (1641–1660). Zur Stadtgeschichte im Dreißigjährigen Krieg* (Jülich: Verlag der Joseph-Kuhl-Gesellschaft, 2013)
Black, Jeremy. *European International Relations, 1648–1815* (Basingstoke: Palgrave, 2002)
Black, Jeremy. *From Louis XIV to Napoleon: The Fate of a Great Power* (London: UCL Press, 1999)
Black, Jeremy. *A History of Diplomacy* (London: Reaktion books, 2010)
Bodensten, Erik. *Politikens drivfjäder: Frihetstidens partiberättelser och den moralpolitiska logiken* (Lund: Lunds universitet, 2016)
Bois, Jean-Pierre. *De la paix des rois à l'ordre des empereurs, 1714–1815: Nouvelle histoire des relations internationales*, 3 (Paris: Seuil, 2003)
Bolzern, Rudolf. *Spanien, Mailand und die katholische Eidgenossenschaft: Militärische, wirtschaftliche und politische Beziehungen zur Zeit des Gesandten Alfonso Casati (1594–1621)*, Luzerner Historische Veröffentlichungen, 16 (Lucerne: Rex, 1982)
Bonney, Richard. *The King's Debts: Finance and Politics in France, 1589–1661* (Oxford: Clarendon Press, 1981)
Bonney, Richard, ed. *Economic Systems and State Finance* (Oxford: Oxford University Press, 1995)
Bonney, Richard, ed. *The Rise of the Fiscal State in Europe, c. 1200–1815* (Oxford: Oxford University Press, 1999)
Bosbach, Franz. *Monarchia Universalis: Ein politischer Leitbegriff der Frühen Neuzeit*, Schriftenreihe der Historischen Kommission bei der Bayerischen Akademie der Wissenschaften, 32 (Göttingen: Vandenhoeck & Ruprecht, 1988)
Brandon, Pepijn. *War, Capital and the Dutch State (1588–1795)* (Leiden: Brill, 2015)

Braubach, Max. *Die Bedeutung der Subsidien für die Politik im spanischen Erbfolgekriege* (Bonn and Leipzig: Kurt Schroeder Verlag, 1923)

Brewer, John. *The Sinews of Power: War, Money, and the English State, 1688–1783* (New York: Alfred A. Knopf, 1989)

Browning, Reed. *The War of the Austrian Succession* (New York: St Martin's Griffin, 1993)

Burkhardt, Johannes. 'Die Friedlosigkeit der Frühen Neuzeit: Grundlegung einer Theorie der Bellizität Europas', *Zeitschrift für Historische Forschung* 24 (1997), 509–574

Burschel, Peter. *Söldner im Nordwestdeutschland des 16. und 17. Jahrhunderts: Sozialgeschichtliche Studien* (Göttingen: Vandenhoeck & Ruprecht, 1994)

Burt, Ronald S. *Structural Holes: The Social Structure of Competition* (Cambridge, MA: Harvard University Press, 1992)

Cornette, Joël. *Le roi de guerre: Essai sur la souveraineté dans la France du Grand Siècle* (Paris: Éditions Payot & Rivages, 1993)

Corvisier, André. *L'armée française de la fin du 17e siècle au ministère de Choiseul*, 2 vols (Paris: PUF, 1964)

Corvisier, André. *Les Français et l'armée sous Louis XIV* (Vincennes: Ministère de la défense, Etat Major de l'Armée de terre, Service historique, 1975)

Dafflon, Alexandre. *Die Ambassadoren des Königs und Solothurn: Ein 'vierzehnter Kanton' am Ufer der Aare, 16. bis 18. Jahrhundert* (Solothurn: Zentralbibliothek Solothurn, 2014)

Dehing, Pit. *Geld in Amsterdam: Wisselbank en wisselkoersen, 1650–1725* (Hilversum: Verloren, 2012)

De Jong, Michiel. *'Staat van oorlog': Wapenbedrijf en militaire hervorming in de Republiek der Verenigde Nederlanden, 1585–1621* (Hilversum: Verloren, 2005)

Droste, Heiko. 'Patronage in der Frühen Neuzeit – Institution und Kulturform', *Zeitschrift für Historische Forschung* 30 (2003), 555–590

Edelmayer, Friedrich. *Söldner und Pensionäre: Das Netzwerk Philipps II. im Heiligen Römischen Reich*, Studien zur Geschichte und Kultur der iberischen und iberoamerikanischen Länder, 7 (Vienna: Verlag für Geschichte und Politik, 2002)

Ehrenberg, Richard. *Das Zeitalter der Fugger: Geldkapital und Creditverkehr im 16. Jahrhundert*, 2 vols (Jena: Gustav Fischer, 1896)

Ekholm, Lars. *Svensk krigsfinansiering 1630–31* (Uppsala: Acta Universitatis Upsaliensis, 1974)

Elmroth, Ingvar. *För kung och fosterland: Studier i den svenska adelns demografi och offentliga funktioner 1600–1900* (Lund: Bibliotheca Historica Lundensis, 1981)

Emich, Birgit. 'Staatsbildung und Klientel – politische Integration und Patronage in der Frühen Neuzeit', in *Integration. Legitimation. Korruption. Politische Patronage in Früher Neuzeit und Moderne*, ed. by Ronald

G. Asch, Birgit Emich, and Jens Ivo Engels (Frankfurt am Main: Peter Lang, 2011), pp. 33–49

Ernst, Hildegard. *Madrid und Wien 1632–1637: Politik und Finanzen in den Beziehungen zwischen Philipp IV. und Ferdinand II.*, Schriftenreihe der Vereinigung zur Erforschung der Neueren Geschichte e.V., 18 (Münster: Aschendorff Verlag, 1991)

Ernstberger, Anton. *Hans de Witte: Finanzmann Wallensteins*, Vierteljahrschrift für Sozial- und Wirtschaftsgeschichte, Beiheft 38 (Wiesbaden: Steiner, 1954)

Fahlborg, Birger. *Sveriges yttre politik 1660–1664* (Stockholm: P.A. Norstedt & Söner, 1932)

Forrest, Alan. *The Legacy of the French Revolutionary Wars: The Nation-in-Arms in French Republican Memory* (Cambridge: Cambridge University Press, 2009)

Friedeburg, Robert von. 'In Defense of Patria: Resisting Magistrates and the Duties of Patriots in the Empire from the 1530s to the 1640s', *Sixteenth Century Journal* 32 (2001), 357–382

Gantet, Claire. *Guerre Paix et construction des États, 1618–1714: Nouvelle histoire des relations internationales*, 2 (Paris: Seuil, 2003)

Gaunt, David. *Utbildning till statens tjänst: En kollektivbiografi av stormaktstidens hovrättsauskultanter* (Uppsala: Almqvist och Wiksell, 1975)

Gelderblom, Oscar. *Zuid-Nederlandse kooplieden en de opkomst van de Amsterdamse stapelmarkt (1578–1630)* (Hilversum: Verloren, 2000)

Gelderblom, Oscar, Joost Jonker, and Clemens Kool, 'Direct Finance in the Dutch Golden Age', *Economic History Review* 69 (2016), 1178–1198

Gillard, Lucien. *La Banque d'Amsterdam et le florin européen au temps de la République néerlandaise (1610–1820)* (Paris: Éditions de l'École des Hautes Études en Sciences Sociales, 2004)

Glete, Jan. *Navies and Nations: Warships, Navies and State Building in Europe and America, 1500–1860*, 2 vols (Stockholm: Stockholms Universitet, 1993)

Glozier, Matthew and David Onnekink, eds. *War, Religion and Service: Huguenot Soldiering, 1685–1713* (Aldershot: Ashgate, 2007)

Graham, Aaron, and Patrick Walsh, eds. *The British Fiscal Military States 1660–c.1783* (Farnham: Ashgate, 2016)

Graham, Aaron. 'The War of the Spanish Succession, the Financial Revolution, and the Imperial Loans of 1706 and 1710', in *The War of the Spanish Succession: New Perspectives*, ed. by Matthias Pohlig and Michael Schaich (Oxford: Oxford University Press, 2018), pp. 299–321

Granovetter, Mark. *Society and Economy: Framework and Principles* (Cambridge, MA: Harvard University Press, 2017)

Grell, Ole Peter. *Brethren in Christ: A Calvinist Network in Reformation Europe* (Cambridge: Cambridge University Press, 2011)

Groebner, Valentin. *Liquid Assets, Dangerous Gifts: Presents and Politics at the End of the Middle Ages* (Philadelphia: University of Pennsylvania Press, 2002)

Groebner, Valentin. *Gefährliche Geschenke: Ritual, Politik und die Sprache der Korruption in der Eidgenossenschaft im späten Mittelalter und am Beginn der Neuzeit*, Konflikte und Kultur – Historische Perspektiven, 4 (Constance: UVK Universitätsverlag Konstanz, 2000)

Grosjean, Alexia. *An Unofficial Alliance: Scotland and Sweden 1569–1654* (Leiden: Brill, 2003)

Gugger, Rudolf. *Preußische Werbungen in der Eidgenossenschaft im 18. Jahrhundert* (Berlin: Duncker und Humblot, 1997)

Gustafsson, Harald. *Makt och människor: Europeisk statsbildning från medeltiden till franska revolutionen* (Gothenburg: Makadam, 2010)

Gustafsson, Sofia. *Leverantörer och profitörer: Olika geografiska områdens och sociala gruppers handel med fästningsbygget Sveaborg under den första byggnadsperioden 1748–1756* (Helsinki: Societas Scientiarum Fennica, 2015)

Haan, Bertrand. *Une paix pour l'éternité: La négociation du traité du Cateau-Cambrésis*, Bibliothèque de la Casa de Velázquez, 49 (Madrid: Casa de Velázquez, 2010)

Haas, Philip. *Fürstenehe und Interessen: Die dynastische Ehe der frühen Neuzeit in zeitgenössischer Traktatliteratur und politischer Praxis am Beispiel Hessen-Kassels* (Darmstadt and Marburg: Quellen und Forschungen zur Hessischen Geschichte, 177, 2017)

Häberlein, Mark, and Christof Jeggle, eds. *Materielle Grundlagen der Diplomatie: Schenken, Sammeln und Verhandeln in Spätmittelalter und Früher Neuzeit*, Irseer Schriften: Studien zur Wirtschafts-, Kultur- und Mentalitätsgeschichte new series 9 (Constance, Munich: UVK Verlagsgesellschaft, 2013).

Harding, Richard, and Sergio Solbes Ferri, eds. *The Contractor State and Its Implications, 1659–1815* (Las Palmas de Gran Canaria: Universidad de Las Palmas de Gran Canaria, 2012)

't Hart, Marjolein. *The Dutch Wars of Independence: Warfare and Commerce in the Netherlands 1570–1680* (London and New York: Routledge, 2014)

Hartmann, Peter Claus. *Geld als Instrument europäischer Machtpolitik im Zeitalter des Merkantilismus 1715–1740* (Munich: Kommission für Bayerische Landesgeschichte, 1978)

Hatton, Ragnhild. 'Gratifications and foreign policy: Anglo-French Rivalry in Sweden during the Nine Years War', in *William III and Louis XIV: Essays 1680–1720 by and for Mark A. Thomson* (Liverpool: Liverpool University Press, 1968), pp. 68–94

Haug, Tilman. *Ungleiche Außenbeziehungen und grenzüberschreitende Patronage: Die französische Krone und die geistlichen Kurfürsten (1648–1679)*, Externa: Geschichte der Außenbeziehungen in neuen Perspektiven, 6 (Cologne, Weimar, and Vienna: Böhlau Verlag, 2015)

Haug, Tilman, Nadir Weber, and Christian Windler, eds. *Protegierte und Protektoren: Asymmetrische politische Beziehungen zwischen Partnerschaft und Dominanz (16. bis frühes 20. Jahrhundert)*, Externa: Geschichte der Außenbeziehungen in neuen Perspektiven, 9 (Cologne, Weimar, and Vienna: Böhlau Verlag, 2016)

Hitz, Benjamin. *Kämpfen um Sold: Eine Alltags- und Sozialgeschichte schweizerischer Söldner in der Frühen Neuzeit* (Cologne: Böhlau, 2015)

Höbelt, Lothar. 'Vom militärischen saisonnier zum miles perpetuus: Staatsbildung und Kriegsführung im ancien régime', in *Krieg und Gesellschaft*, vol. 2, ed. by Thomas Kolnberger and Ilja Steffelbauer (Vienna: Mandelbaum, 2010), pp. 59–79

Holenstein, André, Thomas Maissen and Maarten Prak, eds. *The Republican Alternative: The Netherlands and Switzerland Compared* (Amsterdam: Amsterdam University Press, 2008)

Holt, Mack P. *The French Wars of Religion, 1562–1629*, 2nd ed. (Cambridge: Cambridge University Press, 2005; first published in 1995)

Ingrao, Charles W. *The Hessian Mercenary State: Ideas, Institutions, and Reform under Frederick II 1760–1785* (Cambridge: Cambridge University Press, 1987)

Israel, Jonathan. *The Anglo Dutch Moment: Essays on the Glorious Revolution and Its World Impact* (Cambridge: Cambridge University Press, 1991)

Israel, Jonathan. *Dutch Primacy in World Trade, 1585–1740* (Oxford: Clarendon Press, 1989)

Jespersen, Knud J.V. and Ole Feldbæk, *Revanche og neutralitet, 1648–1814: Dansk udenrigspolitiks historie*, 2 (Copenhagen: Gyldendal, 2002)

Jouanna, Arlette. *La France du XVIe siècle, 1483–1598* (Paris: Presses Universitaires de France, 1996)

Kampmann, Christoph. *Europa und das Reich im Dreißigjährigen Krieg: Geschichte eines europäischen Konflikts* (Stuttgart: Kohlhammer, 2008)

Kapser, Cordula. *Die bayerische Kriegsorganisation in der zweiten Hälfte des Dreßigjährigen Krieges 1635–1648/49* (Münster: Aschendorff, 1997)

Kellenbenz, Hermann. 'Hamburg und die französisch-schwedische Zusammenarbeit im 30jährigen Krieg', *Zeitschrift des Vereins für Hamburgische Geschichte* 49/50 (1964), 83–107

Kettering, Sharon. *Patrons, Brokers, and Clients in Seventeenth-century France* (New York: Oxford University Press, 1986)

Killingray, David, and David Omissi, eds. *Guardians of Empire: The Armed Forces of the Colonial Powers, c.1700–1964* (Manchester: Manchester University Press, 1999)

Klein, Peter W. *De Trippen in de 17e eeuw: Een studie over het ondernemerschap op de Hollandse stapelmarkt* (Assen: Van Gorcum, 1965)

Kohler, Alfred. *Expansion und Hegemonie: Internationale Beziehungen 1450–1559*, Handbuch der Geschichte der Internationalen Beziehungen, 1 (Paderborn: Ferdinand Schöningh, 2008)

Krüssmann, Walter. *Ernst von Mansfeld (1580–1626): Grafensohn, Söldnerführer, Kriegsunternehmer gegen Habsburg im Dreißigjährigen Krieg* (Berlin: Duncker & Humblot, 2010)

Lemnitzer, Jan Martin. *Power, Law and the End of Privateering* (Basingstoke: Palgrave, 2014)

Lesaffer, Randall. 'Amicitia in Renaissance Peace and Alliance Treaties (1450–1530)', *Journal of the History of International Law* 4 (2002), 77–99

Lesaffer, Randall, 'Defensive Warfare, Prevention and Hegemony: The Justifications for the Franco-Spanish War of 1635', *Journal of the History of International Law*, Part I, 8.1 (2006): 91–123, Part II, 8.2 (2006): 141–179

Lesaffer, Randall, ed. *Peace Treaties and International Law in European History: From the Late Middle Ages to World War One* (Cambridge: Cambridge University Press, 2004)

Lindström, Peter and Svante Norrhem. *Flattering Alliances: Scandinavia, Diplomacy and the Austrian–French Balance of Power, 1646–1740* (Lund: Nordic Academic Press, 2013)

Lorenz, Gottfried. 'Schweden und die französischen Hilfsgelder von 1638 bis 1649: Ein Beitrag zur Finanzierung des Krieges im 17. Jahrhundert', in *Forschungen und Quellen zur Geschichte des Dreißigjährigen Krieges*, Schriftenreihe der Vereinigung zur Erforschung der Neueren Geschichte e.V., 12 (Münster: Aschendorff Verlag, 1981), pp. 98–148

Lundkvist, Sven. 'Svensk krigsfinansiering 1630–1635', *Historisk Tidskrift* 2 (1966), 377–417

Lynn, John A. *Giant of the Grand Siècle: The French Army 1610–1715* (Cambridge: Cambridge University Press, 1997)

Lynn, John A. *Women, Armies, and Warfare in Early Modern Europe* (Cambridge: Cambridge University Press, 2008)

Maillet-Rao, Caroline. *La pensée politique des dévots Mathieu de Morgues et Michel de Marillac: Une opposition au ministériat du cardinal de Richelieu* (Paris: Honoré Champion, 2015)

Mann, Michael. *The Sources of Social Power, I: A History of Power from the Beginning to A.D. 1760* (Cambridge: Cambridge University Press, 1986)

Menk, Gerhard. *Georg Friedrich von Waldeck (1620 – 1692): Eine biographische Skizze*, Waldeckische Historische Hefte, 3 (Arolsen: Waldeckischer Geschichtsverein, 1992)

Metcalf, Michael F. *Russia, England and Swedish Party Politics 1762–1766: The Interplay between Great Power Diplomacy and Domestic Politics during Sweden's Age of Liberty* (Stockholm: Stockholm University, 1977)

Morera, Raphaël. *L'assèchement des marais en France au XVIIe siècle* (Rennes: Presses Universitaires de Rennes, 2011)

Morera, Raphaël, 'Du commerce au finances: la fortune de Jean Hoeufft entre la France et les Provinces Unies', *Revue d'Histoire moderne et contemporaine* 63.1 (2016), 7–29

Murdoch, Steve. *Britain, Denmark-Norway and the House of Stuart, 1603–1660* (East Linton: Tuckwell Press, 2000)

Murdoch, Steve, ed. *Scotland and the Thirty Years' War, 1618–1648* (Leiden: Brill, 2001).

Nexon, Daniel H. *The Struggle for Power in Early Modern Europe: Religious Conflict, Dynastic Empires, and International Change* (Princeton: Princeton University Press, 2009)

Nilsson, Sven A. *På väg mot reduktionen: Studier i svenskt 1600-tal* (Stockholm: Natur och kultur, 1964)
Nilzén, Göran. *Studier i 1730-talets partiväsende* (Stockholm: Stockholms universitet, 1971)
Noldus, Badeloch. 'An "unvergleichbarer Liebhaber": Peter Spierinck, the Art-dealing Diplomat', *Scandinavian Journal of History* 31 (2006), 173–185
Norrhem, Svante. *Mercenary Swedes: French Subsidies to Sweden 1631–1796* (Lund: Nordic Academic Press, 2019)
Oakley, Stewart P. *William III and the Northern Crowns during the Nine Years' War, 1689–1697* (New York and London: Garland, 1987)
Olofsson, Sverker. *Gustav II Adolf* (Stockholm: Atlantis, 2007)
Olson, Mancur Jr, and Richard Zeckhauser, 'An Economic Theory of Alliances', *The Review of Economics and Statistics* 48.3 (August 1966), 266–279
Ormrod, Mark, Margaret Bonney, and Richard Bonney, eds. *Crises, Revolutions and Self-Sustained Growth: Essays in European Fiscal History, 1130–1830* (Stamford: Shaun Tyas, 1999)
Parker, Geoffrey. *The Thirty Years' War* (London: Routledge, 1984)
Parrott, David. *The Business of War: Military Enterprise and Military Revolution in Early Modern Europe* (Cambridge: Cambridge University Press, 2012)
Parrott, David. *Richelieu's Army: War, Government and Society in France 1624–1642* (Cambridge: Cambridge University Press, 2001)
Percy, Sarah V. *Mercenaries: The History of a Norm in International Relations* (Oxford: Oxford University Press, 2007)
Price, Leslie. *Dutch Culture in the Golden Age* (London: Reaktion Books, 2011)
Redlich, Fritz. *The German Military Enterpriser and His Work Force: A Study in European Economic and Social History*, Vierteljahresschrift für Sozial- und Wirtschaftsgeschichte, Beihefte 47/48, 2 vols (Wiesbaden: F. Steiner, 1964–1965)
Reinhard, Wolfgang. *Geschichte der Staatsgewalt: Eine vergleichende Verfassungsgeschichte Europas von den Anfängen bis zur Gegenwart* (Munich: C.H. Beck, 1999)
Riley, James C. *The Seven Years War and the Old Regime in France: The Economic and Financial Toll* (Princeton: Princeton University Press, 1986)
Roberts, Michael. *The Age of Liberty: Sweden 1719–1772* (Cambridge: Cambridge University Press, 1986)
Roberts, Michael. *The Swedish imperial experience, 1560–1718* (Cambridge: Cambridge University Press, 1979)
Rogger, Philippe. *Geld, Krieg und Macht: Pensionsherren, Söldner und eidgenössische Politik in den Mailänderkriegen 1494–1516* (Baden: Hier und Jetzt, 2015)
Rogger, Philippe, and Nadir Weber, eds. *Beobachten, Vernetzen, Verhandeln: Diplomatische Akteure und politische Kulturen in der frühneuzeitlichen*

Eidgenossenschaft, Itinera – Beihefte zur Schweizerischen Gesellschaft für Geschichte, 45 (Basel: Schwabe, 2018)

Rowlands, Guy. *Dangerous and Dishonest Men: The International Bankers of Louis XIV's France* (Basingstoke: Palgrave Macmillan, 2014)

Rowlands, Guy. *The Financial Decline of a Great Power: War, Influence, and Money in Louis XIV's France* (Oxford: Oxford University Press, 2012)

Rystad, Göran. *Karl XI: En biografi* (Lund: Historiska media, 2001)

Salm, Hubert. *Armeefinanzierung im Dreißigjährigen Krieg: Der Niederrheinisch-Westfälische Reichskreis 1635–1650* (Münster: Aschendorff, 1990)

Schaufelberger, Walter. *Marignano: Strukturelle Grenzen eidgenössischer Militärmacht zwischen Mittelalter und Neuzeit*, Schriftenreihe der Gesellschaft für militärhistorische Studienreisen, 11 (Frauenfeld: Huber, 1993)

Schilling, Heinz. *Konfessionalisierung und Staatsinteressen: Internationale Beziehungen 1559–1660* (Paderborn: Ferdinand Schöningh, 2007)

Schindling, Anton. *Die Anfänge des Immerwährenden Reichstags zu Regensburg: Ständevertretung und Staatskunst nach dem Westfälischen Frieden*, Veröffentlichungen des Instituts für Europäische Geschichte Mainz, 143 (Mainz: Verlag Philipp von Zabern, 1991)

Schmid, Alois. *Max III: Joseph und die europäischen Mächte: Die Außenpolitik des Kurfürstentums Bayern von 1745–1765* (Munich: Oldenbourg, 1987)

Schmidt, Peer. *Spanische Universalmonarchie oder 'teutsche Libertet': das spanische Imperium in der Propaganda des Dreißigjährigen Krieges*, Studien zur modernen Geschichte, 54 (Stuttgart: Franz Steiner Verlag, 2001)

Schröder, Stephan Michael. 'Hamburg und Schweden im 30-jährigen Krieg – vom potentiellen Bündnispartner zum Zentrum der Kriegsfinanzierung', *Vierteljahrschrift für Sozial- und Wirtschaftsgeschichte* 76.3 (1989), 305–331

Schulte, Regina. 'Rüstung, Zins und Frömmigkeit: Niederländische Calvinisten als Finanziers des Dreißigjährigen Krieges', *Bohemia: Zeitschrift für Geschichte und Kultur der böhmischen Länder* 35 (1994), 46–62

Schumpeter, Joseph Alois. 'The Crisis of the Tax State', *International Economic Papers* 4 (1954), 5–38

Schweizer, Karl W., and Matt J. Schumann. 'The Revitalization of Diplomatic History: Renewed Reflections', *Diplomacy and Statecraft* 19 (2008), 149–186

Scott, Hamish M. *The Emergence of the Eastern Powers, 1756–1775* (Cambridge: Cambridge University Press, 2001)

Scott, Hamish. 'The Seven Years War and Europe's Ancien Régime', *War in History* 18.4 (2011), 419–455.

Sewell, William H. Jr. *Logics of History: Social Theory and Social Transformation* (Chicago: University of Chicago Press, 2005)

Shaw, L.M.E. *The Anglo-Portuguese Alliance and the English Merchants in Portugal, 1654–1810* (Aldershot: Ashgate, 1998)

Sherwig, John M. *Guineas and Gunpowder: British Foreign Aid in the Wars with France, 1793–1815* (Cambridge, MA: Harvard University Press, 1969)

Snyder, Glenn H. *Alliance Politics* (Ithaca: Cornell University Press, 1993)
Sonnino, Paul. *Louis XIV and the origins of the Dutch War* (Cambridge: Cambridge University Press, 1988)
Sonnino, Paul. *Mazarin's Quest: The Congress of Westphalia and the Coming of the Fronde* (Cambridge, MA: Harvard University Press, 2009)
Sowerby, Tracey. 'Early Modern Diplomatic History', *History Compass* 14.9 (2016), 441–456
Stettler, Bernhard. *Die Eidgenossenschaft im 15. Jahrhundert* (Menziken: Markus Widmer-Dean, 2004)
Stiegung, Helle. *Ludvig XV:s hemliga diplomati och Sverige 1752–1774* (Lund: CWK Gleerup, 1961)
Stollberg-Rilinger, Barbara. *Des Kaisers alte Kleider: Verfassungsgeschichte und Symbolsprache des Alten Reiches* (Munich: C.H. Beck, 2008)
Stolleis, Michael. *Pecunia nervus rerum: Zur Staatsfinanzierung in der frühen Neuzeit* (Frankfurt am Main: Klostermann, 1983)
Storrs, Christopher, ed. *The Fiscal-military State in Eighteenth-century Europe: Essays in honour of P.G.M. Dickson* (Farnham: Ashgate, 2009)
Storrs, Christopher. *War, Diplomacy and the Rise of Savoy, 1690–1720* (Cambridge: Cambridge University Press, 2007)
Szabo, Franz A.J. *The Seven Years War in Europe, 1756–1763* (Harlow: Pearson, 2008)
Taylor, Peter Keir. *Indentured to Liberty: Peasant Life and the Hessian Military State, 1688–1815* (Ithaca: Cornell University Press, 1994)
Thiele, Andrea. 'The Prince as Military Entrepreneur? Why Smaller Saxon Territories Sent "Holländische Regimenter" (Dutch Regiments) to the Dutch Republic', in *War, Entrepreneurs, and the State in Europe and the Mediterranean, 1300–1800*, ed. by Jeff Fynn-Paul (Leiden and Boston: Brill 2014), pp. 170–192
Thomson, Janice E. *Mercenaries, Pirates and Sovereigns: State-building and Extraterritorial Violence in Early Modern Europe* (Princeton: Princeton University Press, 1994)
Tischer, Anuschka. *Französische Diplomatie und Diplomaten auf dem Westfälischen Friedenskongreß: Außenpolitik unter Richelieu und Mazarin*, Schriftenreihe der Vereinigung zur Erforschung der Neueren Geschichte e.V., 29 (Münster: Aschendorff Verlag, 1999)
Tilly, Charles. *Coercion, Capital and European States, AD 990–1990* (Oxford: Basil Blackwell, 1990)
Ulbert, Jörg. 'Französische Subsidienzahlungen an Hessen-Kassel während des Dreißigjährigen Krieges', in *Frankreich und Hessen-Kassel zur Zeit des Dreißigjährigen Krieges und des Westfälischen Friedens*, ed. by Klaus Malettke, Veröffentlichungen der Historischen Kommission für Hessen, 46 (Marburg: N.G. Elwert Verlag, 1999), pp. 159–174

Upton, Anthony F. *Charles XI and Swedish Absolutism* (Cambridge: Cambridge University Press, 1998)
Vann, James Allen. *The Making of a State: Württemberg, 1593–1793* (Ithaca: Cornell University Press, 1984)
Watkins, John. 'Toward a New Diplomatic History of Medieval and Early Modern Europe', *Journal of Medieval and Early Modern Studies* 38.1 (2008), 1–14
Wilson, Peter H. 'Financing the War of the Spanish Succession in the Holy Roman Empire', in *The War of the Spanish Succession: New Perspectives*, ed. by Matthias Pohlig and Michael Schaich (Oxford: Oxford University Press, 2018), pp. 267–297
Wilson, Peter H. 'The German "Soldier Trade" of the Seventeenth and Eighteenth Centuries: A Reassessment', *The International History Review* XVIII.4 (1996), 757–792
Wilson, Peter H. *German Armies: War and German Politics 1648–1806* (London: UCL Press, 1998)
Wilson, Peter H. 'The Politics of Military Recruitment in Eighteenth-century Germany', *English Historical Review* 117 (2002), 536–568.
Wilson, Peter H. *The Thirty Years War: Europe's Tragedy* (London: Penguin, 2009)
Wilson, Peter H. *War, State and Society in Württemberg, 1677–1793* (Cambridge, Cambridge University Press, 1995)
Windler, Christian, '"Ohne Geld keine Schweizer": Pensionen und Söldnerrekrutierung auf den eidgenössischen Patronagemärkten', in *Nähe in der Ferne: Personale Verflechtungen in den Außenbeziehungen der Frühen Neuzeit*, ed. by Hillard von Thiessen and Christian Windler (Berlin: Duncker und Humblot, 2005)
Winter, Martin. *Untertanengeist durch Militärpflicht? Das Preußische Kantonsystem in brandenburgischen Städten im 18. Jahrhundert* (Bielefeld: Verlag für Regionalgeschichte, 2005)
Winton, Patrik. 'Denmark and Sweden in the European Great Power System, 1720–1765', *Revue d'histoire Nordique – Nordic Historical Review* 14.1 (2012), 39–62
Winton, Patrik. 'Parlimentary Control, Public Discussions and Royal Autonomy: Sweden, 1750–1780', *Histoire & Mesure* XXX.2 (2015), 51–78
Winton, Patrik. 'Sweden and the Seven Years War, 1757–1762: War, Debt and Politics', *War in History* 19.1 (2012), 5–31
Wood, James B. *The King's Army. Warfare, Soldiers, and Society during the Wars of Religion in France, 1562–1576* (Cambridge: Cambridge University Press, 1996)
Würgler, Andreas. 'Symbiose ungleicher Partner: Die französisch-eidgenössische Allianz 1516–1798/1815', *Jahrbuch für Europäische Geschichte* 12 (2011), 53–75
Wyn Jones, Dwyryd. *War and Economy in the Age of William III and Marlborough* (Oxford: Basil Blackwell, 1988)

Yun-Casalilla, Bartolomé, Patrick K. O'Brien, and Francisco Comin, eds. *The Rise of Fiscal States: A Global History, 1500–1914* (Cambridge: Cambridge University Press, 2012)

Zunckel, Julia. *Rüstungsgeschäfte im Dreißigjährigen Krieg: Unternehmerkräfte, Militärgüter und Marktstrategien im Handel zwischen Genua, Amsterdam und Hamburg* (Berlin: Duncker und Humblot, 1997)

Zürcher, Erik-Jan, ed. *Fighting for a Living: A Comparative History of Military Labour 1500–2000*, Work Around the Globe, 1 (Amsterdam: Amsterdam University Press, 2013)

Index

When names and concepts that occur in the running text also appear in footnotes, references to the latter have been omitted.

Abbenhuis, Maartje 72n
Adlercrona, Johan 106, 107, 114
Adler-Salvius *see* Salvius, Johan Adler
Affolter, Andreas 148n
agents 5, 23, 71, 74, 81, 82, 83, 203, 213, 214, 218, 219, 220, 221, 224, 227, 228, 230, 231, 232, 249, 253
Albrecht, Dieter 46n
Albrecht, Johann Matthäus 186
Alexander VII, pope 203n
Allemann, Gustav 157n, 165n, 166n, 167n
alliances 8, 11, 13, 19, 22, 28, 41, 47, 60, 121, 124, 126, 131, 148, 150, 152, 153, 166, 177, 190, 192, 197, 201, 205, 207, 213
Alvarez, David 86n
Amalia Elisabeth, landgravine of Hesse-Cassel 46, 47n, 49n, 51, 53n, 65n
Åmark, Karl 98n, 99n, 108n, 124n, 125n, 128n, 130n, 132n, 134n, 137n, 140n, 141n, 142n, 143n
Amoretti, Guido 174n
Amsterdam 23, 214, 215, 216, 217, 218, 219, 220, 221, 222, 223, 224, 225, 226, 227, 228, 229, 230, 231, 232, 233, 237, 241, 242, 244, 247, 248, 250, 251, 252, 253, 255, 256, 257

Anderson, Matthew Smith 9n, 136n
Anderson, R.C. 75n
Andersson, Magnus 251n
Andriaenssen, L.F.W. 238n
Anhalt-Zerbst, family 181
Anne, princess of Orange 184n
Ansbach-Bayreuth, family 181
Appelboom, Harald 255
Arbel, Benjamin 173n
Aretin, Karl Otmar von 177n, 190n
Arielli, Nir 72n
Arlington, Henry Bennet, earl of 199
armies
 foreigners in 12, 73, 84, 85, 86, 88, 103
 recruitment 14, 23, 72, 82, 102, 175, 190, 205
 'standing' 78, 174
arms industry 224
 see also weaponry
Arnoldsson, Sverker 253n
Artéus, Gunnar 123n
Asch, Ronald G. 177n, 182n, 190n
Asche, Matthias 182n, 183n
Asker, Björn 114n
Åström, Sven-Erik 213n
Atwood, Rodney 133n
Aubery du Maurier, Benjamin 235n
Austria, army 82, 85, 87, 135
auxiliaries 80, 88, 89, 90, 91
Avaux, Claude de Mesmes d' 39, 51n, 57n, 58, 236n, 248, 256n
Awty, Brian G. 238n

Babel, Rainer 25n, 34n
Badalo-Dulong, Claude 194n, 234n
Ballard, Kyle M. 177n
Bamberg, prince-bishopric 186
bankers 1, 6, 7, 14, 71, 214, 221,
    228, 232, 234, 235, 238, 247,
    253, 256
Barbier, Edward 17n
Barthas, Jérémie 5n
Bartolotti, Guillaume 235n, 253
Bärwalde, treaty of 35, 36n, 101,
    215, 231, 242, 247, 247n
Baugh, Daniel A. 143n, 144n
Baumann, Reinhard 78n
Bavaria, soldiers from 87, 126
Bavel, Bas van 238n
Baxter, Stephen B. 121n
Bayard, Françoise 242n
Becker-Huberti, Manfred 203n
Beeck, Pieter van 231, 239, 241,
    242
Behr, Andreas 155n, 157n
Belgium 87
Bellièvre, Pomponne de 169
Bély, Lucien vii, 8n, 9n, 19n, 31
Benedict, Philip 239n
Berg, Tor 253n
Berghaus, Peter 196n
Bern 151, 154, 155, 158, 160, 162,
    163, 168
Bernhard, duke of Saxe-Weimar 49,
    51, 54, 55, 56, 60, 77n, 87,
    102, 113n
Bielke, Sten 103, 111
bills of exchange 6, 76, 77, 217,
    220, 221, 223, 227, 248, 249,
    251, 252
Birken, Sigmund von 64
Black, Jeremy 2n, 9n, 118n, 125n,
    134n, 136n, 139n, 140n, 142n
Blommaert, Samuel 217, 221, 225,
    230, 241, 242
Böckenförde, Ernst-Wolfgang 177n,
    190n
Bodensten, Erik 22, 123n, 127n,
    129n, 132n, 142n
Bodin, Jean 26
Boëthius, Bertil 103n, 125n, 127n,
    128n, 130n, 137n, 141n
Böhme, Jakob 63n
Bois, Jean-Pierre 9n
Bolzern, Rudolf 152n, 153n, 155n,
    156n, 169n

Bonde
    Gustav (1620–1667) 94
    Gustav (1682–1764) 19n, 94,
        128n
bonds 76
Boneauschöld, Abraham 107, 114
Bongars, Jacques 235n
Bonney, Richard 2n, 7n
Borkelo 197
Bosbach, Franz 28n, 39
Bottin, Jacques 235, 236n, 239n
Bouthillier, Claude 243n, 245n, 254
Boyne, battle of the (1691) 90
Brandenburg-Prussia 88, 120, 122,
    132
Braubach, Max 10, 30n, 31, 32n,
    76n, 188n, 203n, 204n, 205n,
    206n, 208n
Brandon, Pepijn 16n, 76n, 183n,
    230n, 238n
Brasset, Henri 256
Braun, Bettina 196n, 209n
Braun, Hans 161n, 162n
Braunschweig see Brunswick
Breda 249, 257
Breisach 56
Brett, Edward M. 86n
Brewer, John 70, 173n
Brinkmann, Carl 176n, 197n
British Auxiliary Legion 86
Broadberry, Stephen 7n
Browning, Reed 136n
Brunelle, Gayle K. 239n
Brunswick 31, 32, 176, 179, 180,
    181, 200, 201, 207
Bücheler, Heinrich 56n
Bullion, Claude de 244, 245, 247,
    248
Bundi, Martin 83n
Burgundy 5, 146, 150
Burkhardt, Johannes 1n, 41n, 175n,
    188n, 189n
Burlamachi, Philip 215, 215n, 229,
    241
Burschel, Peter 188
Burt, Ronald S. 237
Busch, Michael 27n, 149n
Büsser, Nathalie 153n, 156n, 158n,
    166n, 183n

Calandrini, Jeremie 256
Canstein, Benno von 180n
capitulations 82, 155

Index

Capol, Hercules 83
Carl, landgrave of Hesse-Cassel 175, 179, 185n
Carl Eugen, duke of Württemberg 134
Carlsson, Ingemar 128n
Caspary, Gundula 62n
Cateau-Cambrésis, treaty of 34, 35
Catherine de Medici, queen of France 166
Celle 88
Chambord, treaty of 34
Charles II, king of England etc. 17, 90, 199n
Charles V, Holy Roman emperor 34
Charles IX, king of France 166
Charles XI, king of Sweden 128
Charlot, Claude 242
Charnacé, Hercule de 242n, 243, 243n, 245n
Chavigny, Léon de Bouthillier, comte de 242n, 244, 245, 250
Christensen, Lars 129n
Christian V, king of Denmark *see* Kristian V
Christina, queen of Sweden 97
Clement X, pope 209
Cleves 196, 204, 205
Colbert
   Jean-Baptiste (1590–1663) 57n, 252n, 253n, 255, 256
   Jean-Baptiste (1619–1683) 110
   Nicolas 252n, 253n
Cologne
   electorate 11, 37, 37n, 87, 136, 206, 207, 208, 210
   Joseph Clemens, archbishop of 203, 204, 206, 207, 208
Compiègne, treaty of 35
confessional aspects 16, 19, 47, 59, 61, 147, 154, 157, 165, 168, 187, 202, 209
conscription 72n, 74, 85, 178
contractor state 75, 213
contracts 10, 49, 54, 69, 72, 73, 74, 75, 79, 80, 82, 90, 98n, 153, 172, 176, 179, 180, 186, 187, 222, 223
   see also troop conventions
contributions (war tax) 44, 46, 75, 99, 117, 200
Cornette, Joël 29n, 261
Corpus Helveticum 147, 148, 150n

Corvisier, André 86n
Courbouson, Simon de 160
Courtin, Honoré 40n
credit 6, 16, 17, 23, 58, 71, 183, 214, 216, 217, 219, 220, 223, 225, 226, 227, 228, 229, 232, 238, 240, 242, 244, 245n, 249, 251, 253, 256, 257
Cromwell, Oliver, lord protector 174
Cronstierna, Henrik 107
Curtius, Jean 238
Cysat, Renward 164, 165, 166, 169

Dafflon, Alexandre 155n
Danish-Swedish War (1643–1645) 33, 75
Dannert, Leif 123n, 141n
Danzig 214, 217, 218, 221, 222, 253, 254
Dardel, Pierre 239n
De Boer, Michael G. 229n
debt 2, 7, 8, 14, 29, 35, 74, 76, 106, 109, 123n, 135, 164, 165, 166, 167, 168, 169, 170, 176, 181, 197, 200, 208, 217, 227, 241n, 251, 252
De Geer, Louis 75, 76n, 215, 220, 226, 227, 228, 229, 230, 232, 237, 238, 240, 257
Degenfelt, family 178
Dehing, Pit 217n, 219n, 220n, 247, 248n
De Jong, Michiel 229n, 231n, 241n, 247
DelaFosse, Marcel 239n
De la Gardie, Magnus Gabriel 100n, 105, 115
Delft 252, 253, 254n
Denmark 2, 18, 19, 33, 78, 82, 95, 97, 105, 122, 129, 132, 139, 172, 189, 211, 221, 229
Dessert, Daniel 239n, 242n
Dillen, Johannes G. van 226, 226n, 227n, 250n
Dilthey, Wilhelm 70n
diplomacy 1, 2, 3, 8, 9, 10, 13, 17, 18, 21, 24, 25, 29, 38, 71, 92, 103, 105, 109, 155, 189, 190, 192, 194, 196, 205, 206, 234, 236, 237, 257
Dordrecht 252
Droste, Heiko 182n, 255n
Duchhardt, Heinz 40n

Duke, Alastair 62n
Dutch Republic
  army 28, 39, 40, 83, 84, 88, 90, 113, 184, 197, 200, 224
  see also Netherlands; United Provinces
Dwyer, Philip G. 58n, 94

East Frisia 46
Echenberg, Myron 73n
Edelmayer, Friedrich 78n, 149n
Ehmer, Joseph 149n
Ehrenberg, Richard 17
Eighty Years' War (1568–1648) 78
Ekeblad, Johan 100n
Ekholm, Lars 98n, 242n, 243n
Eldon, C.W. 2n, 68n, 139n
Elizabeth (Stuart), queen of Bohemia 176
Elmroth, Ingvar 114n
Emanuele Filiberto, duke of Savoy 168
Emich, Birgit 156n, 182n
entrepreneurs 1, 13, 16, 22, 71, 75, 96, 117, 150, 156, 175, 201n, 206, 214, 215, 216, 226, 227, 228, 229, 230, 232, 233, 238
Ernst August, duke of Brunswick 31
Ernst, Hildegard 3n, 30n
Ernstberger, Anton 215n
Eugene of Savoy, field marshal 174

Fahlborg, Birger 111n
Falkenberg, Melchior 103, 217, 218, 224, 225
Fann, William R. 86n
Fayard, Janine 8, 10
Feldbæk, Ole 3n, 129n, 132n, 139n
fiscal-military instruments
  definition 69, 79, 86, 91
  forms of 21, 69, 74, 75, 77, 92
fiscal-military state 69, 74, 119, 120n, 122
fiscal-military system 22, 69, 71, 74, 80, 214, 215, 217
Fleury, André-Hercule, cardinal 111
Flurschütz da Cruz, Andreas viii, 22, 119n, 201n
Foreign Enlistment Act (1819) 86
Forrest, Alan 79n
France
  army 29, 83, 85, 86, 87, 88, 194, 208

pays subsidies 2, 4, 10, 12, 17, 18, 19, 21, 22, 23, 27, 29, 31, 33, 34, 35, 36, 37, 41, 42, 44, 45, 48, 55, 77, 78, 87, 93, 96, 97, 98n, 99, 105, 106, 107, 108, 115, 116, 117, 120, 121, 124, 125, 126, 127, 128, 132, 139, 140, 142, 143, 152, 166, 208, 215, 221, 235, 236, 244, 246, 250, 255
François I, king of France 6, 7, 146, 152, 159
Franconia 56
Frederik Hendrik, prince of Orange 244n
Frei, Gabriela A. 72n
French, Doug 251n
Frensdorff, August von 183, 185n
Frey, Linda 10, 11, 12n
Friedeburg, Robert von 65n
Friedrich I, king of Prussia 121
Friedrich II, king of Prussia 58, 137
Friedrich V, Elector-Palatine 58, 176
Friedrich Carl, duke of Württemberg 180, 186n
Friedrich Wilhelm, elector of Brandenburg 121, 196, 201
Friedrich Wilhelm I, king of Prussia 58
friendship (between subsidizers and recipients) 19, 20, 40, 152, 201

Gabel, Helmut 40n
Gagliardi, Ernst 160n
Galen, Christoph Bernhard von, prince-bishop of Münster 189, 190, 196, 199, 200, 201, 203, 204, 207, 208, 209, 210, 211, 212
Gantet, Claire 9n, 147n, 154n
Garibaldi, Giuseppe 87
Gaunt, David 114n
Gedda, Niklas Peter von 111
Gelderblom, Oscar 222n, 248n, 252n
Geneva 168
Georg Christian, landgrave of Hesse-Homburg 190, 193, 196
Georg Friedrich, duke of Brunswick-Lüneburg 200
George II, king of Great Britain 180
George III, king of Great Britain 184

Index

George, Robert H. 184
German Confederation (1815–1866) 73
Gillard, Lucien 248n
Glaser, Michel 160, 161, 162
Glauser, Franz 164n
Glete, Jan 14, 123, 124, 134, 140, 143
Göhring, Martin 191n
Gorgas, Johann Georg von 200
Gräf, Holger Th. 69n, 181n
Graham, Aaron 75n
Grana, Otto Heinrich von Caretto, marquis of 209
Granovetter, Mark 237n, 239
Gravel, Robert Vincent de 191, 195
Great Britain
  army 18, 87, 88
  kingdom 22, 107, 108, 121, 123, 125, 130, 131, 133, 134, 136, 138, 139, 141, 142, 143, 144, 173, 174, 176, 180, 181, 184n, 187
  soldiers from 82
Greece 87
Greengrass, Mark 2
Grell, Ole Peter 229n, 241n
Grey Leagues *see* Grisons
Gripenstierna, Joel 107, 114
Grisons 83, 84, 147n, 154
Groebner, Valentin 150, 158n, 162n, 163n
Groenveld, S. 251n
Grönberg, Peter 103, 114n
Grosjean, Alexia 114n
Groß, Frederic 12n, 94n, 185n
Grotius, Hugo 20, 20n, 99n, 254
Gugger, Rudolf 81n
Günderode, Hans Heinrich von 52
Gustafsson, Harald 14n
Gustafsson, Sofia 96n, 115, 116n
Gustav II Adolf, king of Sweden 101, 102, 104, 113, 215, 226, 231, 242, 243, 253, 254
Gustav III, king of Sweden 143
Gutmann, Myron P. 238n

Haan, Bertrand 35n
Haas, Philip 177n
Häberlein, Mark 183n
Haehl, Madeleine 235n
Häggman, Jean 123n
Hald Galster, Kjeld 90n

Hamburg 23, 103, 214, 215, 217, 218, 219, 220, 221, 222, 223, 224, 226, 230, 231, 237, 245, 247, 248, 250, 252, 253, 254, 255, 256
Hanover, soldiers from 87, 88
Hanschmidt, Alwin 197n
Harding, Rickard 216n
Hart, Marjolein 't 16n, 220n, 224n, 238n
Hartmann, Anja Victorine 252n
Hartmann, Peter Claus 58n, 68n, 118n, 126n, 213n
Hastings, Adrian 65n
Hatton, Ragnhild 8n, 10
Haug, Tilman viii, 11, 22, 34n, 37n, 52n, 148n, 149n, 152n, 176n, 193n, 206n, 210n
Helfferich, Tryntje ix, 21, 30n, 32n, 44n, 94n
Heltscher, Peter [Rosenbaum] 254
Henri II, king of France 6, 34, 154, 164
Henri III, king of France 6, 164, 165, 166, 168, 169, 170
Henri IV, king of France 6, 7, 35
Hesse-Cassel, soldiers from 19, 186
Hesse-Hanau, family 181
Hille, Karl Gustav von 64
Hintereicher, Margarethe 193n, 195n
Hintze, Otto 14n, 70n
Hitz, Benjamin 151n, 166n, 169n
Höbelt, Lothar 12n, 95n, 185n
Hochheimer, Albert 85n
Hoeufft
  Diederick 241
  Jean 23, 115, 215, 221, 222, 229, 230, 231, 235–258
  Mattheus 23, 222, 229, 230, 231, 246, 249, 253–257
Holenstein, André 147n, 148n, 150n, 151n, 154n, 155n, 158n
Holt, Mack P. 164n
Holy Roman Empire, princes of 12, 77, 79, 85, 174, 176, 179, 191, 193, 255
Hoppe, Peter 157n
Horn, Arvid 112
Horn, Klas 103
Höynck, Paul Otto 210n
Hughes, Ben 86n

Huguenots 88
Hulle, Inge van 72n

Ilisch, Peter 196n
industrialization 73
Ingrao, Charles W. 12, 17n, 57n, 69n, 95n, 96n, 118n, 119n, 132n, 133n, 134n, 142n
Innhausen und Knyphausen, Dodo zu 102
Israel, Jonathan 8n, 223n
Ivetic, Egidio 4n, 178n

Jägerskiöld, Olof 125n, 127n, 129n, 130n, 131n, 132n, 137n, 140n, 143n
Jambu, Jérôme 249n
James II, king of England etc 18, 87
Jaensen, Cornelius 239n
Jarren, Volker 40n
Jeannin, Pierre 236n
Jerven, Morton 7n
Jervis Jones, William 65n
Jespersen, Knud J.V. 3n, 129n, 132n, 139n
Johann Georg I, elector of Saxony 59, 60n
Jonker, Joost 248n, 252n
Jouanna, Arlete 164n
Jucker, Michael 155n, 166n
Judges, Arthur V. 215n, 241n
Juel, Jens 100n
Julius II, pope 160
Jülich, town 192, 195

Kaiser, Michael 196n
Kälin, Urs 156n, 157n, 163n
Kampmann, Christoph 210n, 215n
Kant, Immanuel 8–9, 10
Kapp, Friedrich 57n, 172n
Kapser, Cordula 45n
Keblusek, Marika 183n
Kellenbenz, Hermann 218n, 222n, 231, 256n
Kernkamp, Gerhard W. 225n, 228n
Kette, Adam von der 210, 211n
Kettering, Sharon 206n
Killingray, David 73n
Kinderen, Florens der 200n, 201n
King's German Legion 87, 88
Klein, Peter W. 224n, 227n, 237, 241n

Klerk, Marianne ix, 22, 23, 72n, 96, 237, 242
Knight, Roger 75n, 216n
Kohl, Wilhelm 196n, 197n, 198n, 201n, 208n, 211n
Kohler, Alfred 159n, 264
Kohlndorfer-Fries, Ruth 235n
Kool, Clemens 248n, 252n
Körler, Theodor 209, 209n
Korff-Schmising, Friedrich 202n, 208
Körner, Martin H. 3n, 153n
Krantz, Olle 7n
Kreis, Georg 148n
Krischer, André 211n
Kristian V, king of Denmark 129
Kroener, Bernhard R. 178n
Krosigk, Adolf Wilhelm von 48, 49n
Krüger, Kersten 44n, 98n
Krüssman, Walter 55n, 82n
Kümin, Beat 161n
Kunisch, Johannes 176n
Kury, Patrick 151n

Lademacher, Horst 40n
Landberg, Georg 122n
Langemeyer, Gerhard 196n
Langerak, Gideon van den Boetzelaer, heer von 241, 256
Lansson, Julien 256
Lapeyre, H. 239n
Larsson, Erik [von der Linde] 217, 218, 221, 225, 231, 232, 242, 243
Lau, Thomas 30n, 35n
Laveau, Claude 239n
law
  international 71, 177
  local 82
Leeuwenberg, H.L.Ph. 251n
Lefèvre de la Boderie, Matthieu 51n, 52, 65n
Le Goff, T.J.A. 143n
Leijonankar, Daniel 107, 114
LeJeune, Jean 238n
LeLong, Jacques 243n
Lemnitzer, Jan Martin 72n
Lenman, Hans 109, 115
Leonhardt, Gustav 235n
Leopold I, Holy Roman emperor 27n, 31, 32, 33, 121, 179, 209
Lesaffer, Randall 19, 20n

Index

Leuhusen, Johan 103
Lindström, Peter ix, 95n, 123n, 129n, 131n, 132n, 139n, 213n, 265
Lionne, Hugues de 40, 195n, 204n, 205, 207
Livet, Georges 11n
loans 6, 14, 74, 75n, 76, 77, 99, 117, 165, 217, 241, 249
Lombardy 146, 159
London 197, 198, 229
Longueville, Henri II d'Orléans, duke of 59
Lopez, Alphonse 250
Lorenz, Gottfried 3n, 30n, 31n, 38n, 39n, 218n, 243n
Loriga, Sabina 85n
Lorraine 160, 240
Lossky, Andrew 10
Louis XIII, king of France 8, 20n, 35, 45, 51, 52, 57n, 221, 243, 243n, 244, 250
Louis XIV, king of France 4, 6, 8, 12, 17, 18, 29, 32, 37, 40, 41, 57, 85, 87, 127, 129, 174, 185, 188, 189, 202, 204, 205, 208n
Louis Napoléon Bonaparte, king of Holland 184
Louvois, François Michel Le Tellier, marquis de 207, 208n
Lucerne 153, 156, 164
Lumague, banking family 253
Lundgren, Sune 234n, 255
Lundkvist, Sven 98n, 99n, 102n, 215n
Lutz, Heinrich 159n
Luxembourg, Philiberta of 160
Lynn, John A. 28n, 87n, 183n

Mackay, Donald, first lord Reay 102
Maillet-Rao, Caroline 20n
Mainz *see* Mayence
Malcolm, Noel 59n
Mann, Michael 14n
Mansfeld, Ernst, count of 55, 82
Marc(us)
  Jacob 183
  Philip 183
Marignano 146, 147, 159, 162
Marks, Adam 82n
Marquardt, Ernst 196n
Maurer, Hans-Martin 12n, 95n, 185n

Maurice, prince of Orange 58, 201
Max Heinrich, archbishop and elector of Cologne 203, 204, 206, 207, 208
Maximilian, emperor of Mexico 87
Maximilian Emanuel II, elector of Bavaria 126
Mayence 11, 136
Mazarin, Jules 33n, 36, 39, 49n, 149, 193, 194, 195, 236, 237
McCormack, John 85n
McKay, Derek 2n, 8n, 122n, 132n
McClure, James E. 251n
Melander, Peter, count of Holzappel 52, 53, 53n, 65
Menk, Gerhard 179n, 201n
mercenaries
  interpretations 10, 67
  numbers 151, 153
  geographic origins 5, 30, 35, 147, 150, 155
  recruitment 35, 151, 153, 158, 159, 162, 169
merchants 71, 94, 103, 106, 107, 109, 113, 114, 117, 214, 215, 216, 220, 221, 223, 224, 228, 230, 234, 235, 238, 240, 242, 246, 248, 251, 254, 256
Mesa, Eduardo de 81n
Messmer, Kurt 157n
Metcalf, Michael 130n, 139n, 143n
Metz 34, 37
Meulles, Claude de 221, 256
Mexico 87
Middelburg 252
Milan 5, 148, 150, 157, 158, 159, 162
militias 224
Mollat, Michel 239n
Morera, Raphaël 229, 235, 236, 240, 249n, 257
Moser, Johann Jakob 180n
Müller, Leos 222, 228n
Müller-Wolfer, Theodor 165n, 167n, 168n, 169n
Münster
  prince-bishopric 136, 186, 188, 190, 200, 202, 204, 205, 208, 210, 212
  town 38, 189, 196, 198, 221
Murdoch, Steve 82n, 265
Musgrave, Richard Abel 70n

Naples, kingdom of 5, 83, 87, 159
Napoleonic Wars 72, 86, 87, 91, 137n, 142
nationalism 65, 73
navies 75
Netherlands (republic)
  pays subsidies 22, 98n, 173, 179, 187, 231
  republic 173, 174, 179, 180, 183, 187, 190, 197, 200, 201, 205, 209, 211, 240, 250, 254
  see also Dutch Republic; United Provinces
  networks 15, 16, 17, 22, 76, 83, 115, 156, 157, 161, 183, 190, 198, 200, 206, 211, 214, 215, 219, 228, 231, 232, 236, 237, 253, 255, 256
Neumark, Georg 64n
neutrality 24, 72, 73, 81, 207, 208
Nexon, Daniel H. 15, 16, 265
Nikula, Oscar 123n, 141n, 143n
Nilsson, Sven A. 99n
Nilzén, Göran 131n
Nine Years' War (1688–1697) 31, 85, 87
Noldus, Badeloch 183n, 254n
non-state actors 23, 69, 71, 72, 73, 74, 75n, 77, 215
Nordencrantz, Anders 93, 94, 97
Nordlund, Roland 243n
Norrhem, Svante ix, 22, 93n, 95n, 123n, 129n, 131n, 132n, 139n, 213
North America 12, 94n, 181

Oakley, Stewart P. 3n, 18n
officers
  pay 52, 53, 78, 101, 117, 200, 246
  as recruiters 46, 50, 81, 87, 234
Olofsson, Sverker 113n
Olson, Mancur Jr 13
Opgenoorth, Ernst 189n, 204n
Opitz, Martin 64n
Ormrod, Mark 2n
Oschmann, Antje 189n
Osnabrück 31, 38, 218
Ottoman empire 27n, 121, 128, 143, 174
Oxenstierna
  Axel 99n, 101, 102, 103, 103n, 215, 217, 222, 227, 242n, 243, 254, 255
  Johan 39

Paas, John Roger 66n
Palatinate 82
papacy
  army 86
  paying subsidies 44
Paris 38, 103, 105, 107, 111, 167, 168, 208, 214, 217, 218, 221, 231, 241, 242, 243, 244, 246, 247, 249, 254, 256
Parker, Geoffrey 215n, 223n
Parrott, David 44n, 45n, 56n, 60n, 80n, 88n, 214n, 215, 216n, 228n, 229n, 230, 234n, 244n
patronage 11, 15, 17, 22, 84, 156, 157, 158, 170, 182, 190, 205, 206, 207, 212
Pavia 146, 159
pensions 4, 9, 31, 33, 49, 50, 52, 53, 54, 57, 77, 78, 148, 149, 150, 151, 152, 152n, 153, 154, 156, 157, 158, 160, 161, 162, 163, 165, 166, 167, 169, 169n, 170, 171, 193
Percy, Sarah V. 76n
Petersen, E. Ladewig 70n
Petry, Christine 34n
Peyer, Hans Conrad 151n, 163n
Pfister, Ulrich 156n, 157n, 161n
Philipp Wilhelm, duke of Palatinate-Neuburg 191, 192, 193, 194, 195, 197, 207
Pitner, Ernst 87n
Place, Richard 11
Poitou 251
Polak, M.S. 251n
Polisensky, J.V. 82n
Portugal 90, 122, 139
Pribram, Alfred F. 191n
Price, Leslie 223n
Prussia
  army 81, 85, 86, 133
  foreign recruitment 81, 82, 85, 88
  influence 120, 121, 123, 132
Pufendorf, Samuel von 57

Ranke, Leopold von 70
Ranum, Orest 62n
Reagans, Ray E. 237n
recruitment
  agents 5, 74, 81, 82, 83
  forms 79, 80, 82, 83
  and religion 81
Redlich, Fritz 45n, 80n, 149n, 189n, 200n, 236n

Index

Reenstierna
  Abraham 107, 114
  Jakob 107, 114
Rees Jones, James 41n
Reinhard, Wolfgang 14n, 174n
Reinhardt, Nicole 156n
religion *see* confessional aspects
Renaudin, Marie-Felicia 210n
resource mobilisation, forms of 117, 228, 233
resource transfer, forms of 20
retainers 78
Rheinberg 206
Richelieu, Jean Armand du Plessis, cardinal duke of 20n, 28, 29, 35, 99n, 215, 235, 236, 237, 240n, 241n, 244, 245, 247, 250n, 251, 258
Ridolfi, Leonardo 7n
Riley, James C. 143n, 266
Riley, Jonathan 90n
Rindlisbacher, Sarah 155n, 168n
Rivet, André 257
Roberts, Michael 97n, 123n, 124n, 125n, 127n, 130n, 131n, 137n, 139n, 140n, 142n, 143n, 144n, 213n
Roelcke, Thorsten 63n
Rogger, Philippe ix, 4n, 22, 30n, 148n, 150n, 151n, 155n, 156n, 157n, 158n, 161n, 162n, 163n
Röse, Bernhard 56n
Rosén, Jerker 124n
Rouen 239
Rowlands, Guy 37n, 79n, 221n, 234, 234n
Russia
  army 109, 123, 129, 133
  Swedish war against 127, 128, 132, 136, 140, 144
Rutz, Andreas 188n
Rystad, Göran 99n, 105n, 128n

Saint-Chamond, Melchior Mitte de Chevrières-Miolans, marquis de 50, 54, 55, 252
Salm, Hubert 44n
Salvius, Johan Adler 38, 221, 248, 254, 255, 256n
Sander-Faes, Stephan Karl 4n, 174n
Sandler, Todd 13n
Savoy-Piedmont 83, 120, 121, 122, 125, 126, 132, 134
Schaufelberger, Walter 146n, 159n, 160n
Schilling, Heinz 9n, 177n
Schindling, Anton 27n, 183n
Schläppi, Daniel 163n, 171n
Schmid, Alois 118n, 135n
Schmidt, Alexander 62n
Schmidt, Georg 65n
Schmidt, H.D. 68n
Schmidt, Hans 191n, 192n, 193n, 195n
Schmidt, Peer 28n
Schmölz-Häberlein, Michaela 183n
Schönborn, Johann Philipp von, archbishop and elector of Mayence 33, 194
Schorer, Catherine 163n
Schnur, Roman 195n
Schröder, Stephan Michael 254n
Schulte, Regina 215n, 229n, 238n
Schulz, Kristina 151n
Schumann, Matt J. 10n
Schumpeter, Joseph Alois 70n
Schweizer, Karl W. 10n
Schwencke, Alexander 88n
Scott, Hamish 2n, 122n, 123n, 134n, 137n, 139n, 141n, 142n, 143n
Servien, Abel 33n, 40, 193, 194n, 236n, 256
Sewell, William 4n
Sforza
  Ludovico 159
  Massimiliano 159
Shaw, L.M.E. 139n
Sherwig, John M. 91n, 134n, 137n, 138n, 144n
Sherwood, Joseph 198, 199
Sneckensköld, Jakob 107, 114
Snyder, Glenn H. 13n
Solbes Ferri, Sergio 16n, 216n, 234n
'soldier trade' 57n, 69n, 172
Solothurn 30, 151, 152, 153, 154, 155, 162, 168, 169
Sonnino, Paul 47, 205, 205n, 207n
sovereignty 26, 27, 29, 54, 67, 70, 72, 73, 77, 177
Sowerby, Tracey 10n
Spain, army 193
Spanish Civil War (1833–1840) 86
Spanish Succession, War of (1701–1714) 31, 37, 85, 87, 90, 121, 124, 126, 142, 221
Spicer, Andrew 62n, 65n

Spiegel, Käthe 210n
Spierinck, Pieter [Silfvercrona] 253, 254, 255
Spooner, Frank C. 251
Sprekelsen, Lukas van 253
Stadler, Peter 168n, 169n
Städtler, Erhard 181n
Stanisław I Leszczyński, king of Poland 109
state building 13, 14, 15, 21, 23, 26, 36, 38, 41, 42, 97, 154
state formation 14, 16, 17, 22, 23, 24, 117, 233
states system 22, 41, 68, 122, 123, 125, 133, 141
Stearns, Steven J. 82n
Steiger, Heinhard 177n
Stein, Barbara H. 3n
Stein, Leon 63n
Stein, Stanley J. 3n
Sternberg, Wratislaus von 100n
Stettler, Bernhard 146n
Stiegung, Helle 143n
Stollberg-Rilinger, Barbara 176n
Stolleis, Michael 41n
Störning, Gerdt 107
Storrs, Christopher 3n, 52n, 95n, 119n, 120, 121n, 122n, 126n, 132n, 133n, 134n, 137n
Stradling, R.A. 81n
subsidies
  definition 4, 21, 22
  interpretation 10, 11, 12, 14, 15
  purpose 8, 15, 18, 19
  treaties 34, 35, 45, 46, 46n, 54n, 56, 60, 79n, 101, 104, 106, 107, 108, 108n, 110, 111, 115, 124, 127, 128, 131, 132, 140, 151, 152, 153, 168, 175n, 180, 181, 183, 187n, 197, 206, 215, 231, 242, 245, 246, 247, 253
Sveaborg 96n, 115
Sweden
  army 102, 103, 144, 223, 243
  council of the Realm 19n, 97, 99, 100, 110, 111, 112, 124, 127
Swiss Confederation, troops from 2, 5, 30, 150, 152, 153, 154, 155, 158, 159
Switzerland 73, 85
Symcox, Geoffrey 121n, 122n, 126n, 132n

Szabo, Franz A.J. 132n, 137n, 139n, 142n, 144n

taxation 2, 15, 44, 70, 99, 117, 154
Taylor, Peter Keir 69n, 172n, 173n
Temple, William 198, 199, 199n, 205
Teuscher, Simon 157n, 161
Thiele, Andrea 12, 13n, 18n, 55n, 96n, 119n, 179n
Thirty Years' War (1618–1648) 4, 19, 21, 23, 30, 31, 32, 33, 35, 36, 37, 38, 41, 43, 58, 62, 66, 75, 78, 87, 101, 107, 113, 176, 188, 189, 213, 215, 217, 220, 229, 231, 234, 236
Thiessen, Hillard von 156n
Thommen, Rudolf 151n, 153n, 154n
Thomson, Erik 22, 23, 96, 213, 215n, 217n, 218n, 221n, 222, 229n, 231, 232
Thomson, Janice E. 72n
Thun, Ludwig von 183
Tilly, Charles 13, 14, 14n, 97, 97, 214
Tischer, Anuschka 21, 28n, 33n, 36n, 40n, 41n, 195n
'total war' 73
Torres-Sánchez, Rafael 16n, 75n
Toul 34, 37
Transylvania 38, 236
Treasure, Geoffrey R. R. 11n
Trier 136
Trip
  Elias 215, 224, 225, 226, 227, 230, 252n
  Pieter 215, 226, 240
Trolle Bonde, Carl 19n, 94n, 128n
troop conventions 79, 90, 91

Ulbert, Jörg 11n, 30n, 31, 36n, 48n, 50n, 51n, 78n
uniforms 85
United Provinces
  pays subsidies 2, 18, 19, 121, 133, 136, 184
  republic 7, 8, 12, 35, 189, 200, 204, 236, 239, 241, 244, 245, 246, 249, 255, 256
  see also Dutch Republic; Netherlands
Upton, Anthony F. 128n

Index

Vann, James Allen 57n
Venice
  army 88, 178, 181
  pays subsidies 133, 173
  republic 174, 178, 187
Verdun 34, 37
Verspohl, Theodor 197n
Viotti, Andrea 87n
Vittorio Amedeo II, duke of Savoy
  121, 122, 126, 132, 137
Vogel, Hans 229n
Vries, Jan de 251n
Vultejus, Johannes 46n, 47, 53n

Waldeck
  Carl, count of 183, 184
  Friedrich Carl August, prince of
    175, 181, 182, 184
  Georg Friedrich, count (from
    1682 prince) of 179, 185n, 186,
    201
  Heinrich Wolrad, count of 178
  Josias II, count of 178
  principality 22, 172, 173, 177,
    179, 180, 181, 185, 186, 187,
    201, 203
warships
  construction 110
  supply of 71, 75
wartgeld *see* retainers
Watkins, John 10n
weaponry 75, 214, 216, 224, 225
  see also arms industry
Weber, Nadir 148n, 152n, 155n,
  176n
Weber, Wolfgang 19n
Wedgwood, C.V. 60
Weimar, town 63
Wendt, Einar 254n
Westphalia
  congress of 25, 28, 33, 33n, 36,
    38, 40n, 41, 255, 256
  treaty of 37, 43, 59, 177, 188,
    189, 190, 191, 193, 201, 210,
    212, 252n
Wettin, family 179
Whaley, Joachim 64n
Whitelocke, Bulstrode 101n
Wicquefort, Joachim de 48
Wieland, Christian 156n
Wiens, Eberhard 211n

Wiksell, Knut 251n
Wilcox, Martin 75n, 216n
Willem IV, stadtholder of the
  Netherlands 184
Wilhelm, duke of Saxe-Weimar 102
Wilhelm V, landgrave of
  Hesse-Cassel 45, 50, 52, 77
Wilhelm VIII, landgrave of
  Hesse-Cassel 131
Wilhelm Egon, count (from 1664,
  prince) of Fürstenberg-
  Heiligenberg 204n
William III, king of England etc
  (Willem III of Orange) 18, 90,
  180
Wilson, Arthur M. 125n
Wilson, Peter H. x, 2n, 8n, 12, 17n,
  21, 22, 23, 57n, 71n, 72n, 75n,
  76n, 78n, 81n, 90n, 93, 95n,
  96n, 118, 119n, 120n, 121n,
  122n, 126n, 132n, 133n, 134n,
  135n, 136n, 141n, 142n, 143n,
  144n, 145, 175n, 180n, 215n,
  217n, 224n, 237, 243n
Windler, Christian 3n, 11n, 17n,
  77n, 152n, 153n, 154, 154n,
  156n, 157n, 158n, 170n, 176n
Winter, Martin 85n
Winton, Patrik 3n, 123n, 132n,
  137n, 138n, 139n, 140n, 141n,
  142n, 144, 145n
Wishon, Mark 87n
Wittrock, Georg 242n
Wood, James B. 164n, 165n
Woude, Ad van der 251n
Wrede, Heinrich Alexander von 197,
  199
Würgler, Andreas 147n, 148n, 152n,
  154n, 155n, 156n, 157n, 158n,
  165n, 166n
Wüthrich, Ernst 147n
Wyn Jones, Dwyryd 2n, 95n, 173n
Würzburg, prince-bishopric 186

Zandvliet, Kees 230n
Zuckerman, Ezra 237n
Zunckel, Julia 76n, 215, 216n,
  238n
Zürich 151n, 153, 154, 158, 161,
  162, 168
Zwingli, Huldrych 158

EU authorised representative for GPSR:
Easy Access System Europe, Mustamäe tee 50,
10621 Tallinn, Estonia
gpsr.requests@easproject.com

www.ingramcontent.com/pod-product-compliance
Ingram Content Group UK Ltd.
Pitfield, Milton Keynes, MK11 3LW, UK
UKHW021824140426
5217IPUK00004B/76